WASHINGTON'S
U STREET

WASHINGTON'S
U STREET
A BIOGRAPHY

BLAIR A. RUBLE

Woodrow Wilson Center Press
Washington, D.C.

The Johns Hopkins University Press
Baltimore

EDITORIAL OFFICES
Woodrow Wilson Center Press
One Woodrow Wilson Plaza
1300 Pennsylvania Avenue, N.W.
Washington, D.C. 20004-3027
Telephone: 202-691-4029
www.wilsoncenter.org/press

ORDER FROM
The Johns Hopkins University Press
Hampden Station
P.O. Box 50370
Baltimore, Maryland 21211
Telephone: 1-800-537-5487
www.press.jhu.edu/books/

2 4 6 8 9 7 5 3 1

Library of Congress Cataloging-in-Publication Data

Ruble, Blair A., 1949–

Washington's U Street : a biography / Blair A. Ruble.
p. cm.
Includes bibliographical references and index.
ISBN 978-0-8018-9800-6 (hardcover)
1. U Street (Washington, D.C.)—History. 2. Shaw (Washington, D.C.)—History.
3. Shaw (Washington, D.C.)—Biography. 4. African Americans—Washington
(D.C.)—History. 5. African Americans—Social conditions—Washington (D.C.)
6. African Americans—Intellectual life—Washington (D.C.) 7. Washington
(D.C.)—History. 8. Washington (D.C.)—Social conditions. 9. Washington
(D.C.)—Biography. 10. Washington (D.C.)—Intellectual life. I. Title.
F203.7.U2R83 2010
975.3—dc22
2010028331

Title page illustration: Robert H. McNeill. Used with permission by the
Estate of Robert H. McNeill and the Kiplinger Research Library,
Historical Society of Washington, D.C.

Woodrow Wilson
International
Center
for Scholars

The Woodrow Wilson International Center for Scholars is the national,
living U.S. memorial honoring President Woodrow Wilson. In providing
an essential link between the worlds of ideas and public policy, the Center
addresses current and emerging challenges confronting the United States and
the world. The Center promotes policy-relevant research and dialogue to
increase understanding and enhance the capabilities and knowledge of leaders,
citizens, and institutions worldwide. Created by an Act of Congress in 1968,
the Center is a nonpartisan institution headquartered in Washington, D.C.,
and supported by both public and private funds.

Conclusions or opinions expressed in Center publications and programs are
those of the authors and speakers and do not necessarily reflect the views of
the Center's staff, fellows, trustees, or advisory groups, or any individuals or
organizations that provide financial support to the Center.

The Center is the publisher of *The Wilson Quarterly* and home of Woodrow
Wilson Center Press and *dialogue* television and radio. For more information
about the Center's activities and publications, including the monthly
newsletter *Centerpoint*, please visit us on the web at www.wilsoncenter.org.

Lee H. Hamilton, President and Director

For Nasar, James, Allyn, Kelly, Maze, and Joseph
Thanks for the music!

In spite of all the injustices, and horrors, and stupidity, beauty always survives, and there will never be a higher mission than making the world richer and purer by adding more beauty to it.

—Olga Grushin, *The Dream Life of Sukhanov*

CONTENTS

PROFILES

MAPS

FIGURES

PREFACE

First, culture is forever.
It is politics and ego that fade.

—Robert Farris Thompson,
Tango: The Art History of Love, 2005

Very early on a Sunday morning a decade ago, my wife Sally and I were making our way down the decrepit staircase that winds its way to Twins Jazz, a club that perches over Jumbo Pizza overlooking U Street just down from 14th Street north of downtown Washington. A blanket of the city's warm, heavy, slightly rancid summer air enveloped us—but hardly dampened our spirits—as we moved toward the door. Since early evening that Saturday, we had enjoyed some of the best local jazz combined with the easy fellowship of the staff and regulars who had moved with the club from the far reaches of the city's Upper Northwest quadrant to be part of its reemerging U Street scene.

The conversation that night had more of an edge than is typical in the commodious club. The new Ellington Condominium had just opened down the street, with its million-dollar apartments and its spanking-new tanning salon staring out on the street. The tanning salon—which didn't last very long—was more of an affront to the Twins Jazz regulars than the huge price tag on each bedroom. U Street, they felt, was theirs—but they were losing it, building by building, block by block. As I proclaimed to Sally on the stairs that morning, this was a subject that deserved a book.

My conversations that muggy night at Twins made me appreciate the reality that the story of U Street transcends both Washington and the nation. The musicians performing so well that evening were creating beauty, and they were doing so against all odds that they could. As I entered the world of U Street, I came to appreciate more and more that its history is about how human beings strive for beauty in the face of stupidity, folly, injustice, and brutality.

No matter how confident I was walking down the stairs from Twins that evening, I have had to confront the certainty that this is a foolhardy book. I am and must remain an outsider to the community about which I am writing. I am not a historian. I am not an academically trained specialist on the United States. I am not a native-born Washingtonian. I am not African American. So this book and the views it contains will always be those of an outsider, no matter how much I have striven to give voice to those who live in the U Street community. I can only hope that my outsider's perspective resonates with those for whom U Street is home in ways that add dignity to their community and value to their already considerable achievements.

So how did a white, New York–born specialist on Russian affairs with a doctorate in political science from a Canadian university come to write about a historical subject of such importance for Washington and for African Americans? As with most writing, the answer is deeply personal, even autobiographical. Sally and I have lived for more than three decades in Washington's Dupont Circle neighborhood, a distinct community all its own located just a mile or two away from U Street, NW; we have close colleagues and coworkers who have grown up and lived around U Street; we have driven through the area as it has been transformed from a violence-scarred zone of urban "failure" to a "hot" and "trendy" real estate market; we have frequented Twins and other jazz clubs around the corner of 14th and U streets; and we have done all this for years.

There is a professional connection as well. Having written about cities in the former Soviet Union and elsewhere, I have become convinced that my own adopted hometown of Washington is a rich source of insights about the urban condition. All too frequently, Americans dismiss the District of Columbia as too special to have any meaning beyond its diminutive borders. But, as argued in the text to follow, this view is a product of racism and, in turn, only reinforces the disfranchisement of the city's predominantly African American population.

I do not wish to imply that everyone who embraces a sense of Washington's exceptionalism is a racist. The problem is far more insidious. Notions dismissing Washington as a true city—that is has no "genuine" urban life, has no "real" history, and is not a "city" like other urban communities—emerged at about the same time that blacks and whites first settled around what would become U Street along the northernmost boundary of the territory encompassed by Pierre L'Enfant's and Benjamin Banneker's original surveys for the nation's capital. Like the myth that home rule was suspended in the 1870s because of local corruption, the denial that the District of Columbia is a living, breathing community inhabited by tens of thousands of citizens of the United States justified the suspension of local political control in this first large American city with a majority African American population.

The hundreds of scholars from abroad—primarily from Russia and Ukraine—who have worked at the program that I have run at the Woodrow Wilson Center for more than twenty years have had no problem whatsoever thinking of Washington as a formidable city with a fascinating history in its own right. Among the immeasurable debts that I owe these exceptional scholars who have worked at the Kennan Institute during my tenure has been the realization that I need not travel a third of a globe away for the sights and sounds of everyday life to challenge my thoughts about cities. In the end, the U Street story is about nothing more or less than what it means to be human.

Being human is not always ennobling or uplifting. I should note, for example, that I reproduce materials throughout this volume that have been taken from the period under discussion. A small handful of these passages—such as quotations by, or attributed to, Jean Toomer, Stokely Carmichael, Marion Barry, Ralph "Petey" Greene, and various voices from the streets of Washington during 1968—include language that will offend many readers (such as variations on the "N-word," the "F-word," the "S-word," and racial epithets about white people—the "H-word"). Those who used such expressions intended their language to evoke strong emotions. Therefore, I want to warn readers that they will encounter these passages should they choose to read further. I apologize for any offense that they may give.

It is perhaps fitting that a project that began with affable conversations in a bar would depend first and foremost on the work of those who have come before. My approach to writing this neighborhood biography necessarily builds upon the work of the many historians who have studied Washington; U Street, NW; and its neighborhood. The study of the city remains fragmented, at the fringes of mainstream American urban history. But the corpus of scholarship on the city's history—like that history itself—is richer and more varied than conventional wisdom might allow. Much scholarship on the city remains captured in master's theses and doctoral dissertations, obscure reports, and local publications. My final wish is that readers, having had a glimpse at this very important body of work, will follow my references to those authors and scholars who have come before.

WASHINGTON'S
U STREET

INTRODUCTION

Washington's Contact Zone

I would say that the whole U Street story is
a story of families. It's a story of people. It's a
story of churches. It's a story of hard work.

—Rohulamin Quander, 2004[1]

Washington is a city of spirits—but not the Hollywood demons of pulp fiction that are exorcized on film and television screens to the delight of millions. It is a city of the spirits of the African field-workers owned by Notley Young who farmed the lowlands on the future site of the Jefferson Memorial, of the human chattel who endured the horrors of one of America's largest slave markets set down on the land where the Department of Energy now stands, of slaves and poor market workers who were shuttled along streets long since buried under the Federal Triangle's government offices, and of the thousands of terrorized slaves who fled across the front lines of the Civil War, America's bloodiest, to become figuratively and legally nothing more than "contraband."[2] Centuries later, their spirits still animate Washington's political, social, and cultural life.

Washington, or, alternatively, the District of Columbia—familiarly, the District, or D.C.—is not merely the artifice of an eighteenth-century rationalist mind, cast out like a board game across a landscape rendered absent of distinguishing characteristics by the plans of a French military engineer, Pierre L'Enfant. Yet the image of Washington as an architectural apparition rather than a place soon took hold in the American imagination, even as that engineer was molding his plans to the area's topography to enhance the prominence of a handful of the most significant government buildings, such as locating the Capitol Building on Jenkins Hill.[3] Instead, as this book seeks to reveal, Washington is a real city, a messy city—a city that indeed has something that so many have wanted to ignore: a history all its own.

Washington has been denied its own story for as long as it has been without its own representation in the federal Congress.[4] For many Americans, Washington has never been—and even today is not—a "real" city. And therefore, white elites have been able to argue all too easily that the city does not "deserve" the same political rights as the rest of the country. The city is living proof of the observation by the Nobel Prize–winning economist Amartya Sen that "the asymmetry of power between the ruler and the ruled, which generates a heightened sense of identity contrast, can be combined with cultural prejudice in explaining away failures of governance and public policy."[5]

Sen continues on to note a "general tradition of finding explanations of disasters not in bad administration, but in the culture of the subjects."[6] This point will immediately be understood by African American Washingtonians. Their city has nurtured urban communities that have produced more than their fair share of local stories, including accomplishments and misdeeds that have altered the nation. These "real" African American urban communities exist in the District of Columbia, with "authentic" American urban tales to tell. But more often than not, they have been ignored or denigrated by the white authorities, both local and national—that have simultaneously dismissed the stories of the complex and diverse white communities that have also formed in the city of Washington ever since it was established more than two centuries ago.

Many of these local stories can be traced back to a handful of city blocks along what is now known as U Street (figure I.1), in the city's Northwest quadrant, abbreviated "NW" (throughout, addresses, except as noted, are followed by the standard designations for the city's four quadrants—NW, NE, SW, and SE; see map 1).[7] This U Street neighborhood's most celebrated offspring, Edward Kennedy "Duke" Ellington, fondly recalled growing up near 13th and T streets, NW, in his memoirs, *Music Is My Mistress*. (T Street is a block south of U Street, following the city core's generally alphabetical layout of main east-west streets, which run across its eastern and western quadrants and are repeated in its northern and southern ones. Its numbered streets run north-south, with the same

FIGURE I.1
U Street in the 1930s, with Griffith Stadium in the Background

Photograph by Robert H. McNeill, from the Kiplinger Research Library, Historical Society
of Washington, D.C. Used with permission.

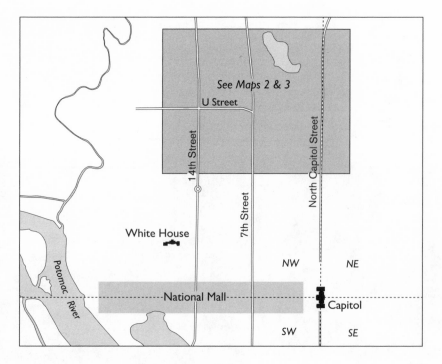

MAP 1
The U Street Neighborhood in Relation to the Rest of Washington
Map by William Nelson.

numbers generally repeated in each quadrant.) An elderly Ellington reflected on taking his first piano lessons from Mrs. Marietta Clinkscales; selling peanuts, popcorn, candy, and cigars at ball games at nearby Griffith Stadium; exploring the city with his cousin Sonny; and playing sandlot baseball on a vacant lot along 16th Street in front of the solitary figure of President Teddy Roosevelt on his horse.

Readers who are having difficulty imagining Ellington's Washington as a "real" city have probably missed his description of Frank Holliday's poolroom next to the Howard Theatre on T Street between 6th and 7th. Holliday's place, Ellington wrote, "was not a normal, neighborhood-type poolroom. It was the high spot of billiard parlors. . . . Guys from all walks of life seemed to converge there: school kids over and under sixteen; college students and graduates, some starting out in law and medicine

FIGURE I.2
A Diverse Cast of Characters at a Billiard Hall

Photograph by Robert H. McNeill, from the Kiplinger Research Library, Historical Society
of Washington, D.C. Used with permission.

and science; and lots of Pullman porters and dining-car waiters."[8] This poolroom was a home away from home for a diverse cast of characters—Dr. Charles Drew, who became famous for his work with blood plasma; a hustler named Clarence "Snake" Cabiness; scores of porters and waiters; and—most important for the young Ellington—the best piano players in town (figure I.2).

Holliday's poolroom was the sort of social mixing bowl that marks "real" cities—urban communities where people build "real" lives. In the United States, citizens of cities with meeting places such as Holliday's usually have full democratic rights—but not so Washington. No public official in the Washington of Duke Ellington's childhood faced an electorate—the entire District of Columbia having been disfranchised by an act of Congress in 1874.

Ellington's U Street neighborhood was only a generation or so old when he was growing up. Slaves who escaped from the Confederacy during the early months of the Civil War were among the area's first settlers. Not quite free, these fugitive slaves literally became "contraband." And their presence established a tone of ambiguity that has lasted ever since.

The stretch of U Street more or less between 3rd and 18th streets, NW, has always been a space "in between."[9] Like Moscow's famous Bohemian Arbat, the notion of "U Street" has embraced an entire world of neighboring streets, alleys, and landmarks.[10] As the center of Washington's "Secret City," the U Street neighborhood emerged as an elite area for a repressed minority, a point of forced interaction between blacks and whites, as well as among descendants of field slaves black as any African night and tan self-anointed grandees who asserted their status based on the lightness of their "colored" skins.[11] More recently, U Street has been caught up in a social maelstrom of communal violence and urban decay, followed by unrelenting gentrification.

This city was not really a "secret" to anyone who wanted to see it. African American Washington has a long, distinguished, and visible history, which blacks have known about and rightfully taken pride in for some time. The African American city was only a "secret" to whites who never bothered to look for it. Indeed, very few neighborhoods have been home to as many people of distinction as the general area adjacent to U Street. It was, as the former *Washington Post* writer Juan Williams observed, a place where "being there meant being somebody."[12]

A local business owner and the unofficial "mayor of U Street," John "Butch" Snipes, made a similar observation several years later, at the beginning of the twenty-first century. "You were privileged," Snipes told a reporter, "just to be in that vicinity."[13] U Street was the kind of neighborhood where parents dressed their kids up to go outside to play in the front yard. The area remained special even in a city full of numerous, well-established African American communities impinged upon by the complexities of racial segregation, such as Georgetown, Foggy Bottom, Southwest, and Deanwood east of the Anacostia River.[14]

U Street Luminaries

Among those people of distinction who have lived for a considerable time within a block or two of U Street have been any number of prominent whites and blacks, such as the founder of the American Red Cross, Clara Barton (who resided at 926 T Street, NW, between 1878 and 1892); the aforementioned musician, Duke Ellington (who lived in several houses in the neighborhood between 1899 and 1920); the founder of the American Federation of Labor, Samuel Gompers (who called a house near the Howard University campus at 2122 1st Street, NW, his home between 1901 and 1919); and the opera diva Lilian Evans-Tibbs (who inherited her father's house at 1910 Vermont Avenue, NW, in the early twentieth century). The great performing artists Pearl Bailey, Harry Belafonte, Diana Ross, Billy Taylor, and that neighborhood youth named "Duke" all made their stage debuts in U Street's theaters and clubs. And the Broadway stars Chita Rivera, George Faison, and Hinton Battle learned their dance steps nearby.[15]

Ahmet Ertegun, the teenage son of the Turkish ambassador to the United States during the mid-1930s, discovered jazz haunting local clubs, and eventually founded Atlantic Records.[16] More recently, the comedian Dave Chappelle and the fearsomely talented young jazz lion Allyn "Sugar Fingers" Johnson enjoyed some of their earliest successes on U Street's stages.

In the world of sports, Walter "Big Train" Johnson, "Cool Papa" Bell, Josh Gibson, and "Buck" Leonard threw and hit baseballs for the home teams harder and farther than all but a handful of human beings in the entire history of the American "national pastime."[17] "Slingin'" Sammy Baugh revolutionized how professional football would be played by perfecting the forward pass as an offensive weapon.[18] The basketball legends Elgin Baylor and Dave Bing learned their game playing pickup hoops with other neighborhood children.[19] By doing so, they continued a local tradition dating from the formation of the first African American basketball league, which had been established in 1907 at True Reformer Hall on the corner of 12th and U streets.[20]

Nonviolent means of protesting racial segregation got their start along U Street in the late 1930s as local activists including the future Nobel Prize winner Ralph Bunche—among many—invented forms of resistance that would change the course of American constitutional history during the civil rights movement a quarter-century later.[21] Mary McLeod Bethune founded and ran the National Council of Negro Women from her house at 1318 Vermont Avenue, NW, until her death in 1955. She was joined in many causes by her neighbor and sister activist Mary Church Terrell, who lived in nearby LeDroit Park before moving to the Strivers' Section late in her life.[22] The future Supreme Court justice Thurgood Marshall learned the law at Howard University in the area, and he perfected his winning arguments for the famous 1954 *Brown v. Board of Education of Topeka* case at meetings convened in the John Wesley African Methodist Episcopal Church at 1615 14th Street, NW.[23]

In 1870, the first public high school for African Americans in the United States opened its doors near U Street as the Preparatory High School for Colored Youth.[24] The school was later renamed for the poet Paul Laurence Dunbar, who lived nearby at the end of the nineteenth century.[25] This prominent academic school was joined by the city's leading technical and commercial high schools for African American students, Armstrong and Cardozo high schools, producing rivalries that resonate to this day. The literary stars Georgia Douglas Johnson, Horace Gregory, Alain Locke, Jean Toomer, and Langston Hughes invented what became known as the "Harlem Renaissance" in the drawing rooms of houses surrounding Howard University.[26] And the popular contemporary detective story author George Pelecanos writes about U Street,[27] as does the Pulitzer Prize winner and master short story teller Edward P. Jones.[28]

The U.S. Army's first African American general, Benjamin O. Davis Sr., made the 1700 block of S Street, NW, his home. Dr. Drew, from Ellington's visits to Holliday's poolroom, explored the uses of blood plasma at more or less the same time as Davis was living nearby. The District of Columbia's future nonvoting delegate to Congress, Eleanor Homes Norton, grew up here, and the future Atlanta mayor and U.S. ambassador to the United Nations Andrew Young spent his college days in the neighborhood, as did the dancer Debbie Allen and her sister, the actress Phylicia Rashad.[29] George Washington University, Frelinghuysen University, Wayland Seminary, Miner Teachers College (one of the founding institutions of today's University of the District of Columbia), and Howard University all got their start around U Street; with Howard remaining a vital international, national, and neighborhood presence to this day.[30] Freedmen's Hospital and Children's Hospital were among Washington's most important public health facilities for years, and the U.S. Department of State occupied the buildings of the equally important Washington City Orphan Asylum at 14th and S streets, NW, for a decade following the Civil War.[31]

Such a cursory listing fails to mention the hundreds more leading performers, entertainers, thinkers, writers, politicians, athletes, and everyday Washingtonians who have appeared, worked, and played at the U Street area's universities, theaters, clubs, sports fields, churches, associations, shops, and businesses over the past century and a half.[32] Many of the area's individual achievers have been honored many times over. Duke Ellington, for example, appears on a commemorative 25-cent coin, and several onetime U Street residents—including Clara Barton, Mary McLeod Bethune, Ralph Bunche, Anna Julia Cooper, Benjamin O. Davis Sr., Paul Dunbar, Charles Drew, Josh Gibson, Samuel Gompers, Patricia Roberts Harris, Langston Hughes, Zora Neale Hurston, Walter Johnson, Ernest Just, Thurgood Marshall, and Carter Woodson—have appeared on commemorative postal stamps. Such recognition, though important, largely ignores the connections of time, place, and community that advanced these people's individual accomplishments. Bringing the U Street community into view underscores how this compact urban area has long been one of those rare patches of real estate that has nurtured an unending stream of people who have shaped the world in profound ways.

Zone of Contact—and Creative Crucible

The U Street area has fostered this creativity by bringing a variety of people who often could barely tolerate one another crashing together while coming and going to their homes, apartments, places of worship, doctors' offices, funeral parlors, restaurants, cafés, bars, theaters, stores, stadiums, and schools. Because the area is located within the city's original boundaries, it never fell prey to the formal discriminatory restrictions and racial covenants imposed by private developers in such post-Reconstruction areas as Anacostia and Mount Pleasant. Therefore, the neighborhood remained more interracial in reality than its image might suggest. It has constantly been an unwelcome zone of contact "unprotected" from racial propinquity by formal legal constraints.

The U Street neighborhood is an area reminiscent, at times, of Tokyo's Asakusa district, as the Nobel Prize–winning author Yasunari Kawabata described it in his wanderings as a young man throughout the late 1920s and early 1930s: "In Asakusa, everything is flung out in the raw. Desires dance naked. All races, all classes, all jumbled together forming a bottomless, endless current, flowing day and night, no beginning, no end. Asakusa is alive. . . . The masses converge on it, constantly. Their Asakusa is a foundry in which all the old models are regularly melted down to be cast into new ones."[33]

Both Asakusa and U Street, to borrow from Robert Alter, have been "compelling arenas of incoherence."[34] They are spaces that bring together those with purpose and those without, thereby defining a city's meaning for its residents. Writing about another such area—the *calle* Corrientes neighborhood in Buenos Aires, which gave birth to the Tango king Carlos Gardel, among many other leading cultural figures— Jason Wilson observed, "to stroll this crucial and symbolic street is to get to know the heart of popular Buenos Aires. Night and day it is packed with wanderers."[35] As U Street demonstrates as well, promoting seemingly aimless wandering may be one of the most creative functions of any city street.

Contemporary social scientists "problematize" such places of intense group interaction as "zones of contact," a notion, first used by Mary Louise Pratt in the early 1990s, that nicely fits the story of U Street. For Pratt, such zones are the spaces where "cultures meet, clash, and grapple with each other, often in contexts of highly asymmetrical relations of power, such as colonialism, slavery, or their aftermaths."[36] She observes that although they are "commonly regarded as chaotic, barbarous, lacking in structure," such zones are often full of improvised relationships and a "copresence" that mark the coming into contact of peoples "geographically and historically separated, . . . usually involving conditions of coercion, radical inequality, and intractable conflict."[37]

The notion of contact zones is particularly important in relation to African American neighborhoods. Kevin J. Mumford argues, for example, that interracial vice districts—or "interzones"—have frequently been located in the black neighborhoods of American cities.[38] Stephanie Barbara Frank goes further, observing that U Street historically has stood at the center of an interracial vice district that has featured heterosexual as well as homosexual sites of interaction and, therefore, represents precisely the sort of neighborhood described by Mumford.[39]

Whether described as a "compelling arena of incoherence," "zone of contact," or "interzone," U Street should be widely recognized as an American equivalent of Kawabata's Asakusa. This neighborhood has proven itself to be one of the most inventive plots of American soil, together with the likes of Cambridge's Harvard Square, New York's Greenwich Village, Chicago's Hyde Park, and Berkeley's Telegraph Avenue. Like Kawabata's Asakusa of old, the neighborhood around U Street became "a foundry in which the old models [were] regularly melted down to be cast into new ones." As the historian Kathryn S. Smith recorded in the journal *Washington History*, "Here was a community that, despite acknowledged divisions based on color and class, functioned well for its members. Shaw [of which U Street is a part] was a dense weave of personal acquaintances and lifelong friendships based in strong families, churches, schools, fraternal and social clubs, black-owned businesses, and other local institutions."[40]

Outlines of a Hidden History

Very few neighborhoods of such distinction have been as little recognized as has U Street, at least until very recently. Mary Louise Pratt's appreciation of asymmetrical power relationships becomes critical for understanding why this happened. As recently as 2004, loud voices have proclaimed that Washington somehow has "no history" of its own, and certainly no history to which anyone would want to pay the least attention.[41] The painful yet undeniable reason for such scorn is more straightforward than twenty-first-century Americans would care to admit: The U Street story is first and foremost about African American creativity. And like so much African American achievement, U Street has been ignored, mislabeled, and simply discounted. For most Americans, this street and its environs have indeed been, as Constance McLaughlin Green told her readers four decades ago, a "Secret City."[42]

Significantly, white folks have also been part of the U Street story. Whites shaped U Street in the almost metaphysical sense that white power brokers in Congress, the White House, and the local business community set down rules that denied African Americans a full voice in their own community, rules that prohibited African Americans from pursuing specific careers and living in particular neighborhoods, and rules that abolished African American political rights. White authority figures, from judges down to street cops, forcefully—and, all too frequently, brutally—exerted a form of social control designed to exclude African Americans from local political, economic, and social respectability. White professional sports franchise owners kept African Americans off their teams, even at the cost of fielding some of the most pathetic squads in the histories of their leagues. White shopkeepers sold their goods throughout much of U Street's history; while white neighbors came and went, living on local streets and alleys before the full impact of Washington-style apartheid was felt. More recently, whites and immigrants of many hues and colors have been integral to the neighborhood's resurgence that began in the 1990s.[43]

The achievements of the "Secret City"—and of U Street in particular— were created by the complex and often malevolent relationship between whites and blacks, rich and poor. Howard University, the Howard Theatre, and Howard University Hospital would be very different institutions in a city untouched by overt and institutionalized racial discrimination. U Street is a rare crack in a world crisscrossed by the walls—visible and invisible—that separate human beings one from another on the basis of race, class, language, ethnicity, religion, and any number of other criteria that are limited only by the constraints of human imagination.

Once, when describing his hometown of Covington, Louisiana, Walker Percy observed that it was a place where one could "live happily as a bug in a crack in the sidewalk," a place where someone "can mosey out now and then and sniff the air just to make sure this is not just any crack in any sidewalk."[44] Communities benefit from spaces where a protected public meeting can take place. Cities need such places even more, those sorts of places where different kinds of people can come and go and interact with one another.

As the Barcelona philosopher and urban thinker Josep (Pep) Subirós has noted, heterogeneity in and of itself does not produce a "civic" environment.[45] A city must simultaneously accept differences and provide shared points of reference if a genuine civic identity and urban culture are to emerge. For *civitas* to reign, local legends and memories, and the telling of history, must go beyond divided understandings of society to embrace pluralism.

Cities fragmented by race, ethnicity, and religion benefit from a Percy-esque "crack in the sidewalk" more than most. Indeed, a city like Washington, so long divided by the harsh reality of race, has nurtured far too few such cracks in its sidewalks for an overall sense of shared community to emerge. The city's blacks and whites have lived in distrustful isolation from one another ever since it was founded on the site of slave-farmed plantations at the end of the eighteenth century.[46]

U Street has been one of a very few, very imperfect meeting grounds for various groups throughout the city's difficult history. At one end, the street was crossed by the pretentiously upscale "Avenue of the Presidents" (16th Street, NW), and at the other it was crossed by the raucous 7th Street, NW. So at times U Street became an unrecognized middle ground—a "contact zone," a meeting place, and a "crack in the sidewalk"—in a town divided since the very beginning by race and class.

The U Street area has brought people together in very much the same way that the Ukrainian city of Kyiv brought Jews, Ukrainians, and Russians crashing into one another during the early twentieth century. As Natan M. Meir has noted, such contact was driven more by necessity than by admiration and respect: "Against a backdrop of centuries of interethnic tension, government-sponsored segregation, rising nationalism, and sporadic violence, [Kyiv's] ethnic and religious groups got along better than might have been expected in the period before [the *pogroms* of] 1905 and even, to some extent, in the years after."[47]

The U Street story begins with the emergence of a robustly diverse community, which included residents of different races and economic classes, during and after the Civil War. A new period of segregation, resulting from "Jim Crow" customs, came to Washington beginning in the mid-1880s, after the Compromise of 1877 ended the Reconstruction Era. Riots—initiated by white soldiers and sailors—rocked the neighborhood in 1919 during the "Red Summer" that swept the country following the "Great War," World War I. U Street emerged during these years as an increasingly energetic center of African American life in a city that was ever more segregated by race. Simultaneously, the creation of a middle class and elite largely centered on institutions near U Street encouraged differentiation within the African American community by skin tone and economic class.

In spite of the surrounding racially segregated city, the proudly black-centered U Street community thrived throughout the 1920s, 1930s, and 1940s, until landmark judicial decisions marked the beginning of the end for officially sanctioned segregation in housing, education, and public accommodations. These years were marked by an economic boom and bust, massive in-migration from the rural South, social protest, intellectual ferment, and court actions promoting African American claims to full citizenship. Local residents and institutions assertively confronted the nation for its failure to extend the benefits of personhood to African Americans.

Along with political and social strife, this era was also one of boisterous nightlife—the moment when U Street earned the nickname "Black Broadway." The U Street area's vibrant club, theatrical, and musical life attracted both blacks and whites to hear the likes of Duke Ellington and watch ball games at Griffith Stadium. The resulting mixture of classes and races—though tentative and often resented—brought more whites to U Street even as Washington generally remained sharply segregated by custom and law.

U Street, like many of the city's in-town neighborhoods, fell on hard times following World War II as the area entered a period of transition. The African American and white middle classes began to move away from the center of the city, taking entertainment and retail districts with them. Harsh political struggles over racial desegregation tore apart the social underpinnings of the world that had come to flourish along U Street. The neighborhood continually teetered on the edge of collapse throughout the 1950s and 1960s, reaching a disastrous nadir in the communal violence of 1968 after the assassination of the Reverend Martin Luther King Jr.[48]

The U Street of old never recovered from the April 1968 civil disturbances. The area seemingly fell victim to decay, urban misman-agement, and a cascade of urban problems, including growing poverty, illegal drug trading, and rising crime. Yet the reality was considerably more complex, and often more positive. U Street did not disappear so much as it moved indoors, primarily into the area's illustrious churches, which retained their congregations even as their parishioners moved to the suburbs. The U Street community remained precisely that, a community in every sense of the word, where longtime residents found ways to support one another.

After holding on for almost twenty years, the neighborhood finally saw the beginning of a renaissance based on its residents' activism as well as on religious and educational institutions with deep roots in the U Street community following the opening of the Frank D. Reeves Municipal Center at the corner of 14th and U streets in 1986, and then the inauguration of service at a Metrorail subway station in May 1991. Tensions emerged as younger, wealthier, and whiter residents moved into the neighborhood, claiming it as their own. The area's older, poorer African Americans, who had lived through so many abrupt turnarounds in wealth and social standing, often found themselves excluded.

For better or for worse, the transition period of the 1970s and 1980s led to unrelenting gentrification, simultaneously building on and consuming the area's past. In recent years, rising real estate prices and rents have threatened to drive all but the middle class and wealthy out of the area, undermining the street's historic function as a place in between for the city's various groups.

The final test for the U Street neighborhood, Washington's "crack in the sidewalk," will be whether the area's new bourgeoisie demands that the space for mixing be protected and nurtured or paved over and "beautified." Can this latest incarnation of the city's historic zone of contact bring together those groups in the city beyond the already privileged? Perhaps—but only if the entire sweep of its incredibly rich, difficult, and complex history is known and appreciated by all.

An Overview of the Book

The story of the U Street neighborhood that follows can be as large or as small as the reader might wish. At one level, this book presents a straightforward tale about the lives of those who have inhabited a rather small and confined community for more than a century and a half. Some—such as those whose parents and grandparents attended Dunbar, Cardozo, or Armstrong high schools—may be fascinated to discover in the pages that follow just how important those medals from a military drill competition fifty years ago were to those who hid them away with care in the family trunk. Others who are interested in the history of Washington will find a retelling of that story from a slightly different angle that places African Americans center stage, rather than from the perspective of the city as the nation's capital.

Those seeking to understand the urban experience of African Americans will find in this book a biography of U Street as an emblematic neighborhood for all the different moments, contradictions, and achievements that have been found in dozens of American cities over the past fifteen decades. Similarly, the American national response to the question of race is visible on every page. This neighborhood, by virtue of the fact that it is located just a few blocks from the Capitol to the east and the White House to the west, has often become the object of experimentation by those who hold national power. Such meddling has known few bounds in a city that has been denied control over its own fate, having been relegated by the nation's founding documents to little more than a plaything for congressional power brokers. African Americans intent on shaping that experiment have sought out U Street just to be close to that power. This city and this neighborhood thus not only embody the African American urban experience but also stand starkly exposed to the latest fashionable policy proscriptions being imposed on them.

Each possible reading would more than justify a book such as this. But the stories in this book of diverse people's lives illustrate how U Street's history transcends both Washington and the nation—how human beings strive for beauty in the face of stupidity, folly, injustice, and brutality. There has not been a moment during this history when many of the street's residents have not been seeking to create beauty. Indeed, the U Street story is as much about the human condition as it is about American circumstances, African American reality, and the life of the city of Washington.

In the seven chapters that follow, this book first delineates U Street's ambiguous roots, and traces the neighborhood's early formation in the context of the growth of the very Southern city of Washington. Then it tells the stories of a few of the determined U Streeters who changed America—and the world—in its heyday during the early twentieth century. Next it turns to U Street's more recent cultural accomplishments, its political radicalization, and its challenges and triumphs as the city was granted home rule. Finally, the book considers today's ambiguous future for a revitalizing yet gentrifying U Street. At the end of each chapter, two profiles of characteristic U Streeters give close-ups of the people who have made the street such a crucible of great Washingtonians—and Americans.

CHAPTER 1

Ambiguous Roots

It has been said, apparently with a great deal of truth,
that the capital has more intelligent, cultured,
well-to-do colored people than any other American city.

—Joseph West Moore, *Picturesque Washington*, 1884[1]

Nestled in a crook of the escarpment marking the Potomac River's fall line, a ridge encircling what became the downtown part of the City of Washington, the land on which U Street would be built lies just within the northern boundary of Pierre L'Enfant's original plan for this federal capital city in the District of Columbia as surveyed by Andrew Ellicott and the African American astronomer Benjamin Banneker in 1791.[2] Up until the Civil War, the "city" in this part of the District of Columbia existed more often than not as a theoretical statement deduced from surveyors' maps. It was, as the historian Marcia McAdoo Greenlee reminded her readers, "in the woods."[3] Once the war began, the Union Army erected camps in this area precisely because the land was so vacant.[4]

Washington's population more than doubled during the four years of the Civil War, while its African American community grew by more than fourfold. This expansion caused the prewar city to burst out of its physical and social boundaries.[5] Before the outbreak of hostilities in 1861, Washington had been a distinctly "Southern" town, with three-quarters of its highly transient nonnative population having moved there from Southern states.[6] Antebellum Washington became distinctive among American cities—even Southern towns—for the relatively large number of free blacks residing in both Georgetown and Washington City.

Because the District of Columbia had originally been carved out of two plantation states—Maryland and Virginia—which together accounted for more than half the slave population of the United States at the time of the country's first census in 1790, slavery and the slave trade had been a constant feature of the city's life from the very beginning. Given its location midway along the Atlantic Coast, the city quickly became a major depot and auction site for slave traders.[7] Nearly a quarter of its population was African American in 1800, of whom only about 5 percent were free.[8] Intense political disputes and social unrest eventually led to the outlawing of the slave trade within the federal capital as part of the Compromise of 1850.[9]

Freeing slaves was relatively easy within the District of Columbia, with residence by free blacks thereafter being permitted.[10] As a consequence, the ratio between free blacks and slaves residing in the District began to shift to the advantage of those African Americans who were not held in bondage. If, in 1800, 783 of the District's African American population of 4,027—and, in 1830, 6,152 of 12,351 African Americans—were free, by the outbreak of the Civil War the free Negro population stood at 11,131, as opposed to 3,185 slaves.[11] Washington was just one of three cities—together with Saint Louis and Baltimore—in which a majority of the black population were not slaves.[12] Only Baltimore could rival Washington's vibrant free black community in total size as well as percentage of the total African American population.[13]

Life for free blacks was never easy in Washington, or anywhere else in the country. Law and custom confined employment for African Americans primarily to trade and services because the apprenticeships so necessary for entry into many sectors of the labor market remained tightly controlled to keep blacks out.[14] Nonetheless, an increasingly robust and autonomous African American community set down roots. Black businessmen and professionals assumed leadership positions and developed local cultural traditions.[15] They opened churches (such as Asbury Methodist Church, Mount Zion United Methodist Church, Metropolitan African Methodist Episcopal Church, Nineteenth Street Baptist Church, Saint Augustine's Catholic Church, and the First Colored Presbyterian Church); created other critical institutions, such as the first YMCA organized for blacks; and established a nascent school system for African American children.[16] Government jobs—particularly at the Navy Yard—emerged as another mainstay of African American employment during this time.[17]

The founding of the YMCA illustrates the dynamism of the local African American community.[18] The Young Men's Christian Association had been organized in London in 1844 by George Williams, a dry goods entrepreneur concerned with the morals of his workers. Americans attending the London World's Fair of 1851 brought the idea back to Boston, where Thomas V. Sullivan founded the first American YMCA at the end of the year.

Three young Washingtonians similarly concerned with the rise of gambling, delinquency, alcoholism, and vice of all forms—Thomas Duncan, William Rhees, and William Chauncey Langdon—established a YMCA in Washington a year later. Langdon met Anthony Bowen while working at the Patent Office. Bowen, a freed slave born in 1805, had purchased his freedom from his owner in Prince George's County for $425 in 1830. He had become the Patent Office's first African American employee and, by the 1850s, had established himself as a leader of the local African American community.

Bowen helped to found Saint Paul's Church as well as a Sunday evening school for free blacks during the 1840s, and he frequently harbored escaped slaves fleeing along the Underground Railway at his home near 9th and E streets, SW. Working with Langdon, Bowen established the first African American YMCA in 1853, only a dozen months after the first Y had opened in the United States in Boston. Bowen, who would live until 1872, served the country with distinction during the Civil War. He steadfastly promoted African American public education as the war raged on and helped to recruit three regiments of African American soldiers to fight for the Union. He ended his career by serving on the Washington City Common Council from 1870 until his death.

Washington's community of free blacks was thus well established by 1862, when streetcar lines moved out along 7th and 14th streets, NW, into the urban hinterland above K Street for the first time. New development, and white residents, quickly followed.[19] As the Civil War progressed, the city filled with military personnel and clerks for an expanding wartime government so that, for the first time since its founding, Southerners became a minority in Washington City.[20] Thousands of escaped slaves (more than 40,000 by the end of hostilities) from the Confederacy and nearby Maryland made their way to Washington. These pressures meant that the city could only be built in a haphazard manner throughout the war, waiting to become formalized once hostilities had ceased.

Contraband Human Beings and the First Freed

The District of Columbia remained slaveholding territory until a special act of Congress in April 1862 provided compensation for local slave owners.[21] The date on which this law took effect—April 16—immediately became a city holiday; while the moniker of "first freed" bestowed special status on the city's blacks.[22] These celebrations, which were often attended by the president and senior members of Congress and Cabinet officials, over time took on national as well as local significance.[23]

Slaves elsewhere remained the property of their owners. Accordingly, slaves fleeing neighboring states to the District technically remained "fugitives" until the Emancipation Proclamation of 1863.[24] The newcomers' legal status had been uncertain at first.[25] Many Union Army commanders simply turned away fugitive slaves seeking refuge in their camps, and some ordered their troops to forcibly return such human property to their "rightful" Confederate owners.[26]

However, one Union general, Ben Butler, commander of Fort Monroe in Virginia, was unwilling to release fugitive slaves to their owners and thus declared the question to be "simply whether they shall be used for or against the Government of the United States." Accordingly, Butler held "these Negroes as *contraband* of war."[27] He later explained his decision as one of humanity. Viewing the fugitives as "deserted, thrown away, abandoned like the wrecked vessel upon the ocean," he confided to Major General Oliver Otis Howard after the war, his duty "as a humane man [was] very plain. I should take the same care of these men, women, and children—houseless, homeless, and unprovided for—as I would for the same number of men, women, and children, who, for their attachment to the Union, have been driven or allowed to flee from the Confederate States."[28]

Following Butler's lead, refugee slaves reaching the District of Columbia and elsewhere were declared "contraband," and hence, wards of the Union Army in June 1861.[29] And the Washington Military District established a special Contraband Department, located at 12th and O streets, NW, under the control of the Reverend D. B. Nichols, the former director of the Chicago Reform School.

"Contraband" camps grew up in the shadow of the various Union Army's encampments, forts, hospitals, and warehouses scattered about the city as the fleeing slaves believed—generally correctly—that the soldiers would protect them from racist violence as well as from Southern sympathizers who would try to return them to the previous owners. The fifty-six forts surrounding the city that had been built just after the war began provided easy shelter as well as plundered construction materials for informal settlements.[30]

Significant "contraband" communities formed along Duff Green's Row on East Capitol Street (the future site of the Folger Shakespeare Library on Capitol Hill), on Analostan (now Roosevelt) Island in the Potomac River opposite Georgetown, next to the Navy Yard on the city's Southeast Anacostia River waterfront, near Campbell Barracks (at what is now 7th Street and Florida Avenue, NW), and around Camp Barker (which, like Campbell Barracks, was located near the future U Street at what would become the intersection of Vermont Avenue at 12th Street, NW).[31] Following an outbreak of smallpox in 1863, the authorities tried to disperse the "contrabands" to more distant suburban locations within the District.[32]

Meanwhile, Congress had established the Bureau of Refugees, Freedmen, and Abandoned Lands—or the "Freedmen's Bureau"— to assist refugees and freedmen to begin a new life and to manage confiscated lands in the former Confederate States, various border states, Indian Territories, and the District of Columbia.[33] The war secretary, Edwin Stanton, appointed Major General Oliver Otis Howard to head the bureau as its first commissioner.[34] Howard was surprised by the offer, noting later that, "naturally, as the great war drew to a close, I had been pondering the subject of my future work. Should I remain in the army or not? What as a young man of thirty-four had I better do? The opportunity afforded by this offer appeared to me at once to answer my anxious inquiries. Indeed, it seemed providential."[35]

The young warrior, viewing his appointment as the product of divine guidance, dove into his work, leading the agency throughout its tumultuous history until Congress abolished the Freedmen's Bureau seven years later in response to growing hostility among Southern whites. The bureau eventually supported more than 4 million "wards" by providing medical assistance to more than 1 million former slaves, and by establishing African American schools and colleges throughout the states and territories under its mandate.

The Military District (and, subsequently, the Freedmen's Bureau) was responsible for helping the city's newly freed blacks find jobs, receive an education, and generally get along. The agency operated its Washington Freedmen's Hospital under the direction of Dr. Alexander T. Augusta, a U.S. Army major and surgeon. The hospital, which was located at 13th and S streets, NW, when it opened in 1862, would serve Washington's African American community for more than a century. It moved several times before settling on Howard University–owned land at 5th and W streets, NW, in 1869, where it remained one of black Washington's most important institutions, before relocating one last time in 1975 to the former site of Griffith Stadium at Georgia and Florida avenues, NW (where it became part of an enlarged Howard University Medical School complex).[36] The Freedmen's Bureau simultaneously converted army barracks in the area into tenements, and the Association for the Relief of Destitute Colored Women and Children built an orphanage nearby.[37] Such facilities guaranteed the area's importance as a major employment and residential center for freed slaves.

In 1867, Commissioner Howard of the Freedmen's Bureau secured a congressional charter and budget for the first university south of the Mason-Dixon Line dedicated to a biracial education.[38] Howard, several local notables, and leading members of the city's Congregational churches foresaw the need for an institution that would train African American teachers, lawyers, doctors, and collegians. Their thinking about the institution that would become Howard University grew more ambitious during ongoing conversations throughout late 1866 and early

1867. With the congressional charter in hand, Howard and his friends purchased the 150-acre farm of John A. Smith on a hill overlooking the city, just beyond the area covered by the original L'Enfant Plan,[39] for the seemingly outlandish price of $1,000 an acre.[40]

Howard University, with a large initial investment from the Freedmen's Bureau, emerged as one of African America's leading higher educational institutions.[41] The Freedmen's Hospital, together with Howard University, firmly secured this corner of the nation's capital as one focal point for the city's rapidly growing African American community.

By the end of the 1860s, what had been largely vacant land when the decade began had been transformed into a powerful magnet for Washington's blacks and for many whites as well. U Street, like the city at large, retained a pattern of racial residential propinquity that predated the war. Whites and blacks (both free and slave before 1862) shared many neighborhoods.[42] The poor and unskilled of both races frequently inhabited alley dwellings, while more prosperous black and white residents lived on houses facing streets.[43]

In *Neglected Neighbors*, a classic early-twentieth-century report on the distinctive Washington alley dwelling, Charles Frederick Weller described this "city within a city" as

> unique, with few if any parallels in other American cities. . . . Many of the deep building lots of Washington have houses at both their front and rear ends. One set of dwellings face outward upon the streets and avenues, the others front inward upon hidden alley streets. . . . Their inhabitants have no connection whatever with those of the streets and avenues. The hidden dwellings are reached by distinct, winding roadways. Resourceful people live for years in the attractive residences on the avenues without knowing or affecting in the slightest degree the life of the alley hovels just behind them.[44]

Part of what the residents of the streets did not realize, according to modern historians, is that the lives lived in the alleys behind their houses were not all that different from their own. Archeologists, for example, have uncovered remnants of the city's alley life that indicate a steady reduction in household income differentials over time.[45] Alley dwellers began to approach the material living standards found in the houses facing the streets through collective and household survival strategies, as opposed to a reliance on the single incomes earned by household heads in the houses facing streets. Such findings—especially those related to different dietary and food preparation practices—point to varied value systems and consumer choices rather than absolute differences in material well-being. A middle class of sorts was taking shape facing both the streets and the back alleys. This was so even if the street gazers ate bone-cut beef dismembered by cleavers while the alley dwellers ate sawn-bone pig parts and opossum accompanied by heaping portions of greens.

The fast-growing U Street neighborhood had its share of alleys and alley dwellings, and its array of more prideful street residences.[46] African American men living both on streets and in alleys began to enter such trades as carpentry, masonry, smithing, cabinetmaking, shoemaking, painting, barbering, and retail in larger numbers; while African American women from streets and alleys alike were gaining steady employment in domestic service.[47] And a disproportionate number of the growing African American middle class—buoyed by steady employment—increasingly settled around U Street.

In the U Street area, the local institutions—which, more and more, were African American institutions, established in response to white hostility—attracted people and commerce from across the city, a trend accelerated by increasingly popular streetcars.[48] Most important for the future, the once-bedraggled "contraband" camps developed into a full-fledged urban community tied to major organizations that served a variety of African American socioeconomic and professional groups—ranging from orphans and day laborers dependent on the goodwill of others to the intellectual elite associated with Howard University.

Radical Reconstruction

These physical changes in the city took place against a backdrop of a venomously vitriolic local political scene, where old-time Southern whites were pitted against Radical Republican white reformers, newly enfranchised blacks, and an emergent conservative Republican business community.[49] Originally, the District of Columbia was divided into several jurisdictions: Georgetown, a settlement of 10,000 with a charter predating the founding of the District; the City of Washington, which had been chartered by Congress in 1803 and was bounded by the Potomac River to the south, Rock Creek to the west, the Anacostia River to the east, and the outer edge of L'Enfant's original plan—Boundary Street (now Florida Avenue)—to the north; Alexandria City, a tobacco port like Georgetown situated on the Potomac's western shore, together with unincorporated lands under the jurisdiction of Alexandria County; and Washington County, largely unsettled areas with a few crossroads scattered about, such as Tenleytown and Reno to the north and Uniontown across the Anacostia River to the east.[50] Alexandria City and County received scant federal attention and returned to Virginian jurisdiction through retrocession in 1846.[51]

Although the District's residents were denied full voting representation in Congress, Georgetown and Washington City did elect mayors, council members, and other officials, though neither granted wide suffrage.[52] Women and African Americans were prohibited from voting in D.C., just as they were nearly everyplace else in the country. Property restrictions and high poll taxes further limited the voting rolls, especially in Georgetown.[53] Given the small size of the population eligible to vote in Washington County, the farmland and large estates of the area remained under the control of the Levy Court.[54]

Georgetown retained a largely Southern political and social culture throughout the period, while Washington City came to represent the dynamism of the North before and during the Civil War. The diminutive size and racial intolerance of local electorates became obvious in late 1865, when Washington City voters opposed a referendum granting African American suffrage by a vote of 6,591 to 35, and Georgetown voters by a tally of 712 to 1.[55]

Congressional oversight of the District of Columbia remained fitful during the first six decades of its existence. As Steven Diner has concluded, "Benign neglect by Congress characterized the political system that evolved in the District between 1800 and the outbreak of the Civil War. Congress devoted only limited attention to the District and provided funds for public needs stingily and haphazardly."[56]

Such cozy arrangements collapsed at the outbreak of war. The Military District of Washington dominated local administration during hostilities, while congressional Radicals came to view the city as a testing ground for postwar Reconstruction policies once the war had ended.[57] Prompted by a Radical Republican senator from Massachusetts, Charles Sumner, Congress granted African American males full suffrage within the city—over both the bitter objections of the local white community and a presidential veto by Andrew Johnson.[58]

African Americans responded to the opportunity to vote by registering in large numbers.[59] By 1867, they represented nearly half the electorate in Washington City, and a significant percentage of the Georgetown electorate as well.[60] Newly registered African American voters helped to elect a Radical-dominated Washington City Council in late 1867, as well as several Radical candidates to a variety of top city posts.[61] Their victory presaged a brutal mayoral election contest the following year between the Democratic mayor, Richard Wallach, and a Radical Republican tub-thumper, Sayles Jenks Bowen.[62]

Wallach, a native of the city, strongly supported the Union despite owning slaves himself and his vocal opposition to abolition. He became mayor in 1861, after his predecessor, James G. Berret, had refused to take an oath of loyalty to the government of the United States. Wallach had become increasingly dismayed, as had many white Washingtonians, by the rapid wartime influx of African Americans into the city.[63]

Bowen—the postmaster of Washington and a strong supporter of the embryonic African American school system in Washington City and County—moved to the District from Pennsylvania in 1845 to work at the Treasury Department. He eventually lost his government job for distributing antislavery propaganda. Like Radical Republican senator Sumner, Bowen was impassioned about the right of African Americans to all the privileges of U.S. citizenship.[64]

Wallach and Bowen and their supporters fought one of the most savage election campaigns and postelection legal battles in American history. Chaos seemingly reigned following flawed balloting in June, which proved to be too close—and too compromised—to produce a clear winner despite recounts, stormy City Council meetings, wild courtroom confrontations, and fisticuffs.[65] At various moments over the next few weeks, separate Republican and Democratic councils and mayors simultaneously claimed victory and tried to govern the city as if the other side did not exist. But by late November, Bowen and the Radical Republicans secured victory by successfully requesting congressional and judicial intervention.

This Bowen-Wallach contest and other similar early post–Civil War election campaigns revealed how easily Washington's blacks took to politics. As Robert Harrison has observed, "The most striking feature of black political activity in post-bellum Washington was the high level and intensity of participation, most obviously manifest in the impressive rates of electoral registration and turnout. It was evident also in the attendance at Republican ward clubs, which met weekly in the months before elections and intermittently at other times."[66]

Harrison continued that Washington's African Americans "looked to the Republican Party not only to pass legislation in their favor or to facilitate their acquisition of jobs but also as a medium of personal expression and civic education. They regarded political participation as a way of acclimatizing themselves to the procedures of democracy and, in a broader sense, to the culture of freedom."[67] Accordingly, during this period black political life in Washington became inexorably linked to church organizations, with the increasingly important pre–Civil War churches being joined by newly established (and eventually prominent) churches such as Shiloh Baptist and Saint Luke's Episcopal.[68]

The behavior of African American voters underscored the centrality of community in the worldviews of newly freed former slaves. Katherine Mazur has thoughtfully explored a distinct conception of citizenship among Washington's African Americans, which found ready expression in their political activities—namely, a set of collectivist values that emerged from survival strategies embedded in the slave experience: "The central rubric through which African Americans sought to reconstruct their world after emancipation was that of community integrity. Freed people moved immediately to reunite families, assert control over their own labor, and create and consolidate such institutions as churches and voluntary associations."[69]

Mazur develops her point further, adding that "the complex relationships among private property, race and 'the public' made residential neighborhoods sites of continuous struggle over citizenship. While African Americans sought safety and independence in their own spaces, white property owners often used the language of economic progress and taxpayer rights to justify incursions into African Americans' private spaces. As black people resisted scrutiny and attacks by police and other unfriendly whites, they insisted on the right to build communities and institutions outside the surveillance of the state."[70] This fundamental commitment to the protection of a broader African American community has animated the story of U Street ever since.

The mayoral conquest by the Radical Republican Sayles Jenks Bowen—who was viewed by many in the city as having been placed in office by judges and members of Congress rather than by the local electorate—proved short-lived. His administration collapsed under a cloud of inefficiency and corruption charges by the time the need for reelection loomed in 1870.[71] Bowen's ineptitude was symbolized for many by the seizure on behalf of a local merchant of the furniture in the mayor's own office to compensate for the city's nonpayment of an outstanding invoice.[72]

Breakaway Republicans opposed to the ineffectual Radical Republican Bowen nominated a city alderman, Matthew Emery, as their next candidate. Emery, who was originally from New Hampshire, had come to the city to practice his trade as a stonemason in 1855, and remained throughout the Civil War.[73] He both benefited from, and represented, the District's astonishing growth during the conflict and its aftermath. As the favored candidate of the conservative Republican business interests who were profiting from the city's spectacular growth, Emery won election with heavy business and African American support. Significantly for the future of the city, a new local power broker—Alexander Robey Shepherd—backed Emery's candidacy.

Enter the "Boss"—Alexander Robey Shepherd

Alexander Robey Shepherd, a plumber who had been elected to the City Council with the backing of local merchants to promote infrastructure improvements, capitalized on his personal friendship with President Ulysses S. Grant to become the dominant player in Washington politics.[74] Shepherd was never the Radical advocate of African American rights that Bowen had been. He and his stalking-horse minions, such as Emery, nonetheless commanded pivotal support among the city's black voters as they traded the promise of jobs on massive public works projects for votes.[75]

Old-line conservative white Washingtonians bided their time for the right moment to undermine growing black political power. Many local whites used every opportunity to distance themselves from their African American neighbors. The social, associational, religious, and educational aspects of the city's life became increasingly segregated. Strikingly, institutions connected with the Congregational Church— as a consequence of titanic struggles between the Congregationalist Major General Howard and his segregationist comembers—remained integrated.[76] The Roman Catholic Church—which placed an African American, Father Patrick Healy, at the head of its prestigious college in Georgetown in 1868—offered another notable exception to a citywide pattern of racial separation.[77] More generally, two distinct and separate urban communities—one white and one black—were forming behind the facade of the Radical Republican experiment.

U Street took shape during this period on the semi-abandoned lands of the urban fringe. In the words of the historian John Karl Byrand, U Street immediately became "an eclectic mix of individuals: blacks and whites of all classes and occupations." This mixing, Byrand continued, "was not necessarily from racial harmony, but more out of a need for housing that was increasingly difficult to find as the District's population swelled."[78] The area's forced juxtaposition of black and white, rich and poor, professional and laborer, intellectual and shop owner powerfully marked the neighborhood as an unusual middle ground in the city from its origins rooted deep in the turmoil of the nation's Civil War.

Shepherd never concerned himself with creating an urban middle ground; nor did he favor vibrant elected institutions. In 1871, the "Boss" managed to maneuver Congress into instituting a "territorial government" for the District of Columbia, combining all the jurisdictions within the District's boundaries into a single governing structure. Georgetown, Washington City, and Washington County were folded into a new Territorial Government administration dominated by an appointed Board of Public Works.[79] The president appointed all local officials save for the small number who were elected to the lower house of the Territorial legislature, making subsequent congressional charges of electoral corruption especially droll.

With fewer elected officials, the conduct of municipal affairs became less accountable to local citizens, either white or black. A stormy period followed, ending with the suspension of home rule less than three years later as congressional grandstanders blamed those who were elected for the misdeeds of those who were not. Congress would not again give the District's residents control over their local affairs for almost a hundred years.

Shepherd secured his own appointment to the Territory's all-powerful Board of Public Works.[80] The board, from which he dominated the city together with other probusiness "improvers," initiated a massive public works program. The District of Columbia had become notorious for its inadequate infrastructure. Hardly any street was paved, and the city had completed an aqueduct system to supply potable water only a few years before. That system had taken eleven years to construct under the direction of Montgomery C. Meigs, an Army engineer who simultaneously directed an extension of the Capitol Building and the construction of its iconic dome.[81] Meigs, who served as quartermaster general for the Union Army during the Civil War, continued his distinguished career in Washington overseeing the construction of many vital infrastructure projects as well as prominent buildings such as the Pension Building (now the National Building Museum).

Meigs's substantial achievements were oriented toward serving the federal presence. Shepherd and his colleagues focused on the city and its neighborhoods. For example, President Ulysses S. Grant appointed the architect Adolf Cluss to the Board of Public Works in October 1872. Cluss, who had left his native Germany following the unsuccessful revolutions of 1848, was a longtime friend of Karl Marx and the Marx family.[82] Once in the United States, Cluss settled in Washington, bonded with his new homeland, and eventually turned his back on his friendship with Marx. But he retained a deep commitment to architectural design as a tool of social reform. He would become best known for his revolutionary designs for the city's schools and markets, as well as for the Smithsonian's National Museum (now the Arts and Industries Building) on the National Mall.[83]

Cluss, whose distinctive and somewhat fantastical red brick structures were covered with what are now identified as "Victorian" gewgaws, defined a local vernacular style.[84] He exerted a powerful influence on the Board of Public Works, eventually serving as the city's chief municipal engineer. He subsequently broke with Shepherd and spoke before several congressional committees about waste, fraud, and abuse among contractors with ties to the Republican Party.[85]

As Cluss testified, the board profligately spent federal funds to grade streets, pave sidewalks, build bridges, and tunnel sewer systems with little regard for budgetary constraints.[86] The historian Alan Lessoff observed, in reviewing Shepherd's legacy more than a century later, that "Shepherd and his allies embody that strand in Reconstruction Republicanism which had come to emphasize progress in physical and economic development at the expense of political and ethical progress, the other pillar of the original Republican vision."[87]

Shepherd was the local version of a new type of urban American— the businessman politician who parlayed municipal power into a machine for providing the public infrastructure necessary for economic growth.[88] As a "pragmatic pluralist," Shepherd would look for support wherever he could. He welcomed African Americans into his coalition, rewarding them in turn with employment, even though he might not have welcomed them into his home.[89]

Shepherd's authoritarian and assertive style quickly began to wear thin among better-heeled city residents and with members of Congress.

Journalistic critics discerned parallels with the infamous Boss Tweed Ring in New York, whose corrupt practices had just been uncovered.[90] Criminal allegations stuck to the Territorial Government, even though any number of congressional investigations failed to uncover wrongdoing beyond profligate spending.[91] Shepherd's work crews didn't help the District's case when, following a congressional recess in late 1872, senators George Edmunds of Vermont and Thomas Bayard of Delaware returned to their respective mansions along Massachusetts Avenue only to discover their homes perched precariously ten feet above the newly regraded street.[92]

Shepherd, who was supported by large segments of the city's African American community, provided the excuse for antiblack whites in the city and in Congress to deny suffrage to local African Americans. A national depression following the stock market crash of 1873—together with the death of Charles Sumner in March 1874—removed the financial and political underpinnings for the Radical Republican experiment in the District's governance. Restive congressional Democrats launched a series of hearings and investigations to identify malfeasance in Territorial affairs.[93] Rather than disenfranchising blacks alone, conservative Democrats used race-baiting attacks centering on corruption charges to suspend all local government within the District of Columbia.

Congress terminated the Territorial Government on June 20, 1874, abolishing the District's nonvoting congressional delegate in the process.[94] Congressionally approved commissioners assumed receivership for District affairs, while Senate and House leaders tried to develop a new system for administering the national capital. Symbolically, given the racial implications of the move, the new commissioners enacted a law establishing chain gang labor on municipal projects on their first day in office, September 4, 1874.[95]

Four years later, the Organic Act of 1878 converted the District of Columbia into a congressional fiefdom by establishing a municipal corporation governed by three presidentially appointed commissioners (two were to be civilians, and one was to be appointed from the U.S. Army Corps of Engineers). Much to the delight of the white business community, Congress agreed in return to make an annual federal payment in lieu of taxes to compensate for those District services that supported the federal presence in the city.[96] This commissioner form of government was to last ninety-nine years.[97] The abolition of municipal suffrage accompanied the creation of the commissioner system, further extending congressional control over the District.

These actions were partially a consequence of the Compromise of 1877, under which Southern members of the commission established to determine the disposition of the November 1876 presidential election granted twenty disputed electoral votes to Republican Rutherford B. Hayes over the Democrat Samuel Tilden in exchange for Hayes's agreement to withdraw the remaining federal troops from the South. The Compromise marked the end of Reconstruction and the beginning of a rollback of federal policies protecting equal rights for former slaves.

With the nation's postwar commitment to African Americans revoked, local and state governments once again began to restrict black political, social, and economic rights.[98] This slow but steady erosion of black rights eventually led to the establishment of the segregationist "separate but equal" system throughout the South known as "Jim Crow." Many correctly view the denial of voting rights to residents of the District of Columbia as one of numerous betrayals that combined to become a "great betrayal" to the country's newly freed black citizens.[99]

Other factors were also at work. In part, by "removing" the District of Columbia's municipal government from "politics," Congress was lending early support to a broad "progressive" movement to reform municipal governance in the late nineteenth century by converting the management of a city from a political to a "scientific" footing.[100] Even so, there is no escaping the fact that race, class, and gender lurked at every turn—the very essence of what is now called identity politics.

Mazur underscores the stakes involved:

> Post–Civil War discussions of suffrage rights were premised
> on the knowledge that the polling place was already a space of
> class mixing among men. The space was already disorderly and
> volatile, as elite men and laborers came together in a ritual of
> manhood. The prospect of expanding the suffrage then raised

three main problems. First, many white elites contended that white men and black men would be unable to share the space of the polling place without resorting to violence. Second, they argued that black men's voting rights would lend inevitably to greater "social" mixing between the two races and, ultimately, to interracial sex. Finally, they claimed that especially if black men were enfranchised, the polling place was no place for women. In each instance, voting rights could not be divorced from the social interactions involved in the act of voting itself.[101]

The Territorial Government left behind a legacy of racial mistrust among congressmen and senators, as well as enormous public debt. Representatives and senators have found it convenient ever since to bemoan corruption and inefficiency as a screen for opposition to black power in the nation's capital.[102]

The District's tremendous growth during the postwar period more than offset the failures of either the elected municipal governments or subsequent Territorial administration. Shepherd's infrastructure improvements, along with the growth of the federal government following the Civil War, inspired an enormous real estate boom that created a number of row house neighborhoods surrounding the central city, including the area around U Street. Future District tax payers proved able to manage the debt built up under Boss Shepherd's administration with relative ease.[103] A modern city with the latest urban infrastructure and amenities sprang almost full-blown from Shepherd's audacious public works programs.[104]

Some sense of Shepherd's legacy lived on well after his departure from office.[105] A century and a quarter later, the Washington press corps presented departing D.C. mayor Anthony A. Williams with a miniature statue of Shepherd as a gesture honoring the various improvements Williams had brought about in the city's life.[106]

Yet in an America sliding into an era of increasingly contentious racial politics, such an accomplishment could never be acknowledged.[107] And so U Street and the other neighborhoods created by Boss Shepherd's audacious construction projects came to symbolize all that had gone wrong in the city during the Reconstruction years following the end of the Civil War.

A Vibrantly Integrated Urban Community

U Street and its surrounding district entered the 1880s as an attractive, increasingly upscale urban neighborhood despite the fact that a number of prominent building lots remained empty.[108] These blank spaces later provided sites for the country's leading African American architects— such as John Lankford, Isaiah T. Hatton, and William Sidney Pittman (Booker T. Washington's son-in-law)—to design and to build a number of the area's most significant institutional buildings, including True Reformer Hall, the Industrial Bank, the Twelfth Street YMCA, and the Whitelaw Hotel. Nonetheless, as the historian John Karl Byrand has observed, the area already had become distinctly urban, consisting "of an eclectic mix of individuals: blacks and whites of all classes and occupations." And as already noted, Byrand simultaneously cautioned that "this mixing was not necessarily from racial harmony, but more out of a need for housing that was increasingly difficult to find as the District's population swelled."[109]

To the east, a fancy enclave of recently built ornate gabled mansions known as LeDroit Park stood just off Rhode Island Avenue next to a growing Howard University. Major General Oliver Otis Howard had sold the land off to a group of private developers headed by the asphalt and future automobile magnate Amzi L. Barber, a member of the university's Board of Trustees; Barber's brother-in-law, Andrew Langdon; and the architect James McGill. Barber and his partners marketed the houses to affluent whites, erecting a high fence around their complex to keep African American students and faculty from the neighboring campus safely off their carefully cultivated streets. The "LeDroiters" successfully withstood court challenges to their early gated community, although neighbors pulled down their fences as quickly as they could be built until the last barbed-wire rendition was dismantled in 1890.[110]

By the turn of the century, the last Caucasian owners in the once exclusively white LeDroit Park had sold out to wealthy African American professionals. Barber, meanwhile, moved on to develop an area to the northwest that would become known as Columbia Heights.[111] LeDroit Park continued to evolve, becoming home to many of the prominent African Americans who would contribute to the U Street area's cultural explosion during the early twentieth century.[112]

To the west, Mary Henderson and her husband, the former Missouri senator Colonel John Brooks Henderson, would build a "castle" at the corner of Boundary Road and 16th Street, just a block or two north of the intersection of U and 16th streets. Their huge home, originally named "Boundary Castle," became a focal point for white Washington society until Mrs. Henderson's death in 1931.[113] She was known as the "Queen of Sixteenth Street," and her megalomaniacal plans for the neighborhood would exert a powerful influence over this corner of the city well into the twentieth century.[114]

The Henderson's heavily rusticated, turreted stone pile, which came to be known as Henderson Castle, loomed over the city from the pedestal of Meridian Hill even before it was completed in 1888 (figure 1.1). Senator Henderson was widely known as the author of the Thirteenth Amendment abolishing slavery, and as one of the critical legislators who had cast his ballot against the impeachment of President Andrew Johnson in 1868. Henderson and his wife relocated to Washington permanently in 1872 after he was defeated by critics of his vote in the Johnson impeachment trial. They eventually purchased farmland along 16th Street, NW, which is one of the city's central axes and is known for its spectacular view of the monumental city below. From the Henderson's house, at the top of Meridian Hill, the street ran straight downhill to end at Lafayette Square a dozen blocks away, with the White House directly across Pennsylvania Avenue. Their sprawling hulk of a home thus provided the perfect perch from which Mrs. Henderson could set about securing an equally domineering promontory on the Washington social scene.[115]

Mrs. Henderson liked her servants to be formal (all female servants were to wear ankle-length skirts), and her guests and neighbors to be

FIGURE 1.1

A View of "Henderson Castle" on 16th Street, NW, above Florida Avenue

Photograph from the Washington Historical Image Collection, Washingtoniana Division,
Martin Luther King Jr. Library, Washington. Used with permission.

white.[116] Senator Henderson used his political connections to enlist the assistance of the city's congressional commissioners to evict black families from his immediate surroundings. Reluctant longtime African American residents of the area who resisted the city's initial eviction notices had their houses assessed out from under them by overzealous tax collectors.[117]

In between the ivory bookends of Barber's LeDroit Park and Henderson's Meridian Hill stretched a dynamic neighborhood of three- and four-story brick homes in what would later be recognized as the "Victorian" style. These vainly eclectic dwellings were filled with successful white, black, and immigrant families of a rising middle class, which sought out the modern amenities provided by Boss Shepherd's work crews. Lively commercial strips developed along the trolley routes down 14th and 7th streets, with businesses beginning to appear on U Street. And an increasingly black community of unskilled manual laborers found entry into the city's life via densely packed communities hidden away in intimidating back alleyways.[118]

The surface power of the neighborhood obscured a set of racial pathologies that would long beset U Street and the entire city. If one stepped off a main street into a back alley, one was likely to be confronted with alley communities of poverty that were becoming overwhelmingly African American. Inhabitants living next door to one another were trying to find their own ways in the city. Separate cultural, economic, and religious institutions were taking shape for whites and blacks, and, within the African American community, for light-skinned and dark-skinned blacks (and also between the descendants of the city's pre–Civil War Freedmen's community and the former slaves who had moved from surrounding Virginia and Maryland).[119] Economic and occupational divisions further fragmented local society.

By 1880, the area was, as the historian James Borchert would observe, an urban community which "served as a home base for blacks, whites, and mulattos; wealthy and poor; and educated and non-educated individuals."[120] However, it was "a neighborhood on the brink of racial and economic change."[121] The story of U Street during this period largely parallels the evolution of the larger Washington African American community. Allan Johnston, in a study of changes in the city's black community between 1860 and 1880, argues that the broad social patterns in place by the end of the period would last throughout the rest of the nineteenth century. Washington already had moved well "along the road to complete separation of the races."[122]

Johnston continues by observing that, "while total segregation seems to have been a long way off, significant areas of the city had already acquired a strong black 'flavor.'"[123] Later on, he adds, "a black world hidden from the view of an increasing number of whites" was taking shape—a "secret city" that was itself divided by class and skin color.[124] U Street was a center of this separate community, one that increasingly defined the tormented relationship between blacks and whites. U Street could not exist unless whites wanted to ignore the black city, to make it "secret"; nor could it exist unless blacks were willing and able to establish their own vigorous "secret" life.

The divisions noted by Johnson, Borchert, and others had yet to find physical expression, in part because the full impact of the loss of home rule only had begun to be felt. Previously passed civil rights legislation had yet to be overturned; Jim Crow segregation had yet to find its full stride.[125] A city government fully accountable to an increasingly Southern-dominated Congress—rather than to its own citizens—had yet to discover how little Congress could care about people who lived in neighborhoods such as those along U Street. Efforts to integrate the school system had yet to collapse fully. Another handful of years would still be required before segregated schools could hold racially defined residential patterns in place for decades. Racially separated churches, though the rule, were not yet an exclusive model for worship.[126] And successful black businessmen were just beginning to be expunged from city registers.

All this would soon change. The "Secret City" would become firmly ensconced within just a few years. The area that had been "in the woods," as Marcia McAdoo Greenlee had characterized it during the 1860s and 1870s, was about to become, at least in part, known as "Hell's Bottom."[127]

Profile

Major General Oliver Otis Howard (1830–1909)

Major General Oliver Otis Howard (figure 1.2) was born in Leeds, Maine, on November 6, 1830. He grew up in Maine, the son of a farmer who would die when Oliver was only nine. Howard attended local public schools and graduated from nearby Bowdoin College in 1850. Upon graduation from college, he taught school while considering various careers. An uncle, who was a member of Congress, arranged for Howard's appointment to the United States Military Academy at West Point. He graduated as a second lieutenant of ordnance in 1854, but he left military service after two years and returned to West Point as a civilian mathematics instructor.

At the outbreak of the Civil War in 1861, Howard accepted a commission as a colonel in the Third Maine Infantry. He eventually fought with various units in some of the war's fiercest battles, including the First Battle of Manassas (Bull Run), Fredericksburg, Chancellorsville, Antietam, Gettysburg, Chattanooga, Lookout Mountain, Missionary Ridge, and Atlanta. He led the right wing of William Tecumseh Sherman's March to the Sea through Georgia and the Carolinas into Virginia. He lost his right arm early in the war at the battle of Fair Oaks, Virginia, during the Peninsula Campaign of 1862 (three decades later, Howard would be awarded the Congressional Medal of Honor for heroism at Fair Oaks).

Howard was not always liked by either his fellow officers or his own troops, and he quarreled at times

FIGURE 1.2
Major General Oliver O. Howard

with his superiors. He suffered significant setbacks on the battlefield (particularly at Chancellorsville and Gettysburg). His strongly moralistic tone—which included advocating temperance—earned him the not-always-complimentary sobriquet of the "Christian Soldier."

Howard was appointed commissioner of the Freedmen's Bureau in 1865, a position he held throughout the life of the bureau. As commissioner, he was especially active in Washington, launching an agricultural settlement in the city's Southeast quadrant for freedmen known as Barry Farms; fighting for the continued racial integration of the Congregational Society's Washington congregations; and, in 1866, establishing what would become Howard University. He sent his daughters to the school, and he used his position at the Freedmen's Bureau to secure a congressional charter for the university. Howard served as the university's president between 1869 and 1874, and he led the city's YMCA between 1867 and 1871.

Howard went west following the closure of the Freedmen's Bureau, fighting in the Indian Wars (including the 1877 Nez Perce expedition in Oregon). He served as superintendent of his alma mater, West Point, between 1880 and 1882. He retired from military service in 1894, one year after receiving the Congressional Medal of Honor for his heroism at Fair Oaks. He subsequently founded Lincoln Memorial University in Harrogate, Tennessee, in 1895.

Reflecting upon the university named in his honor, Howard recorded near the end of his life that he considered the institution "as of the first importance as an object lesson—a complete exhibit in its organization and in its operation of the higher grade of school work. Here," he continued, "I tried to foster its life in the social as well as in the literary sphere, recognizing as far as it could be done the manhood of the Negro scholar, teacher, and professor."[128]

Howard wrote several books following his military service. He died in Burlington, Vermont, on October 26, 1909.

ALEXANDER ROBEY "BOSS" SHEPHERD (1835–1902)

Alexander Robey Shepherd (figure 1.3) was born in the District of Columbia on January 31, 1835, a time in local history when the city hardly seemed to belong among the ranks of even the rawest of American towns. One of seven children, Shepherd grew up in a semirural corner of Southwest Washington that was cut off from the rest of the city by a filthy and smelly canal. After the death of his father when Shepherd was thirteen, he found work in a series of low-paying jobs ranging from store errand boy to carpenter's apprentice. By the age of seventeen, he had created a niche for himself in the city's largest plumbing company and rose quickly from accountant to partner to owner.

The Civil War does not seem to have interfered much with Shepherd's increasingly lucrative business dealings. After a brief time in the local militia, he married, and then purchased a large estate in Washington County—a section of Northwest Washington now known as Shepherd Park near what is today Walter Reed Hospital and Georgia Avenue. He aggressively used his contacts in the building trades to buy and sell real estate, constructing some

FIGURE 1.3
Alexander Robey "Boss" Shepherd

Photograph from the Washington Historical Image Collection, Washingtoniana Division, Martin Luther King Jr. Library, Washington. Used with permission.

1,500 homes for speculation during the 1860s. He capitalized on his new riches and local knowledge for entree into the clubs of the local elite, befriending President Ulysses S. Grant in the process.

Shepherd became a strong advocate for public improvements, foreseeing the day when Washington would extend to fill and overtake the boundaries of the District of Columbia. In 1871, he worked closely with Grant and other powerful friends to engineer the suspension of municipal governance in the City of Washington, Georgetown, and Washington County. In their stead, Congress established a unified Territorial Government for the District of Columbia in its entirety. Critical decisions fell to a newly established Board of Public Works appointed by the president. Shepherd secured appointment as chair of this board, taking control of local politics (and public expenditures). He served as the territorial governor in 1873 and 1874, and his administration built 157 miles of roads, 123 miles of sewers, 39 miles of gas mains, and 30 miles of water mains, overspending local budgets by more than $16 million and leaving a modern and seemingly bankrupt city in its wake.

The Territorial Government proved to be short-lived. Congress lost patience with rampaging public expenditures, as well as with the growing prominence of African Americans in local affairs. Congress suspended the Territorial Government in 1874, abolishing any pretense of local home rule for the next ninety-nine years.

Shepherd fled Washington, arriving in Batopilas, a small city in the Copper Canyon of Mexico, in 1880. He spent the remainder of his life building a silver empire, discovering rich veins of ore in mines long thought to have been worked out. His Batopilas Mining Company extracted more than 20 million ounces of silver between 1880 and 1906, and built miles of rail lines, aqueducts, and tunnels. He supervised the construction of a hydroelectric plant that still operates today—and that enabled Batopilas to become the second city in Mexico after the capital to be electrified.

Shepherd returned to Washington in 1887 for a brief stay marked by a parade up Pennsylvania Avenue, followed by a hero's reception for thousands at the posh Willard Hotel. For Washingtonians, Shepherd remained the man who had modernized their city. He died in Batopilas in 1902.

CHAPTER 2

A City "Like the South"

> But Washington is like the South. It has all the prejudices
> and Jim Crow customs of any Southern town, except that
> there are no Jim Crow sections on the street cars.
>
> —Langston Hughes, *The Big Sea*, 1940[1]

The poet Langston Hughes overstated the extent of Jim Crow racial segregation in Washington while reflecting on his time in the city during the early 1920s. He could not go see any plays as he had in New York because people with his skin tone were banned from Washington's dramatic theaters; he couldn't go to restaurants as he had in Paris and in Italy because people with his skin tone were banned from nearly all of Washington's restaurants (except for a few serving the "colored"); he couldn't stay at the same hotels and rooming houses as folks of another skin color as he had in Mexico.[2] But he could do more than ride in the front of streetcars sitting next to white folk. He could visit the National Zoo, see a ball game at Griffith Stadium next door to Howard University, sit in the reading rooms of the Library of Congress and of the city's public library, and roll eggs on the White House lawn on Easter Monday.[3] However, he would not have been able to bury a family dog or cat in a cemetery reserved for the pets of whites.[4] Such was the extent of interracial mixing in the capital of the world's most ambitious democracy at the close of the "War to End All Wars" in 1918.

Hughes was also offended by the city's African American high society, which tried to define itself by lighter skin color; by family lineage back to either "first freed" slaves or "free persons of color" a half-century before; and by not having to work with their hands.[5] "These upper-class colored people," Hughes observed about a group of people that included some of his own cousins and mentors, "were on the whole as unbearable and snobbish a group of people as I have ever come in to contact with anywhere. They lived in comfortable homes, had fine cars, played bridge, drank Scotch, gave exclusive 'formal' parties, and dressed well, but seemed to be altogether lacking in real culture, kindness, or good common sense."[6]

The two faces of Hughes's detested Washington—those of Jim Crow and of his Langston cousins—were only vaguely visible along U Street in 1880.[7] By 1920, U Street, its culture, and its society would be emblematic of the dramatic transformations that had washed over the city with the collapse of home rule. "Prior to 1880," the historian John Karl Byrand would observe, "many of the city's black residents were confined to mini-ghettos within alleys; however, around the turn of the century, specific sections of the city underwent the process of racial concentration, forming large, predominantly black enclaves."[8] What happened?

The historian Thomas Johnson gets to the heart of the matter in a study of race relations in Washington following the Civil War. "Viewed from the perspective of a century," he concludes, "Reconstruction was a dismal failure, in Washington no less than in the nation. The slave remained emancipated, but in nearly all other respects Negro civil and political rights returned to ground zero. After a relatively brief period of excitement, political progress vanished."[9]

Johnson observed further that "the political and social revolutions that seemed to career back and forth with vigor in 1868 slowed perceptibly during the next several years, and finally, like waters on the shore, receded back to the old line. The process seemed to Washingtonians to be as inevitable as time and tide—the folkways of the nation could not be changed."[10] The loss in Washington, from Johnson's perspective, was greater than elsewhere in the country because "perhaps no other American city possessed the potential that Washington did to attain a fair amount of racial harmony and tolerance. But Reconstruction ultimately failed in the capital, and this failure became a harbinger of later disasters in the South."[11]

With local power resting in the hands of an increasingly Southern-dominated, prosegregationist Congress representing a white United

States not at all embarrassed by its crude racism—together with the emergence of a local Southern-dominated commercial and political elite by the turn of the century—the city turned its back on laws passed by the Territorial Government in 1872 and 1873 prohibiting discrimination in public accommodations, increasingly experiencing custom-enforced racial segregation in its place.[12] This reversal took place just as rural migrants—nearly all African American—arrived in record numbers. The result was achievement and tragedy, with upper-class African Americans—denied entry into white elite society—seeking to shut themselves off from their increasingly déclassé neighbors.[13] By 1920, the first signs of a newly assertive African American self-image molded out of the pain and frustration of a Jim Crow world would mark the initial stirring of an era of protest. U Street stood at the epicenter of these developments.

Enter Mr. Crow

"Jim Crow" was a popular term for laws, customs, and public policies intended to segregate and disfranchise African Americans throughout the American South between the 1880s and 1960s. Supported by courts, politicians, and mob violence, Jim Crow practices relegated Americans of the slightest African heritage to the status of second-class citizen.

The name "Jim Crow" appears to have been derived from a character created by Thomas "Daddy" Rice, a popular white minstrel singer of the 1830s. Rice performed in black face, mocking the dignity of African Americans through song and buffoonery. His character's name, "Jim Crow," became a term of racial disparagement widely used by whites to denigrate African Americans. For example, railway cars reserved for African Americans in the years leading up to the Civil War were popularly known as "Jim Crow Cars."[14]

Two Supreme Court rulings during the late nineteenth century permitted states, counties, and municipalities to pass Jim Crow laws of racial exclusion and segregation. In 1883, the Court ruled the Civil Rights Act of 1875—which had guaranteed equal access to public services and conveyances—to be unconstitutional. Interestingly, this ruling did not apply to Washington (until a subsequent Supreme Court decision in 1914) because the District of Columbia is not a state.[15] Thirteen years later, the Court upheld a Louisiana law stipulating that African Americans could be denied access to public transportation services designated for white passengers (in this instance, streetcars) so long as service was "separate but equal." The standard of "separate but equal" established by the 1896 Supreme Court decision in the case of *Plessy v. Ferguson* remained the law of the land until it was overturned in 1954 by the Supreme Court's decision in the *Brown v. Board of Education* case concerning the Topeka, Kansas, school system.[16]

The District of Columbia did not adopt the same sort of legislation that swept through the South after 1883. Rather, school and residential segregation, denial of access to employment, exclusion from restaurants and theaters, and many other restrictions were enforced by custom, physical force, and administrative fiat. The white commissioners appointed by Congress and the Army Corps of Engineers to manage the city—together with their various minions, including judges—ignored questions of equal access. As a consequence, Washington increasingly became divided by discriminatory practices that were sanctioned unofficially rather than by the power of law.[17] With a very few notable exceptions such as the streetcars and library reading rooms, Washington began to function as a racially segregated city within a remarkably short period of time.[18]

Both racial segregation and the final abrogation of home rule following the Organic Act of 1878 were a consequence of the Compromise of 1877. As already noted, the presidential election the previous year between Democrat Samuel J. Tilden of New York and Republican Rutherford B. Hayes of Ohio ended in a dead heat, with a number of electoral seats falling under dispute. The House of Representatives took control of the election, establishing a commission to adjudicate claims among contested electors. The Democrats agreed to support the claims of the Republican Hayes to a majority in the Electoral College in exchange for the removal of federal troops from the former Confederate States, as well as the appointment of Democrats to key government posts. Republican acceptance of this compromise permitted the coming to power of "Redeemer" governments—local administrations dedicated to reestablishing white supremacy regimes—throughout the region.[19]

The Democrats justified their policies in part on the basis of so-called misrule of the nation's capital by Shepherd and the city's black electorate.[20] Against this broad political backdrop, the days were numbered for even an imperfectly racially integrated neighborhood such as those that had grown up around U Street.

The Undisputed Center of American Negro Civilization

Several distinct forces shaping the city created U Street during the two decades following the start of the Civil War: War brought people flooding into the District of Columbia; street cars spread those settlers out over a considerably larger settlement footprint; the physical city expanded more slowly than the number of people who were arriving; Northerners undermined the city's antebellum Southern culture; freedmen enhanced Washington's African American community. The local government simultaneously constructed a modern urban infrastructure and bankrupted the city. National leaders, for their part, reined in as many of these forces as possible by suspending home rule. All these developments solidified the city's function as the national capital just as the role of the national government was expanding within American life.[21] The city's overall population more than doubled from 75,080 in 1860 to 177,624 in 1880, while its African American population exploded from 14,328 to 59,596.[22] U Street was just one of many communities affected by the profound changes that were redefining Washington as a city.

The next forty years between the suspension of home rule in 1878 and the end of World War I in 1918 spurred even greater transformations as the city's population grew at an ever faster pace. By 1920, census takers could find 437,571 residents of the District of Columbia, including 109,966 African Americans.[23] This black metropolis included within it large numbers of government employees and more than 1,500 professionals, who formed the core of a vibrant middle class.[24]

Halfway through the period, around 1900, Washington had become the largest African American city in the country.[25] The city was "the undisputed center of American Negro civilization."[26] And U Street, a once-vitally diverse mix of races and classes, became the undisputed heart of this undisputed center.

The notion of U Street as a center of a civilization would have struck some Washingtonians of the era—especially white Washingtonians—as absurd. One area around the corner of 11th and R streets, NW, was widely known as "Hell's Bottom" because of its perceived role as a major vice and crime center.[27] Within just a few decades, however, the streets generally located around U Street would go from being known as "In the Woods," to "Hell's Bottom," and eventually "Quality Row."

Marcia McAdoo Greenlee argues that none of these labels were deserved in terms of either the reality of daily life in the area or the neighborhood's evolution over time.[28] She correctly reminds her readers that

> certain aspects of its character remained remarkably constant. . . . White men were responsible for the initial subdivision of the squares, . . . and for most of the construction after 1877. . . . Black men, however, also participated in the area's development. . . . The most intense period of development was between 1874 and 1880, when the number of homes along [11th] Street more than doubled. City beautification under the Territorial Government, increased city services and improved transportation to outlying areas of the city, enhanced this growth. It took thirty-three years for the same number of new homes to be constructed after 1880 as had been completed in the six previous years. Between 1913, by which time the area had become known as "Quality Row," and . . . 1930, there were only six instances of new construction or major renovation. Houses once erected tended to remain as they were.[29]

If the houses were basically the same in 1880 and in 1913, 1920, or 1930, what was changing? Superficial traits placed the neighborhood somewhat out of step from the tenor of the times. For example, the large number of saloons, bars, and taverns confronted bourgeois sensibilities at a time when the temperance movement was gaining strength. As a consequence, Congress closed drinking establishments within proximity of the National Old Soldiers' Home in the nearby Petworth neighborhood to the north.[30]

More profoundly, the racial composition of the area's inhabitants changed, thereby prompting "proper" white—and often openly racist—Washingtonians to perceive physical and moral decline regardless of the realities on the ground. African Americans moved in, rented, purchased, and built homes, businesses, social institutions, and communities. Whites—less hemmed in by restrictive covenants, laws, custom, and violence—took advantage of the city's growing network of streetcars to move to newer neighborhoods to the north.[31] As these changes took place, LeDroit Park at the east end of the U Street neighborhood—and an area bounded by 15th and 18th streets, R Street, and Florida Avenue to the west that would become known as the "Strivers' Section"—passed from well-manicured white to well-manicured African American hands.[32]

Perceptions did not follow reality. The poet Paul Laurence Dunbar captured the profound misconceptions about African American Washington in an article appearing in *Harper's Weekly* during the early days of 1900. "That the pleasure and importance of Negro life in Washington are overrated by the colored people themselves is as true as that it is underrated and misunderstood by the whites," Dunbar observed. "To the former," he continued, "the social aspect of this life is a very dignified and serious drama. To the latter it is nothing but the most amusing and inconsequential farce. But they both are wrong: it is neither the one thing nor the other."[33]

Just as the neighborhood was associated with a level of iniquity that did not exist, many Washingtonians thought of the area around U Street as completely black. This too was not quite the case. The adjacent "Hell's Bottom" neighborhood studied by Greenlee, for example, was transformed from 54 percent white in 1880 to 85 percent black in 1900.[34] In some instances, older white residents remained, as did some of their children. White owners of small businesses stayed near their stores, shops, and other commercial operations.[35] In Washington, as in America, perceptions of race nonetheless mattered more than reality.

The integrated U Street of 1880 had become a "colored" neighborhood by 1900.

This particular Washington neighborhood was hardly alone in experiencing the gathering storm of racial segregation. The historian Allan Johnston reports that there were no census tracts in the city inhabited entirely by blacks in 1880 (although two were more than 75 percent African American).[36] Within just a few years, disparate communities in Southeast's Anacostia, in Northwest's Foggy Bottom and Iowa (now Logan) Circle, along H Street in Northeast, and around 4½ Street in Southwest would become Jim Crow neighborhoods surrounded by an ever-hardening color line.[37] Though some of these areas had long histories as neighborhoods of African American settlement, none previously had been completely segregated by race. In the case of U Street, a tipping point was passed around 1890, thereby nurturing ever-growing racial hostility.[38]

With every new Jim Crow racial practice accepted as custom and law, segregation tossed up ever higher invisible walls separating African Americans from whites who chose not to look their way. Black Washington had its own heroes and villains, its own successes and failures, its own rich and poor, and very much its own distinct identity. As Dunbar observed, "It is the middle-class Negro who has imbibed enough of white civilization to make him work to be prosperous. But he has not partaken of civilization so deeply that he has become drunk and has forgotten his own identity. The church to him is still the centre of his social life, and his preacher a great man. He has not—and I am not wholly sorry that he has not—earned the repression of his emotions, which is the mark of a high and dry civilization."[39]

The Alleyways of African American Poor People

Pierre L'Enfant's design of intersecting radials and grids for the city of Washington created an urban geography in which individual blocks grew to abnormally large proportions. So deep were some lots that they could contain within them dense networks of alleys hidden from public view behind the grand facades that lined major thoroughfares.[40] As population pressures increased during and following the Civil War, these byways became home to growing numbers of migrants fresh from the countryside.[41] Such small corners of rural life provided protected preserves in which the country played hide-and-seek with the proud official buildings and pretentious houses of the federal city.[42] Alleys emerged as the place where racial separation within the city began in earnest.

Always poor, the alley communities were either white or black—and sometimes both mixed together—around the time of the Civil War. They became reception points wherein migrants from the rural South and elsewhere began their life in the city.[43] Most African American alley dwellers were born in neighboring states and came to the city in search of a better life.[44]

By 1880, backstreet communities were among the first in the city to become segregated by race.[45] In 1897, for example, 90 percent of the 19,000 alley residents—the highest number ever recorded—were African American.[46] This was a time when the requirements for the care and feeding of horses—and, later, the parking and repair of automobiles— began to push alley inhabitants from such relatively middle-class areas as U Street.[47]

Alley communities remained a prominent feature of the city's life for another few decades, despite constant agitation by civic reformers pressing for their elimination. The city's new Board of Health began condemning alley shanties as early as the 1870s, while the U.S. Congress imposed the first of many restrictions on alley construction in 1894.[48]

Civil society, both black and white, responded. Shortly after arriving from Florida to become pastor of the powerful African American Shiloh Baptist Church, John Milton Waldron established and served as president of the Alley Improvement Association.[49] The conditions of the alleys became one of several impetuses prompting the establishment of the white Washington Civic Center, which was modeled after a similar alliance of civic and charitable organizations in Chicago known as the Civic Federation.[50] The center commissioned some of the most extensive studies of Washington's alley communities of the late 1890s under the direction of the anthropologist Clare de Graffenried, the civic leader Charles Weller, and others.[51]

Weller, the executive secretary of the Associated Charities of Washington, took up the charge to increase business engagement on the issue.[52] He simultaneously organized investigations of alley communities to determine the precise contours and scale of the "problems" they posed.[53] His resulting volume, *Neglected Neighbors*—which appeared in 1909 with a foreword by President Theodore Roosevelt—became a classic among early American efforts to employ new social science methodologies in the search for solutions to pressing social problems.[54]

Weller ends his report with a highly unusual call for popular suffrage in the city, a singular and heartfelt appeal demonstrating an all-too-rare appreciation for the linkage between democracy and civic virtue that embraced both whites and blacks. "Although it may seem a 'far cry' to bring a consideration of popular suffrage into a study of this character," Weller wrote,

> this summary of the writer's fundamental ideals for the National Capital cannot be complete without it. For the establishment of an adequate policy regarding housing and living conditions it is essential that public opinion should be developed. The community must be enabled to act more and more as a self-conscious whole. At present, large sections of Washington are absolutely without any effect upon the government which controls them. Their lack of power is accompanied by a corresponding lack of interest. It is doubtless true that a comparatively small number of resourceful citizens—who know what they want and are trained in the effective expression of their desires—can exert greater influence upon local government here than would be possible in other American cities.

"There is nothing, however, to enlist the interest and influence of the less resourceful masses," he continued.[55] "The local bugbear, the presence of a large colored population, should not be deemed a conclusive argument against popular suffrage in Washington, for in any democratic government it is not safe in the long run to exclude any group of citizens from this educational relationship in the community's life."[56] Three-quarters of a century would pass before a majority of the members of Congress would heed Weller's eloquent concluding words.[57]

Although singular in its concern for democratic inclusion, Weller's examination of the harsh conditions of life in Washington's alleys did not stand alone. Numerous studies commissioned by a variety of civic and governmental groups and agencies appeared at the time.[58] According to the historian James Borchert, research sponsored by another group of concerned Washingtonians—the Monday Evening Club—estimated that 240 blocks of inhabited alleys could be found in the city in 1912.[59] These areas contained 3,201 alley houses—nearly all built before 1892—housing 16,000 residents.[60] Borchert reports further that, "although the number of houses decreased by nearly 40 percent by 1927, 1,346 alley dwellings remained occupied in Northwest and Southwest alone."[61]

Such houses eventually became targets for the Alley Dwelling Authority, which was established in 1934 by Congress "to provide for the discontinuance of the use as dwellings of the buildings situated in alleys in the District of Columbia."[62] Ironically, at the beginning of the twenty-first century, laws restricting residences in alleys would become the object of protest by gentrifiers looking for centrally located, inexpensive housing that they could convert into trendy in-town residences.[63]

The lasting images of African American poverty, disease, degradation, and perceived vice used by reformers to mobilize support for their cause became fixed in the minds of the city's white population. African American communities of all economic statuses—including the middle-class neighborhood around U Street—became associated in white minds with degradation and decay (when white minds reflected on their African American neighbors at all).

Leading "mainstream" newspapers such as the *Washington Post* and the *Evening Star* reinforced these images by the absence of coverage of African Americans. The *Post* remained particularly aggressive in its statements about—and coverage of—the black community well into the 1950s, if not beyond.[64] The *Evening Star*, the local Republican paper, generally proved to be friendlier to African Americans during this period. Even the *Evening Star*, however, steadily reduced its mention of African Americans between the 1880s and 1920s.[65] Overall, the iconography of racial segregation proved to be as powerful as it was misplaced and misguided.

Recognizing the danger of romanticizing the life of the poor, historians looking back on the lost world of the Washington alley discover communities that were rich in what social scientists have come to call "social capital."[66] The city's alley community provided dense networks of contacts that supported its members. Rather than being the dens of iniquity that reformers believed them to be, alleys were play areas for children, outdoor laundries for women, refuges for men, and conversation pits for all. The informal social world of the alley sheltered inhabitants from the humiliations and hardships of the wealthier and whiter world beyond. Residents drifted in and out of the alley every day.

These rural oases in the city—often inaccessible to outsiders—sustained many new Washingtonians; even as they crushed others.[67] Borchert concludes, "intolerable conditions do not necessarily lead to dehumanization. . . . Despite the intolerable conditions, alley residents were able to shape and control their own lives within the economic, social, and political limits imposed by the dominant white society."[68]

The powerful images of urban debasement associated with the alleys were too readily transferred onto largely middle-class and stable neighborhoods of longtime city residents, such as U Street. Reality, once again, was very different. As Greenlee concludes, "the absence of white residents after 1913 . . . did not result in the deterioration of the street, as is so frequently the expected result from such shifts in population. . . . The quality of neighborhood life," she continued, "in what became known as 'Quality Row,' was the result of black people committed to acquiring and holding property while improving all they could of their environment."[69] In fact, better-off African Americans created their own ways in which they could control their own lives, despite the social, economic, and political walls being erected by the city's whites.[70]

The Equally Hidden World
of the African American Middle Class

Jim Crow segregation increasingly meant that Washington's African Americans had to fend for themselves. Constance McLaughlin Green argues that, by the turn of the century, the city's once-fragmented and largely disorganized African American community was beginning to "yield to community effort."[71] African American businesses and nonprofit community groups offered commercial and civic services unavailable from the larger white city, published magazines, produced plays, opened restaurants, designed theaters, built hotels and apartment buildings, sold automobiles, and created YMCAs and other institutions to offer community services.[72]

African American women, many of whom were employed in domestic service, emerged as stalwarts of associations, societies, and religious institutions.[73] They became an ever more vital presence in the community once the "live in" service of the nineteenth century began to give way to "live out" employment. This transformation played itself out as the city's white middle and elite classes adjusted their lifestyles to higher costs, smaller houses, and labor-saving home technologies.[74] Reconfigured—and altogether new—institutions developed alongside the continued vigor of such traditionally strong pillars of African American Washington society as the dozens of vibrant churches, some of the best "colored" schools in the country, the Freedmen's Hospital, and Howard University.[75]

Michael Andrew Fitzpatrick warns against overstating the changes that were taking place. In a work that chronicles the evolution of African American commerce in the Shaw neighborhood that includes U Street, he wrote that "it would be misleading to imply that it was only after the events of the 1870s and 1880s, and the growth of a business-oriented ideology of racial advancement, that blacks in Washington were engaged in business."[76] African Americans had been engaged in commerce as mechanics and skilled artisans, operated stores, and driven cabs since the founding of the city. What was changing throughout the city in general—and around U Street in particular—is that the white racism so evident in the 1880s prompted African Americans to view business as a vehicle of self-preservation.[77] The number of African American businesses in the Shaw neighborhood (of which U Street is a part) increased from just 15 in 1886 to more than 300 by 1920.[78]

African Americans establishing companies occupied niches ever higher up the urban economic hierarchy. Black businessmen founded business associations, banks, and other financial institutions that would serve their community well throughout the coming decades, including the National Negro Business League, the Capital Savings Bank, the True Reformers' Bank (founded in Richmond), the National Benefit Life Insurance Company, and the Industrial Building and Savings Association (which still exists after several reorganizations and resurrections).[79]

Community business leaders embraced the Twelfth Street YMCA, which has provided invaluable community service since it was founded as the first black branch of that organization by the former slave turned educator Anthony Bowen in 1853.[80] The cornerstone of a grand new headquarters building for the organization was put into place on Thanksgiving Day 1908 by President Theodore Roosevelt at 1816 12th Street, NW, near the corner of 12th and S streets, with a speech praised by many in the community as an "honest, open, frank tribute to this race of ours, always earnest and sincere."[81] The building opened its doors in 1912. The Phyllis Wheatley YWCA a few blocks away at 9th Street and Rhode Island Avenue, NW, opened in 1905, offering a similarly wide range of programs to African American women.[82]

The headquarters buildings of many of these associations and enterprises—such as the Twelfth Street and Wheatley Ys; the True Reformer Building built in 1903 at the corner of 12th and U streets (designed by the country's most prominent African American architect, John A. Lankford, whose own office was around the corner at 12th and V streets); the Laborer's Building and Loan Association, initially at 12th, and later at 11th and U streets; and the Lincoln Memorial Building Company's offices nearby—were described by the *Washington Bee* as "the new Emancipation Proclamation," symbolizing an emboldened and increasingly assertive African American entrepreneurial class intent on providing community services as well as making money.[83] The handful of

African American business establishments and civic associations in the
neighborhoods surrounding U Street in 1880 had become hundreds by
1920.[84]

Thick networks of businesses and civic and religious institutions
became one way in which African Americans could exert influence over
the broader community. In the pernicious and supercharged world of
Washington race relations, these African American organizations often
would be distinguished from their white counterparts by assuming the
title of "civic associations." White organizations, by contrast, frequently
were called "citizens associations."[85]

The Organic Laws of 1878 disfranchised blacks and whites alike,
of course. Whites were less concerned, even welcoming the change.
Wealthy white Washingtonians met federal power brokers in clubs, in
offices, and through family connections. They could push their agendas
via any number of informal mechanisms that were often more effective
than formal city government might have been.[86] It is small wonder that
Mark Twain and Charles Dudley Warner titled their 1873 satire of the
city and its folkways *The Gilded Age* (a label that would eventually stick
to all of American society during the era).[87]

Beyond personalistic and informal ties, white citizens and business
leaders organized their own network of associations and commissions,
exerting powerful control over the city. More specifically, they benefited
directly from the increased federal payment to support the District
government, which had been included in the suspension of local rule
because the new arrangements lessened their tax burdens.[88]

Downtown businessmen formed the powerful Washington Board
of Trade in 1889 just as New Hampshire Republican Henry Blair
introduced the final failed congressional effort to extend the right to
vote to the city's residents.[89] The board—which still exists as the Greater
Washington Board of Trade—combined real estate, commercial, and
utilities leaders in a potent lobby on behalf of real estate development
interests.[90] Over time, Congress looked to the board to speak for the
entire city, a role that reached its zenith with the 1901 McMillan
Commission appointed by the Senate to devise a plan to reinvigorate
L'Enfant's original plans for the monumental city.[91]

Meanwhile, blacks were being driven out of jobs with the District government. African Americans filled only 9 of 450 positions when the newly constructed District Building opened in 1908, which helps to explain the proposal by the *Washington Bee* that the words "discrimination is the greatest evil that can creep into municipal administration" be etched across the building's ornate facade in large gold letters.[92] This low level of African American employment in local public-sector jobs was a far cry from the Reconstruction administration of Mayor Bowen just four decades before. Institutions and arrangements dependent on snug relationships among business and political leaders steadily marginalized poor whites and all blacks from city affairs.

Businesses, civic associations, churches, social groups, cultural organizations, and educational institutions provided a protective wall as important to the black middle class as the refuge provided by alley life was for the city's black poor.[93] As a community under attack by the city's and country's white majority, African Americans living, working, and playing along U Street needed every resource they could muster to survive and to thrive. With each passing year between 1880 and 1920, the urban society of U Street in Washington became ever more African American. Self-sufficient entrepreneurs—encouraged in part by philosophies of economic separatism—provided more and more services to African Americans denied access to the white economy.[94] The black bourgeoisie produced by these developments took advantage of white migration further out into previously countrified areas of the District of Columbia to lay claim to prestigious enclaves such as LeDroit Park, the Strivers' Section, and Iowa (later Logan) Circle.[95] LeDroit Park, which in 1880 had been an ivory bookend at the eastern limit of a racially mixed neighborhood, now became a symbol of pride in the segregated black society of 1920, as did the Strivers' Section to the west.[96]

When U Street Was in Vogue

All was not well within the U Street community. Between 1925 and 1927, a former principal of M Street (later Dunbar) Colored High School and head librarian at Howard University, Edward Christopher

Williams, published a series of anonymous articles in the form of letters from a fictional character reflecting upon the shortcomings of Washington's African American elite. Appearing under the title "Letters of Davy Carr, A True Story of Colored Vanity Fair" in the black literary journal *The Messenger*, Williams's novel captured many of the foibles of the city's "talented tenth," a self-contained community increasingly held up in their segregated neighborhood around U Street. Often described as an African American *Great Gatsby*, Williams's masterful novel criticized much of the same behavior that was drawing the ire of two of the author's friends, Jean Toomer and Langston Hughes. His work would be forgotten with the passage of time, only to resurface some seventy-five years later as single volume published under the editorship of Adam McKible.[97]

As an associate of various African American literary societies and cultural institutions around town, such as the prestigious Mu-So-Lit Club, Williams helped arrange for performances of Angelina Grimké's play on the horrors of lynching, *Rachel*; helped organize memorial commemorations for the poet Paul Lawrence Dunbar; helped promote the initial publication of the work of the poet Carrie Clifford; and helped to build the Howard University Library into a major collegiate research center. Williams, who died unexpectedly on Christmas Eve 1929 after having just begun his studies for a doctoral degree at Columbia University, proved himself to be a quiet stalwart of the literary and cultural movement that would later become known as the "Harlem Renaissance."[98]

Williams, Toomer, Hughes, Grimké, Clifford, and many other African American writers of the period engaged the community that the active, vital, socially integrated U Street neighborhood of the 1880s had become by 1920—an internally divided and uncommonly complex mixture of classes and cultures forced together by the accident of skin color and the malevolence of whites. Divisions occurred within the African American community, with mulattoes increasingly experiencing more economic and social success than those with darker skin.[99]

The failures of Reconstruction had prompted this fragmentation along the twin pressure points of class and race, both within the national

African American community in general and within Washington in particular.[100] African American elites sought to distinguish themselves from poorer rural migrants to urban life. Skin color, personal and family histories, education, and wealth became markers separating the "talented tenth" from the rest of the African American community.[101] Simultaneously, as they were increasingly spurned by whites of similar socioeconomic and educational accomplishment, African American elites gained a consciousness of themselves as black.[102]

The historian Jacqueline Moore records that "in 1880, elite blacks based their social status on their ties with prominent whites, their skin color, and their family backgrounds. They were obsessed with being seen as distinct from the race and therefore acceptable to the white community. Their primary concern was their own assimilation. . . . By 1920 they had formed a firmer foundation for social status based on income, education, and the creation of independent institutions. They could now associate with less fortunate members of their race without risking their social status."[103]

Professionals and businessmen were divided over the extent to which Negro communities could and should partition themselves from the white world, and how much "native" Washingtonians should and could separate themselves from recent migrants from the rural South. The tone among the increasingly disputatious local leaders could turn deeply personal, as when the *Washington Bee* published a screed against W. E. B. Du Bois, noting that "when you have said that Prof. Du Bois is a scholar you have said it all. A leader he can never be, for he lacks the first and prime requisite of a leader, to wit: tolerance. Disappointed because the people will not accept and proclaim him leader, he displays his teeth, indulges in personalities, and detracts not only from his peers but his superiors."[104]

Such arguments, in turn, produced a constructive reaction in the form of an increasing appreciation of a shared responsibility to "better the race." In fact, the retrograde social attitudes disparaged by Langston Hughes as he encountered Washington's U Street elite during the 1920s obscured a more profound development: the emergence of a radicalized racial community increasingly intent on justice. The complex racial, social, cultural, educational, and economic landscape of U Street that had been forged by the suspension of home rule locally—and the collapse of Reconstruction nationally—eventually provided a basis for unified political action.

This new world was shaped both by the exclusion and degradation engendered by white indifference and racism, as well as by the self-assertion of African Americans of all castes and classes in response. The increasing segregation and ever more harsh racial stereotypes held by whites during the 1890s led to new survival strategies among African Americans.[105] No longer admitted to white clubs, African Americans formed their own—such as the Lotus Club, Sparta Club, Manhattan Club, and Acanthus Club—aimed at different segments of the black community.[106]

Literary and academic clubs—such as the distinguished Bethel Literary and Historical Society and the Mu-So-Lit Society—followed, uniting prominent public intellectuals such as Frederick Douglass and the brothers Grimké.[107] The Monocan Club, established in 1899, was generally considered the most difficult to join, and hence was regarded in the community as the most exclusive of all.[108] These organizations were joined during the early twentieth century by a lively array of professional associations, elite sororities for African American women, fraternities for African American men, settlement houses, mutual aid societies and mutual benefit associations, charitable and reform clubs, and other civil society organizations.[109]

As with so much else along U Street, the unrelenting pressure of white racism in a post-Reconstruction America and congressionally ruled Washington brought out both the best and worst in African Americans. Such clubs and associations became controversial. Many served as important vehicles for racial uplift that transcended the boundaries of class and skin color. The more prominent often set themselves up as arbiters of virtue and fountainheads of superiority based on lighter skin. Some reformers—such as William Calvin Chase, editor of one of the community's leading newspapers, the *Washington Bee*—severely chastised claims to exclusivity.[110]

Churches remained especially prominent centers of African American life, as had been the case since the city's founding.[111] Clergy such as

Francis J. Grimké at the Fifteenth Street Presbyterian Church, Dabuek Payne at the Metropolitan African Methodist Episcopal Church, Walter Henderson Brooks across town at the Nineteenth Street Baptist Church, John Milton Waldron at Shiloh Baptist Church, and the magisterial Alexander Crummell at Saint Luke's Episcopal Church used their positions to articulate a public identity among African American Washingtonians.[112]

Payne founded the Bethel Literary and Historical Association. Crummell became the animating force behind the establishment of the first black learned society in the country—the American Negro Academy.[113] Having been established by the seventy-eight-year-old Crummell in 1897 as "an organization of authors, scholars, artists, and those distinguished in other walks of life, men of African descent, for the promotion of Letters, Science, and Art," the academy became one of black America's leading institutions. For more than a quarter of a century, academy members included such prominent African American intellectuals and activists as W. E. B. Du Bois, Booker T. Washington, Paul Laurence Dunbar, James Weldon Johnson, Carter G. Woodson, Alain Locke, Arthur Schomburg, and Archibald Grimké.[114]

Congregations often divided the black community as well as uniting the race. "By stressing proper behavior," Moore writes, "the elite churches hoped to distinguish themselves from the more emotional working-class black churches, to which whites pointed as typical indications of why blacks could never assimilate with sedate white society. . . . Elite churches were distinct from mass churches in several ways. . . . Whereas the rural church focused on preparing for the next world, the urban church focused on making this world a better place."[115]

As frustration grew with the world of Jim Crow, some among the city's black elite abandoned Christian churches. The Baha'i movement gained a moment of particular prominence in the years around 1900. Movement leader Abdu'l Baha, visiting from Iran in 1912, spoke before packed audiences at the Bethel Literary and Historical Association and at Howard University.[116] Somewhat later, during the 1930s, Nation of Islam founder Elijah Muhammad established Masjid Muhammad (also known as Muhammad Temple Number 4), serving as minister between

1937 and 1942.[117] The ethical focus on racial and moral uplift among the area's varied religious institutions often served to bridge the very divisions within the black community that the social composition of various congregations had reinforced in years past.

Many Washingtonians and others in the national African American community viewed the city's African American public schools as the best in the country. The schools similarly divided the community into classes based on educational achievement.[118] The nationally renowned M Street High School for Colored Youth (later Preparatory, and subsequently Dunbar, High School) and Howard University attracted middle-class African American families to the city generally, and to the U Street neighborhood more particularly.[119] M Street High, which was founded in the basement of the Fifteenth Street Presbyterian Church in 1870, was the nation's first high school for African American youth; and for many years, its best. Faculty included graduates of the country's leading universities—often at the postgraduate level. The school's alumni filled major African American institutions with talented staff.[120] Its neighborhood location—together with nearby Armstrong High specializing in technical subjects and, much later, Cardozo High in business, as well as Howard University—meant that many among this elite remained close by throughout their careers and lives.[121]

Controversies surrounding education were deep, in part reflecting an ideological battle between supporters of Booker T. Washington's "industrial" approach favoring vocational skills, and advocates of more classical curricula with a focus on higher educational achievement who were drawn to the arguments of Du Bois.[122] National debates played themselves out slightly differently in Washington given the proximity of congressional scrutiny and the absence of home rule. Black appointees sat on the local school board together with whites, often having final approval over hiring and firing in the "colored" schools.[123] Ultimate authority rested with white school superintendents for the public schools—and white regents and university presidents at Howard—who were inclined to "dumb down" curriculum for blacks.[124]

Despite serious financial problems, supply shortages, inadequacies in physical plant, and constant warfare over curriculum, the city's record in black education set a national standard. Between 1870 and 1910, the African American illiteracy rate fell in the city from 80 percent to under 20 percent, despite the constant inflow of poorly educated and undereducated migrants from the rural Jim Crow South.[125] Once again, African American community institutions—public schools, private schools, the Miner Normal School (the city's principal school for black teachers),[126] and Howard University—united even as they divided the community by differentiating within the African American community according to educational achievement and values. Black educational institutions instilled a fierce race pride that would carry Washington's blacks forward in the decades to come.

FIGURE 2.1
Edward Kennedy "Duke" Ellington

Photograph from the Washington Historical Image Collection, Washingtoniana Division, Martin Luther King Jr. Library, Washington. Used with permission.

The distinguished composer and musician Edward Kennedy "Duke" Ellington (figure 2.1) recalled the importance of school-instilled pride in his memoirs, writing that "Negro History was crammed into the curriculum, so that we would know our people all the way back. They had pride there, the greatest race pride, and at that time there was some sort of movement to desegregate the schools in Washington, D.C. Who do you think were the first to object? Nobody but the proud Negroes of Washington, who felt that the kind of white kids we would be thrown in with were not good enough."[127]

Stable employment rather than educational or occupational achievement mattered most in calculations of social status. A job with the federal government was highly valued despite the fact that most were menial. The presence of the federal sector helped to distinguish Washington's African American community from others around the country, contributing mightily to the well-being of those who lived around U Street.[128] For this reason, among many others, the overtly racist employment policies of the

Woodrow Wilson administration exerted especially deleterious effects throughout the city's African American neighborhoods.[129]

A Spirit of Enterprise

African American leaders fought back in every way that they could. Debates within Washington's black community reflected the national divide developing between the relatively more accommodationist stance of Booker T. Washington and the more assertive black nationalism of W. E. B. Du Bois.[130] Numerous community leaders and business owners—such as William Calvin Chase, John W. Cromwell, and the Reverend Alexander Crummell—embraced racial economic nationalism in the face of the white exclusionary onslaughts.[131] Local African American leaders and opinion makers encouraged a movement for patronage of black businesses, creating banks and other financial institutions and supporting black entrepreneurs in every possible manner.[132]

The community's professionals, businesses, and leaders—both men and women—became less dependent on white patronage as whites refused to seek out their services.[133] Forced to rely on their own resources, African American Washingtonians developed networks and institutions, together with a separatist philosophy that encouraged residents to patronize black-owned businesses.[134] Early-twentieth-century business leaders such as Andrew Hilyer became especially passionate advocates for racial resistance.[135]

The ideology of racial separatism evident among the business community had deep roots along U Street.[136] John W. Cromwell, editor of the *People's Advocate* (1878–84), and William Calvin Chase, the acerbic editor of the longer-lived *Washington Bee* (1882–1922), constantly sounded the call for racial unity and cooperation.[137] They sharply attacked what they saw as an accommodationist elite enamored with distancing themselves from their less fortunate racial brethren.[138]

Although there is considerable justification for Cromwell's and Chase's frustrations, the so-called integrationist elites were no less aware of the hardening barrier between white and black Washington. The debates—reflective of the division nationally between supporters of

W. E. B. Du Bois on the one hand and Booker T. Washington on the other—were more about tactics than goals.[139] All community leaders were deeply angered by their treatment at the hands of white Washington and of the federal government. Their shared contempt for the divided city—combined with the intensity of neighborhood debates in what was at the time the nation's largest African American community—forged many of the leaders who eventually would join together to form the National Association for the Advancement of Colored People in 1909.[140] Black-owned businesses in the city exploded in number and deepened in sophistication. By 1910, hundreds of African American businesses in the U Street vicinity were listed in the city's business directories—including many financial institutions.[141] Black developers built apartment and office buildings around the neighborhood, as well as the swank Whitelaw Hotel.[142]

This entrepreneurial trend nurtured a thriving neighborhood economy and, by the early decades of the twentieth century, cultural life and sports as stores, theaters, and financial institutions catered to the needs of neighborhood residents.[143] Black and white entrepreneurs competed for the growing purse of the early-twentieth-century black middle class. Whites opened the Howard Theatre near the intersection of 7th and T for live performance; black businessmen responded with the Minnehaha Theater for movies (the present site of Ben's Chili Bowl).[144] A little later, in 1922, the Lincoln opened next door to the Minnehaha as a "first-run" movie house, with live performances offered in the Lincoln Colonnade located at the back of the building in the basement.[145]

In sports, the Twelfth Street YMCA basketball team dominated the first African American basketball league in the nation during the years leading up to World War I, outrunning Brooklyn's Smart Set Grave Diggers 24 to 15 for the initial national championship among black hoopsters in 1910.[146] Clark Griffith built a stadium for his baseball team in 1912. His ballpark towered over U Street for half a century, playing home to such baseball teams as the white Senators and the black LeDroit Tigers, Pilots, Elite Giants, and famous Homestead Grays, as well as the Redskins football team.[147] The celebrated "Black Broadway" of the 1920s and 1930s (see chapter 4) was being born as early as the 1910s.[148]

Large, stable family networks sustained a U Street elite produced by neighborhood institutions and businesses. Parents mobilized personal and community resources to advance their children's life possibilities within a social class that invested heavily in the emotional capital of proper genealogy, proper schooling, and proper jobs. Among the beneficial aspects of the swaggering attitude that so distressed Langston Hughes were close familial ties that sustained people in the midst of a constantly hostile general environment.[149]

The always perceptive Paul Lawrence Dunbar perhaps caught this distinctive feature of Washington African American community life earlier than most observers when, in 1900, he wrote that

> the influence which the success of a few men will have upon a whole community is indicated in the spirit of venture which actuates the rising generation of this city. A few years ago, if a man secured a political position, he was never willing or fit to do anything else afterward. But now the younger men, with the example of some of their successful elders before them, are beginning to see that an easy berth in one of the departments is not the best thing in life, and they are getting brave enough to do other things. Some of these ventures have proven failures, even disasters, but it has not daunted the few, nor crushed the spirit of effort in them.[150]

Dunbar's children of U Street's—and Washington's—black and tan elite trained for community service and achievement independent from white society. The interaction between aggressive white intransigence and assertive black autonomy produced a stronger, more self-reliant community.[151]

On the negative side, African Americans did not always treat one another well simply because they were all victims of ever sharper white racism. Status-conscious African Americans became concerned about the image of their community among the larger white society. For example, the Emancipation Day parades celebrating the April 16, 1862, freeing of the city's African Americans from servitude emerged as an ever increasing point of contention. Fearful that whites might misinterpret these raucous demonstrations, "proper" black elites withdrew support from the holiday.[152] Outbreaks of violence in the late 1890s prompted the School Board to disallow children taking time off to watch and to participate. Public celebrations ceased in 1901, to lie fallow for nine decades before being reinstituted during the early 1990s by All Souls Unitarian Church parishioners led by Wesley and Loretta Carter Hanes, as well as the Smithsonian Institution's Anacostia Museum, Howard University, and the District government.[153]

More importantly, skin color increasingly divided the U Street community into what Byrand has called a "three-ringed racial and residential pattern," in which the outer rings were whites of decreasing occupational mobility, the middle were primarily blacks on their way up, and the center in closest proximity to U Street itself formed a mulatto core of the well off.[154] Often, these circles were virtually on top of one another.

Seventh Street

Try as black elites might, whites would not permit voguish African Americans to set themselves apart from their less prosperous racial brethren. The flip side of stylish U Street was downscale Seventh Street.[155] As described in *Cane*—Jean Toomer's classic collection of poetry, short stories, drama, and prose linking rural and urban African American culture—Seventh Street was "a crude-boned, soft-skinned wedge of nigger life breathing its loafer air, jazz sounds and love, thrusting unconscious rhythms, and black reddish blood into the white and whitewashed wood of Washington."[156] Seventh Street was where poor African Americans claimed their right to their city by their simple physical presence.[157]

Toomer, a native of Washington and graduate of Dunbar High School, was himself a product of the "talented tenth." Although he was the grandson of the African American acting governor of Louisiana during Reconstruction, Pickney Benton Stewart Pinchback, Toomer's racial descent was mixed.[158] Eventually declaring that all racial classifications were inappropriate, Toomer lived in affluent white neighborhoods and attended white schools in New Rochelle, New York, and in Washington, before moving to African American neighborhoods and schools following family financial setbacks. *Cane*, a literary landmark of the Harlem Renaissance, is seen as the first attempt to express the rich lives, culture, and language of rural African Americans in belles lettres. Toomer's enthusiastic embrace of black working-class culture in the early 1920s nurtured a fascination with Seventh Street culture.

Divisions ran deep within African American Washington—even along the stretch of U Street that defined so much of local black culture and society. One of Toomer's major accomplishments in *Cane* was to capture the influence and continuity between working-class rural and urban black culture. Seventh Street was the place where rural field hand life came to town, much to the approbation of whites and the embarrassment of middle-class blacks.[159] Seventh Street and U Street represented the "crack in the sidewalk" of black Washington, in which cultures and values collided with and enriched one another. The hostility of whites forced the highly class-conscious African Americans of Washington to think about themselves as being bound together. Along Seventh Street, African Americans from alley slums and proper townhouses ran into one another, interacted with one another, and became a shared community.[160]

Whites—white society, white power structures, and white racists— were implicated in this collision. African American intellectual and business leaders might never have come to acknowledge any responsibility for the semi-urban African American proletariat if whites had permitted them to escape into biracial bourgeois respectability. Instead, the African American middle class—spurned by and excluded from "mainstream" (i.e., Caucasian) Washington—came to embrace "racial uplift" during the early years of the twentieth century.

The result was a tense conflict between norms and attitudes that melded into an explosively creative mix of class and background. U Street probably never would have emerged as one of the most creative places in America had it not been for Seventh Street. The literary and musical art of Toomer, Hughes, and Duke Ellington captured—and was the product of—these deep tensions within African American society.

Toomer, Hughes, and Ellington were more or less contemporary products of the nation's nascent African American middle class, with personal stories tied by family to U Street and to its churches, schools, and community life. Toomer's *Cane*, Hughes's 1927 poem "Fine Clothes to the Jew," and Ellington's homage to Holliday's pool hall reflect the rough-and-tumble street life of Seventh Street with its rich and juicy language and musical tradition.[161] Hughes absorbed the bluesy feel of the place through such verse as:

> I'm goin' down to de railroad, baby
> Lay ma head on de track
> I'm goin' down to de railroad, babe,
>
> **Lay ma head on de track—**
>
> But if I see de train a-comin',
> I'm gonna jerk it back.[162]

Seventh Street was the space—both physical and metaphysical—in which Toomer, Ellington, and Hughes embraced the African American experience in all its hues and classes. As Hughes recalled in his memoir *The Big Sea* just a few years later,

> From all this [that of the "talented tenth"] pretentiousness Seventh Street was a sweet relief. Seventh Street is the long, old, dirty street, where the ordinary Negroes hang out, folks with practically no family tree at all, folks who draw no color line between mulattoes and deep dark-browns, folks who work hard for a living with their hands. On Seventh Street in 1924 they played the blues, ate watermelon, barbecue, and fish sandwiches, shot pool, told tall tales, looked at the dome of the Capitol and laughed out loud. . . . And I went to their churches and heard the tambourines play and the little tinkling bells of the triangles adorn the gay shouting

tunes that sent sisters dancing down the aisles for Job. . . .
Their songs—those of Seventh Street—had the pulse beat of
the people who kept on going. . . . I liked the barrel houses
of Seventh Street, the shouting churches, and the songs. They
were warm and kind and didn't care whether you had an
overcoat or not.[163]

The intensity of U Street—and much of twentieth-century African
American and American culture—originated with just such a collision
between black elites and plain black folk. This encounter would continue
along U Street for the next century.

Toomer penetrates the heart of the matter in a passage about the
Howard Theatre, which played such an important role in Ellington's

FIGURE 2.2
The Howard Theatre with Its Manager, Andrew J. Thomas

Photograph from the Washington Historical Image Collection, Washingtoniana Division,
Martin Luther King Jr. Library, Washington. Used with permission.

life and was located next door to Holliday's billiard room (see figure 2.2). "Life of nigger alleys, of poolrooms and restaurants and near-beer saloons," Toomer wrote, "soaks into the walls of Howard Theatre and sets them throbbing to jazz songs. Black-skinned, they dance and shout above the trick and trill of white-walled buildings. At night, they open doors to people who come in to stamp their feet and shout. At night, road-shows volley songs into the mass-heart of black people. Songs soak the walls and seep out to the nigger life of alleys and near-beer saloons, of the Poodle Dog and Black Bear cabarets."[164]

The Howard Theatre was named after the acropolis of African American intellectual life—the university more or less across the street. Griffith Stadium—a temple of a different sort—stood nearby, luring whites into the neighborhood. Like New York's Harlem, New Orleans' Storeyville, Memphis's Basin Street, and Chicago's Bronzeville, Seventh Street is where modern American—and not just African American— culture was being born. Excluded by whites, African Americans of all colors and classes were creating the dominant sounds of the United States of the twentieth century.

The Niagara Movement and Washington

African Americans needed to find a voice before they could create their sound. By 1900 or so, national and Washington black leaders began to search for ways to bridge their deep divisions—discord reflected in the differences between Seventh Street and U Street, between Booker T. Washington and W. E. B. Du Bois, between progress through accommodation with white power and confrontation with white bigotry. The national drama of post-Reconstruction segregation caught up many prominent Washingtonians and U Streeters in the politics of race.

On May 18, 1895, Booker T. Washington opened the Cotton States International Exhibition with a dramatic speech proposing what became known as the "Atlanta Compromise."[165] Declaring that blacks and whites could "be as separate as fingers" while remaining part of "one hand," Washington proposed that African Americans would accept "Southern customs" in exchange for being left in peace.[166]

Booker T. Washington had emerged as the most prominent African American leader of the time by advocating industrial and agricultural vocational education for freed slaves. His Tuskegee Institute in Alabama became a beacon for white and black reformers and philanthropists. Yet his—and Tuskegee's—pragmatic focus on vocation skills rather than on a more traditional higher educational curriculum would come to be viewed by his African American opponents as a means for keeping blacks in economically secondary positions.

Many prominent African American leaders—including Washingtonians Francis Grimké and Mary Church Terrell—accepted invitations to speak at Tuskegee and came away impressed with what they saw.[167] As Terrell recalled years later in her memoir *A Colored Woman in a White World,*

> After I had seen Tuskegee with my own eyes I had a higher regard and a greater admiration for its founder than I had ever entertained before. I realized what a splendid work he was doing to promote the welfare of the race, and that he was literally fulfilling "a long-felt want." From that day forth, whenever those friends tried to engage me in conversation about Tuskegee who knew that "way down deep in my heart" I was a stickler for higher education, and that if it came to a show down I would always vote on that side, I would simply say, "Have you seen Tuskegee? Have you been there?"[168]

The authority vested in Booker T. Washington on the basis of the success of the "Tuskegee system" gave his Atlanta proposal great weight. Moderates of both races embraced his broad invitation, while more radical voices—such as that of the young W. E. B. Du Bois—were silenced by the reality that black America had few options left.[169] White racists across the American South, however, viewed Washington's speech as a sign of weakness and pushed ever harder for racial exclusion.[170]

The era was turning into a killing season. Lynchings—vigilante executions by hanging without trial—were reaching epidemic proportions. An average of 100 Americans—by far the majority of whom were African

American—was being hung to death each year by mobs throughout the South. In 1892 alone, whites hung 161 blacks and 69 whites without any trial.[171] In November 1898, emboldened whites murderously overthrew the elected interracial municipal government of Wilmington, North Carolina, in the only successful armed coup d'état in American history.[172] White Americans were not only separating themselves from black Americans; some were hanging them from trees. The Atlanta Compromise increasingly seemed pointless.

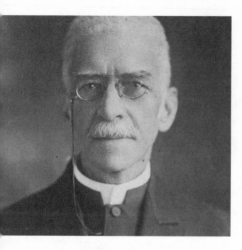

FIGURE 2.3
The Reverend Francis Grimké

Photograph from the Moorland-Spingarn Research Center,
Howard University, Washington. Used with permission.

Francis Grimké, a distinguished pastor, was the first major African American leader to speak out against Washington's views (figure 2.3). He did so in a series of sermons delivered from his pulpit at the prominent Fifteenth Street Presbyterian Church, which was regularly attended by many among the U Street elite.[173] Francis and his lawyer-diplomat brother Archibald (both former slave children born to a South Carolina planter and his slave mistress) were becoming powerful intellectual leaders in black America.[174] Francis Grimké's remarks touched a deep cord of discontent over the Atlanta Compromise.

Archibald Grimké, living in Boston at the time and writing forcefully about the rapid rise in lynchings throughout the South, entered into an extended correspondence with Booker T. Washington. Their exchanges defined an embittered gulf within elite African America between the "talented tenth" and the "Tuskegee Machine."[175] Mark Perry, the historian of the Grimké family, records that "in truth, the Washington-Grimké exchange was far less a debate than a long-distance presentation of competing monologues, but by 1903 it was clear that the two leaders were set on a collision course that threatened to split America's black leadership."[176]

The Grimké brothers were moderates in comparison with younger voices coming to the fore. As Perry observes, Francis and Archibald never cut themselves off personally from fellow ex-slave Washington. More strident leaders such as William Monroe Trotter and W. E. B. Du Bois were less inhibited and respectful because they never shared the experience of slavery.[177] In 1903, the brilliant Du Bois launched his own damaging salvo against Washington in his extraordinary and compelling volume *The Souls of Black Folk*.[178]

Du Bois's collection of wide-ranging essays provided a biting critique of the place of race in American society. He argued forthrightly against the vocational orientation of Booker T. Washington's educational philosophy. Instead, Du Bois declared that the race issue was the central challenge of the twentieth century. He did so by contending that the color line extended worldwide, thereby foreshadowing the anticolonialism of the mid–twentieth century. Du Bois forcefully maintained that African Americans should pursue higher education in order to combat white control over their lives. He thereby explicitly formulated an alternative strategy for racial liberation to that which had been proclaimed by Washington and other advocates of the "Tuskegee Model."

Open warfare broke out within prominent African American organizations—such as the Afro-American Council, the Washington-based American Negro Academy, and the Howard University Board of Regents—as both sides battled for control of institutional resources.[179] Though the disagreement was national in scope, prominent members of the U Street elite became increasingly embroiled in local conflicts. And just as important for U Street, the eventual resolution of these conflicts provided new institutional resources for black Washington to draw upon as they mobilized for a protracted struggle for equality.

Booker T. Washington seemed to be the first to back down ever so slightly by calling for a national conference of reconciliation among African American leaders. The conference, which was convened in New York City's Carnegie Hall in January 1904, brought together the era's major leaders of black America, including Booker T. Washington, W. E. B. Du Bois, Archibald Grimké, T. Thomas Fortune, Emmet Scott, William H. Morris, Clement Morgan, and Hugh Browne. The gathering lasted for three days against the backdrop of increasing white violence toward African Americans. Andrew Carnegie spoke first, lavishing praise on Washington. The "Wizard of Tuskegee" and Du Bois followed—both expressing their willingness to find shared ground.[180]

Archibald Grimké brokered a common strategy that would dominate the civil rights movement for much of the next century. The participants agreed to speak out against lynching, pursue the right to vote, support a legal strategy of filing lawsuits against segregationist practices and laws, accept the validity of both industrial and higher education, and call for all Americans to work together to resolve racial problems.[181] The Carnegie Hall conference ended with the naming of a twelve-member "Committee of Safety," which included Washington, Du Bois, and Archibald Grimké.[182]

Du Bois rejected the compromise almost immediately after he left New York, resigning from the Committee of Safety within a month. On July 10, 1905, Du Bois and his allies met at the Erie Beach Hotel across the Niagara River from Buffalo in Ontario, Canada. Among those present were *Washington Bee* editor Calvin Chase, together with fellow Washingtonians Henry L. Baily and W. H. H. Hart. The Niagara Movement, which met a second time in Harper's Ferry on August 1906, was chartered in Washington.[183]

Previously moderate African American leaders associated with Washington's U Street community were becoming ever more radicalized by events both national—such as the especially violent 1906 Brownsville, Texas, riots by whites against African American soldiers wrongly accused of shooting a white bartender and a white policeman[184]—and local—such as the highly unfortunate Howard University presidency of a white racist, John Gordon. Protests against Gordon turned into open student rebellion that was quelled brutally by the all-white D.C. police force. The Howard University imbroglio had an especially chilling impact on Washington's black elites—and particularly on Francis Grimké, who was then serving as a university trustee.[185]

Francis's brother, Archibald, was now living in Washington with his daughter, Angelina—a schoolteacher, poet, playwright, and novelist—after having served as U.S. consul general in Santa Domingo.[186]

Archibald published his seminal article on American racism, "The Heart of the Race Problem," just as the Niagara Movement was gathering for the second time in West Virginia. In this, his most influential work, he argued that the propensity of white men to rape and sexually intimidate African American women stood at the center of the American racial conundrum.[187]

The Founding of the NAACP

By 1909, the Niagara Movement's leaders had decided that more concerted action was necessary against white racism and Jim Crow laws and policies. The movement disbanded after voting to establish the National Association for the Advancement of Colored People (NAACP), under the leadership of W. E. B. Du Bois, Ida Wells-Barnett, Henry Moskowitz, Mary White Ovington, Oswald Garrison Villard, William English Walling, and Archibald Grimké.[188] The NAACP established a District of Columbia chapter in 1913.

Intense struggles over control of the powerful D.C. NAACP chapter broke out almost immediately.[189] With easy access to the federal government and to the city's prosperous African American community, the Washington organization represented a potential alternative power base to the national NAACP headquarters in New York. Struggles over control of the D.C. chapter would continue until a bitter 1942 court battle definitively resolved the chapter's status as subordinate to the national organization.[190]

This conflict over control of the NAACP in Washington was more than just a conflict over internal organizational rights and privileges. The organization was caught up in the emerging efforts of a rising professional class within the city's African American community to seize community leadership away from its well-entrenched pastor-politicians. After some missteps under the ineffectual leadership of Shiloh Baptist Church pastor John Milton Waldron, Archibald Grimké took control of the fledgling D.C. NAACP chapter.[191] Over much of the next decade, Grimké built the D.C. chapter into the largest and strongest of all the NAACP's local organizations.[192] The chapter, in turn, became one more of U Street's robust institutions that nurtured and provided leadership to the city's African American community.[193]

Joining—let alone leading—the NAACP at the time required courage. Mary Church Terrell observed, "There is no doubt that when the Association was formed there were many colored people who believed in the principles for which it stood, who hesitated or refused to join it because they feared membership in it would cause them to lose their jobs or hurt their influence in the communities in which they lived."[194]

This was a lesson that Archibald Grimké—and many subsequent U Street leaders—would learn well. In 1919, the federal government initiated an investigation for disloyalty against Grimké, who ironically was a former American consul in Santo Domingo.[195] Many other prominent figures in the U Street story throughout the remainder of the twentieth century similarly would fall prey to federal suspicion, investigation, and harassment.

The hostility of the federal government to the nation's own citizens was hurting more than a handful of intellectual activists. The first Southern-born president since the Civil War, Woodrow Wilson, launched a devastating attack on the world of U Street. He segregated the federal Civil Service, effectively denying federal employment to African Americans. This action—which evidently was prompted by his wife's "shock" at discovering African American men working alongside white women in the Post Office Department—lay waste to a community in which the stability of a government job could mean the difference between respectability and penury.[196] More than half of all twentieth-century legislation restricting the rights of African Americans in the District of Columbia became law during Wilson's presidency, earning long-lasting enmity among U Streeters for the Democrats whose policies, the *Washington Bee* had long maintained, promised the "everlasting damnation to the colored Americans in this country."[197]

Many among Wilson's white supporters and compatriots shared the president's harshly racist attitudes. Racial tensions heightened as the United States entered World War I, and the atmosphere of white violence against African Americans intensified after the war.[198] Communal violence—often in the form of white attacks on blacks—erupted as the soldiers returned home from the front. And one of the worst of these outbreaks was centered at the intersection of Seventh Street and U.

July 1919: A Community Defined

The violent events of July 19 to 23, 1919,[199] mark a turning point in the history of U Street.[200] A neighborhood that had once been racially mixed became defined through this violence as the home of African Americans (even as a small number of whites continued to live and to own businesses in the area). An African American community that had once been economically divided, in turn, redefined itself as unified, with shared interests in opposition to the white world beyond. A neighborhood elite that had once been passive was radicalized into action. A business community that had once been nonexistent was poised to become a national center for African American enterprise. And an enclave that had once been disorganized now stood at the center of a dense community network of religious and educational institutions, and cultural and civic organizations.

Though already unfolding before July 18, 1919, these developments had not generally been recognized within the neighborhood—let alone in the city at large.[201] Yet in just a matter of days, the harsh reality of white assault burned away many misperceptions of what U Street was and would be. The glory days to follow were built on the coming of age of an urban community under attack.

African American veterans had returned home from World War I emboldened by their experiences abroad.[202] Whites, concerned with the unfolding Bolshevik Revolution in Russia and seeing omnipresent radical threats to their domination of American society from immigrants and blacks, disliked the enhanced self-confidence they sensed in many African Americans. The racist policies of the Wilson administration encouraged such enmity.[203] Violent attacks by whites against blacks broke out in many American cities—including Charleston, Knoxville, and Omaha—throughout the "Red Summer" of 1919.[204] But one of the most important outbreaks of racial violence for defining an African American identity occurred in the area around

U Street (followed only days later by another round of deadly racial confrontations in Chicago).[205]

The tensions evident throughout the United States were inflamed in Washington by the recent arrival of large numbers of rural Southerners, both black and white, during World War I. The arriving dispossessed African Americans placed considerable strain on the "Secret City's" charitable capacities, while poor Southern whites became increasingly angry about the presence of blacks who were so much better off than themselves.[206] These pressures were enhanced by hateful Southern servicemen returning home from the war, an irresponsibly jingoistic white press led by the *Washington Post*, and a Negrophobic police force under the command of the bigoted Major Raymond Pullman.[207]

On July 19, 1919, false reports that African American men had been attacking white women prompted angry white men to act.[208] Gangs of white thugs led by enlisted servicemen answered the call of the *Washington Post* to organize a "cleanup" of the city.[209] Following the paper's instructions, vigilantes "spontaneously" gathered at a small Knights of Columbus building at Seventh Street and Pennsylvania Avenue, NW, as lynch mobs often did in the South. They moved out quickly to descend on the U Street neighborhood.[210]

"At the corner of Eleventh and Eye Streets Northwest," reported the *Washington Bee*,

> a mob of about three hundred assembled, looking for colored citizens to come down in [street]cars. A telephone message was sent to [police] headquarters and all the satisfaction that the informant got was "I thank you." No officer came in this section—in fact, none could be seen. The mob, not seeing any colored people alight from the cars, or upon the streets in the neighborhood, then broke out and ran in the vicinity of Eleventh and K Streets Northwest, followed by hundreds of white women and while children—looking for some unprotected colored citizens to assault, no doubt. Similar conditions were witnessed in the vicinity of Eleventh and F, Ninth and G, and Seventh and G Streets.[211]

The white press, led by the *Washington Post*, set out their coverage of these events against the backdrop of a supposed inability among city authorities to combat crime, as a consequence of congressional unwillingness to pay for sufficient numbers of police to control the streets.[212] The media initially implied, for example, that an underpaid, largely absent police force had failed to contain the initial violence following the arrest of an African American man.[213]

Some subsequent press coverage acknowledged the role of white military men in the violence. On July 22, the *Washington Post* reported that "thousands" of white men in soldiers' and sailors' uniforms had taken to the streets the night before to attack African Americans.[214] However, reports in the *Washington Times* and the *Evening Star* the same day accentuated African American attacks on whites.[215] In particular, reporting in the William Randolph Hearst–owned *Washington Times* emphasized black violence against whites.[216] "About 7:30 o'clock in the evening, a crowd of about 400 Negroes stopped a street car at Eleventh and U Streets Northwest and started to take the motorman off," the paper reported, "while several in the crowd threw stones through the windows of the car."[217]

President Wilson and official Washington, characteristically, were slow to respond, bringing in troops to quell the violence only after days of white rampaging through black neighborhoods.[218] When they did act, police officers arrested blacks who were protecting their neighborhood rather than the whites who were looking for blacks to beat up. Of the hundred or so people arrested during the riots, fewer than a dozen were white.[219] Eventually, four hundred cavalrymen from Fort Myer and four hundred Marines from Quantico under the command of the Spanish American War hero General William G. Haan—who reached out to African American community leaders—were able to reassert government control over the area with the assistance of heavy rains.[220] By the end of the upheaval, some thirty people had died and untold numbers had been wounded.[221]

The U Street community, in contrast to the government, responded immediately. African American veterans organized a sophisticated defense of their neighborhood. Light-skinned veterans in uniform circulated in white neighborhoods to collect intelligence; veterans organized the importation of arms—including machine guns—from Baltimore, and constructed barricades to keep the marauding whites at bay; an estimated 2,000 armed blacks fanned out across the neighborhood in organized resistance; and reinforcements were called in from the large African American community in Baltimore.[222] Historians have generally acknowledged what that era's white press did not: The story of the 1919 violence was one of African Americans defending their community from white marauders, rather than of the government, police, and the military containing black aggression.[223]

African Americans at the time had no doubt that their own self-organization had saved their community. In a postdisturbance editorial titled "They Started It," the *Washington Bee* argued that "soldiers and marines started the riot against the colored citizens for no cause whatever. It is so strange that every effort was made to disarm defenseless colored citizens and no effort made to disarm the whites. Men were arrested for carrying concealed weapons because they had weapons in their houses—that is, colored men. . . . The police department could not protect the colored citizens, so they were forced to protect themselves."[224]

The NAACP's James Weldon Johnson concluded his investigation of the violence by arguing that black self-defense both prevented even worse damage to the community and encouraged a sense of black unity and pride.[225] For Johnson, a new assertiveness and an unprecedented appreciation of shared destiny marked U Street after the disturbances.[226] He informed readers of the NAACP's journal *The Crisis* that "when we reached the Northwest Section of the city, I found the whole atmosphere entirely different. I had expected to find the colored people excited and, perhaps, panicky; I found them calm and determined, unterrified and unafraid. . . . They had reached the determination that they would defend and protect themselves and their homes at the cost of their lives, if necessary, and that determination rendered them calm."[227]

This newfound self-confidence was evident in African American demands for a full accounting of official incompetence and intransigence during the July violence.[228] As the *Washington Bee* declared, "The black man is loyal to his country and its flag, and when his country fails to protect him, he means to protect himself."[229]

All the components that enabled the U Street community to respond to threat so quickly had been put into place during the four decades since the collapse of home rule. U Street stood at the center of African American Washington in every respect. As James A. Miller reminds twenty-first-century readers, the "noise and music from the traffic, storefront churches, barber shops, liquor stores, flophouses, and lunch counters mingled together punctuated by the enormous audiences crowding into the matinees and evening performances at the Howard Theatre around the corner on T Street. After the curtain fell on the Howard stage shows, the beat went on well into the night at the Dreamland Café, Café Deluxe, Club Harlem, and the Old Rose Social Club. At the Southern Dining Room at 1616 Seventh Street, Mrs. Hettie Gross served down home southern cooking in a workingman's bucket."[230]

In response to white-imposed segregation, African Americans had gained the organizational skills and created the tight institutional base they needed to support a self-sustaining community. The tensions of class and skin tone had not been eliminated—only a few years would pass before Langston Hughes would come to town and experience what he saw as an absence of "real culture, kindness, or good common sense" among the local self-proclaimed leaders of black Washington.[231] Nonetheless, the mix of the haughty descendants of the "first-freed" and the flood of migrants from the rural South—the potent blend of U Street and Seventh Street—had already begun. The churches, universities, schools, theaters, clubs, social groups, fraternities and sororities, charitable organizations, activist groups, legal scholars, and businesses and financiers that would define U Street in the years ahead were in place.

Alain Locke was already at work encouraging African American literary culture at Howard; Carter G. Woodson was creating the field of African American history. Angelina Grimké, Jean Toomer, Langston Hughes, Edward Christopher Williams, and so many other writers already had arrived, or would come to U Street in just a little while. The

D.C. chapter of the NAACP, fortified by Angelina's father Archibald, was about to launch its historic drive for African American civil rights, which would involve, among many, the diplomat and future Nobel Prize winner Ralph Bunche and the future U.S. Supreme Court justice Thurgood Marshall. A resplendent and effervescent society had replaced the fledgling community of a half-century before.

Profile

Archibald Grimké (1849–1930) and Francis Grimké (1850–1937)

Archibald Grimké (figure 2.4) and Francis Grimké were born into slavery as the first and second of Henry and Nancy Weston Grimké's three sons. Henry was the offspring of a prominent Charleston family and the brother of the famed abolitionists and suffragettes Sara and Angelina Grimké. Angelina's husband, the Reverend Theodore Dwight Weld, was one of the leading American progressive activists of the early nineteenth century. Nancy was Henry's slave.

Henry moved to the Cane Acre plantation in Saint Paul's Parish, near Beaufort, South Carolina, during the 1840s following the death of his wife. He and Nancy established a household despite her status as chattel. Upon Henry's death in 1852, ownership of Nancy and her sons transferred to Montague Grimké, Henry's eldest son by his legal marriage. Montague transported his brother's household to

FIGURE 2.4
Archibald Grimké and Angelina Grimké
Photograph from the Moorland-Spingarn Research Center, Howard University, Washington. Used with permission.

Charleston, allowing them to live a modest existence as his property. Archibald and Francis joined the Union Army upon its occupation of Charleston. Following the Civil War, they made their way north, entering Lincoln University in Pennsylvania. The brothers established relations with their previously unknown relatives, Sara and Angelina, and were joined by their mother Nancy. Their younger brother John moved to Florida to lead a quiet life, estranged from his family until his death in 1915. Nancy died in Washington in 1895.

Archibald entered Harvard Law School following his studies at Lincoln University. He married Sarah Stanley, the daughter of a prominent white abolitionist clergyman from Michigan. The marriage proved to be tumultuous. Sarah left Archibald after the birth of their daughter Angelina Weld Grimké in 1880. Archibald lived alone in Boston, earning an excellent reputation as a lawyer, biographer (he published well-received volumes on William Lloyd Garrison and Charles Sumner during these years), and Republican Party activist. He broke with the party to support the Democratic presidential candidacies of Grover Cleveland in 1888 and 1892. Archibald eventually settled in Washington, after serving as U.S. consul in Santo Domingo between 1895 and 1898. His daughter Angelina—a poet, playwright, and novelist—became one of the leading contributors to the "Harlem Renaissance." She lived with her father in Washington, teaching in the D.C. public schools, and she died in obscurity in New York City in 1958.

After a brief period of study at Howard University Law School, Francis transferred to Princeton Theological Seminary. He became the assistant pastor of Washington's Fifteenth Street Presbyterian Church in 1877, as the city was entering a period of increasing racial segregation. At this time, he married Charlotte Forten, and he remained associated with the church for the remainder of his life (save for a brief unhappy period in Jacksonville during the mid-1880s). With his fame as a gifted orator and prolific writer, his sermons circulated widely within the African American community.

Archibald and Francis became leading figures in Washington's African American intellectual and political activist communities. Both were noteworthy contributors to the arguments between Booker T. Washington and W. E. B. Du Bois, and both were active in the Niagara Movement leading to the establishment of the NAACP. They played decisive leadership roles in the organization, with Archibald serving for many years as the head of the NAACP's all-important D.C. chapter.

Archibald's essay, "The Heart of the Race Problem," was the first major examination of the relationship between race and sexuality in the United States. Archibald passed away in Washington in 1930; Francis died in Washington seven years later.

Profile

MARY CHURCH TERRELL (1863–1954)

Mary Church Terrell (figure 2.5), the daughter of Robert Reed and Louisa Ayers Church, was born in Memphis during the Civil War. Her father's owner, Captain Charles B. Church, allowed his son-slave to work on riverboats as a young man. Because Robert was a hard worker with notable organizational skills, he rose from dishwasher to procurement steward.

Following Emancipation, which came the year of Mary's birth, her father opened a saloon in Memphis. He was shot and left for dead during racial violence following the war. Though he survived, he was tormented by bouts of pain for the rest of his life. Mary's mother Louisa ran a successful hair salon frequented by affluent white women. Combining their assets, the Churches entered the real estate market and accumulated considerable wealth.

The Churches wanted to ensure that their daughter would have a first-rate education. They sent young Mary to Ohio, where she studied at the Antioch College Model School and, subsequently, in the Oberlin public schools. Mary matriculated in

FIGURE 2.5
Mary Church Terrell

Photograph by Addison Scurlock, from the Scurlock Studio Records, Archives Center, National Museum of American History, Smithsonian Institution, Washington. Used with permission.

Oberlin College, which she completed in 1884. She taught languages at Wilberforce University in Ohio between 1885 and 1887, before moving to Washington to join the faculty of the prestigious Colored High School. She later earned her master's degree at Oberlin, and left for a two-year tour of Europe.

In 1891, Mary moved back to Washington to marry Robert Herberton Terrell, the principal of the city's Colored High School. Robert, an honors graduate of Harvard College, soon entered Howard University Law School. He would remain a prominent member of the Washington African American community throughout his life. He became the city's first black municipal court judge, being named to his position by four consecutive presidents from both political parties. He simultaneously taught at his alma mater, Howard Law School, until his death in 1925.

Mary was prohibited from teaching by virtue of the fact that she was married. She turned to community activism, and to parenting a daughter and adopted son. Moved by anger following the 1892 lynching of Tom Moss, a close friend in Memphis, Mary formed the Colored Women's League of Washington, which eventually merged with other similar organizations to form the national Colored Women's League.

Mary was appointed to the District of Columbia School Board in 1895, serving until 1901, and again between 1906 and 1911. She was a founder of the Lincoln Temple Congregational Church and a prominent area resident (first as the second black family to move into LeDroit Park, and later into the Strivers' Section). At the age of eighty-six, she was elected chair of the Coordinating Committee for the Enforcement of D.C. Anti-Discrimination Laws.

Her various leadership positions made her an internationally recognized celebrity and provided a platform from which she addressed many of the leading racial and women's suffrage issues of the day. She worked with Frederick Douglass, Booker T. Washington, and W. E. B. Du Bois, and was a charter member of the NAACP.

In her 1940 autobiography, *A Colored Woman in a White World*, Mary Terrell scoffed at the notion that Washington was "the Colored Man's Paradise." Indeed, she hoped that "the angels in Heaven will be a little more kindly disposed towards me than some of the good people in my home town."[232]

CHAPTER 3

Confronting the Nation

In Washington, bell-boys and elevator operators
in every large building may be seen casting their eyes,
at odd moments, into books that have no connection
whatever with their occupation.

—Helen Nicolay, *Our Capital on the Potomac*, 1924[1]

Charlie Houston changed America. He was not alone. Other U Street intellectual, professional, business, sports, and cultural leaders redefined themselves and their relationship with white America, and in the process they changed the world. As the neighborhood was coming out of the violence of 1919, its leaders, its institutions, and its everyday residents were finding their own voices. Their shouts could no longer be contained within one corner of one city. U Streeters were moving out into the world, changing American—and later global—conceptions of the rule of law; changing how American sports and music would be played; changing how Americans would be taught; changing how the world would view entire continents; and changing how global diplomacy would be conducted.

Charles Hamilton Houston was a child of U Street (figure 3.1).[2] He was the son of William Houston, a lawyer educated at Howard University who had moved to Washington from Indiana to take a job as a clerk in the War Department.[3] William married Mary Hamilton of Xenia, Ohio, who had graduated from Wilberforce College. Like Duke Ellington, who was three and a half years younger, Charles grew up in the relatively protected environment of Washington's "talented tenth." After being honored as class valedictorian at M Street (later Dunbar) High School, he entered Amherst College at the age of sixteen and graduated with equal speed, after having been elected to the Phi Beta Kappa national honor society.[4] Following his academic success in college, he returned to the city to teach

FIGURE 3.1
Charles Houston in a Courtroom
Photograph from the Moorland-Spingarn Research Center, Howard University,
Washington. Used with permission.

English at Howard and at Dunbar High before signing on for service in the U.S. Army during World War I.[5]

The Army brought an end to the protective bubble that had elevated Charles Houston above white hostility. After earning a commission as a first lieutenant in a segregated infantry unit, he resigned as an officer and entered artillery school. He shipped off to France in September 1918, just shy of the Armistice a few weeks later.[6] He returned home on the eve of the 1919 attacks by whites on African Americans in his old stomping grounds. In the fall of 1919, he finally was able to fulfill his dream of following his father's career at the bar, trundling off to Harvard Law School.[7]

Houston was a standout student at Harvard, becoming the first African American male to be elected to serve on the *Law Review*. He became a favored student of the legendary future Supreme Court justice Felix Frankfurter and graduated in the top 5 percent of his class.[8] Houston stayed at Harvard to earn his doctor of juridical science, thereby cementing his status as a Frankfurter protégé. He returned to Washington to join his father's law firm in 1924, after having added a doctorate in civil law from the University of Madrid to his credentials.[9]

Houston was a remarkable man, but no less so than many others growing up in and around U Street at the time.[10] His cousin William Hastie surpassed Houston in almost everything he did. Hastie, who grew up in Tennessee, followed his elder cousin by nine years to Amherst, where he graduated magna cum laude. Like Houston, Hastie continued on to Harvard, where he too earned both a law degree and a doctorate in juridical studies. Hastie—who would be the first African American to serve as a federal magistrate—joined the faculty of Howard University Law School in 1931.[11]

Houston and Hastie returned to Washington just as Mordecai Johnson had become the first African American president of Howard University in 1926.[12] An imperious personality, Johnson re-created Howard during his thirty-four years at the helm, turning it into a first-rate higher educational institution (figure 3.2).[13] He brought Houston, Hastie, and other top African American scholars—such as the philosopher and Rhodes Scholar Alain LeRoy Locke, the zoologist Ernest E. Just, the chemist Percy Julian, the poet and literary critic Sterling Brown, the economist Abram Harris, the sociologist E. Franklin Frazier, the political scientist and later diplomat Ralph Bunche, the medical researcher Charles R. Drew, and the historians Rayford W. Logan and John Hope Franklin—to the faculty in a remarkable period of growth during the 1930s.[14]

The Capstone of Negro Education

Mordecai Johnson's hardscrabble childhood in Tennessee could not have been further away from the protected world of U Street's black and

FIGURE 3.2
Howard University President Mordecai Johnson Welcoming
Interior Secretary Harold Ickes to the Campus

Photograph from the Moorland-Spingarn Research Center,
Howard University, Washington. Used with permission.

tan bourgeoisie. Johnson, the son of a former slave and mill worker, clawed his way through school and university to national prominence, beginning in his backwater hometown of Paris, Tennessee. He left Paris to pursue a better education at the Roger Williams University Academy in Nashville. His fledgling academic career was disrupted when the academy burned down, forcing him to continue his high school education at the Howe Institute in Memphis. His oratorical gifts were catching the attention of his teachers by this time, landing him at the preparatory school of Morehouse (Atlanta Baptist) College. After finishing high school, Johnson remained at Morehouse for his undergraduate studies, which he completed in 1911.

Johnson continued his education, earning a second bachelor's degree from the University of Chicago and entering the Rochester Theological Seminary. He became pastor of Rochester's Second Baptist Church and launched a successful career as a Baptist minister. He earned a reputation as a brilliant speaker and community organizer while at the First Baptist Church of Charleston, West Virginia. He received two doctor of divinity degrees, one from Harvard University and another from Gammon Theological Seminary. His commencement address on African American religious beliefs at the Harvard University Divinity School in 1922 cemented his reputation as a leading African American religious figure.

Johnson burned with a passion to improve the condition of African Americans. As adept at evaluating political power relationships as he was at speaking, he reached out to whomever could advance a cause. His experiences at Chicago, Rochester, and Harvard enabled him to move easily between white and black worlds.[15] He was just the sort of person the trustees of Howard University were seeking as they set out to find a new president for the university in 1926.

Howard had been beset by a major crisis around this time. Many of its schools lacked accreditation, while debates between followers of Booker T. Washington and W. E. B. Du Bois paralyzed hiring decisions. The school, known as the "Dummies' Retreat" of U Street's snooty elite, was in trouble.[16] To make matters worse, the latest in a string of white presidents—James Stanley Durkee—regularly insulted the students, faculty, and trustees while running the school aground in one scandal after another. The time had arrived for a school that claimed to be the leading African American university in the country to have its first African American chief executive officer.[17]

If Johnson was a fitting candidate for Howard, Howard was a fitting institutional home for him. Despite its chronic financial and administrative crises, Howard had the best physical facilities of any black college, was sitting in the middle of one of the wealthiest and most intellectually engaged African American communities to be found anywhere, and was a brief streetcar ride away from the corridors of national power.[18] The shrewd and pugnacious Johnson intuitively understood how to capitalize on these assets to enable Howard to actually achieve its self-proclaimed status as "the Capstone of Negro Education."

The scale of Johnson's accomplishments at Howard was enormous. As Richard Kluger writes,

> The year he became its president, Howard University received $216,000 from Congress; when he left thirty-four years later, it got $7 million and would get $12 million the year after. Before he came, Congress had appropriated a total of about $900,000 for buildings and other capital expenditures; by the time he left the total was nearing $42 million. And he did not do it by eating humble pie before Congressmen and other white warhorses. In fact, he seemed to make a point of delivering at least one pugnacious speech a year noting how little America was doing to improve the lot of its deprived masses.[19]

Johnson was an authoritarian—even messianic—visionary and tough taskmaster who drove his faculty and trustees to fits of anger.[20] The same combativeness that enabled him to climb from abject provincial poverty to the leading position in African American higher education just as easily outraged talented academics who were themselves no shrinking violets.[21] Johnson was committed to "the Hill," as the university was known for its location on a ridge just above U Street.[22] He strove to turn the school into a beacon of black education, winning loyalty in pursuit of that goal even from those who could not stand him personally.

Johnson's greatest achievement may have been his ability to identify and to recruit brilliant scholars who were pushing at the edges of their disciplines.[23] Their work often was explicitly interdisciplinary at a time when strict divisions among fields of thought dominated university intellectual life. And even more important for the story of U Street as a zone of contact among various economic groups and races, Johnson's faculty proved themselves to be radical activists challenging the status quo in a segregated city and nation each and every day.

Jonathan Scott Holloway—in a perceptive study of the careers of Abram Harris Jr., E. Franklin Frazier, and Ralph Bunche at Howard during the 1930s—captures what made the university such a creative institution: "Howard University became the leading site, despite internal and external pressures to the contrary, of black intellectual radicalism in academe during the interwar era. Harris, Frazier, and Bunche represented the leading edge of social science radicalism—a modernist project that brought the latest social science theories to bear upon lived conditions, organizational structures, and federal policy. Not only were they radicals for their time, they were also trend setters in their fields."[24]

The impact of Howard on the world at large is perhaps most evident in jurisprudence, as Howard faculty and students transformed conceptions of race and rights, formulating the legal strategy for the American civil rights movement and, internationally, creating what is now known as a "rights-based approach" to the law. As Holloway notes, "Howard scholars were engaged in cutting edge work that would influence American cultural sensibilities and improve opportunities for black contributions to American and world culture. Charles Houston and William Hastie were legal radicals who trained and mentored a generation of attorneys and jurists who reshaped society in profound ways, most famously through the work of protégés like Thurgood Marshall."[25]

A Living Laboratory of Civil Rights

Larger-than-life personalities congregated around Johnson's Howard, beginning with Mordecai Johnson himself. They added vitality to the African American community throughout the city and around nearby U Street. The synergetic relationship between town and gown reinvigorated many disciplines, starting with the field of law.

Howard's Law School was ripe for a makeover under Johnson's leadership. The school's reputation had remained mediocre at best under the leadership of a retired white judge and a sitting African American municipal judge as dean and vice dean.[26] Johnson started asking around about young hotshot attorneys who might be able to shake his Law School to its core. He very quickly discovered Charles Houston, who was practicing law with his father in the neighborhood.

Johnson and Houston were interested in more than upgrading the value of a Howard law degree. They wanted to transform an entire American legal system that was predicated to the core of its being on racial inequality. As Kluger observed in his history of American civil rights law, *Simple Justice*,

> A law school for Negroes was different from a medical school for Negroes or, say, an engineering school for Negroes. Hearts and lungs and glands worked the same inside blacks as in whites. And the principles of thermodynamics or the properties of the hypotenuse did not vary with the color of the man contemplating them. But the laws of the United States did not operate to provide equal justice for whites and blacks, and so it would not do just to learn them in general and in principle. Charles Houston set out to teach young Negroes the difference between what the laws said and meant and how they were applied to African Americans. His avowed aim was to eliminate that difference.[27]

Houston ripped the Howard Law School apart, closing down the night school that had enabled many in the community (including his own father) to earn a law degree while working during the day. He and Johnson set the standards for entry into the Law School as high as at any school in the country, and higher than most. Seeking to place the social activist credo of Houston's mentor, the Supreme Court justice Felix Frankfurter—and of Frankfurter's mentor, Louis Brandeis—within the context of race relations, Houston and Johnson reinvented the Howard legal education as one in which students both would master their profession and would develop the skills needed to mold social relations. The Howard lawyer would become more than a talented reader of legal codes or a courtroom rhetorician; the Howard law graduate would become a model of social engagement.[28]

The Law School's entering class size shrank to a dozen or less, and quality rose. Among Houston's first student recruits was the future Supreme Court justice Thurgood Marshall, the son of a Baltimore & Ohio dining car waiter from the integrated Druid Hill neighborhood of Baltimore. Marshall attended Pennsylvania's Lincoln University with a fellow Baltimorean, the singing star Cab Calloway, as well as future presidents Nnamdi Azikiwe of Nigeria and Kwame Nkrumah of Ghana.[29]

Simultaneously, Johnson and Houston attracted arguably the best African American legal minds in the country, including Houston's younger cousin William Hastie, Texan James Madison Nabrit Jr. (who would succeed Johnson as Howard's president in 1960), and Ohioan Leon A. Ransom.[30] The school was becoming a laboratory for the best and the brightest—both faculty and student—to join together in reconceptualizing the American legal order. In 1931—just two years after Houston had taken over, and just one year after the arrival of the school's most illustrious student, Thurgood Marshall—Howard University Law School won full accreditation from the whites-only American Bar Association and was granted membership without qualification in the Association of American Law Schools.[31] Houston's growing reputation earned him an appointment to the District of Columbia Board of Education in 1933.[32]

NAACP president Walter White lured Houston from Howard to become the association's litigation director in 1935, a position Houston retained until his untimely death just shy of his fifty-fifth birthday in 1950. Houston, in reality, did not go far as his appointment had the effect of unifying the NAACP's legal team and the talented faculty and students at the university into a single center for leading the battle for equal rights. These relationships were strengthened when Hastie assumed leadership of the law school in 1939; and when Marshall joined the NAACP's legal office. As Kluger records, Howard University "would now become the command post of black militancy and, welded to NAACP headquarters in New York, part of a double-edged drive for black equality that would gather strength and confidence for the next three decades."[33]

This tightly organized group of lawyers shuttling back and forth between the Howard campus in Washington and NAACP headquarters in New York fought and, for the most part, won the major civil rights legal battles of the era, from Houston's first victory before the Supreme

Court in *Missouri ex rel. Gaines v. Canada* (1938) to Marshall's success leading the winning legal team in the landmark *Brown v. Board of Education of Topeka* case in 1954.[34] Of local significance, Houston argued successfully before the Supreme Court in 1948 against the enforcement of restrictive covenants on housing deeds that prohibited the sale of property to African Americans and other excluded groups. His victory in *Hurd v. Hodge* marked the beginning of the end of legalized racial segregation in the city's housing.[35] The NAACP legal strategy took shape in good measure in the classrooms of Howard University and the basement halls of U Street's churches.

U Street was more than the happenstance venue where high-flying law professors and their talented students happened to meet. Houston, Hastie, Nabrit, Ransom, Marshall, and many other Howard faculty—such as Locke, Just, Julian, Brown, Harris, Frazier, Bunche, Drew, Logan, and Franklin—lived their lives among U Street's byways, churches, lunch counters, streetcars, libraries, jazz clubs, and pool halls. The Twelfth Street YMCA, for example, was a major meeting place in which African Americans of varied economic levels gathered, and where young people found role models among people of achievement.[36]

Duke Ellington's favorite place in town—Frank Holliday's poolroom next to the Howard Theatre on T Street between 6th and 7th streets—was a regular haunt of the medical researcher Charles Drew, a blood plasma specialist.[37] U Street was where the historians Rayford Logan and John Hope Franklin met Carter G. Woodson, whose Association for the Study of Negro Life and History and its principal publication, *The Journal of Negro History*, quite literally were inventing the field of African American history.[38] These and other intellectuals undoubtedly gathered from time to time with porters, maids, preachers, and charlatans to enjoy the good food at Harrison's Café at 455 Florida Avenue, NW, and at the Southern Dining Room run by Hettie Gross at 1616 7th Street, NW.[39] Many were engaged in the volatile politics swirling around the powerful Washington Branch of the NAACP.[40] Together, they fretted over their community's negative coverage in the local white press and did all they could to support African American alternatives.[41]

Most important, every waking minute of every waking day, the brilliant African American scholars and administrators at Howard struggled with the reality of racism and second-class citizenship, just as everyone else did on U Street. As James W. Quander—who would earn a PhD in economics later in the century—recorded in his memoir, U Street "was an all-black world, and very limited, despite my residing in the capital of the nation."[42]

The profound class divisions within the U Street community that had been so visible a generation before became increasingly submerged by the reality of race in the Jim Crow city.[43] This simple fact of American reality made life at Howard different from that at other elite universities, in that its faculty and students could never withdraw into an ivory tower. "Throughout their tenure at Howard," the historian Zachery Williams writes, "the University's scholars and activists felt the sting of racism and segregation, both in academia and outside its hallowed walls. As a result, it was easy for Howard professors to see a natural connection between life in the academy and in the black communities. Many professors lived in the heart of the black community and had their everyday lives centered around its institutions, namely churches, schools, and other businesses. They knew intimately the concerns of the community and its needs."[44]

The U Street Barber

Charles Houston's legal strategy came together with the realities of segregated life in his neighborhood around the figure of Gardner "Bish" Bishop, who was widely known as "the U Street Barber."[45] Bishop didn't think too much of white people—in fact, he had grown to hate them after suffering a series of injustices growing up in Rocky Mount, North Carolina—and he didn't think too much of pretentious black people and their self-important organizations such as the NAACP either. What he cared deeply about was his daughter, Judine, who was getting an increasingly shoddy education at Browne Junior High School, even though nearby Eliot Junior High for whites was emptying out as local whites began their postwar exodus to the suburbs.[46]

Distrustful of most organizations, Bishop and some other parents at Browne Junior High formed their own group—the Consolidated Parents Group, Inc.—to challenge the unequal treatment of their children in the District of Columbia's segregated schools. The group periodically petitioned the Board of Education and its offices downtown, piling forty or so children into taxis that were made available by their drivers for free to head downtown to confront local officials.[47] One night, Bishop walked to a nearby church for a meeting of the NAACP and encountered Houston, who seemed nothing like the fancy African American intellectuals he so resented. Houston offered his legal services. That evening, the two went to Houston's house at 1744 S Street, NW, where they joined forces in a plan to desegregate local schoolyard playgrounds.[48]

Houston already was suffering from the heart condition that would cut his life short and, on his deathbed, passed the case on to Howard law professor James Madison Nabrit Jr., who pursued it to the Supreme Court. Nabrit, a top graduate of Northwestern University's Law School, gave up a successful legal practice in Texas representing Native Americans in fights over land and oil claims to join the Howard University Law faculty.[49] The future Howard University president was in constant contact with the NAACP legal staff, including many who were directly associated with Howard, such as Houston, Marshall, Robert Carter, and Spottswood Robinson.[50]

On September 11, 1950, Bishop led a group of eleven African American children—including twelve-year-old Spottswood Thomas Bolling Jr.—to the sparkling John Philip Sousa Junior High School, which had just opened in the Anacostia neighborhood of Southeast Washington.[51] The children were refused admission. Nabrit filed suit in 1951 in a case that would become known as *Bolling v. Sharpe.*[52] Nabrit's case eventually was folded into a cluster of similar cases—including *Brown v. Board of Education of Topeka*—that were argued before the Supreme Court in December 1952.

In challenging the constitutionality of segregation, Nabrit went further than the legal team on the *Brown v. Board of Education of Topeka* case, which merely proposed that Topeka schools for African Americans were not equal to those for whites. Nabrit's arguments before the Supreme

Court on Bolling's and Bishop's behalf were among the most powerful in support of the proposition that separate can never be equal in the provision of education. Though *Bolling v. Sharpe* was decided together with the famous *Brown* decision on May 17, 1954, the *Bolling* case had a more important impact on the District of Columbia.[53]

The coming together of pathbreaking legal thinkers such as Houston and Nabrit with poor but proud neighborhood residents such as Bishop and Bolling stands at the core of the accomplishments of the U Street community during the years following the 1919 disturbances leading up to the historic Supreme Court decisions of three and a half decades later. The civil rights cases and legal strategies that emerged from the Howard University Law School are but one corner of a much larger tapestry in which white hostility, customary segregation, and racist laws forced African Americans of very different life experience and social status to come together to defend their collective dignity. U Street was the zone in which that contact took place.

Activist Scholarship

Among many new Howard faculty, Mordecai Johnson appointed three young social scientists to head up university departments. The economist Abram Lincoln Harris arrived in 1927 to take over the Economics Department, while still completing his doctoral degree at Columbia University; the future Nobel Peace Prize laureate Ralph Bunche came a year later to become chair of the Political Science Department while still working on his PhD at Harvard (figure 3.3); and the sociologist E. Franklin Frazier joined the Howard faculty in 1934 after earning his doctoral degree at the University of Chicago and a teaching stint at Morehouse College in Atlanta.[54]

Harris, Bunche, and Frazier were acknowledged as being at the forefront of a new radical social science that sought to understand society in order to change it. They participated in national meetings on race issues, such as the Second Amenia Conference organized by the NAACP in 1933; they served as consultants to national academic and philanthropic organizations, such as the Social Science Research Council

FIGURE 3.3
Ralph Bunche

Photograph from the Moorland-Spingarn Research
Center, Howard University, Washington.
Used with permission.

and the Russell Sage Foundation; and they hosted a major national conference on the impact of the New Deal on African Americans, which convened at Howard in 1935.[55]

All three were exemplars of an approach to social science combining intellectual excellence with social activism in response to the social and economic upheavals of the Great Depression, all three were trained at the very best graduate departments in their fields, and all three were among the very first of their race to earn PhDs in their disciplines.[56] They were dedicated to exploring the intersection between the explosive issue of race and socioeconomic class in America.[57] They thought and argued about the place of the Negro in the world at large, contributing to fledgling discussions about the nature of colonialism while linking their thinking about the fate of the black person in the United States to the fate of black people everywhere.[58]

Frazier engaged in a seminal debate with the University of Chicago anthropologist Melville Herskovits over the retention of African culturalisms by African Americans (Frazier, a student of the sociologist Robert Park, minimized African cultural influences on Americans of African descent).[59] Bunche was sent on a fellowship from the Social Science Research Council for postdoctoral training on African issues at the London School of Economics and Political Science—where he studied with the famed anthropologist Bronislaw Malinowski, was a fellow student of Jomo Kenyatta, and befriended Paul Robeson—and the University of Cape Town—where he took anthropologist Isaac Schapera's seminar on African social organization. Bunche, it turns out, visited the South African Native College at Fort Hare just one year before Nelson Mandela entered as a freshman.[60] Like their colleague in Howard's History Department, Rayford Logan, they were radicals who came to be viewed as conservatives—even reactionaries—with the passage of time.

Logan grew up at 20th and K streets, NW, prayed at the Nineteenth Street Baptist Church, was valedictorian of his class at M Street High School, and graduated with distinction from Williams College.[61] He served in World War I, fighting in the Argonne Forest campaign, but rebelled in the face of harassment of African American officers and enlisted men by their white commanders. He remained in France following his discharge in 1919 to work as a currency trader, partaking in the vibrant African American cultural scene that was developing in Paris in the months after the war. He became involved in the Pan-African movement; participating in the Second Pan-African Congress (he had missed the first congress because he was on active duty at the time).

Logan returned to the United States in 1925 and joined the faculty of Virginia Union University in Richmond. But he was too radical for the paternalistic whites who oversaw the school, so he left to pursue a PhD in history at Harvard, writing about American policy toward the Caribbean and the history of education in Haiti. Gaining a reputation as a "bad Negro with a PhD" upon graduation from Harvard, he moved back to Washington in 1932 and joined the staff of Carter G. Woodson's Association for the Study of Negro Life and History.[62] He accepted an appointment on the Howard faculty in 1938 after teaching briefly at Atlanta University. He remained at Howard for the remainder of his long career, closing out his association with the university by writing its official centenary history.[63]

Beyond scholarship, Logan was active in many racial advocacy organizations, including the NAACP and the Alpha Phi Alpha fraternity. His description of the years between Reconstruction and World War I as "the nadir" of African American life in his 1954 book *The Betrayal of the Negro* has come to be accepted as an important label for the period, while his 1944 collection of fourteen essays by prominent African American intellectuals, *What the Negro Wants*, was a battle cry for activism.[64]

Despite this record of social engagement and lifelong concern for the fate of postcolonial societies in Africa, Logan is perhaps most remembered today for his vociferously stubborn rejection of the term "black" during the upheavals of African American intellectual life in the late 1960s.[65] With this stance of rejection, Logan was accused of failing to keep pace with the times—as was Frazier, whose work on the decline of the African American family would cause him to be labeled as hostile to his race after it was picked up following his death by Daniel Patrick Moynihan and others; and as was Bunche, whose highly visible and remarkably successful diplomatic career would similarly attract criticism.[66]

However, the real story is more complex than one in which these leading intellectuals fell behind the times. Frazier, Harris, Bunche, and Logan led lives of achievement and distinction despite the very real barriers placed in their way. They never denied the harsh realities of American racism. Frazier embraced Kwame Nkrumah's call for black liberation, while Bunche's final speech in Honolulu in July 1969 argued that the world faced a "steady tendency toward polarization of the white and nonwhite peoples of the world which can lead to ultimate catastrophe for all."[67] Bunche, in fact, turned down senior appointments in the U.S. government to remain at the United Nations in New York so that he did not have to return to Jim Crow Washington.[68] Frazier, Bunche, and Logan became increasingly bitter toward the end of their lives. Harris, in this regard, was something of an exception, because he identified ever more closely with the neoliberal free market philosophies of the University of Chicago's Economics Department that he had joined in 1946.[69]

Frazier, Harris, Bunche, and Logan did not reject the racial radicalism of their youth so much as they rejected racial nationalism. Over the course of their careers, all four sought to understand and to confront racial segregation by placing themselves against an intellectual backdrop that transcended their own lives and immediate community. All flirted with Marxism and class-based theories of subjugation in the 1930s, and they found sustenance in looking to a wider world.[70] Harris relied on economic theory to explain the difficulties that he and other African Americans faced; Frazier and Logan turned to the African experience; and Bunche's distinguished diplomatic career confronted racism and racialism on a global scale.

In this regard, these four were like Alain Locke—their Howard colleague living at 13th and R streets, NW, during the 1930s—who did as much as anyone to promote a distinctive African American cultural achievement, even as his intense Bahá'í faith taught him the universality of humankind.[71] They were not accommodationist "Uncle Toms" as much as they were antinationalists who embraced a view of their humanity over time that rejected human degradation in all of its forms. They represent a strong and honorable tradition in the African American community—and on U Street as well.[72]

Yet theirs was not the only reaction among U Street intellectuals to the humiliations they and their fellow African Americans faced in a segregated Washington run by hostile whites. Many intellectuals and activists in the U Street neighborhood did embrace African American nationalism with enthusiasm.

Creating Black History

Carter G. Woodson, the son of former slaves, was born into abject poverty in central Virginia (figure 3.4). He moved to West Virginia to pursue an education as he approached adolescence because no schools were available to him in the rural Buckingham County of his birth. He worked on the railroad and in mines to earn sufficient funds to keep his brother and himself together while attending Douglass High School in Huntington, West Virginia. He made his way to little Berea College in Kentucky, a socially progressive school founded by abolitionists on the eve of the Civil War. Berea still admitted African American students, despite the closing in of the state's Jim Crow laws.

Woodson earned enough credits to graduate from Berea after taking additional courses at the University of Chicago and Lincoln University. Following graduation, he accepted a high school teaching position in the Philippines to escape the racial restrictions of the United States. Making his way home via Europe, he enrolled in classes at the Sorbonne, before arriving in America in late 1907. He entered graduate school at the University of Chicago, earning a joint bachelor's and master's degree, before continuing on for his PhD in history at Harvard University in

1912. He was only the second African American to earn a doctoral degree in the discipline (W. E. B. Du Bois having been the first).[73]

Woodson's advisers at Harvard—Edward Channing and Albert Bushnell Hart—argued that African Americans had no history—a position that would drive Woodson to dedicating his life to a demonstration of the contrary.[74] Hart, who served on the Howard University Board of Trustees for twenty-three years, went so far as to argue that "the theory that the Negro mind ceases to develop after adolescence perhaps has something in it."[75] Unsurprisingly, in the face of such attitudes, Woodson later would claim that he needed at least two decades to recover from his miseducation at Harvard.[76]

FIGURE 3.4
Carter G. Woodson

Photograph by Addison Scurlock, from the Scurlock Studio Records, Archives Center, National Museum of American History, Smithsonian Institution, Washington. Used with permission.

Woodson moved to Washington to teach American history, French, Spanish, and English at M Street High School before he completed his degree at Harvard. Rayford Logan was enrolled as a student at the school while Woodson was on the faculty. Woodson served as principal of Armstrong Manual Training School, M Street's great rival, for a year before joining the Howard faculty at the time of the 1919 racial confrontations.[77] He was elected to the American Negro Academy upon completion of his doctoral studies, an affiliation that brought him into social contact and intellectual interaction with Washington's African American intellectual elite.[78]

Woodson's career at Howard came to an abrupt end just as he was settling into his new life on its faculty. He had taught the first courses ever offered in African American history at the school when the university and its then-president, James Stanley Durkee, came under attack in Congress for promoting "Bolshevik" ideas.[79] Woodson found Durkee's response cowardly, and he did not hesitate to complain about the absence of support for Howard faculty under attack by white know-nothings. During a showdown over Woodson's display of disloyalty, Durkee produced a letter from Secret Service agents accusing Woodson of communist tendencies. Durkee tried to recruit Woodson to spy on his fellow faculty members.[80] Woodson quit instead, moving to West Virginia Collegiate Institute (now West Virginia State College) in 1920.

Meanwhile, Woodson—together with Jesse E. Moorland—had established the Association for the Study of Negro Life and History in 1915. This effort was intended to confront the ignorance and hostility toward African American history that was so dominant in white America, beginning with his own dissertation advisers at Harvard.[81] Woodson rounded up enough money to keep the association and its new publication, *The Journal of Negro History*, operating throughout the difficult years of Woodrow Wilson's anti–African American hold over life in the District of Columbia. The association opened a small office on U Street and, in 1921, founded the Associated Publishers to promote works exploring African American history. The association ran a popular lecture and seminar program at the nearby Twelfth Street YMCA and Phyllis Wheatley YWCA throughout this period.[82] In 1922, Woodson landed the first of several major grants from the Carnegie Corporation of New York, the Laura Spelman Memorial Fund, the Social Science Research Council, and the Rockefeller Foundation. He left teaching behind for good, returning to Washington from West Virginia to dedicate his life to promoting African American history through the association's speaker programs, press, journal, and other activities.[83]

Woodson used his operation to support and to encourage bright young African Americans to explore their culture. At various times, the folklorist Zora Neale Hurston, the historian Rayford Logan, and the writer Langston Hughes—among many future intellectual leaders of the black community—worked for Woodson.[84] Woodson was publishing his own works—such as *The Education of the Negro Prior to 1861*, *A Century of Negro Migration*, *The History of the Negro Church*, and the landmark *The Negro in Our History*—leading up to the appearance of perhaps his most important work, *The Mis-Education of the Negro*. In 1926, Woodson, operating through the Association for the Study of Negro Life and History, established Negro History Week during the second week of February to coincide with the birthdays of Frederick Douglass and Abraham Lincoln. Fifty years later, in 1976, Negro History Week would evolve into Black History Month, which is celebrated throughout February each year.[85]

Woodson's promotion of African American history and studies as legitimate fields of inquiry represented a different response to the white hostility that had pushed Frazier, Harris, Bunche, and Logan to find solace in theories that accentuated the universality of the human experience. Woodson's initiatives were intended to counter white ignorance and hatred by demonstrating the accomplishments of the African American past. This inclination to look within his community for sustenance and hope was accentuated in the 1930s.

White financial backers withdrew from supporting his activities due to skepticism about a supposed radicalization of the Association for the Study of Negro Life and History and its journal, as well as falling investment portfolios in the wake of the stock market crash of 1929.[86] Woodson would not be deterred, and reached out to raise small amounts of money from large numbers of contributors through the NAACP and African American fraternities, sororities, community associations, professional organizations, and church groups. The crisis initiated by the withdrawal of white money transformed the Association for the Study of Negro Life and History into a broad movement within the African American community to foster pride based on the past accomplishments of the race.[87]

The differences among Woodson, Frazier, Harris, Bunche, and Logan reflected deep divisions within the African American and U Street communities more generally between the broadly accommodationist approaches of a Booker T. Washington and the more combatively independent stance of a W. E. B. Du Bois. Woodson became embedded in a U Street community that was becoming more assertive about its own place in the world. He tapped into a vibrant business environment and civil society that were rooted in the enterprises, associations, and churches of U Street. His vision survived through the depths of the Great Depression because African Americans in communities such as U Street found the money to support his ventures despite the period's harsh economic deprivations. He pulled together the various strains of the U

Street and national African American communities under the large tent of racial pride.

Woodson and the people who disagreed with him, such as Logan, were members of the same community. They lived on the same streets, conducted their research in the same integrated reading rooms at the District's Public Library and at the Library of Congress, ate at the same handful of the city's eateries that would serve them, watched films at the same segregated theaters, were members of the same associations, rode the same streetcars, and watched the same ball clubs at Griffith Stadium. Woodson had taught Logan in high school, and the two of them fought many a battle against the same racists dominating the local Harvard alumni community. Logan assumed stewardship of Woodson's Association for the Study of Negro Life and History and editorship of its *Journal of Negro History* when his mentor passed away in 1950.[88] Whatever their differences—and no matter how much they may have wanted to escape one another—Woodson, Logan, and the other prominent African American intellectuals such as Frazier, Harris, and Bunche were bound together by life in one and the same zone of contact.

Woodson's Association for the Study of Negro Life and History, *Journal of Negro History*, and Negro History Week survived and grew precisely because they were rooted in a complex community that brought together intellectuals and rural migrants, people from the middle class and working class, business people and entertainers, and people who frequented Seventh Street as well as those who were denizens of Fourteenth Street. Whites played their role as well—initially with some important start-up funds, but also by constantly challenging the ideas that drove Woodson. No one can know if Woodson might have pursued these interests if his own dissertation advisers at Harvard had been open to the notion that the African American had a history. The point is that they were not—and Woodson responded.

These crosscurrents came together in the person of Carter G. Woodson, and in the neighborhood where he lived out much of his adult life. U Street served as a vital zone of contact among many contradictory social forces and human beings. Woodson's activities depended on local churches and the YMCA to promote the programs of the Association for the Study of Negro Life and History, on Howard faculty and students to provide intellectual sustenance and challenge, on associations such as the NAACP to sustain his work, and on small financial contributions from African American schoolchildren and workers to uncover a past in which they could take pride and sustenance. Everything that Woodson did was a product of the same U Street community that had taken shape before World War I, and that had defended itself so fiercely during the riots of 1919. Not surprisingly, Woodson's efforts reinforced a growing social and political radicalization that was sweeping through the community.

"Don't Buy Where You Can't Work"

On September 3, 1933, a small article on page 10 of the day's edition of the *Washington Post* told readers that "The 'New Negro Alliance,' comprising young men and women graduates of Eastern colleagues, associated with others in education work here, have organized to 'protect employment of Negroes under the NRA program.' A series of boycotts have been conducted by them during the past week." The article continued on to list, among many, H. [*sic*] A. Davis as the group's administrator, Jesse Lewis of the Howard School of Finance as treasurer, and William Hastie as counsel.[89] Carter G. Woodson was among the group's earliest supporters. He soon found himself attracted to ever more radical causes, including the National Negro Congress formed two years later.[90]

The New Negro Alliance's assertiveness harkened back to the neighborhood's embrace of racial economic nationalism a generation earlier.[91] Local African American business leaders and opinion makers such as William Calvin Chase, John W. Cromwell, Andrew Hilyer, and the Reverend Alexander Crummell had encouraged a movement to foster patronage of black businesses at the turn of the century, creating banks and other financial institutions, and supporting black entrepreneurs in every possible manner.[92] Because they had been forced by Jim Crow laws and customs to turn to community networks and institutions developed within African American Washington, they advocated a separatist philosophy that encouraged residents to patronize black-owned businesses.

The issues facing the community by the 1930s were different. Previously, advocates of racial economic nationalism were responding to a growing African American business and financial sector that could increasingly meet the needs of their community.[93] Now the primary issue was more simply employment in a deepening national Depression that was closing many of those same businesses that were being supported by an earlier generation of racial economic nationalists. People throughout the United States were losing their livelihoods, with African Americans frequently being the first to be turned out onto the streets.

Woodson was primed to embrace racial economic radicalism after having been mugged on Pennsylvania Avenue on Friday, January 13, 1933, as he was returning home from the Library of Congress.[94] The experience jolted Woodson out of his "ivory tower" complacency. He took immediate action, speaking to the white managers of the local A&P and Sanitary (future Safeway) grocery stores about hiring blacks as well as whites. After beseeching these whites—who were earning their livelihoods from segregated blacks along U Street—Woodson became convinced that only community action would change the economic fortunes of local African American residents.

Other U Streeters were shaken by less harrowing personal experiences than a mugging, events that amplified the difficulties in securing steady incomes among their racial compatriots. A recent Williams College graduate, John Aubrey Davis, was disillusioned by the inattention to economic issues being exhibited by the local NAACP. Davis was the son of a government employee who had lost a secure income as a federal worker when he was fired during Woodrow Wilson's campaign against African Americans.[95] Davis graduated from M Street High School before completing Williams summa cum laude. His brother Allison Davis would become a member of the sociology faculty at the University of Chicago.[96]

In August 1933, Davis and his colleagues initiated a campaign of picket lines in front of businesses in the neighborhood that refused to hire African Americans.[97] They selected a local hamburger place on U Street before moving on to the A&P and Sanitary supermarkets that had raised Woodson's ire.[98] William Flintier, the white owner of the Hamburger

Grill at 1211 U Street, invited the protest when he dismissed three young African American employees, Joseph Dacons, James McArthur, and Alfonso Bradley.[99] Dacons and McArthur were enrolled at Howard. Davis and other activists mobilized Howard students to join the protest, and the New Negro Alliance was born. Within days, Dacons, McArthur, and Bradley were back at work, and the alliance's "Don't Buy Where You Can't Work" campaign was launched.[100]

Davis moved his protest to the *Washington Star* in a successful effort to get the paper to hire African American newspaper boys.[101] Picket lines formed at the Temple Restaurant in the Masonic Temple Building, at local A&P grocery stores, at the High Ice Cream Company (prompting local children to stop eating ice cream), at Peoples Drugs, and at Kaufman's Department Store downtown.[102] Their campaign spread to other cities.[103] In September 1940, the U.S. Post Office opened a special branch at 14th and T streets to allow black postal workers to secure higher-paying window service jobs denied them elsewhere in the city by Jim Crow regulations left over from the Wilson administration.[104] Prominent community members such as Mary McLeod Bethune proudly had their photos taken on the picket lines.[105] William Hastie brought fellow Howard Law professor James Nabrit and his own cousin Charles Houston to the alliance's picket lines.[106]

Some stores refused to give in to the New Negro Alliance's picket lines. The Peoples Drug chain withstood the protests for two years, and the Sanitary Grocery Company sought an injunction rather than hire African American employees.[107] The resulting court case eventuated in a U.S. Supreme Court decision upholding the constitutionality of the alliance's picket lines under the Norris-LaGuardia Anti-Injunction Act of 1932.[108]

Not everyone was supportive of the New Negro Alliance's campaign. Abram Harris and Ralph Bunche were particularly concerned that the protests would alienate black and white workers from one another. Bunche attended a discussion group at an alliance meeting on March 16, 1935, after which he spoke out against the alliance. The alliance, in return, launched broadsides against academics who viewed the world through theory rather than through the realities of the street.[109]

Other protests followed in Washington and elsewhere, with the New Negro Alliance finding itself outflanked by the National Negro Congress, which was affiliated with the Communist Party and was vociferously protesting the kangaroo-court-style trial of the so-called Scottsboro Boys.[110] John P. Davis's and Robert Weaver's Joint Committee on National Recovery—an alliance of twenty-two community organizations— vigorously pursued economic goals as well.[111] These new, more combative groups challenged older organizations such as the NAACP for leadership and sharpened the focus of African American community leaders on economic issues and employment.[112] The New Negro Alliance's success eventually prompted the D.C. chapter of the NAACP to take up similar economic protest strategies a few years later under the leadership of former alliance administrator Eugene Davidson.[113]

Economic boycotts and campaigns against segregation continued in the U Street community following World War II.[114] One of the most important was led by community doyenne Mary Church Terrell.[115] She had arrived in Washington in the 1890s after marrying Robert Terrell, the principal of M Street High School, who would become the city's first African American municipal court judge. She served for several years on the city's appointed school board and became a leading civil rights activist in her own right.[116] The Terrells' LeDroit Park home at 326 T Street, NW, became a primary meeting place and parlor for activists and neighborhood elites both before and after Robert's death in 1925.[117]

Thinking her life done as she approached her eighties, Terrell published her exceptionally eloquent memoir about living in segregated Washington and America, *A Colored Woman in a White World*.[118] The book turned out to be somewhat early, because Terrell lived to ninety-one, passing away just after the Supreme Court's 1954 landmark decision in the *Brown v. Board of Education* case.

Mary Church Terrell was not someone who let age get in her way. She continued her activism, defending and mobilizing support for many victims of segregation until the end of her long and distinguished life.[119] As a staunch supporter of the New Negro Alliance and the economic boycotts they had launched, she took up many a cause throughout the 1940s. For example, she formed a "National Committee to Free the

Ingram Family" on behalf of a Georgia sharecropper, Rose Ingram, and her two sons, who were sentenced to death for killing a white man in self-defense.[120]

Locally, Terrell's last major attempt to end segregation began in 1949 when she joined with a Jewish activist, Annie Stein, and others to launch a new campaign to desegregate public services.[121] Her initiative, which included pickets and boycotts, prompted a law suit against Thompson's Restaurant after it had denied service to Terrell and other protesters on February 28, 1950.[122] The resulting June 1953 Supreme Court decision in *District of Columbia v. Thompson Co.* held that the District had the power to pass and enforce laws prohibiting discrimination in restaurants. The *Thompson* case—together with Houston's 1948 victory removing restrictive housing covenants in *Hurd v. Hodge*, and Nabrit's success in removing bans on integrated schools through the *Bolling v. Sharpe* decision a year later—marked the beginning of the end of the Jim Crow regime in Washington.

Community Organization from Above and Below

While Howard law professors and students were inventing the legal strategy of the postwar civil rights movement—and as young U Street radicals were inventing the economic strategy—the extensive networks of church, social, professional, and business associations that had taken root in the neighborhood before World War I were sustaining their community and their neighbors in the face of the harsh realities of Depression-era African America.[123] The challenges confronting the community were growing exponentially.

The economic and demographic balance among middle-class, working-class, and poor rural migrants in the U Street area remained stable throughout the first half of the twentieth century.[124] Federal employment provided a bedrock for the city's and neighborhood's African American middle class.[125] Meanwhile, the city overall was changing more quickly than U Street and its surrounding area.

Washington's African American population grew from 109,966 in 1920 to 132,068 in 1930, 187,266 in 1940, and 280,803 in 1950.

This rate of increase surpassed that of whites and the city's population generally, which increased from 437,571 in 1920 to 802,178 in 1950.[126] The city's growth spurt was largely a consequence of migrants from the depressed rural South pouring in looking for economic opportunities.[127] The impact of the arrival of migrants was greatest in the poorer African American neighborhoods such as those in Southwest Washington.[128]

As a consequence of these trends, the city was becoming blacker and poorer throughout the first half of the twentieth century, a pattern that placed greater demands on African American organizations.[129] The housing and employment situation for Washington's blacks remained dismal, despite some growth in jobs following World War II.[130] These realities forced communities such as U Street to rely on themselves for survival rather than to look to local or national governments, despite the growth of federal social programs under Franklin Delano Roosevelt's New Deal.[131]

One change that took place throughout the era is that community groups became better organized and, whenever possible, began to work with the small number of whites who were interested in helping their African American neighbors. As early as 1929, the powerful Board of Trade endorsed the initiative of some white—largely Jewish—business owners to create a unified "Community Chest" that would raise money for all local charities, both white and black.[132] Franklin Delano Roosevelt's uncle, Frederic A. Delano, and a longtime Howard University dean, Kelly Miller, accepted key leadership positions in the effort. Their initiative gained strength after two hundred representatives of eighteen social service and international organizations from around the community met in Washington under the auspices of the Social Science Research Council in December 1928. But the effort floundered in the face of the stock market crash ten months later.

The attempt to create the Community Chest with links to social science analysis elevated Washington as a suitable laboratory for new social policies once Roosevelt swept his Democratic Party to power in 1932. The secretary of the interior, Harold Ickes, took a particular interest in African American Washington, U Street, and Howard University; as did the first lady, Eleanor Roosevelt.[133] Both encouraged the administration to use executive orders to integrate parts of the city (as when the Interior Department's National Park Service opened up federally operated golf courses to blacks as well as whites and, later, when fellow Democrat Harry S. Truman ordered an end to discrimination in the government in February 1948).[134]

The appointment of African Americans to high-level positions throughout the bureaucracy by both the Roosevelt and the Truman administrations forced changes in internal customs and arrangements— as when future secretary of state Dean Rusk invited Ralph Bunche to the War Department's whites-only Officers' Dining Room in 1948.[135] Similarly, U Street resident Benjamin O. Davis Sr.'s commission as the first African American general in the history of the U.S. Armed Forces in 1940 initiated a process of slow racial integration throughout the military.[136] Such efforts gradually turned the clock back on the damage inflicted by President Wilson on local African American communities.

More important, national activism was growing—and gaining limited results. A threatened march on Washington in 1941 led by Bayard Rustin, A. Philip Randolph, and A. J. Muste to protest racial discrimination in the military was headed off by a last-minute agreement. Rustin, Randolph, Muste, and others held many of their organizational meetings at U Street institutions, such as the Twelfth Street YMCA. New York City mayor Fiorello LaGuardia, negotiating for President Franklin Delano Roosevelt, was able to use their efforts to pressure the president to issue Executive Order 8802—which was later known as the "Fair Employment Act"—establishing the Committee of Fair Employment Practice within the Office of Production Management.[137] Other executive orders abolished racial segregation in the military in 1948, with more to follow as an intransigent Congress dominated by Southerners refused to pass civil rights legislation. These measures gradually expanded the space within which African Americans could seek employment, helping residents of neighborhoods such as U Street find a more secure living.[138]

Groups like the New Negro Alliance and those supporting the canceled march on Washington recognized that the problems faced by Washington's and the nation's African Americans fundamentally stemmed from poverty and exclusion. The Great Depression cut through neighborhoods such as U Street in many pernicious ways. People lost jobs, which they could not reclaim. Middle- and upper-class African American households around U Street saw the value of their homes and other investments plummet, leaving them bereft of resources that could have counterbalanced the growing difficulties on the job market.[139]

African American female migrants from the South, who frequently worked as domestic servants, suffered particular hardships. Their livelihoods were undermined both by the reduction of white households with the means to employ them, and by new patterns of "living out" of the employer's household, which threw them into a difficult housing market.[140] The demands of living on one's own after hours threatened the savings of many domestic workers, undercutting the ability of the once-vibrant and widespread mutual-benefit associations known as "penny savers' clubs."[141]

Local churches remained at the center of an extensive support network throughout the U Street community. Somewhere around a hundred churches were active in the neighborhood at midcentury, ranging from brick architectural masterpieces to storefront halls.[142] African American churches in areas such as U Street gained strength from the refusal of white Protestant churches to reach out to their parishioners.[143] As a result, congregations retained their wealthiest parishioners even as their community was buffeted by the economic upheavals of the Depression.

Churches such as the John Wesley African Methodist Episcopal Church on 14th Street, NW, made their facilities available to social groups such as the NAACP.[144] Elder Lightfoot Solomon Michaux's Temple of Freedom under God, Church of God—which opened in a Georgia Avenue storefront in 1928 and gained a national audience through its *Happy Am I* program on the CBS Radio Network—saved the bankrupt Howard Theatre by moving in during the difficult years at the outset of the Depression in 1930 and 1931. And Michaux's church refinanced the failed Industrial Bank and Savings Association at 11th and U streets in 1933.[145]

Improvising around Failed Local Government

Congregations were forced to step into the breach because the District of Columbia government faced its own difficulties. Congress had established the District's federal payment at $9 million in 1925, a figure that proved woefully insufficient to meet the growing social demands brought on by the Great Depression.[146] (As noted in chapter 1, the federal payment was made to the city in lieu of property taxes for the large proportion of tax-exempt land in the city owned by the federal government.) The absence of elected representation became an ever more evident omission in an era when concern for democracy was growing internationally. The District's three appointed commissioners divided administrative responsibilities for various agencies among themselves, while Congress fitfully served as the District's legislative body. The failures of this governing system became increasingly glaring under the pressures of the Depression and World War II. Between 1934 and 1941, Congress undertook thirty reviews of how best to organize the city's affairs.[147]

The city's residents became increasingly vocal in their demand for home rule, while a number of unsuccessful bills were introduced in Congress to remedy the situation.[148] The Southern-dominated Democratic Party refused to consider any measures that would expand the role of the city's African American community in its own governance. A 1952 reorganization plan issued by President Harry S. Truman under his authority to reorganize federal agencies streamlined some procedures. This action nonetheless failed to address the fundamental issue of local control.[149]

The federal government under presidents Roosevelt and Truman responded to the city's concerns through a series of stopgap measures tied to larger national social policies. In the field of housing, the Capper-Norton Alley Dwelling Act of 1934 established the Alley Dwelling Authority, which was the first public housing authority in the country.[150]

John Ihlder had advocated the idea of such an institution for several years. Ihlder, a Georgetown homeowner, remained active in local housing initiatives throughout the 1930s and 1940s, establishing the

Committee on Housing of the Washington Council of Social Agencies in 1929, as well as the Washington Committee on Housing under the honorary chair of first lady Eleanor Roosevelt in 1933. He and his associates promoted legislation in Congress to address local housing conditions, including the Capper-Norton Act.

The Alley Dwelling Authority, with Ihlder as its executive director, served as a model for the U.S. Housing Act of 1937. The authority— and its successors, the Washington Housing Authority and the National Capital Housing Authority—advanced greater understanding of the notion that philanthropic efforts alone could not solve the city's housing problems. Its assertive inspections of housing conditions alleviated and eventually eliminated the shameful conditions of the city's alley communities, particularly in the Foggy Bottom area of Northwest Washington and various neighborhoods in the Southeast quadrant of the city.[151] These agencies served as a model for the nation's massive postwar public housing programs.[152] They gave a start to many prominent careers, including that of future D.C. mayor and Howard University graduate Walter Washington.[153] Furthermore, they paved the way for the creation of the D.C. Zoning Advisory Committee in 1954, which would play an important role in shaping the future of the U Street neighborhood following desegregation.[154]

More broadly, the National Capital Planning Act of 1952 reformed federal decisionmaking affecting development and redevelopment throughout the entire capital region.[155] The act replaced the National Capital Park and Planning Commission, which dated from the 1920s, with a new National Capital Regional Planning Council containing representatives from all the region's jurisdictions.[156] A few years later, in 1957, the city and suburban jurisdictions in Virginia and Maryland formed the Metropolitan Washington Council of Governments to better coordinate regional policies, such as those affecting transportation.[157] Such agencies and initiatives promoted the creation of a regionwide parkway system, and eventually planned for regional highway and mass transit networks that would transform U Street in the decades ahead.[158]

Following the departure of Army Corps of Engineer major general Ulysses S. Grant III—the grandson of the Civil War hero and

Reconstruction-era president General U. S. Grant—as one of the District's commissioners, successive commissioners worked closely with the Council of Governments in staunchly advocating regional decentralization plans promoted by the federal government's national security agencies as a means for better defending the city against an air attack.[159] The council's policies—combined with the National Highway Act of 1956 establishing the Interstate Highway Program and the May 1948 Supreme Court decision in *Hurd v. Hodge* against restrictive covenants limiting African American access to housing in the District of Columbia—accelerated postwar white flight from the city.

Similar improvisational measures were taking place in the field of education as public schools in the city suffered from declining city revenues in the face of the Depression, and none more so than African American schools. In 1936, President Roosevelt appointed Mary McLeod Bethune to serve as director of the Division of Negro Affairs at the newly formed National Youth Administration.

Already near sixty, Bethune was a prominent African American educator and outspoken proponent of anti-lynching legislation.[160] She had moved from picking cotton in her native South Carolina to graduating from the Scotia Seminar in neighboring North Carolina. After a year at Dwight Moody's Institute for Home and Foreign Missions in Chicago—where she discovered that there were no opportunities for African Americans to serve as missionaries in Africa—she moved to Georgia, where she taught and started a family. In 1904, she relocated once again—this time to Daytona Beach, Florida—founding the Daytona Literary and Industrial School for Training Negro Girls (which would eventually become Bethune-Cookman College).

Bethune organized voter registration drives and urged African American women throughout the South to fight against school segregation. By the mid-1920s, she had become president of the National Association for Colored Women's Clubs and a national leader in the women's and civil rights movements. She moved back to Florida when the National Youth Administration was abolished in 1944, returning to Bethune-Cookman College and writing a sharp-edged column for the *Chicago Defender*.[161] She maintained a residence in Washington on Vermont Avenue just off of

U Street, which served as her office for running the National Council of Negro Women until the end of her life.[162]

Bethune used her time in Washington to promote African American education, stressing the importance of learning job and business skills. Under her leadership, the National Association for Colored Women's Clubs operated scholarship programs and other initiatives to encourage African American women to pursue educational opportunities. They were joined in the U Street neighborhood by a number of other formal and informal initiatives.

Miner Teachers College on Georgia Avenue was the principal training school at the time for the city's African American teachers.[163] Having been founded in 1875 and named in honor of Myrtilla Miner, an abolitionist white educator from New York who established the School for Colored Girls in 1851, Miner remained the most accessible institution of higher learning for the city's African American community until it merged in 1955 with the white Wilson Teacher's College.[164] Both institutions eventually formed the core of the University of the District of Columbia. Similarly, Anna J. Cooper founded Frelinghuysen University, a night school offering classical education to working-class African Americans. Faced with growing financial constraints during the Depression, in 1931 the school moved many of its operations to Cooper's LeDroit Park residence at 2nd and T Streets, NW, where it remained until closing during the late 1950s.[165]

These private and community initiatives responded to the needs of an increasingly inadequate and ineffectual public school system struggling under the economic exigencies of a faltering economy combined with inattention from the whites who controlled funding. Protests and boycotts organized by the NAACP and other organizations failed to move the white-dominated school board to release sufficient funds to black schools to close the gap between African American and white education.[166]

Efforts early in the century to promote and to sustain evening adult schools began to suffer from budget cuts as well.[167] Many U Streeters long maintained that Washington's African American public schools were among the best in the country throughout the era of segregation. But best, in this instance, was not good enough, because the city's growing impoverished population of blacks newly arrived from the South stretched local resources and demanded more innovative curricula.

The increasing failure to sustain systemwide excellence in education accentuated the bankruptcy of Jim Crow policies. African Americans faced humiliation every day, whether in the classroom, in dining rooms to which they were denied entry, in their choice of housing, and in their access to theaters and clubs. In the most notorious incident of the era, in 1939 the internationally acclaimed opera diva Marian Anderson was prohibited from performing in the city's primary concert venue—Constitutional Hall of the Daughters of the American Revolution. Harold Ickes and Eleanor Roosevelt intervened, arranging for a free concert on the steps of the Lincoln Memorial on Easter Sunday.[168]

In 1936, Ralph Bunche greatly embarrassed his longtime friend Todd Duncan—the original Porgy in George Gershwin's *Porgy and Bess*—when he was forced to decline an invitation to attend a performance of the opera at the National Theater downtown.[169] The National Theater was particularly known for its hostility to black patrons, hiring African Americans to spot their racial brethren who were trying "to pass" in order to enter the theater. A benefit performance of the Pulitzer Prize–winning play *The Green Pastures*, about life in a heaven where God is black, was canceled at the National Theater just a few years earlier in 1933 after court cases failed to open up seats in the audience for African Americans.[170] Many white Washingtonians appear to have agreed with a letter writer to the *Washington Post*, who observed that "the theaters, night clubs and restaurants in Washington are the only places that we can escape mingling with Negroes so be sure and keep it that way."[171]

Bunche and Duncan were so outraged in this particular instance that they organized a picket line, which eventually opened the theater to African American ticket purchases for this one opera.[172] Three years later, Bunche was out on the picket line again, leading protests against the showing of *Gone with the Wind* at the prestigious Lincoln Theatre on U Street.[173] The showing of a film glorifying the South at one of the premier African American theaters in the country was simply more than he or many other U Streeters could abide.[174]

Anna Julia Cooper (1858–1964)

Anna Julia Haywood Cooper was born into slavery in Raleigh on August 10, 1858. Cooper was the daughter of a white master, George Washington Haywood, and his slave, Hannah Stanley, and she was accepted into a teacher's training program at the age of seven. She began to teach to pay her way through Saint Augustine's Normal School and Collegiate Institute in Raleigh, which at the time prepared men for the ministry. The curriculum for women eschewed advanced courses oriented toward academic achievement. But she successfully demanded access to the same classrooms as her male counterparts.

In 1877, she married the Reverend George C. Cooper, a fellow former slave and tailor who had been ordained into the ministry in Nassau, the Bahamas. The couple met when Anna enrolled in a Greek course being taught by George. Anna, who was a dozen years younger than her husband, left the classroom because married women were prohibited from teaching in schools at the time. George—only the second African American to be ordained as a minister in North Carolina's Episcopal Church—died suddenly two years later.

Finding herself without family and career at the age of twenty-one, Cooper set out for Ohio. She enrolled in predominantly white Oberlin College, graduating in 1884 together with African American coeds Mary Eliza Church and Ida A. Gibbs. Cooper earned a master's degree in mathematics from Oberlin the following year and then accepted a position at Ohio's Wilberforce University. She moved to Washington in 1887 to join the faculty of M Street High School. She became the school's principal in 1901, only to be dismissed five years later for her insistence on academic excellence. She taught at Lincoln University between 1906 and 1910.

Cooper published her first and best-known book, *A Voice from the South: By a Woman from the South*, in 1892. The volume advocated self-determination for African American women through education. As an eloquent advocate for what would become black feminism, Cooper argued that African American women were essential to the struggle for equality. She was the only woman elected to the American Negro Academy at its founding in 1897.

Cooper entered a doctoral program at New York's Columbia University in 1914. Following her mother's death the next year, she adopted her half-brother's five children. She completed her doctorate at the University of Paris–Sorbonne in 1924, becoming, at sixty-five, only the fourth African American woman to hold a PhD. Her dissertation— *The Attitude of France on the Question of Slavery between 1789 and 1848*—appeared in print a year later.

Cooper worked closely with Frelinghuysen University in Washington, which had opened in 1907 to provide educational opportunities for the city's "colored working people." The school was originally housed in the home of its founders, Jesse and Rosetta C. Lawson, at 2011 Vermont Avenue, and it was named in honor of white New Jersey senator Frederick T. Frelinghuysen, a staunch Reconstruction-era advocate of policies assisting freedmen and freedwomen. The school moved around the city throughout the 1920s and gained full accreditation in 1927. Cooper became the university's president in 1930 following the death of founder Jesse Lawson. Financial constraints forced Cooper to move the school into her LeDroit Park home at the height of the Depression. After losing its accreditation in 1937, Frelinghuysen eventually closed at the end of the 1950s.

Cooper retired from Frelinghuysen in 1942 and remained active until her death at the age of 105 on February 27, 1964. She was buried next to her husband in Raleigh. In 2008, the U.S. Postal Service commemorated Cooper by issuing a postage stamp in her honor.

Profile

WILLIAM HENRY HASTIE JR. (1904–1976)

William Henry Hastie spent the first dozen years of his life in his native Knoxville, where his father—William Henry Hastie Sr.—worked as a clerk in the U.S. Pension Office. The family moved to Washington in 1916 following his father's transfer to the nation's capital.

Hastie entered M Street High School just a few years after his elder cousin Charles Hamilton Houston had graduated as class valedictorian. Hastie followed in Houston's footsteps, graduating as class valedictorian in 1921 and moving on to Amherst College, where he graduated Phi Beta Kappa with highest honors in mathematics as class valedictorian in 1925. He taught high school for two years before entering Harvard Law School, where he was elected to *Law Review*.

Hastie moved back to Washington in 1930 upon graduation from Harvard, joining his cousins' firm Houston and Houston. He began teaching at Howard Law School at the same time, taking time off to earn his doctorate in juridical science from Harvard Law School in 1933. The newly elected President Franklin Delano Roosevelt appointed Hastie as assistant solicitor in the Department of the Interior, the first among his numerous distinguished federal appointments. Roosevelt appointed Hastie to the U.S. District Court for the Virgin Islands in 1937, making him the first African American to serve as a federal judge. Hastie left federal service two years later to become dean of Howard Law School.

Government service beckoned once again as the likelihood of a new war loomed larger and larger. In 1940, Hastie left Howard to become a senior civilian aide to Defense Secretary Henry Stimson. Hastie used his position to advance desegregation in the American military. But he became frustrated by the slow pace of reform and quit in protest in 1943, the same year he was awarded the NAACP's Spingarn Medal, and returned to the Howard faculty.

Hastie continued to teach at Howard throughout his various government appointments, simultaneously serving on the NAACP's Board of Directors. Together with his cousin Charles Houston and his former student Thurgood Marshall, Hastie was active in civil rights litigation and supported numerous advocacy organizations such as the New Negro Alliance. He argued several crucial civil rights cases with Houston and Marshall during the late 1930s and early 1940s, at times presenting the winning argument before the Supreme Court.

Hastie was inaugurated as the first African American governor of the Virgin Islands in 1946. Three years later, President Truman nominated him to the prestigious Third United States Circuit Court of Appeals in Washington, the highest judicial appointment of an African American before Marshall's appointment to the Supreme Court in 1967. President John F. Kennedy considered appointing Hastie to the Supreme Court in 1962, backing away in the face of fierce opposition from the segregationist chairman of the Senate Judiciary Committee, James Eastland.

Hastie served on the Third Circuit for twenty-one years, becoming the circuit's chief judge in 1968. He authored some four hundred decisions before retiring to senior status in 1971. He died in suburban Philadelphia in 1976.

CHAPTER 4

"Black Broadway"

Perhaps what the interrupted, deceiving, sometimes
drunken voice of the urban night is telling its laced-up
daytime twin is that the real source of a city's magic,
and the strongest force of its survival, is the permanence
of human desires and the indefatigability of human will.

—Mark Caldwell, *New York Night:*
The Mystique and Its History, 2005[1]

U Street between the world wars was a place where simply "being
there meant being somebody."[2] Its theaters, clubs, businesses, pool
halls, barbershops, and drugstores provided African Americans with
the meeting places they were denied elsewhere in the city (map 2). The
picketers outside the Lincoln Theatre for the opening of *Gone with the
Wind* were protesting more than a single movie. They were claiming U
Street's sparkling entertainment district as their own.[3]

Marya Annette McQuirter, in a groundbreaking study of African
Americans and leisure in Washington, argues that recreational activities
emerged as "one of the principal arenas in which African Americans
formed, transgressed, and struggled over what it meant to be black
in the first half of the twentieth century."[4] McQuirter goes further to
suggest that defining Washington as a "segregated" city "ignores the
city's complex and varied racial landscape."[5] Using the language of
the current historiography on the emergence of U.S. public culture—
and examining the city in its entirety—she portrays the world of
leisure as a place of confrontation,[6] by looking at how Washington's
African Americans visited libraries, read newspapers, watched movies,
went to amusement parks, sought equal access to department stores

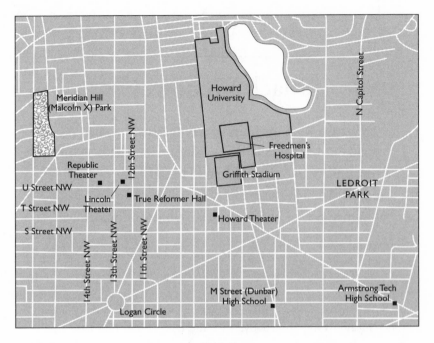

MAP 2

The U Street Neighborhood in the Mid–Twentieth Century

Map by William Nelson.

downtown, and used public places "as stages for the performance of urban identities."[7] Her city becomes a "zone of contact," and much of that interaction transpired in the area around U Street.

McQuirter's perspective on U Street finds important parallels in other cities divided by class and race around the world. For instance, writing about contemporary Rio de Janeiro, James Freeman underscores a concept of public space in which conflict is ever present, and positive. "The real public sphere," he writes, "is political in a messy, conflictual, and unjust way. In addition to being convivial, there is an undercurrent of struggle. . . . Class distinctions are refined and reproduced in conversations that rarely cross social lines."[8] But, he continues, public space matters because it provides a stage on which it is difficult to exclude the poor and the dark of skin. As McQuirter shows, U Street provided just such a stage in the Washington of the early twentieth century.

Claiming the City

McQuirter begins her study by recounting the reflections of Shirley Ridgely Banks about growing up black in Washington during the early 1930s. Banks—McQuirter records, with words similar to Duke Ellington's recollections about exploring the city a generation before— "recalled her and her friends' frequent jaunts throughout *their* city. These jaunts took them to one of the churches in their immediate neighborhood for movies, midtown to visit the main public library, downtown to the Mall for the museums and monuments, and on streetcars which gave them a view of different neighborhoods in all four quadrants of the city."[9] Banks and other African Americans did not allow whites to take Washington away from them. They contested white control by claiming public space just as they picketed white businesses, explored African American history, and developed new legal strategies.

Sometimes, African Americans could claim public space simply by walking down the street. Recalling the native Washington poet Sterling A. Brown's character "Sporting Beasley," McQuirter writes about the real-life "Sportin' Daniels," whose "stylin'" became a visible fixture of the city's Depression-era life. Daniels, McQuirter asserts, was "a walking embodiment of a particular kind of urban masculinity. Washingtonians reminiscing about the past will invariably mention Sportin' Daniels and recount how he was always impeccably dressed. He was a ubiquitous presence, particularly around U Street. Similar to movie theaters that changed shows daily, Sportin' Daniels changed his clothing several times a day."[10] For an aspiring "Washington monument" like Daniels, U Street was the place to be.

As McQuirter shows, there were other places, too, such as the Suburban Gardens amusement park in the city's Deanwood neighborhood across the Anacostia River, nearby beaches, and the Public Library of the District of Columbia. The library is particularly important for the story of U Street because it was never segregated. It was located just a few blocks down 7th Street, toward downtown on Mount Vernon Square, and it became a valued resource for the city's African Americans. Given that it was open to all Washingtonians, the Public Library remained one of the few shared spaces in the city open to men, women, children, the rich, the poor, black, and white alike.[11]

Reading was a major leisure activity for Washington blacks, especially during the years before the explosion of broadcasting and electronic media. By 1910, more than 80 percent of the city's African Americans were literate (as opposed to 55 percent nationwide).[12] So after opening in 1903 in an elegant granite and marble building funded by Andrew Carnegie, the main Public Library immediately attracted readers.[13] By 1910, one in seven Washingtonians had a library card.[14] The library's Reference Room, just a short stroll or streetcar ride down 7th Street from Howard University, was frequently full of students because the university did not yet have an adequate library facility of its own, and would not until the Founders Library opened in 1937.[15] Public school students similarly used the reading rooms, ensuring that the African American presence in the city was forever visible in this uniquely integrated facility.

McQuirter proposes that participation in leisure activities such as trips to the library as well as access "to a range of city spaces were critical to African Americans' conceptions of themselves as urbanites, to their incorporation into Washington's burgeoning urban culture, and to an understanding of how they helped to shape U.S. public culture."[16] And among these activities, nightlife was serious fun—and no more so than in the theaters, clubs, barbershops, and bars along U Street.

Showbiz, Vice, and Haircuts

By the late 1920s, there were several major motion picture palaces catering to African American audiences in the U Street area—often offering live entertainment together with films—including the top-of-the-line Lincoln at 13th and U, the Republic at 14th and U, and the Dunbar at 7th and T.[17] These three theaters were selling nearly 1.4 million tickets a year during the mid-1920s.[18]

The Howard at 7th and T streets—home to "'high-brown' dancing girls" known as the "Howardettes"—was one of the premier African American live entertainment theaters in the country.[19] The Lincoln

Colonnade in the basement of the Lincoln Theatre, the Murray Palace Casino at 10th and U streets, the Scottish Rite Temple near 11th and R streets, and the Press Club a couple of blocks away were among the best dance halls in the city, opening their doors to more than 3,000 hoofers on a good night.[20]

If someone liked the music, she or he could step into Waxie Maxie's Quality Music Shop at 1836 7th Street, NW.[21] That is precisely what Ahmet Ertegun, the son of the Turkish ambassador to America, did during the late 1930s.[22] Sneaking out of the Embassy at midnight, Ertegun caught a Cab Calloway show at a club along U Street one summer night in 1935. He was hooked. He began scouring the city for recordings of the great artists whom he was hearing at places like the Howard Theatre, Bengasi, the Casbah, and the Crystal Caverns (figure 4.1)—musicians like Duke Ellington, Louis Armstrong, Jimmie

FIGURE 4.1
The Chorus Line at Crystal Caverns

Photograph by Addison Scurlock, Scurlock Studio Records, Archives Center, National
Museum of American History, Smithsonian Institution, Washington. Used with permission.

Lunceford, Fats Waller, and Mary Lou Williams. He became a regular denizen of Max "Waxie Maxie" Silverman's little record store behind the Howard Theatre. These childhood experiences shaped Ertegun's life. He went on to establish Atlantic Records, and to become one of the most successful record producers of American popular music during the last half of the twentieth century.

The Oriental Gardens and the Andrew Thomas Cabaret along R Street and the Phoenix Inn opposite the Lincoln Theatre on U Street offered superior cabaret performances, as did the city's largest cabaret—Café De Luxe—at 7th and S streets.[23] The Dreamland Café and Paradise Café around the intersection of 7th and T provided less wholesome and more disorderly cabaret performances, with some of the "girls" allegedly offering more than drinks for sale in back rooms.[24] The night club Bohemia in the basement of the Davis Drug Store at 11th and U streets similarly failed to maintain standards and "degenerated somewhat because of the demoralizing influences of a class of unscrupulous patrons," while "a number of probation officers have reported" that the Silver Slipper Club in the Pythian Temple Building at 12th and U had become "the 'hangout' of a rather large number of their delinquent girls."[25]

U Street and 7th Street sported many of the city's best billiard parlors—too many to count easily—which the Howard University sociologist William H. Jones told readers in 1927

> are the harbingers of superstition and magic, since luck and chance play an important role in the activity performed. But they also are places where much liberal thought is promoted through discussion, disagreement, and the giving of information. The majority of pool hall patrons are persons who have wide experience, even though they have little formal education. They are men who traveled widely as porters, waiters, chauffeurs, etc. And one only needs to assume a sympathetic attitude to realize that here experience and ideas from the "ends of the earth" are assembled. The contacts of these patrons are truly cultural, though hardly intellectual.[26]

With names such as the Silver Slipper, the Poodle Dog, and the Idle Hour, such places combined casual mixing of classes with games, libations, and, at times, hot piano music.[27]

Conversations that started in pool halls continued at the fourteen barbershops along U Street between 4th Street and Florida Avenue to the east and 14th and U Streets to the west, which similarly were important places for socializing.[28] Informal social clubs, church halls, fraternal groups, sororities, and civic associations of all kinds sponsored entertainment for their members, rounding out a portrait of the neighborhood's vibrant street and cultural life.

Jones concluded his study of African American leisure in the city by adding that there were "play and amusement activities that do not receive the approval of either formal laws or public opinion, because they make for the demoralization of the community. Chief among these forms are the three vices: prostitution, gambling, and alcoholic orgies. These represent the illegitimate and unwholesome side of the play life of any community but constitute in no small degree means of socialization."[29]

Vice, as Jones perceptively recorded, sustained U Street's role as a contact zone between the city's blacks and whites. "The history of vice in practically every American city," he observed, "is intimately connected with the Negro population. With few exceptions, white vice areas have been created in or near settlements of Negroes, and furnish the patterns of behavior for such Negro communities. This tendency of the white population to secret its vice in Negro communities has been due to the lack of resistance which the residents of such communities have offered to its encroachment." He continued by noting that "most Negro communities in Washington are not characterized by solidarity. They lack homogeneity of cultural types. Variety rather than uniformity prevails, and this interferes with the development of like-mindedness from which a strong set of public sentiments and attitudes could arise. The best Negro communities may represent uniformity in economic status but are characterized by pronounced cultural variations."[30]

McQuirter carries the story further into the 1930s, as the Great Depression took hold. African American women employed in the service economy a few years before, during the Roaring Twenties, found themselves displaced by white women who had lost their jobs. Some unemployed women turned to street prostitution. The area along 14th Street between R and S streets became a well-known haunt for streetwalkers, many of whom were African Americans.[31]

Sex on U Street was not limited to men seeking women. McQuirter, picking up on Jones's work, speculates that such apartment houses as the New Rochelle at 1603 U became the favored abode of gay African American men and women.[32] The back room of the Republic Gardens restaurant on U between 13th and 14th streets was known for lively drag shows, and several of the clubs along 7th Street were popular with gay men, white and black alike.[33] Little is known about the largely hidden world of gay Washington at this time. The scant evidence that exists suggests that the entertainment district around U Street brought together gays and straights as well as blacks and whites, young and old, rich and poor.

Inventing the Chitlin' Circuit

The neighborhood's mix of classes, races, and sexual orientations was perhaps most visible at the famous Howard Theatre at 7th and T streets. The magnificent 1,500-seat theater first opened its doors on August 22, 1910.[34] That event proved to be one of the highlights of the year's social calendar, with the usually acerbic *Washington Bee* recording that "the Howard Theatre is no doubt the finest theatre in the city, . . . one of the prettiest theatres in the country."[35] The *Bee* continued that "the private boxes were filled with ladies of society. The orchestra was monopolized with the social elite of Washington, gayly and gorgeously dressed in gowns fit for goddesses."[36] Washington's own Abbie Mitchell—who later created the role of Clara in the Broadway production of George Gershwin's "Porgy and Bess"—was among the performers that evening.[37]

The Howard's manager, Andrew J. Thomas—who ran the theater between 1911 and 1918—launched a tradition of mixed bookings, including vaudeville, musicals, road shows, stock company productions, and even a circus or two that marked the house from its opening until the stock market crash of 1929.[38] Under Thomas's management—and that of the dynamic Shep Allen after 1931—the Howard served the community, offering frequent performances by local musicians and dramatic plays by Alain Locke's Howard University Players.[39] The Howard rightfully could claim to be the premier African American theater in the country before the New Apollo Theater in New York's Harlem emerged as a stage featuring black entertainers in 1934.

The Howard was forced to close for two years at the height of the Depression, becoming temporary home to Elder Lightfoot Solomon Michaux's Temple of Freedom under God, Church of God, in 1930 and 1931. Duke Ellington reopened the theater with a wildly successful three-week run beginning September 26, 1931 (figure 4.2).[40] With Allen, "D.C.'s Dean of Showbiz," now at the helm, the Howard hosted the most famous African American entertainers of the day; and would continue to do so throughout the 1940s.[41]

FIGURE 4.2
Edward Kennedy "Duke" Ellington Performing on U Street

Photograph by Robert H. McNeill, from the Kiplinger Research Library, Historical Society of Washington, D.C. Used with permission.

Rock-and-roll arrived in the 1950s. The Howard's prime clientele began to move out of the neighborhood following the desegregation court rulings early in the decade. White venues elsewhere in the city aggressively sought out bookings with top-flight African American performers.[42] Physical decline set in. The theater's great run came to a close following the April 1968 outbursts of violence following the assassination of the Reverend Martin Luther King Jr., despite fitful attempts to bring new life to the place throughout the 1970s.[43] But during its later heyday, among the performers to play the Howard were Little Anthony and the Imperials, Louis Armstrong, Pearl Bailey, Count Basie, Chuck Brown, Delores Brown, James Brown, Jerry Butler, Cab Calloway, Benny Carter, Sammy Davis Jr., the Delfonics, Fats Domino, the Drifters, Billy Eckstein, Ella Fitzgerald, Aretha Franklin, Marvin Gaye, Lionel Hampton, Woody Herman, Earl Hines, Lena Horne, Ahmad Jamal, Stan Kenton, Gladys Knight and the Pips, Ramsey Lewis, Jimmie Lunceford, the Marvellettes, the Platters, Louis Prima, Artie Shaw, the Supremes, the Temptations, Ike and Tina Turner, Sarah Vaughan, Fats Waller, Dionne Warwick, Dinah Washington, Cootie Williams, and Stevie Wonder.[44]

For all the Howard's significance for African American cultural life throughout the twentieth century, the theater also did attract some whites to its audiences. More important, it was built and owned by whites— initially the National Amusement Company, and later Abe Lichtman, who owned a chain of movie theaters catering to African Americans, including the Lincoln Theatre down the street.[45] The Howard's white proprietors hired African American managers Andrew J. Thomas and Shep Allen, giving them free reign over a program that reflected a coming together of white capital and black savvy. Thomas—who also managed the Minnehaha movie house on U Street near 13th—joined with Sherman H. "Uncle Dud" Dudley in 1914 to take over the American Theater on Pennsylvania Avenue downtown. Their effort to bring African American entertainment to the white business center proved short-lived.[46] By the 1920s, African American movie theater owners had formed the Colored Exhibitors' Association, based in the U Street area, to cater to the needs of black movie audiences around the country.[47]

Dudley, who began his career as a vaudevillian in Texas, organized the Colored Actors' Union and began to expand his chain of movie houses. He eventually operated nearly thirty theaters across the South, East, and Midwest. Following World War I, he began promoting musicals in what became the first black-controlled theatrical circuit in the country, S. H. Dudley Theatrical Enterprises. Uncle Dud retired after the crash of 1929 forced him to sell many of his theaters. He died in suburban Oxon Hill, Maryland, in 1940.[48]

Dudley's entrepreneurial efforts included the Theater Owners' Booking Association (TOBA), which operated a loose group of major African American theaters—primarily in the Northeast and Midwest—that became known as the "Chitlin' Circuit."[49] TOBA theaters included the Apollo in New York, the Regal in Chicago, the Uptown in Philadelphia, the Royal Theater in Baltimore, the Fox in Detroit, and, of course, the Howard on U Street. At one point, TOBA controlled bookings at 80 of the 107 theaters presenting African American performers around the country.[50] TOBA encouraged entertainers to become entrepreneurs, often making it possible for star performers—such as the single-legged tap dancer Clayton "Peg Leg" Bates—to move into successful business careers.[51]

For much of the pre–World War II era, Washington and U Street served as the pivot for various efforts to promote African American film, music, and theater through such homegrown organizations as the Colored Exhibitors' Association, the Colored Actors' Union, S. H. Dudley Theatrical Enterprises, and TOBA. The city and neighborhood were critical to these initiatives because the area was a zone of contact where white and black business interests combined in a variety of creative arrangements, as was evident in the African American management of the white-owned Howard and Lincoln theaters. The result was some of the finest achievements of African American popular culture.

Moving in Beauty

The U Street area's cultural achievements extended beyond popular music and film into the realm of "high culture," such as concert dance. The neighborhood's abundance of vernacular, vaudeville, and staged dance created an environment that nurtured a fledgling concert theatrical black dance tradition as early as the 1930s.[52]

Interest in concert dance was a natural extension of the "New Negro Movement" fostered by Alain Locke and Montgomery Gregory at Howard University. Locke and Gregory sought out young African American talent, particularly in letters and the theater. In addition to their publishing ventures—which led to what is now known as the "Harlem Renaissance"—Locke and Gregory drew on the institutional resources at Howard to encourage a distinctive African American theatrical tradition.[53] Their Howard Players promoted the notion that "the Negro playwright, musician, actor, dancer, and artist in concert shall fashion a drama that shall merit the respect and win the admiration of the world."[54] The Players introduced many exciting playwrights and performers, such as Angelina Weld Grimké, whose plays and poems confronted the horror of lynching and vigilante violence in the American South.[55]

With its special combination of popular dance performance, access to promotional capital from local African American businesses, and institutional support for more classical performance at Howard University, the U Street area became one of the most vital centers for African American dance from the 1920s to the 1960s. As the dance historian Tamara Brown tells the story,

> During the Negro Renaissance period, the U Street Corridor, Black Broadway, provided a venue for the development of black musical theater. Calvin Chase of the *Washington Bee* recognizing the political and economic ramifications if not the cultural wrote extensively about the need for black ownership of theaters. Sherman Dudley established his theatrical circuit here. The Howard Theatre was not a black-owned theater (until the 1970s with the Howard Theatre Foundation, though African Americans had leased it), but in catering to the black community employed African Americans in key management positions and showcased black talent. The nightclubs that offered floor shows also contributed to this

development. The type of dance performed (such as tap and jazz dance) changed the Broadway musical and helped to introduce African American dancers to the concert dance tradition. Women who had performing ambitions often had to overcome negative stereotypes of immorality to pursue their ambitions. Moreover, during the Depression, a performing career could earn a competitive salary.[56]

College-level study of dance at the time took place in university physical education departments. Margaret H'Doubler had offered the first courses in dance at the University of Wisconsin at Madison earlier in the century.[57] Classical ballet was still a rarity in the United States, and would remain so until the arrival of Russian dancers and choreographers displaced by the Bolshevik Revolution such as Anna Pavlova, Mikhail Mordkin, Lydia Lopokova, and Adolph Bohm.[58] Even the mercurial and inventive George Balanchine found himself working for Broadway and Hollywood producers after his arrival in the United States in 1933. Balanchine, for example, joined the composer Igor Stravinsky to compose and to choreograph a pachyderm polka for the Ringling Brother's circus.[59] The cross-fertilization taking place between the theaters and clubs along U Street and the academic dance studios at Howard similarly proved to be groundbreaking within the context of this emergent period in American concert dance.

Around the same time that Balanchine and Stravinsky were relegated to planning the steps of performing circus elephants, the Hampton Institute's Charles Hosten Williams was introducing African dance to America, blending it with local performance traditions to create forms of modern dance.[60] Williams had been driven to Hampton in Virginia from Berea College in 1905 by Kentucky's new Jim Crow laws, which prohibited blacks and whites from attending school together. He completed his college education in physical education in 1909, becoming a standout in football, basketball, and baseball. After a time at the YMCA College in Springfield, Massachusetts, Williams returned to Hampton to become the director of physical training. He soon organized the Central Intercollegiate Athletic Association, bringing together premier African American universities such as Shaw, Lincoln, Virginia Union, and Howard.

Williams was particularly interested in African dance forms. Between 1934 and 1949, his Hampton Creative Dance Group infused the burgeoning modern dance repertoire with African forms. Williams' group became the premier African American college dance company at the time.

Williams' efforts at Hampton were not unique. In 1925, Maryrose Reeves Allen arrived on the Howard campus to join the university's small physical education program. Allen had taught summer dance classes at Hampton beginning in 1922, possibly working with Williams.[61] She came to campus just as Gregory and Locke were establishing the Howard Players' Guild, which later became the Howard Players, to promote African American theatrical arts. Within two years, Allen had formed the Howard University Dance Group in cooperation with the Players. Her group evolved into the Howard University Dance Ensemble, one of the era's most creative African American dance companies.[62]

Allen remained at Howard until her retirement in 1967, expanding the physical education program and making the school one of the centers for training African American dancers and choreographers.[63] She consciously patterned the Howard women's physical education program after those of Wellesley, Wisconsin, Boston University, New York University, and the Sargent School of Physical Education for Women in Massachusetts.[64] She was as innovative in her field as were the other pioneers on Mordecai Johnson's Howard campus, such as Charles Hamilton Houston, William Henry Hastie, Alain LeRoy Locke, Ernest E. Just, Percy Julian, Sterling Brown, Abram Harris, E. Franklin Frazier, Ralph Bunche, Charles R. Drew, Rayford W. Logan, and John Hope Franklin. Like her colleagues in the social and biological sciences, Allen drew on the world around her to reinvigorate American life.

Allen's companies penetrated the world of white concert dance by the 1950s, performing with the National Symphony Orchestra in Washington, and on many integrated stages in New York City.[65] In addition to Williams at Hampton and Allen at Howard, Eugene von

Grona established the American Negro Ballet in Harlem in 1934. Von Grona, born in Germany, had his company perform to a range of music extending from W. C. Handy to Duke Ellington and Igor Stravinsky. The Ballet Theatre formed a women's "Negro Unit" in 1940, while Joseph Rickard established the First Negro Classical Ballet in Hollywood.[66]

Allen and the Howard performers represented the cutting edge when it came to female African American dance. Her students populated major classical and modern dance companies throughout the United States, Broadway stages, and Hollywood studios, as well as—most important—the classrooms of African American schools across both the city of Washington and the country. Graduates and colleagues Doris Jones, Claire Haywood, Therrell Smith, Bernice Hammond, Melvin Deal, Mike Malone, and Louis Johnson created a lively dance scene in Washington that spawned the Capitol Ballet and professional companies associated with the Black Arts Movement during the 1960s and 1970s.[67]

These companies thrived until the John F. Kennedy Center for the Performing Arts began to dominate the local cultural scene during the 1970s. The center, a grand marble pile on the Potomac River west of downtown, opened in 1971 as a living memorial to President Kennedy. Likewise, the white Washington School of Ballet, founded by Lisa Gardiner and Mary Day, staked an almost monopolistic claim on local sponsorship for dance at that time.[68] Yet Allen's legacy lives on at Howard, which became the first historically black university to offer a degree in dance through its Department of Theatre Arts beginning in 1991, a year before her death.

As with other cultural forms thriving along U Street during the 1920s and 1930s, local institutions brought together a range of traditions—formal and informal, African and European, urban and rural—in a enlivening mix that challenged the assumptions of the white society all around them. Culture became one arena in which Washington's African Americans could assert their presence. Sports was another, and—as in theater, dance, music, and literature—U Street was the place to be.

Follow the Bouncing Ball

Although individual African Americans probably played basketball soon after James Naismith invented the game in 1891 to keep athletes in shape while they had to stay inside during the long New England winters, more than a decade would pass before the black game began to develop an organizational framework capable of supporting teams. The first African American basketball teams appeared in New York in about 1905, and along Washington's U Street two years later.[69]

This delay had little to do with a lack of interest on the part of African American athletes. Rather, it reflected the woeful state of organized sports in black America. Of the 30,600 athletes playing all sports in 1906 through 4,150 teams organized at 568 YMCA gymnasiums nationwide, only 88 in six clubs at three gyms were associated with African American Ys. An African American athlete might have pursued sports at a white Y north of the Mason-Dixon line, or at a local, non-Y sports club. Jim Crow laws ensured that African Americans in the South—where more than 90 percent of all black Americans were living at the time—had access to just nine Ys.[70] One of those was the Twelfth Street YMCA in Washington.

Jim Crow made U Street the first center of African American basketball, much as Jim Crow made U Street the focal point of a vital business community and entertainment district. Blacks interested in basketball simply had no place else to go. By 1906, African American teachers fed up with being cut out of competition with local white teams established the Interscholastic Athletic Association to oversee competition among black schools and athletic clubs in Washington and Baltimore. This association organized high school football and baseball competitions as well as African American track meets, much as black business associations formed the backbone of a lively African American business community.[71]

Ed Henderson, the son of a domestic worker and a day laborer, was born into poverty in Washington in 1883. He grew up in Washington, Pittsburgh, and then-rural Falls Church, Virginia, outside Washington.[72] Despite moving around in his youth, Henderson managed to graduate from M Street High School with academic honors and baseball stardom. He entered the local teachers' college for African Americans—Miner Normal—from which he graduated first in his class. After securing a job teaching physical education at M Street, he pursued further education at Harvard during the summers of 1904, 1905, and 1907 to become the first black male physical education student in the United States.[73] He simultaneously earned an undergraduate degree from Howard as well as a master's degree from Columbia University.[74]

Henderson emerged as one of the pivotal figures in the founding of several important African American sports organizations. Back at M Street as a faculty member, he became an animating force behind the establishment of the Interscholastic Athletic Association to promote high school football and baseball leagues.[75] While teaching in Washington, he moved back to a family's farm in Falls Church in January 1915. His arrival prompted the local town council to pass a law forbidding black residents from owning property outside a well-defined boundary. Having been told that he would have to sell his land, he fought the local ordinance all the way to the Supreme Court, despite constant threats of violence directed at himself and his family from neighbors and from the local Ku Klux Klan. These events launched him on a career as a civil rights activist that would last until his death in 1977. As if teaching, organizing, and being an activist didn't fill his days, he became a prolific author, publishing landmark studies of African Americans and sports.[76]

Organized African American basketball may be said to have begun on an evening in late 1907 when Henderson—fresh back from Harvard, where he had learned the game—and Benjamin Brownley walked into the white Central YMCA gymnasium looking for a place to play. A dozen players and the Central Y manager, C. Edward Beckett, drove the black men from the premises with a barrage of racial epitaphs. Henderson swore to set up his own league that would play an even better brand of ball—and he did.[77] On the night after Christmas that year, his new league featuring several teams from Howard University, local high schools, and the African American Twelfth Street YMCA tipped off in the ballroom of True Reformer Hall.[78] The evening's games were followed by a dance.

During the next couple of years, African American Washington's Basket Ball League would play a doubleheader every Saturday night at True Reformer Hall, followed by dances featuring Duke Ellington and his band.[79] The place rocked, as did the games, which were played with more verve and style than white basketball games despite rules that promoted slow and deliberate play (such as a tip off in center court after each basket).[80] Although the game was new, the coaches and players were inexperienced, and the playing conditions were primitive, the quality of play improved quickly. The better teams—such as the Crescent Athletic Club, Armstrong High, the Howard teams, and the Twelfth Streeters—began to look further afield for competition.[81]

Basketball had arrived in New York's African American communities a couple of years earlier than in Washington. And the much-larger metropolis of New York supported more teams, which often played in larger facilities before more fans and, at times, against white competition, given the absence of local Jim Crow ordinances. The Smart Set Athletic Club Five dominated these early leagues and was seeking out new competition on its own. In 1909, Crescent and Armstrong in Washington and Smart Set in New York played the first intercity series among African American teams, with Smart Set traveling to True Reformer Hall, followed by a return series in Brooklyn's Pilgrim Hall.[82] More intercity play followed and, in late March, Ed Henderson led Washington's Twelfth Street Y to a come-from-behind 20–17 victory over Smart Set in a raucous Brooklyn Fourteenth Regiment Armory to garner the first national championship win among African American basketball teams.[83]

Other Washington teams enjoyed considerable success on the court in the years leading up to World War I. The Howard Big Five outscored all the top New York teams by a combined 251–59 points in 1912, before being taken down in a stunning upset by Virginia's Hampton Institute. Howard went on to lose the national championship among African American teams to the Monticello Athletic Association Five from Pittsburgh led by the "slickest black cager around," Cumberland "Cum" Posey Jr.[84] Posey—by far the best African American basketball player at the time, as well as a future Baseball Hall of Fame member—

frequently found himself compared with great fighters and baseball and football players as the finest black athlete of his generation.[85]

Basketball's center of gravity moved to New York during and after World War I. The bigger city's promoters could fill larger arenas with more fans, thereby earning more money in a game that was quickly leaving behind the restrictions of amateurism. The white "Original Celtics," which played on Manhattan's Upper West Side, and the black Renaissance Casino Big Five—the Rens—which played in Harlem, emerged as the decade's best professional teams, despite some competition for the Rens from various Chicago teams.[86] The Rens' victory over the Original Celtics marked the coming of age of black basketball in the early 1920s. The Rens would compile a 2,588–539 record between 1922 and 1949, when they finally disbanded. They were inducted into the Basketball Hall of Fame as a team in 1963.[87]

White America wasn't ready to watch their teams being picked apart by better black players. The primary professional league of the interwar period—the American Basketball League—followed the whites-only policies of major league baseball. One of the league's owners, George Preston Marshall, would move his Boston Braves football team to Washington in 1937, where it would earn infamy as the last team in professional football to begin hiring African American players.[88]

U Street's smaller arenas and Washington's Jim Crow laws and traditions undermined the ability of local clubs to compete nationally. Basketball nonetheless remained central to Washington African American community life. Friday and Saturday night games followed by dances drew big crowds and enthusiastic fans. Though left behind by other emerging basketball centers following World War I, U Street was where black basketball was born. And the U Street game remained alive as future Hall of Famers Dave Bing and Elgin Baylor and scores of other legendary athletes played their first pickup games in the gymnasiums and play yards nearby.

Fields of Glory

The eastern end of the U Street entertainment district had long been home to baseball. The local team added to the National League—appropriately known as the "Nationals"—played ball at Boundary Field (also known as National Park) throughout the 1890s. Big league baseball stayed at the field after Washington switched to the newly formed American League early in the twentieth century. With their field destroyed by fire in March 1911, the team tossed up a new steel and concrete structure by midseason, which they expanded during the next three years to form a new National Park on 7th Street. President William Howard Taft threw out the first ball of the season on opening day in 1912, starting a presidential tradition that would last six decades before a second reincarnation of the Senators left town for Dallas–Fort Worth.[89] In 1920, the 32,000-seat park took on the name of Senators' owner, a parsimonious local businessman, Clark Griffith.[90]

Griffith Stadium was an odd architectural jumble, like many of its contemporary ballparks—Chicago's Comiskey Park (opened in 1911), New York's Polo Grounds (1911), Boston's Fenway Park (1912), Detroit's Tiger Stadium (1912), Brooklyn's Ebbets Field (1913), and Chicago's Wrigley Field (1914).[91] As the first steel and concrete stadiums, these fields were shoehorned into existing urban neighborhoods and sites once used for smaller, wooden grandstands. They were built piecemeal over a couple of seasons, with new stands and upper decks added as crowds grew, light stanchions tossed up beginning in the mid-1930s, and the playing fields set down every which way to conform to the requirements of oddly shaped building lots rather than to the needs of the game of baseball. With the patina of age and years of use by rabid fans, two of these ugly ducking survivors—Fenway Park and Wrigley Field—have turned into swans. But the rest—including Griffith Stadium—were torn down beginning in the 1960s with little fanfare, when they were no longer able to meet the needs of an increasingly suburbanizing fan base.

Griffith Stadium was deformed even within this collection of ballpark freaks. The outfield fences—among the furthest from home plate in all of baseball—lurched inward to avoid five LeDroit Park row houses and an oak tree beyond centerfield. One section of the upper deck grandstands down the third base line was a couple of dozen feet lower than the upper deck seats behind the infield that had been built a few years earlier. The hard cement walls were lethal when unfortunate ballplayers failed to pull up short in their pursuit of fly balls and line drives. This ad hoc accumulation of stands and seats lent a certain endearing quirkiness to the ball yard.[92]

Big league baseball had been a white affair for decades, and Griffith looked to fill his ballpark with white fans who could ride the convenient streetcar service along Georgia and Florida avenues.[93] William H. Jones reported in the late 1920s that local African Americans did not play baseball much, although they followed the Senators with "interest and loyalty."[94] Ungainly Griffith Stadium would not have even entered into the local consciousness if it had only been a baseball playing field. Once his stadium had been built, however, Griffith was more than willing to open it to all sorts of community events, as long as the rent was paid in full.

With this mercenary "desegregation," championship fights featuring African American boxers such as Joe Louis, outdoor jazz concerts with performers such as Louis Armstrong, and the Thanksgiving "Turkey Bowl" football game between longtime African American athletic rivals Howard and Lincoln universities gave African Americans opportunities to embrace the odd stadium looming over their neighborhood.[95] The Armstrong-Dunbar Competitive Military Drill was one of the U Street community's most dazzling events of the year, drawing thousands of spectators to the ballpark.[96]

The Metropolitan Baptist Church organized battalions of high school cadets for exhibition drills in 1892 in preparation for the presidential inauguration the following spring. This initiative required an act of Congress to grant the loan of arms to the "colored cadets," who created a single company of some seventy members.[97] The cadets formed a special escort for the outgoing president, Benjamin Harrison, and marched in the Inauguration Parade for the new president, Grover Cleveland. Their appearance made such a positive impression that the cadets became a personal escort for Cleveland, and they went on to also march in the inaugural parades for Woodrow Wilson and Warren Harding.[98]

Competitive drills began at the Metropolitan African Methodist Episcopal Church in May 1893, with members of the single company dividing into two units under separate command. By 1895, a second company battalion had been formed, with the first competitive drill between the two companies taking place in 1895. This event shifted to the National League Baseball Park—the precursor to Griffith Stadium—in 1897.

By 1902, the drill companies had moved to M Street High School and Armstrong Technical High School. As was noted above, these public schools represented alternative visions for African American education, with M Street advancing a W. E. B. Du Bois–like academic curriculum and Armstrong favoring a Booker T. Washington–style vocational program. Rivalries and resentments between the two schools ran deep, with every moment of competition taking on a wider meaning throughout the community. After 1902, no single event was more deeply infused with meaning than the annual drill competitions.[99]

The drills grew in importance and scale, particularly after World War I. By the 1920s, the Twenty-Fourth Regiment High School Cadets consisted of eleven companies—five at Dunbar High and six at Armstrong High. The number of companies and battalions would fluctuate until World War II. The annual review remained a well-attended community event, at which the high school soldiers in training performed complex drills before senior military officers—including the Army chief of staff in some years—symbolically representing the divisions within the city's African American community between the "talented tenth" and blue-collar families.[100] The award of the Prize Flag and the diamond-covered Teacher's Medal to the victorious battalion's captain elevated the winners to almost mythical status within the community.

William H. Jones communicates something of the excitement surrounding the event in his study of African American leisure in the Washington of the 1920s:

> When about nine hundred youths are in training in preparation for one of the most gala affairs that the Negroes of Washington witness, they are anticipating the representing of more than three thousand school mates, more than one hundred thousand Negro citizens of the District and a host of alumni all over the United States. Moreover, the crowd to which they must address themselves on the day of the event

will number more than twenty thousand. This is an occasion of great promise for each youth, if he makes good. This, indeed, in the true sense of the word, is a conflict, rather than a competition, for there is a conscious effort on the part of each participant to win from the opposing forces. The intense stimulations emanating from the rooter in particular and the entire citizenry in general, sensitize each man to a high degree of esprit de corps.[101]

As Jones notes, the event became a community outing that matched the excitement of the defunct Emancipation Day celebrations of the 1860s, 1870s, and 1880s. "On the day of the drill," Jones continues,

thousands of colored pedestrians pass through the streets of the city, carrying the colors of the school of their choice; hundreds of automobiles, elaborately decorated with school colors and loaded with a group of merrymakers race noisily through the streets, resounding with the joy of their occupants. For the most part, this is a day off for the mothers, fathers, sisters, brothers, sweethearts and friends of the participants in the drill. It is a time when friends from various sections of the city meet and exchange experiences through free conversation; hence, it is a day when much of the pent-up energy of the year is released—a sort of catharsis is in operation—and the older people are restored to normalcy again.[102]

The competitive military drill lost its interest for the community at large as the economic dislocation of the Great Depression took hold, as new migrants from the impoverished rural South moved to town, and as the realities of war came home with the dead and wounded of European and Pacific battlefields after Pearl Harbor. Griffith Stadium continued to play its role as a community center, only to other kinds of events. Beyond sports, Elder Lightfoot Solomon Michaux expanded his ministry into center field from the Georgia Avenue storefront Temple of Freedom under God, Church of God, across the street.[103]

Michaux opened temples in Philadelphia, New York's Harlem, Baltimore, and Newport News, and also launched the WJSV (Willingly Jesus Suffered Victory over the grave) radio station in Alexandria, Virginia, across the Potomac River from Washington, just as the Depression began.[104] By the early 1930s, his *Happy Am I* radio program was being aired on the CBS Radio Network (and continues to be broadcast today).[105] Michaux's church was making major contributions to the community, including saving the Howard Theatre, saving the bankrupt Industrial Bank and Savings Association, and setting up soup lines (the church-run Happy News Café served a quarter-million meals for a penny a plate in 1934).[106] His 150-plus-voice white-robed Cross Choir promoted the New Gospel movement in music. And beginning in 1938, he extended his reach into Griffith Stadium.

For the next quarter-century, until the stadium was torn down, Michaux organized mass baptisms in the middle of the ballpark. His followers set up enormous canvas tanks that were filled with water by the D.C. Fire Department or, on at least one occasion, with water from the River Jordan. The 1948 baptism was televised for the first time. In addition to baptisms, Michaux organized other religious pageants— conversions, mass marriages, and healing ceremonies. Those healed at times ran the baseball bases on a "home run for Jesus," while forty-by-fifty-foot "clouds" ascended from the left-field light towers and the chorus sang "There'll Be Shouting on the Hills of Glory" from the center field bleachers. By the end of the 1930s, Michaux was coming close to attracting more parishioners to the old ballpark than the hapless Senators had spectators.[107]

Other events, however, excluded local residents—at least from the playing field. As was noted above, George Preston Marshall moved his National Football League franchise from Boston to Washington in 1937, changing the team's name from the Boston Braves to the Washington Redskins.[108] Marshall was a notorious racist who refused to integrate his ball club until the time arrived in 1961 to move to the new D.C. Stadium controlled by the federal government. As noted above, the Redskins were the last National Football League team to begin hiring African American players, and the team consistently fell to the bottom of league standings.[109] As the popular *Washington Post* sports columnist Shirley Povich once famously penned, "The Redskins' colors are burgundy, gold, and Caucasian."[110]

The Redskins enjoyed considerably more success when they first moved to town, attracting sold-out crowds as Quarterback Slingin' Sammy Baugh perfected the forward pass as an offensive tactic in the emerging professional game.[111] Between 1937 and 1945, the team played in five league championship games behind Baugh, winning the league trophy in 1937 and 1942 and suffering the biggest defeat in any title game to the Chicago Bears by a score of 73 to 0 in 1940.[112] Baugh wrote the record books at the time, leading the league in passing for six of his fifteen years in the league (1937–52).[113]

But the most legendary Griffith Stadium story about the Redskins had nothing to do with football. On December 7, 1941, as the Redskins were battling the Philadelphia Eagles before a sold-out crowd, announcements began to float over the crowd from the public address system paging generals, Cabinet secretaries, and other military personnel as word of the Japanese attack on Pearl Harbor reached Washington.[114]

Take Me Out to the Ball Game

At the end of the day, Griffith Stadium was a baseball field, and its meaning for the neighborhood was most intimately tied to that game. Griffith's Senators entered the 1920s with one of the best pitchers in the history of baseball, Walter "Big Train" Johnson, who could throw a ball faster than anyone had before. During his twenty-one-year career with the Senators, stretching from 1907 until 1927, he won 417 games (second only to the legendary Cy Young); established a record for career strikeouts—3,509— that would last for more than half a century; had a dozen 20-victory seasons; and set a record for career shutouts, in which the opposing team did not score.[115] He was among the first ballplayers to be elected to the Baseball Hall of Fame, in 1936, and he led the Senators to back-to-back World Series appearances, in 1924 and 1925. The Senators' victory over the New York Giants in the 1924 series unleashed a neighborhood-wide celebration that featured a lively parade down U Street.[116]

Washington's African Americans were as crazy about watching baseball as other Americans seemed to have been at the time. The joys of a championship club combined with a physical presence in the neighborhood, the celebration of community events, days at the ballpark for adults, and jobs as vendors as children (including Duke Ellington) to tie Griffith Stadium closely to the neighborhood's daily life. One way or another, people throughout the U Street area incorporated the stadium and its events into their lives. Standing as it did at the intersection of U and 7th streets—next to the Howard campus—the park became a meeting ground for middle-class, intellectual, and working-class African Americans.

How much Griffith Stadium brought whites and blacks together, however, is a subject of historical dispute. Unlike the downtown theaters, the stadium was officially desegregated. Many African Americans have spoken and written with affection about their experiences at the stadium rooting for the Senators.[117] But others have noted that Griffith rejected black requests for tickets—especially during the team's back-to-back World Series appearances in the 1920s—and generally discouraged African Americans from sitting anywhere other than the far-right-field seats.[118] The truth probably was a little of both. Unlike other public facilities, African Americans could attend big league baseball games with whites while being made to feel uncomfortable by any number of small informal arrangements when they sat anywhere but in "their" section of the stands.

The Senators began to fail as Walter Johnson headed toward retirement. Griffith, always the cheapskate, would not—or could not—spend the money necessary to compete with the rising New York Yankee dynasty forming around the legendary Babe Ruth. The larger-than-life "Bambino" nonetheless filled Griffith Stadium and team coffers because fans everywhere wanted to see this great home-run hitter. U Streeters and other African American Washingtonians took Ruth to their hearts, for many believed him to be one of them. Black Americans during the 1920s and 1930s suspected that the Babe was a "secret brother" passing for white.[119]

The Great Depression, accompanied by falling revenues, drove Griffith to the verge of bankruptcy. The team was saved in part by his close personal relationships with Washington dignitaries, including President Franklin Delano Roosevelt, which meant that his team would always enjoy a modicum of notoriety. Griffith began to recruit inexpensive players from Cuba to fill in the ranks of his failing team.[120] Following one last World Series appearance in 1933, the Senators became one of the worst teams in major league baseball.[121]

Nonetheless, being located in the U Street area, Griffith and his team sat in the middle of one of the largest, wealthiest, and best-educated African American communities in the country at the time, which, as a focal point for an emergent political and legal radicalism, was home to people who would change America. Not unexpectedly, they also tried to change the Senators. And leading the charge was the journalist Sam Lacy, who was U Street bred and a future member of the Baseball Hall of Fame.

Lacy was born into the African American middle class in 1905, moving from Connecticut to U Street as a child. He became a pitching star at M Street High School, and then, after being disciplined for infractions during military drill team practice, stormed from M Street to its archrival Armstrong Technical High School. He led Armstrong to three straight city championships between 1922 and 1924, and continued at Howard with some interruptions as he tried unsuccessfully to continue his pitching career on semiprofessional teams. He dropped out of Howard after a couple of years to become a radio sports commentator and promoter. During the 1940s, his Washington Bruins basketball team, which he owned with Harold Jackson and Art Carter, won major professional tournaments.[122] His distinguished newspaper career included stints as writer and editor at the *Washington Tribune*, the *Chicago Defender*, and the *Baltimore Afro-American*. He remained a fixture in the U Street neighborhood until his death at the age of ninety-nine in 2003.[123]

Lacy was unrelenting in his advocacy of having African American players break the long-standing color line in major league baseball. In cooperation with other journalists, he used every opportunity to write columns, to speak before audiences and on radio, and generally to make sure that the question was not allowed to die.[124] He maintained that Griffith was receptive to the idea of integrating the game, in part because of the baseball owner's willingness to rent out the stadium for community events, and in part because of the community's increasing radicalism. In

December 1937, Griffith obliquely noted in an interview with Lacy that the day of integrated baseball was near. For all these reasons, in April 1938 Lacy spoke out against picketing and boycotting Griffith Stadium.[125]

Griffith seemed to be softening on the issue. In May 1942, he lifted a self-imposed ban on interracial exhibition games to allow an All Star team assembled by the legendary black Kansas City Monarchs pitcher Leroy "Satchel" Paige to face off against an all-white team playing behind retired Saint Louis Cardinals star Dizzy Dean.[126] Most significantly, Griffith began renting his ballpark to the premier team in black baseball, the Homestead Grays.[127] Yet other baseball owners were moving more quickly, looking to change the game and their teams' performance. Thus the Brooklyn Dodgers' president and general manager, Branch Rickey, signed Jackie Robinson to a contract in 1946, dispatching him to the Montreal Royals before bringing him to the big club in 1947.[128]

In retrospect, Griffith and the Senators weren't accommodating at all. Griffith began to transfer power within the Senators' organization to his nephew Calvin, who was an even more unreconstructed segregationist. For Calvin, black baseball was little more than a low-grade diversion, similar to professional wrestling, that helped pay for the stadium's upkeep.[129] The Senators, after all, were profiting nicely from renting their home field to the Grays.[130]

Despite various hints favoring integration, the Griffiths, both uncle and nephew, privately equated efforts to bring African American baseball players into major league locker rooms to a communist plot intended to undermine the game by creating confusion between the races.[131] Seven teams integrated before the Senators brought a black Cuban outfielder, Carlos Paula, onto the team from a minor league club in September 1954.[132] This backdoor approach to integration further alienated an already disgusted local African American fan base.[133]

Calvin Griffith assumed leadership of the team at the time of Clark Griffith's death in 1955 and immediately began lobbying to move the team out of Washington.[134] He begged his fellow owners to let him move because "the trend in Washington is getting to be colored."[135] Griffith's club eventually moved in 1960 to the whitest city in the major league baseball: Minneapolis. As Griffith admitted in a 1978 speech before a local Lions Club, he moved the club to Minnesota "when I found out that you only had 15,000 black people here. Black people don't go to ball games, but they'll fill up a rassling ring and put up such a chant it'll scare you to death. It's unbelievable. We came here because you've got good, hardworking white people here."[136] The American League parachuted a newly formed "expansion" club into the old Griffith Stadium in the wake of the old club's departure.

If Calvin and his uncle Clark had bothered to notice, they could have seen that some of the best ballplayers in the history of the game had been playing right under their noses in their own ballpark. The Homestead Grays were far more than a professional wrestling sideshow prompting bloodcurdling chants. The Grays playing in Griffith Stadium during the 1940s were one of the best teams ever to throw and bat a baseball.

"Only the Ball Was White"

In 1912, Cumberland "Cum" Posey Jr., the African American professional basketball star, as well as baseball standout and local entrepreneur, bought the Homestead Grays, a ball club established by steelworkers in the Pittsburgh-area mill town of Homestead, Pennsylvania, and turned it into a professional club.[137] Drawing on his experience promoting his basketball teams, he widened the circle of the team's opponents beyond western Pennsylvania to the eastern United States and the Midwest and, over time, enhanced the team's reputation. Running an independent professional baseball club became increasingly difficult and, in 1929, Posey affiliated his team with the American Negro League. That circuit folded a year later under the growing economic pressures of the Great Depression. Posey tried to start his own league— the East-West League—in 1932, which similarly failed before finishing its first season. Finally, in 1935, Posey brought his team into the Negro National League—the premier African American professional baseball association in the country.

The Grays played all over the country during their barnstorming years, visiting Griffith Stadium as early as 1921.[138] The Negro Leagues had been reluctant to place a team in Washington because of the strong allegiance of local African American fans to the Senators. As black support for Griffith's teams began to wane, the Grays came through town for the odd game and found growing success at the gate. By this time, the Grays were playing their home games in Forbes Field—the home park of the Pittsburgh Pirates—and were experiencing greater difficulty making financial ends meet. Attracted by the higher incomes of Washington's African Americans, Posey announced after the 1939 season that his team would begin playing half its "home" games in Griffith Stadium and half at Forbes Field. But hosting games at stadiums 263 miles apart took a terrible toll on the players. They would leave Pittsburgh on Saturday night around midnight and arrive in Washington about 11:00 Sunday morning to be on the field for a Sunday doubleheader by 11:30 a.m.[139]

The Grays began to attract local fans two years later, after hiring the African American promoter Art Carter, a native of Southwest Washington.[140] Carter handed out free passes to Howard University faculty, prominent African American federal employees, and local church leaders such as Elder Michaux. The U Street community took the team to heart and began giving up on the Senators. By 1942, the Grays were earning more money than any other team in the Negro Leagues.[141]

The team's performance on the field was far more important to its success than marketing gimmicks. Powered by five future Baseball Hall of Famers—Cool Papa Bell, Ray Brown, Josh Gibson, Buck Leonard, and Jud Wilson—who were surrounded by talented teammates, the Grays won nine consecutive Negro National League championships beginning in 1937 and three Negro League World Series titles.[142] Matches against the Kansas City Monarchs—who were led by Satchel Paige—proved to be among the best baseball games ever played in the nation's capital.[143] Gibson, who was often compared with Babe Ruth, and Leonard, who was mentioned together with Lou Gehrig, matched many of the accomplishments of these white stars. Cool Papa Bell was regarded as one of the most spectacular players to set foot on a baseball diamond.

Local African American fans, encouraged by the local African American press, luxuriated in the experience of seeing the talented

Grays take the field in contrast to the ever more pathetic Senators. But white Washingtonians ignored the Grays, in part because local white newspapers such as the *Star* and the *Post* refused to cover the team and its accomplishments.[144] Thus the Grays were among the "Secret City's" best-kept secrets.

Walter "Buck" Leonard personified the Grays for local fans. Like an increasing number of black Washingtonians, Leonard came to town from an impoverished North Carolina coastal plain, where he had been unable to receive what he felt to be a suitable education or find a job. His talents on the ball field were unmistakable. As a hard line drive hitter and elegant fielder, he was the steady day-in-and-day-out All Star who quietly powered his club to victory after victory. He inspired his fans by his accomplishments and his dignity on and off the field.

Tellingly, Leonard chose not to move into the major leagues after Jackie Robinson broke the race barrier. He felt he was too old and, therefore, no longer capable of achieving the level of professionalism he expected of himself.[145] After a brief stint in the Mexican Leagues, he returned to his native North Carolina, where he lived quietly until his death in 1997. The baseball historian Brad Snyder best captured Leonard's meaning for the city when he wrote that "from 1940 to 1950, Buck Leonard gave the black community of Washington, D.C., relief from feelings of inferiority. He gave them happiness. He gave them disappointment. He gave them love. He gave them identity."[146]

Broadway—and More

Integration destroyed the Negro Leagues, much as it would transform the streets and alleyways around U Street. The Grays lingered on until 1950 under ever-less-successful ownership following Posey's death at the age of fifty-five in 1946. Following a path already evident in basketball, the most talented black baseball players were being recruited by white teams, just as white universities were recruiting the best black faculty, and the most acclaimed black entertainers were being booked by white clubs. The African American middle class that had formed the backdrop to so many of the neighborhood's accomplishments began moving to white neighborhoods from which they previously had been excluded in Upper Northwest Washington. U Street entered what seemed to many to be a prolonged period of decline.

Yet the neighborhood was not dead; it was changing. Most important for what was to follow, African Americans remained loyal to their churches even as they moved outward in the city and beyond to the suburbs. Those churches preserved much of what had made U Street special even as the physical streets on which they were located seemed to deteriorate. In the midst of such transformation, Howard University eventually found a new niche for itself in the city and in American higher education. U Street was different; it was not dying.

Even if the neighborhood had disappeared, its importance for American life in general and African American life in particular had become secure. One small indication of the powerful and diverse role played by community members in national African American affairs during these years is that nine U Streeters won the NAACP's Spingarn Medal for highest achievement in their fields: Archibald Grimké (1919), Carter G. Woodson (1926), Mordecai Johnson (1929), Mary McLeod Bethune (1935), William Hastie (1942), Charles Drew (1943), Thurgood Marshall (1945), Ralph Bunche (1949), and Charles Hamilton Houston (1950).[147] Other winners included an Atlanta surgeon, Louis T. Wright (1939), and a nurse, Mabel Keaton Staupers (1951), who had completed their medical training at Freedmen's Hospital, together with a journalist, Carl Murphy (1955), who had graduated from Howard in 1911.

Among future Spingarn winners tied to the U Street of the era were Duke Ellington (1959), Langston Hughes (1960), the Howard-trained psychologist Kenneth B. Clark (1961), the Dunbar High School graduate and future secretary of the U.S. Department of Housing and Urban Development Robert C. Weaver (1961), the neighborhood child and Howard graduate U.S. senator Edward W. Brooke III (1967), the director of the NAACP's Washington Office Clarence M. Mitchell Jr. (1969), the photographer Gordon Parks (1972), the Howard graduate and Atlanta mayor Andrew Young (1978), the historians Rayford Logan (1980) and John Hope Franklin (1995), the one-time dean of the

Howard School of Religion Benjamin E. Mays (1982), and the Howard Law School graduates Virginia governor L. Douglas Wilder (1990), federal judge Robert L. Carter (2004), and Oliver W. Hill (2005).

U Street became known during the 1930s and 1940s as "Black Broadway." The reference to New York's famous White Way arose because of the area's theaters and nightlife. Yet U Street was more than another Broadway, including not only the Broadway of New York's Midtown theater district but also the Broadway of the Financial District downtown, of the social protest of Union Square, of the fancy residential districts on the Upper West Side, of the great universities Columbia and City College of New York uptown, of the theological centers of Riverside Heights, and of the African American cultural centers in Harlem. Thus U Street was everything that Broadway was, except more so. U Street combined in just a few short blocks what took Broadway half a dozen miles or more to contain stretched out along the spine of Manhattan. And unlike on New York's Broadway, on U Street all the attractions coexisted quite literally on top of each other. This intensity bred a level of contact unknown along Broadway, which organized itself by function as it moved from the Bowery uptown to Washington Heights. U Street brought it all together in one place.

Sterling A. Brown, working as a contributor to the Works Progress Administration's Federal Writers' Project, captured U Street's complexity at the end of the 1930s:

> Poolrooms, short-lived cabarets, beer gardens, and eating places, from fried-fish "joints," barbecue, and hamburger stands to better-class restaurants, do an apparently thriving business. And yet, when the outsider stands upon U Street in the early hours of the evening and watches the crowds go by, togged out in finery, with jests upon their lips—this one rushing to the poolroom, this one seeking escape with Hoot Gibson, another to lose herself in Hollywood glamour, another in one of the many dance halls—he is likely to be unaware as these people momentarily are, of aspects of life in Washington of graver import to the darker one-fourth.

This vivacity, this gaiety, may mask for a while, but the more drastic realities are omnipresent. Around the corner there may be a squalid slum with people jobless and desperate; the alert youngster, capable and well trained, may find on the morrow all employment closed to him. The Negro of Washington has no voice in government, is economically proscribed, and segregated nearly as rigidly as in the southern cities he condemns. He may blind himself with pleasure seeking, with a specious self-sufficiently; he may point with pride to the record of achievement over grave odds. But just as the past was not without its honor, so the present is not without bitterness.[148]

Profile

MARYROSE REEVES ALLEN (1899–1992)

Maryrose Reeves Allen, a native of Louisville, became fascinated by music and dance while growing up in Indianapolis (figure 4.3). Coming of age early in the twentieth century, she was best able to pursue her interest in dance through a career teaching physical education. She earned her college degree at the Sargent School of Physical Education for Women in Cambridge, Massachusetts, teaching summer school at Hampton Institute in Virginia. Her time at Hampton coincided with the institution's emergence as the leading center for the study of African dance in the United States. After a brief period in Trenton, New Jersey, she joined the faculty of Howard University in 1925, where she became the director of the physical education program for women.

Allen was an early advocate of advancing the black female sense of self through the exploration of the unique aspects of the black body. She viewed rhythmical movement as an essential component of bodily aesthetics among African American women and promoted dance in the

FIGURE 4.3
Maryrose Reeves Allen with Students

Photograph from the Moorland-Spingarn Research Center, Howard University, Washington. Used with permission.

Howard physical education program from the very beginning of her time on campus. For her, the purpose of dance education was to strengthen body and mind, teaching physical and moral discipline.

Allen played a leading role in the development of physical education programming at historically black colleges and universities nationwide. Her preference for noncompetitive activities that promoted poise dominated the policies advocated by the National Association of College Women, which had been founded by Mary Church Terrell, following a conference of deans and advisers to women in black universities and colleges held at Howard in 1929.[149]

In 1927, Allen established the Howard University Dance Group, which evolved into the Howard University Dance Ensemble. This ensemble took shape contemporaneously with the evolution of the Howard Players' Guild into the Howard University Players under the leadership of T. Montgomery Gregory in close association with Alain Locke. The Howard Players contributed to the New Negro Renaissance, presenting major works by Willis Richardson, Angelina Grimké, and others.

The dance historian Tamara Brown has observed that Washington was a vital and creative center of African American dance during the mid–twentieth century because of the juxtaposition of academic training at Howard and the numerous theaters along U Street.[150] Graduates of Allen's program populated dance education throughout the Washington area as well as the nation, and included many prominent figures in various forms of dance such as Debbie Allen, Chuck Davis, Melvin Deal, Ulysses Dove, and George Fainson. The George Washington University dance professor Maida Withers described Allen to historian Brown as "a minister of values." According to Withers, Allen promoted the worth of the individual and of being black through dance.

Allen remained active in the Howard and dance communities following her retirement in 1967 until her death in 1992. In 1991, Howard University became the first historically black university to offer a degree in dance through its Department of Theatre Arts.

Walter Fenner "Buck" Leonard (1907–1997)

Known as "The black Lou Gehrig," Walter Fenner "Buck" Leonard was one of the most feared hitters in the Negro National League during the late 1930s and throughout the 1940s (figure 4.4). He was born in Rocky Mount, North Carolina, and he never intended on becoming a baseball player. But facing the impossibility of obtaining either an education or employment in his hometown, he headed north, playing baseball in Portsmouth, Baltimore, and Brooklyn in 1933. He landed a position with the Homestead Grays, the dominant team in the Negro Leagues, a year later.

FIGURE 4.4
Walter Fenner "Buck" Leonard

Photograph by Addison Scurlock, from the Scurlock Studio Records, Archives Center, National Museum of American History, Smithsonian Institution, Washington. Used with permission.

In 1912, Cumberland Posey purchased the Homestead Grays, a recreational team of African American steel workers based in Homestead, Pennsylvania, outside Pittsburgh. Like most Negro teams, the Grays were an independent operation, frequently switching leagues and playing wherever possible. The team joined the Negro National League in 1935, a circuit it would dominate until the league collapsed in 1948 following the integration of major league baseball. Facing financial incertitude in a Pittsburgh that was impoverished by the Great Depression, Posey arranged with Clark Griffith, owner of the Washington Senators, to play in his stadium just off U Street whenever Griffith's white team was not in town. Leonard's career coincided with the seasons throughout the 1940s, when Washington was a second home to the Grays.

Posey assembled an awesome lineup, including the future Hall of Famers Cool Papa Bell, Ray Brown, Jud Wilson, Josh Gibson (known as the "black Babe Ruth"), and Leonard. Gibson and Leonard pounded the ball, with Gibson hitting tape-measure home runs and Leonard lining the ball off Griffith Stadium's cement walls seemingly at will. The team won nine consecutive league titles between 1937 and 1945, with either Leonard or Gibson leading the league in home runs.

Skilled defensively as well as offensively, Leonard was a relatively slight 5-foot-11-inch and 185-pound first baseman. He hit .391 in his best season at bat in 1948. His .341 career average in the Negro National League (plus a .382 average in exhibition games against major league players), earned him election to the Baseball Hall of Fame in 1972.

Leonard was a much admired presence in the Washington African American community during his years with the Grays. He was embraced by local fans as a fine player, a fine human being, and a demonstration of black achievement during a time of segregation and humiliation. Several community leaders—including future Hall of Fame sportswriters Sam Lacy of the *Washington Tribune* and the *Baltimore Afro-American* and Wendell Smith of the *Pittsburgh Courier*—unsuccessfully campaigned for Senators' owner Clark Griffith to integrate major league baseball by adding the power-hitting Leonard to the offensively anemic white club. Lacy—a classmate of William Hastie and Charles Drew at Dunbar High School—was himself something of a local sports hero when he transferred to rival Armstrong Technical High School and pitched his team to three city championships.

Leonard continued to play in the minor leagues and in Mexico after the Grays ceased operation. In 1952 he declined a major league contract, citing age, and in 1955 retired to Rocky Mount, where he continued his lifelong association with baseball as a physical education instructor and as a vice president of a minor league team.

CHAPTER 5

The Last Colony

Would civilization be destroyed?
Would the world really end?
"Not my world," I said to myself.
"My world will not end."
But worlds—entire nations and civilizations—do end.

—Langston Hughes, *I Wonder As I Wander*, 1938[1]

The world of U Street could not survive desegregation. Many of the neighborhood's middle-class residents, having been freed up to move and to attend school as well as to work without legal restrictions, decamped for other areas of the city further away from downtown in the Northwest quadrant and, eventually, to Prince George's County in the Maryland suburbs. Professionals and university professors found jobs in the law and accounting firms downtown as well as at leading white universities around the country. Businesses that catered exclusively to African American customers found themselves in competition with white businesses that had previously refused to serve blacks. An increasingly maladjusted public school system failed to maintain the high standards of some of the area's schools during the process of desegregation. Life appeared to ebb out of the neighborhood. Griffith Stadium closed down, Howard University Hospital absorbed the Freedmen's Hospital, and students and faculty slowly turned away from Howard to prestigious white schools.

This seemingly downward spiral accelerated after the physical devastation of massive communal violence following the assassination of the Reverend Martin Luther King Jr. in April 1968. A crack cocaine epidemic during the 1980s and a decade of highly disruptive subway construction continued the sense of decline. Among the scores of businesses that brought life to the neighborhood in the 1950s, only three—Ben's Chili Bowl, Lee's Flower & Card Shop, and the Industrial Bank—survived the 1968 destruction and its aftermath to remain open when Metro's Green Line finally began running under 7th, 14th, and U streets in 1991.[2] A casual observer driving down U Street in the mid-1980s might easily think of urban decline.

The reality was much more complex. In the context of the additional knowledge of the neighborhood's eventual "revitalization" during subsequent decades, the processes that accompanied desegregation appear to be those of "transition" rather than of "decline." Significantly, the dense social and economic networks that had emerged during the previous century did not disappear, even as social unrest devastated the physical environment.

Life in the U Street area retreated to the refuge of the neighborhood's churches and social institutions more than it ceased to exist. Area congregations retained their parishioners, even as they moved to the outer reaches of the city and into the surrounding suburbs. The churches in particular kept U Street alive, providing the social services and social organization necessary for an eventual vibrant resurgence. The U Street of the "Secret City" did not disappear during the 1960s, 1970s, and 1980s so much as it evolved into a new state of being. Rather than decline, the changes along U Street following desegregation are better thought of as a transition from the relatively closed and protected economy of Jim Crow D.C. to an open neighborhood tied into a globalizing capitalist economy. Much like Latin America in the 1980s and Eastern Europe in the 1990s, U Street found itself exposed to the disruptions of unregulated capitalism for the first time in decades.

How one evaluates such transitions from premodern to postmodern economies depends very much on where one looks. As with other transitional economies, observers concerned with macro-level economic restructuring can see great success. Since the late 1980s, the U Street economy has grown, incomes in the area have risen, the city's tax revenues have soared, and crime has been reduced. The area has emerged as one of the leading "development poles" of the city and region.

Others concerned with the micro-level realities of everyday life see a different picture of an unending string of destroyed lives, as residents have been left behind by economic change that favors newcomers with different skills and life experiences. The challenge of any economic transition is to ensure that the original human beings in a community, nation, or economy benefit from the systemic changes that are creating new wealth and bringing in new residents. According to this measure, the experience of postsegregation U Street has been ambiguous at best.

By any reckoning, desegregation destabilized the U Street community for half a century. Middle-class residents moved out, poorer rural migrants and their descendants moved in, businesses collapsed, schools failed to maintain academic standards, the urban infrastructure deteriorated, and many buildings burned while others were bulldozed.[3] Social fissures exposed at the dawn of the early twentieth century—those dividing U Streeters between the "high" culture of 14th Street and the "low" culture of 7th Street, dividing African Americans between racial separatists and accommodationists, dividing old-timers from newcomers—grew deeper and wider under the pressure of continuing social change throughout the city.

"From Tranquillity to Turmoil"

Soon after World War II, planners and federal officials began to look for ways to improve the increasingly worn Washington urban fabric. By the mid-1950s, they had drawn up a number of highway and urban redevelopment projects that would destroy some of the poorest African American sections of town. Official Washington would achieve its lofty visions by removing African Americans from view. As the editorial writers at the *Washington Post* told their readers, "No doubt many residents of the area will be loath to lose their homes despite the prevailing slum conditions. They should realize, however, that the net effect of this great redevelopment effort will be to make Washington a much more pleasant place in which to live and work."[4]

The postwar era witnessed profound changes in Washington's demographic structure. Pent-up consumer demand from the harsh years of the Great Depression and World War II combined with new highways and accessible housing to lure middle-class city dwellers to the suburbs around Washington, as in other metropolitan areas across the United States.[5] Easing racially restrictive real estate practices enabled the U Street middle class to move to neighborhoods where they had previously been unwelcome (including some of the very same areas of the city being left behind by the suburbanizing white middle class).[6] By 1957, Washington had become the first major U.S. city with a majority African American population.[7]

During these same years, Washington also became a poorer city as wartime and postwar booms lured rural migrants from the coastal South to low-wage service jobs in the city.[8] And as these demographic changes took place, the city's planners destroyed the neighborhood to which many of these migrants initially moved—its Southwest quadrant, between the National Mall and the Potomac River and Anacostia River waterfronts. The Southwest Redevelopment Project sent thousands of desperately poor residents who were ill prepared for urban life into once-middle-class African American neighborhoods along U Street and also into once-middle-class white areas across the Anacostia River.[9] Not unexpectedly, given the scale of these dislocations, currents of fear and anger ran ever more deeply throughout the city. U Street, in the words of Paul K. Williams, moved "from tranquillity to turmoil."[10]

The Washington metropolitan area was well on its way to becoming a suburban-oriented region by the time court decisions were removing the legislative underpinnings of Jim Crow residential and school segregation. More than 1.5 million new residents moved to the area during the quarter-century following the end of the war, but this growth did not find its way into the metropolitan core.[11] The overall regional population grew from 621,000 in 1930 to 1.5 million in 1950, 2.9 million in 1970, and 4.2 million in 1990. By contrast, the city's population first nearly doubled, from 486,869 in 1930 to an all-time high of 802,178 in 1950, but then fell to 756,510 in 1970 and 606,900 in 1990.[12] As a consequence, the city's proportion of the metropolitan population declined from 78 percent in 1930 to 54 percent in 1950, 26 percent in 1970, and 15 percent in 1990.[13]

Some of the city's neighborhoods kept pace with the region's expansion. Its outer areas in Northwest and in Anacostia in Southeast filled with new residents during the first postwar decade.[14] Gentrification began in Georgetown, which became the site of the city's first "large-scale, privately financed neighborhood restoration experience."[15] By the 1950s, the Foggy Bottom neighborhood between Georgetown and downtown began its resurgence, to be followed by Capitol Hill and Kalorama by 1970.[16]

For the most part, however, the city was losing ground economically to the suburbs. Private-sector employment became ever more important in the region throughout the last half of the twentieth century, with the vast preponderance of those new jobs being created in the suburbs.[17] Overall, the city lagged behind other local jurisdictions in per capita personal income, simultaneously consolidating its role as home to the largest share of families living below the poverty line.[18]

The city concurrently became darker and poorer, with African Americans constituting 70 percent of its population by 1970. This increase was both absolute and relative, as the number of African Americans identified by U.S. government census takers as residing in the city increased to an all-time high of 527,705 in 1970 before falling back to the level of the 1920s at 346,382 in 2000 as a consequence of African American suburbanization. Meanwhile, the city's white population plummeted from a high of 517,865 in 1950 to 164,244 in 1980, and has remained more or less stable ever since.[19]

With restrictive covenants on mortgages and land deeds falling away under court pressure—and with whites abandoning in-town neighborhoods for the suburbs—African American middle-class families from the U Street area and elsewhere began to move farther out within the city.[20] This process was neither orderly nor uplifting, as unscrupulous real estate agents engaged in panic tactics persuading white owners to believe that their house would become worthless once African Americans moved onto their street. Brokers began buying up property by the block at discount prices from these panicked whites fearful of neighborhood decline. Then these same agents turned around and resold the properties at higher prices to African Americans. Neighborhoods shifted their racial profiles seemingly overnight in an unseemly process known as "block busting," which only exacerbated already-raw race relations throughout the city.[21] The Brookland neighborhood in Upper Northeast, for example, shifted from being 10 percent African American in 1940 to 85 percent African American in 1970.[22]

Nearly every neighborhood east of Rock Creek Park was affected by these changes, while those west of the park remained in the hands of well-off white people.[23] Some areas—such as Woodridge and Fort Totten in Upper Northwest—became home to middle- and upper-income African American families. Others managed to remain racially mixed for a while. Those spread out between 16th Street, NW, to the east and Rock Creek Park to the west became an elegant "Gold Coast" for the African American elite.[24] Traditional middle-class African American neighborhoods such as LeDroit Park deteriorated. By the 1970s, the average per capita income of residents in the U Street area had fallen well below the city median. Many once-elegant homes fell into disrepair and were converted into apartments and boarding houses by absentee landlords.[25]

Every institution in every neighborhood east of Rock Creek Park bore the brunt of the unprecedented demographic changes whipping through the city. White congregations closed their churches and synagogues as worshippers moved elsewhere.[26] Between 1950 and 1962, for example, seven white churches on Capitol Hill sold or transferred their properties to African American congregations. Other churches throughout the city merged or shut down, destroying long-standing social networks that had held communities together.[27]

The impact of these upheavals on the business community was just as tumultuous. Many traditionally Jewish businesses along Georgia Avenue, and Chinese stores and restaurants around 7th and H streets, NW, moved to the suburbs along with their patrons.[28] Similarly, the U Street commercial district began to deteriorate as its more well-heeled clientele moved elsewhere and as enterprises elsewhere that had once been off limits to nonwhites now opened their doors to a more diverse public. They were being replaced, in the carefully chosen words of analysts at Howard University's Small Business Development Center, by "Negro-owned and -operated" businesses that were "not the types of enterprises" that could sustain the neighborhood economically.[29]

Many landmark U Street enterprises—such as Harrison's Café and its famous Gold Room at 455 Florida Avenue, NW—could not withstand the socioeconomic firestorm unleashed by such massive social change.[30] More symbolically, the area around Mrs. Henderson's lovely Italianate classical gardens along 16th Street on Meridian Hill just above Florida Avenue was transformed from a protected white elite enclave into Malcolm X Park.[31]

"Soulside"

In addition to the suburbanization and metropolitanization that were being experienced in every major American city, Washington became a magnet for poor African Americans from the failed economies of the coastal South. If most African American Washingtonians found their way to the city at the beginning of the twentieth century from nearby Maryland and Virginia, migrants from declining rural economies in the Carolinas and Georgia became an increasingly large presence by the 1940s.[32] Their growing numbers accelerated the city's racial turnover, as its population changed from being two-thirds white to two-thirds African American in two decades.[33]

Newly arriving country folk had difficulty finding a secure place for themselves in the local economy. An ever-increasing income gap opened between the city's small but stable African American middle class and the community of quickly growing African American poor people.[34] On the one hand, one-quarter of all federal jobs in the Washington area were filled by African Americans, thereby providing a base for the growth of a black bourgeoisie.[35] On the other, many of the social institutions that had once provided support for migrants were collapsing under the pressures of growing poverty and larger numbers of migrants.[36]

Migrants largely settled in the old, run-down, historically African American neighborhoods south of the National Mall in the city's Southwest quadrant as well as in other low-lying areas.[37] The city's capacity to accommodate the new arrivals seemed insufficient to the challenges of the day.[38] It had the second-highest infant mortality and the sixth-highest tuberculosis rates relative to U.S. states (as a statistically unique nonstate jurisdiction, the District of Columbia is often compared with entire states, rather than with other large cities), along with the highest gonorrhea infection rate, the second-highest syphilis rate, and the seventh-highest number of narcotics addicts among American cities.[39]

Some observers—such as the 1990s neoconservative urbanist Fred Siegel, in an angry critique of Marion Barry's regime as mayor (see below)—complained bitterly that poor African American rural migrants were unable to respond to urban life as had earlier waves of rural immigrants from Europe.[40] Siegel and other many other authors—including such writers as Alan Ehrenhalt and, most recently, Joseph Berger—have marveled at the ability of immigrant ethnic communities to provide just what immigrants needed to make it in the United States.[41] American cities could have held their own in the global economy, if only African Americans were as self-reliant as foreign immigrants, who often had been just as culturally deprived by rural poverty. Instead, Siegel's argument goes, poor African American migrants to cities such as Washington turned attention away from respectable, middle-class neighborhood leaders to "the street."[42]

Such arguments ignore the profound differences between the experiences of involuntary African migrants and those of other, voluntary immigrants in American cities. African American field hands and their descendants were brought involuntarily to the Americas, often literally in chains, only to be enslaved once on shore. The color of their skin stigmatized them in ways that immigrants' poor clothing and bad accents did not. African American migrants were cast permanently as outsiders with no way to assimilate into mainstream society. Closer to Washington, failed urban plans drawn up by a white power structure insensitive to the needs of African American poor migrants—and accountable to no one within the city, given the absence of home rule—obliterated the very areas within the city that were functioning as the sort of poor, rough-and-tumble engines of urban integration so praised by Siegel and others.

Instead, the city's downtown neighborhoods were becoming a new type of African American neighborhood, which the Swedish anthropologist Ulf Hannerz labeled as "Soulside" in a landmark study based on field research carried out between August 1966 and July 1968.[43] As Hannerz explained, "'Soul' is black. The black people of America's inner cities . . . are soul brothers and soul sisters, listen to soul music, and eat soul food at least occasionally. 'Soul' is said to be the essence of their blackness, shaped by the experience and expressed in their everyday life. 'Soulside,' then, may be as good a name as any for the black side of town."[44] Washington was Hannerz's prototypical soul city; and greater U Street was his prototypical "Soulside."[45]

Soul, it seemed, was becoming ever more concentrated around U Street, as soul brothers and soul sisters were being forced out of traditional African American neighborhoods elsewhere in the city. Communities built by and for poor rural migrants from the South undermined Cold War visions of the good society. Federal and city authorities concerned about notorious rat-infested slums lying within camera range of the Capitol acted to remove soul from view.[46] By 1950, their plans to tear out the city's soulful heart were well under way, beginning with its Southwest quadrant.

"Suburban Wholesomeness with Urban Stimulation"

Washington's Southwest Redevelopment Project—once proclaimed by the prominent architectural critic Wolf Von Eckardt as bringing "suburban wholesomeness with urban stimulation" to downtown— destroyed many of the Siegelesque social networks that had held the city together.[47] A half-century later, the city has still not fully recovered from this misguided planning fiasco. Southwest redevelopment proved to be post–Jim Crow Washington's original sin.

In displacing Southwest's residents as the new Southwest took shape, planners and their construction teams threw thousands of poor African Americans—uprooted in many cases for the second time in their lives— into relatively stable, white middle-class neighborhoods east of the Anacostia River, and into stable African American neighborhoods north of downtown, such as U Street. These inadequately educated rural African American migrants from the coastal Carolinas, Virginia, and Georgia adapted to city life about as well as middle-class Washingtonians of both races would have fared if they had been dropped into a North Carolina tobacco field. These massive demographic disruptions combined with the lingering pathologies of segregation to push the city to the precipice of communal violence. The pent-up anger of thousands of displaced and powerless poor residents continued to build as Washington hurtled toward civic meltdown.

The redevelopment of Southwest was part of a more extensive slum removal and highway construction plan promoted by planners and their congressional allies in the hopes of turning Washington into a model demonstration of how planning can solve urban problems.[48] Three laws enacted by Congress between 1945 and 1952 unleashed regional planners to correct previous mistakes in the city's and region's development patterns.[49] The National Capital Planning Commission sought to secure the regional centrality of a downtown "Metro Center" employment district by aggressively driving a proposed inner beltway through poor African American neighborhoods adjacent to the central city.[50] This inner ring road would be connected by new bridges at 14th Street, Roosevelt Island, and above Georgetown to a suburban system of radial highways tied together by an outer beltway. These ambitious plans included regional parks, public housing, and corporate development, often scattered about in the fashion of the day, following the detached, "radiant city" ideas of the French architect Le Corbusier, with little reference to traditional street plans.

The inner belt highway system would have obliterated much of the area around U Street, along with other African American neighborhoods in Foggy Bottom and Southwest. Similarly, the proposed Three Sisters Bridge would have destroyed wealthier neighborhoods in Georgetown. In actuality, however, only disconnected stumps of the highway in Foggy Bottom and north of the Capitol were built in Northwest Washington, after alliances and coalitions of community groups eventually prevailed in a two-decade battle over road construction.[51] However, planners, real estate developers, and construction interests were able to complete several suburban radial highways, together with the now-famous Washington Beltway, around the entire city in Maryland and Virginia.

The disastrous Southwest Freeway, built as part of that quadrant's redevelopment, and the process followed in realizing the accompanying urban renewal project reveal the National Capital Planning Commission's vision for a city remodeled around highways bringing suburbanites in their cars into and out of the city with hardly a poor or African American neighborhood in view.[52] As Jerome Paige and Margaret Reuss observed, "Middle- and upper-income citizens wanted the slums, which they saw as a reproach to their city, removed. They wanted a clean, sanitary and beautiful environment and they were beguiled by the promise of an increased tax base."[53] Their efforts to build highways and to remove slums echoed initiatives in nearly every major U.S. city at the time. Washington, however, was different. Without home rule, the city was governed by Congress and its appointed commissioners, who were notoriously unconcerned with the preferences of local residents.

This story is more pernicious than the misplaced dreams of misguided planners, however. By 1952, the *Washington Post*'s publisher, Philip Graham, and his well-connected, wealthy white friends on the Federal City Council had pulled together a half-million-dollar plan to create a new city alongside the proposed freeway in Southwest. They enlisted the New York construction magnate William Zeckendorf and a young unknown architect, I. M. Pei, to create a new community of apartments, office buildings, and homes from which they would profit as investors. Local residents were no match against such a powerful array of investors, media moguls, and their congressional sponsors. Only a few skeptical voices would rise above the public relations onslaught promoting the project, as when Eleanor Roosevelt inquired about the fate of the people who had once lived in the area after visiting the project in 1959.[54]

The Southwest slums were particularly unseemly and forlorn, a degradation made more poignant by the presence of the relatively nearby Capitol and national monuments and museums constantly in view. The 113-block project zone south of the Mall and north of the Washington Channel (an inlet of the Potomac River) was home to 22,539 residents in 1950, nearly 80 percent of whom were African Americans.[55] Like U

Street, the area often served as a place of contact among racial groups. But unlike U Street, Southwest lacked the economic diversity and institutional density that enriched daily contact and promoted cultural innovation. Hundreds of buildings had no indoor plumbing; many more were obsolete and below the current building code.[56] But even though the neighborhood was dilapidated, few residents wanted to leave. This area was precisely the sort of down-at-the-heels urban village nurturing poor migrants that so many promoters of an immigrant model for African American assimilation so often praise.[57]

Unfortunately, no one cared to contemplate the answer to Eleanor Roosevelt's query. The National Capital Planning Commission's experiment with urbicide destroyed 99 percent of the buildings within the project area.[58] As a consequence, almost none of the original residents remained. Only a third of the area's more than 20,000 residents were able to secure alternative housing in public projects elsewhere in the city. Approximately 2,000 families moved into private rental units outside Southwest; while others among the displaced remained completely lost from official records. A paltry 391 residents were able to purchase homes, virtually none in Southwest.[59]

Resident reactions to the destruction of old Southwest are suggestively reminiscent of those displaced by the destruction of Cape Town's District Six during the imposition of apartheid policies during the 1960s. District Six residents reported that they lost more than homes when bulldozers cleared away their long-standing neighborhood. They felt at sea in a larger world, losing trust in others and a sense of safety in the world. They felt disappointment, anger, helplessness, and bitterness.[60]

In Washington, a quarter of the expunged residents reported five years after their relocation that they had not made a single new friend in their new neighborhoods. Only 14 percent of these former Southwest residents felt as safe in their new homes as before.[61] By contrast, in 1972, the replacement community had half as many residents, nearly 80 percent of whom were white. They inhabited 5,900 new housing units, of which only 310 were classified as being reserved for low- to moderate-income residents.[62]

Bitter debates still rage over whether or not the Southwest Redevelopment Project "removed unspeakably poor housing, and built an attractive, racially integrated neighborhood" in its place or "destroyed a closely knit neighborhood and removed its institutions."[63] Yet, however lofty the planners' goals, the project's results are unequivocal. A densely organized, poor African American community was replaced by an upper-middle-class, biracial neighborhood. Land use patterns shifted, because the population density of the new community was closer to that of inner suburbs than to those of the city as a whole. Now, half a century later, Southwest is being more thoughtfully renewed again, with carefully planned in-fill projects and other urban interventions designed to draw fresh life to the area. Ironically, some of these initiatives will reconnect streets cut off by the earlier round of "regeneration."

For the city of Washington, the tragic consequences of the Southwest Redevelopment Project extended well beyond the area's immediate surroundings. Twenty thousand unattached poor people scattered across the city, settling where they could. Thousands poured across the Anacostia River, destabilizing middle-class white communities to the east. Thousands more found refuge in once-grand middle-class Victorian homes in and around the U Street area that were being carved up into rooming and apartment houses as their owners moved to newer neighborhoods in Upper Northwest. And these displaced poorest of the poor lost access to the social networks that had developed in Southwest over its decades of receiving new migrants from the South. Racial and class divisions invariably deepened throughout the city.

Creating "Shaw"

Planners had their eyes set on U Street along with Southwest. Their proposed inner beltway would have torn through the community, leaving a swath of urban devastation in its wake. Their reports combined areas of the city once cut off from one another by invisible boundaries of race, class, profession, and ethnicity. The planners often drew their lines atop school district boundaries, as was the case with "Adams Morgan" northwest of 16th and U in 1959, and "Shaw," combining Logan Circle, Bates Street, and U Street in 1966.[64] Some of these new names, such as "Adams Morgan," grew out of community activist links that already had brought together whites and blacks seeking to integrate school districts. Others among these new identities formed slowly. Jim Crow educational districts that appeared contiguous on a map often distinguished between African American and white schools that were worlds apart despite their physical proximity.[65]

The Shaw Urban Renewal Area more or less followed the district boundaries of Shaw Junior High School at Rhode Island Avenue and Q Street, NW. The school was named in honor of the Civil War colonel Robert Shaw, a white officer who died in July 1863 while commanding a famous African American regiment—the Fifty-Fourth Massachusetts Volunteers—on a suicide mission at Fort Wagner, South Carolina.[66] The Shaw district—roughly bounded by North Capitol Street, NW, on the east; 15th Street, NW, on the west; Florida Avenue, NW, on the north; and M Street, NW, on the south—officially included 105 city blocks, embracing much of the historic U Street district while simultaneously extending closer to downtown to the south to include such areas as the O Street Market and Mount Vernon Square.[67] Encompassing 638 acres, the Shaw district was the largest urban renewal district in the United States at the time of its creation.[68]

Like the name "Adams Morgan," the "Shaw" title caught on, redefining the popular understanding of what constituted the U Street neighborhood. The acceptance of "Shaw" as the area's designation advanced its increasing racial and economic homogeneity as the city's "Soulside." And its official recognition as a U.S. Department Housing and Urban Development renewal area in 1968 linked the flow of federal funding to the new boundaries, further consolidating its new status.[69]

The grand notions of planners about how to transform the area included more than merely ramming part of the inner belt highway through the district's neighborhoods. They simultaneously foresaw the transfer of the city's historic downtown away from F Street, NW, between 7th and 14th streets, NW. The older Central Business District appeared to be too close to increasingly impoverished neighborhoods, such as those found in the newly designated Shaw district. Instead, the proposed new downtown would be "closer to high-income residential areas" along K Street, NW, between 17th and 22nd streets, NW.[70]

Having witnessed the destruction of Southwest's neighborhoods, residents in and around U Street wanted no part of expansive designs developed without their input. Lacking the most basic institutions of home rule, the pastors of leading local congregations organized U Streeters by turning for recourse to the community participation provisions of the federal Housing Act of 1954.[71] Many densely woven social networks that somehow had managed to survive rose yet again in defense of local residents.

In 1960, faculty members and students associated with the Howard University's Service Project joined together with local religious leaders organized by the Reverend E. L. Harrison of the Shiloh Baptist Church to rally public, private, and civic resources for community redevelopment.[72] The group conducted two dozen interviews with public and private officials to establish a set of initial policy recommendations and objectives, including stronger enforcement of building codes, the municipal takeover of rental properties with continuing code violations, the formation of "block clubs" of tenants and owners to improve their neighborhoods, increased credit for home improvement to counteract "red-lining" by banks and other financial institutions, and various measures intended to encourage neighborhood residents and churches to take more responsibility for initiating newly arrived families into urban living.

Many clergy and residents responded to these recommendations. The Reverend Walter E. Fauntroy—a young pastor at New Bethel Baptist Church who had grown up in the neighborhood and recently had returned with a divinity degree from Yale University—joined with the Reverend Ernest Gibson to form an alliance of 150 community organizations, churches, and neighborhood groups, named the Model Inner-City Community Organization (MICCO). Fauntroy—who worked closely with the Reverend Martin Luther King Jr. and the Southern Christian Leadership Conference in organizing the August 1963 March on Washington—had considerable experience as a community activist through his participation in the civil rights movement. He cared passionately about his neighborhood and moved energetically to give voice to the concerns of local residents.

Fauntroy drew on an acquaintance with President Lyndon Baines Johnson gained from his work on the march to secure federal funding for MICCO. He reached out to the African American business community through Uptown Progress, a group formed to respond to the displacement of African Americans, and declared 1967 a year of action to develop an alternative vision for U Street and Shaw.

Fauntroy established numerous alliances within the broad Shaw neighborhood, including a union with the Reverend Douglas Moore of the Student Nonviolent Coordinating Committee (SNCC) and with that organization's local director, Marion Shepilov Barry. Moore—who had organized one of the civil rights movement's first "sit in" demonstrations in Durham, North Carolina—led the militant Black United Front; Barry had formed PRIDE, Incorporated, a federally financed self-help organization promoting African American enterprise. MICCO, SNCC, the Black United Front, and PRIDE, Incorporated, were among an intricately connected system of increasingly assertive organizations demanding community empowerment in a city beset by an absence of home rule. Many were based in and around the U Street area. They would form a nucleus around which rebuilding efforts would take shape following the destructive communal violence of April 1968. Moreover, these organizations would provide the city's first generation of elected municipal leaders following the establishment of partial home rule in 1973.

Drawing on business and federal support, Fauntroy hired Reginald Griffith of the Boston Redevelopment Land Agency to head a planning initiative predicated on community participation. Griffith and his team of planners reported to the MICCO Board, which included representatives from a variety of local groups. Griffith conducted a survey about community issues that garnered 9,000 respondents, whose preferences were used to create a general concept plan. MICCO submitted that plan, in turn, to community leaders for further discussion. Having collected these opinions, in 1968 MICCO's leaders submitted their proposals to federal authorities as well as to the presidentially appointed District Council.[73] The end result was a comprehensive overview of how community members saw their future.

These initiatives enabled local residents to challenge proposals by the National Capital Planning Commission to repeat their supposed Southwest "success" along U Street. Similarly, they enabled the community to respond to the devastation inflicted on the neighborhood by the communal violence following the assassination of Martin Luther King Jr. in April 1968. Community leaders arguably proved themselves to be better equipped to deal with the destruction inflicted by those events than either city or federal leaders or institutions.

Carolina in the City

The U Street community being organized by Harrison, Fauntroy, Moore, Barry, and others was different from the historic U Street community that had been organized by Houston, Hastie, Davis, Church, and Bethune a quarter-century before. The area was poorer and closer to rural life than a generation earlier. Local culture was increasingly dominated by downscale 7th Street as upscale 14th Street evaporated in the wake of departures for neighborhoods in Upper Northwest newly opened to African Americans. The differences went well beyond those of income. U Street and many other central city neighborhoods were quickly adapting the cultural folkways and food ways of rural coastal Carolina.

The anthropologist Elliott Liebow selected a street corner in Shaw not too far from U Street to observe the lifestyles of African American men living in poverty. Throughout 1962 and the first half of 1963, Liebow carefully tracked the lives of several men who spent time on the same street corner in Washington's Second Precinct. He converted his resulting dissertation into *Tally's Corner: A Study of Negro Streetcorner Men*, a classic book that has been read by tens of thousands of students over the past four decades.[74]

Following his main subject, Tally, and his friends, Liebow creates a portrait of two dozen men who "are unskilled construction workers, casual day laborers, menial workers in retailing or in the service trades, or are unemployed. They range in age from the early twenties to the middle forties. Some are single, some married men, some of the latter are living with their wives and children, some not."[75] Their lives and networks revolved around the New Deal Carry-Out Shop.

Liebow's description of Tally's neighborhood captures the emerging streetscape of the 1950s and 1960s as the city's dramatic social changes played themselves out in and around U Street. "Walking north from the Carry-Out Shop for three blocks or more," Liebow reports,

> one passes a fairly even mixture of dwelling units (generally old, three story, red-brick row houses, most of them long since converted to rooming and tenement houses), an occasional apartment house, and small business establishments such as liquor stores, grocery stores, barber shops, cleaners, launderettes, beauty parlors, poolrooms, beer joints, carry out shops, pawnbrokers, and others. . . . The cross streets in the immediate area are almost entirely residential. Here, too, are three story brick row houses and an occasional apartment house, but one also finds here and there, a corner grocery, a steeple church or a storefront church, a parking lot, a funeral parlor, or some light commercial enterprise.[76]

Liebow's portrait of the men's lives is complex and textured, full of ebbs and flows not visible to a casual outside observer driving through the neighborhood. Tally "is a brown-skinned man, thirty-one years old. He is six feet tall and weighs just under two hundred pounds." He is a native of Atlanta who had moved to Washington in 1954 and had lived in a variety of neighborhoods around town. He had worked at various wage-grade jobs—including his most recent work as a semiskilled construction worker—taking home paychecks during a little more than half of the year.[77]

The New Deal Carry-Out provided an anchor in lives that were frequently in flux. Liebow observed that

> the Carry-Out offers a wide array of sounds, sights, smells, tastes, and tactile experiences which titillate and sometimes assault the five senses. The air is warmed by smells from the

coffee urns and grill and thickened with fat from the deep fry basket. The jukebox offers up a wide variety of frenetic and lazy rhythms. The pinball machine is standing challenge to one's manipulative skill or ability to will the ball into one or another hole. Flashing lights, bells and buzzers report progress or announce failure. Colorful signs exhort customers to drink Royal Crown Cola and eat Bond Bread.[78]

Most important, a wide sidewalk spread itself out before the Carry-Out, giving the men who wanted to drop by a broad platform for "effortless sociability."[79] Tally and the others gathered to eat and to drink, to enjoy easy talk, to learn what has been going on, to horse around, to look at women and banter with them, to see "what's happening, and to pass the time."[80]

Liebow argued that Tally's corner served in part as "a sanctuary for those who can no longer endure the experience or prospect of failure. There, on the street corner, public functions support a system of values which, together with the value system of the world at large, make for a world of ambivalence, contradiction and paradox, where failures are rationalized into phantom successes and weaknesses magically transformed into strengths."[81] Such pauses in an otherwise harsh urban life relieved the uncertainties posed by the necessity of heading into an alien city every day. Here, on Tally's corner, neighborhoods such as those around U Street enabled new Washingtonians from the South to retain their souls in a strange new world.

Poverty and race set districts such as U Street apart from other areas of the city that were better off economically. Neighborhoods that were not all that far apart geographically—such as Shaw and Georgetown—stood worlds apart as their residents lived different lives.[82] A number of studies of the era reveal that many U Street residents were not "poor" by the statistical measures of the time.[83] Rather than being defined purely by income differentials, "ghetto and non-ghetto people probably differ," the Catholic University of America sociologist Paul Hanly Furfey argued on the basis of field research in and around the U Street of the late 1960s, much more sharply in the sources of their incomes than in the amount of their incomes. Non-ghetto persons are more likely to earn their money in managerial, professional, or highly skilled trades. Quite a few, even those who are far from rich, have some income from stocks and bonds. On the other hand, ghetto people are more likely to be manual laborers, to work in unskilled or semiskilled trades, or, at best, in low-grade, white-collar occupations. Also a significant part of ghetto income comes from illegal activities, from writing numbers, from trading in drugs or bootleg liquor, from prostitution or crimes of violence. . . . The ghetto economy is less stable and systematic than the non-ghetto economy. It is more likely to be on a day-to-day basis.[84]

The constant vicissitudes of life along the U Street of the 1950s and 1960s produced a social ecology that aligned with values differing from those of middle-class life. The middle class looked down on ghetto dwellers as "lazy and shiftless," sexually immoral, and criminal; ghetto residents found the middle class to be "cruel, exploitative, and hypocritical."[85] Given the physical deterioration of U Street and nearby areas, middle-class Washingtonians of both races too easily ignored the positive aspects of local life that were being identified by any number of social science researchers.[86] The neighborhood was not declining so much as it was transforming itself into another stage of its being.

Many of the core community institutions that had sustained the U Streeters remained even as residents of more middle-class sensibilities moved away. New values became ascendant as rural migrants moved to the area after having been displaced by the failing economies of the coastal South, and uprooted by the destruction of Southwest Washington. Liebow's notion of "effortless sociability"—and the corner carry-outs associated with such conviviality—formed the center of neighborhood life. Indeed, conviviality remained a cardinal characteristic of life in and around U Street, even during the harsh days following the communal violence of 1968 and the crack epidemic of the 1980s. This sociability tied to a rural culture had come to town from the Carolinas. It would redefine the meaning of life in the city's central neighborhoods as middle-class African Americans moved elsewhere.

Studying adjacent neighborhoods in nearby Mount Pleasant during the 1970s and 1980s, the anthropologist Brett Williams captured the influence of Carolina folkways that came to dominate the city's central African American neighborhoods during the era.[87] Williams observed that many Washingtonians in the city's downtown neighborhoods had "rebuilt Carolina culture through the shared lore of alley gardens, through the exchange of medicines and delicacies, through fishing and feasting among metropolitan kin, and in visits, exchanges, and the construction of an alternative economy with relatives who bring the Carolina harvest to the city."[88]

Carolina culture, she went on to argue, enabled African American Washingtonians to "construct alternative identities and relationships based on ties of friendship and family, history and place. This symbolic anchor is not without contradictions, given the true grimness of some of the areas former Carolinians have left behind. Nonetheless, in many ways it is a powerfully renegotiated oppositional identity, which knits together neighbors and draws families together across the city."[89] This identity was vitally important to people who simultaneously felt cut off from mainstream Washington and besieged by the difficult social problems visible on the streets outside the front doors of their homes.

The rituals of growing and consuming collards, fixing pig parts (e.g., chitlins, pig's feet, and ham), and catching fish down at the river provided an honorable means for knitting together families and neighbors. As Williams wrote, "when relatives come together to eat, at Thanksgiving, Easter, Father's Day and Mother's Day, the Fourth of July, Labor Day, Christmas, New Year's Day, and occasionally birthdays and Memorial Day, collard greens are almost mandatory. The other compulsory item, again deeply rooted in rural Carolina culture, is pork."[90] Williams goes further, concluding that "Carolina culture celebrates cycles, repetition and texture," by which she means "dense, vivid, woven, detailed narratives, relationships and experiences."[91]

Ulf Hannerz generalized from these cultural patterns—which he identified during his field research on a small street in the vicinity of

7th and U streets—to define "Soul" for an academic audience.[92] Like Tally and his friends, some of the inhabitants of Hannerz's block hung out all hours of the day and night at the local corner King David Carry-Out; like Tally and his friends, their contacts with the outside world were dominated by others.[93] Like Williams' Carolina folk, Hannerz's Winston Street had a natural cycle that bound neighbors together in a constant pageant of men and women talking, children playing ball and riding bikes, and fire hydrants showering hot residents with cool sprays. Such daily dramas were played out against the backdrop of jingling bells from ice cream trucks, Sunday morning hymns and sermons, and the soul music of African American radio stations such as WOL.[94]

As in the past, the large thoroughfares of 7th, 14th, and U streets connected local residents to the larger city. "There are the large chain supermarkets," Hannerz wrote,

> competing with the small street corner groceries; there are bars and restaurants, pool halls and a few movie theaters showing the same movies as the downtown theaters, usually only slightly later and at lower prices; record stores and big churches; clothing and furniture stores, for both new and used merchandise; employment agencies, drug stores, occult advisors, and funeral homes. Interspersed among them are more of the same kinds of small businesses as cluster at the street corners in the Winston Street neighborhood. But the barber shops and carry outs which are routine hangouts for rather stable groups in the neighborhood take on much more urban anonymity on the main streets. There may be fleeting sociability among customers as well as between them and the staff, but there is more reason to 'watch out' as one can not be quite sure what kind of person one is dealing with.[95]

"Soulside" was neither the *Blade Runner* world of white fears nor the proper manners of U Street's historic "talented tenth." A new and vital community of saints (the "respectables," "good people," "model citizens," and "stuck ups"), sinners (the "undesirables," "no goods," "rowdy bunch," "bums," "trash," and "handkerchief heads")—of "mainstreamers," "swingers," "street families," and "corner men"—and every other category of humankind in between busily staked claims to life in the city.[96] Community members did so at a shared disadvantage in the world outside. Uninvolved in relationships of power and livelihood, neighbors and kin were bound to one another by a position of shared weakness.[97] As in Jim Crow Washington, a wellspring of endless frustration with—and hot anger at—the outside world bubbled beneath the surface of daily life no matter how much neighbors, school chums, work buddies, and families valued sociability and conviviality.

"Programmed Retardation"

Few Washingtonians were angrier about race relations than Julius Hobson.[98] And nothing made him madder than the city's postsegregation school system, which he felt was little more than "programmed retardation," purposefully relegating African American children to "the junk heap."[99]

Hobson was a ferocious force of nature. He was born in Birmingham at the height of Jim Crow segregation following World War I, and entered the Tuskegee Institute in 1937. He enlisted in the army just after the start of World War II, and would fly on thirty-five combat missions, earning three bronze stars and several other honors for heroism. He briefly studied in Florence following the war before returning to Tuskegee, where he graduated with a degree in electrical engineering. He continued his education at Columbia University in New York before enrolling in a graduate program in economics at Howard. He subsequently began a career as an analyst and statistician with the federal government, working initially at the Library of Congress and later at the Social Security Administration.[100]

Hobson arrived in Washington having been slighted too many times by whites. His economics graduate training at Howard confirmed his innate radicalism. He spent the remainder of his life as a leading figure in Washington's community politics—heading up the local chapter of the Congress of Racial Equality (CORE), founding the D.C. Statehood

Party, being elected to the first home rule School Board and D.C. Council, and running for vice president of the United States on a People's Party ticket headed by Dr. Benjamin Spock in 1972.[101] Hobson represented a long-standing strain of militancy in the Washington African American community that was distinct from nationalism. The prominent white alternative journalist Sam Smith observed that "Julius remained one of the few leaders in Washington who could lead an effective black-white coalition."[102]

The cigar-smoking, pork-pie-hatted Hobson made great press (figure 5.1). Always operating with panache and flare, he appreciated the power of television before many other activists. In one particularly dramatic

FIGURE 5.1
Julius Hobson Sr. Leading a Demonstration in Front
of the U.S. District Courthouse

Photograph from the Washington Historical Image Collection, Washingtoniana Division,
Martin Luther King Jr. Library, Washington. Used with permission.

episode, he threatened to capture rats in the increasingly rundown alleys around U Street and deposit them in Georgetown and near the White House.[103] One day in 1964, he dramatically strapped a cage on the top of an old station wagon, found a rat, and drove across town with reporters and television cameras on his trail. This political theater resulted in an increase in the federal allocation for rat eradication in the city, despite the fact that Hobson had only managed to capture a couple of rats, none of which were released onto the streets of any neighborhood.

Hobson married a fellow Howard student and settled in the neighborhood to start a family. Schools were still segregated by the time his son, Hobie Jr., was ready to enter elementary school. Angered that he had to walk his son past a much closer and better-kept white school every morning to get to overcrowded Slowe Elementary further away, he joined the local Parent-Teacher Association and quickly found himself elected president. He remained an activist in the newly desegregated Woodridge Elementary School in 1955 and criticized the leadership of the local NAACP for being insufficiently radical.[104]

As has been shown throughout this volume, schools had long been a major point of contention between the city's African American and white communities. And they once again were to become a battleground on which competing visions of Washington's future would be contested.[105]

Political struggles over public schools have continued to this day against the unfortunate backdrop of consistently falling classroom performance. By January 2008, the well-respected national educational publisher Editorial Projects in Education ranked the D.C. public school system the worst in the United States, trailing all state systems in measurements of student achievement, standards and assessments, teachers' pay, and other factors.[106] Political contests over the desegregation of the D.C. public schools would destroy one of the U Street community's most potent important assets, its distinguished neighborhood schools.

The Dwight Eisenhower administration and the public schools led by Superintendent Hobart M. Corning did not resist the court order to desegregate when it came. Many African American children found themselves attending formerly white schools, as did young Hobie Hobson. Officially, racial barriers in employment and student record keeping came to an end as the city's system was touted as a model for desegregation throughout the Jim Crow South.[107]

In retrospect, the initial optimism of the era was unfounded. African American parents such as Hobson were frustrated by what they perceived to be the sluggish effort to integrate their children into white schools; teachers were frustrated by growing tensions within the newly biracial student bodies; and white parents increasingly fled the city for the suburbs, taking their children with them.[108] Those white parents who remained in the city frequently organized protests of their own, as when 2,500 white students at Anacostia Senior High School staged a four-day strike in October 1957 in opposition to attending school with African Americans.[109]

Corning had resigned by that time, having been replaced by Carl Hansen, a committed desegregationist from Nebraska.[110] Hansen was an advocate of a "tracking" system, whereby students would be placed in academic and nonacademic "tracks" on the basis of standardized test scores.[111] Proponents of testing to evaluate and guide student careers predated school desegregation, with the particular plan promoted by Hansen having been developed in the late 1920s. School reformers in a number of districts at the time were pushing for new "efficient" and "scientific" ways for evaluating students so that they could be guided to more "appropriate" educational curricula. Invariably, white pupils found themselves in academically oriented tracks, while African American students were related to nonacademic curricula.[112] More tellingly, the school system never bothered to establish honors and college-bound tracks at some predominantly black schools.[113]

Because Hobson was hypersensitive to racial slights, ornery by nature, and deeply concerned about the quality of his son's education, he needed little convincing that Hansen's track system was a shell game intended to keep the classrooms functionally segregated even as students of both races entered the front doors of the same school buildings each morning. In 1966, Hobson brought suit against Hansen and the school district for using educational tracking as a backdoor method for continuing segregation.[114] Hobson and his lawyer, William Kunstler, were equally matched as showmen.[115] Together, they mobilized their arguments inside and outside the courtroom, relying on a combination of legal argument and public activism.[116]

In June 1967, U.S. Appeals Court judge Skelly Wright ruled that Hansen and the District of Columbia Board of Education had "unconstitutionally deprive[d] Negro and poor public school children of their right to equal and educational opportunity with white and more affluent school children."[117] Accordingly, Judge Wright ordered the school system to stop using the track system, to transport children in overcrowded school districts to underpopulated schools, to abolish certain school zones, and to provide enhanced teacher education.[118] Hansen resigned immediately, while Hobson would pursue additional lawsuits into the 1970s.[119]

Wright's decision prompted Congress to establish an elected school board in 1968. This board became the city's first elected governing body in nine decades. Hobson won a seat on the board, while the local SNCC director, Marion Barry, won elective office for the first time, being selected as the board's founding president.[120] The new board named Hugh Scott as the system's first African American superintendent in 1970.[121]

The school system's problems continued to grow.[122] Simultaneously with the Wright decision, a commission of eighty-one task force members and consultants, ninety-seven graduate students, and six research assistants organized by Columbia Teachers College under the leadership of Columbia University professor A. Harry Passow—and initiated by community groups along with individual Board of Education members critical of tracking—released a 593-page evaluation of the D.C. schools. The board immediately undercut this highly critical and well-documented report by suppressing its findings and recommendations.[123]

However, tests, lawsuits, and expert reports were not needed to show that the city's public school system was highly troubled. Violence was growing in the classrooms, as frustration grew on all sides about the instability and disruptions of the desegregation process and the city's demographic transformation. Animosities spilled out onto the streets and into the local and national press as the city rushed toward open racial conflict.

On Thanksgiving Day 1962, 50,033 fans clambered into the new District (later Robert F. Kennedy Jr.) Stadium behind the Capitol to watch the city's annual high school football championship, the "Turkey Bowl." The game pitted teams representing the nearly all-black public Eastern High (which had only 10 whites among its 2,400 students) against the predominantly white Catholic League winner, Saint John's. With the game winding down and Saint John's comfortably in the lead by a score of 20 to 7, the Eastern players began to vent their frustration with what to them appeared to have been a number of unfair rulings by the referees throughout the game. One of the Eastern linemen lashed out, hitting everyone in sight before teammates could bring him under control. The game continued until time ran out once the Eastern player had been strapped to a stretcher and carried off the field.[124]

Meanwhile, a number of incidents had broken out in the stands. Beyond belligerent taunts and drinking, one white girl had been stabbed in a restroom, and an African American boy had been hit on the head with a bottle. As the gun sounded, marking the end of the game, several hundred African American students rushed onto the field and attacked the Saint John's marching band and fans. Many youths were severely beaten as the melee spilled out onto neighborhood streets. Some fleeing the violence only found refuge by jumping into the nearby Anacostia River.

More than a hundred fans were injured—and ten were arrested— before calm could be restored. Superintendent Hansen established a citizens' committee to investigate. Monsignor John S. Spence, director of education of the Archdiocese of Washington, suspended the much-anticipated public-private high school contest, and this championship game has never been played since, although each year local public high schools decide their own city title in a revived Turkey Bowl. Those in authority ultimately placed the blame on "rowdyism and juvenile delinquency," with little recognition of the social dislocations that had been sweeping through the city in recent years.

Free D.C.

The tensions unleashed at D.C. Stadium that Thanksgiving Day in 1962 were increasingly omnipresent in the city. The city was becoming a magnet for the civil rights movement. In part, the movement was attracted to the city because of its role as the nation's capital; in part, the city's African American community was better placed than many to provide invaluable organizational and financial resources to the movement. And just as significant, the tardiness with which the city was wishing farewell to Jim Crow combined with its absence of home rule to make it an object of intense organizational effort. Numerous young leaders of an increasingly radicalized national African American political movement were coming to Washington.

The August 1963 March on Washington for Jobs and Freedom drew upward of 350,000 marchers to the Lincoln Memorial to hear speeches from such luminaries as CORE president James Farmer, SNCC president John Lewis, NAACP president Roy Wilkins, National Urban League president Whitney Young, and the head of the Southern Christian Leadership Conference, Martin Luther King Jr. The event had been organized by A. Philip Randolph of the Brotherhood of Sleeping Car Porters to parallel plans for the 1941 rally that had been canceled at the last moment (see chapter 3). The marchers lobbied for legislation, which eventually passed as the Civil Rights Act of 1964 and the National Voting Rights Act of 1965, being spurred on by King's historic "I Have a Dream" speech.

This 1963 march, which was national in ambition, simultaneously became local in consequence as the city's churches, religious leaders, and activists such as the Reverend Walter Fauntroy assumed responsibility for logistical details. Many of the behind-the-scenes arrangements that made it possible for so many people to make their way to the Lincoln Memorial depended on the goodwill, enthusiasm, financial well-being, and organizational acumen of U Street residents and institutions.[125]

Among the young African American organizers arriving in the city during this general period were Howard University undergraduate Stokely Carmichael from New York; PhD candidate in chemistry Marion Barry from Tennessee; SNCC sit-in organizer the Reverend Douglas Moore from North Carolina; Urban League activist Sterling Tucker from Ohio; SNCC leaders Ivanhoe Donaldson from Michigan and Kentucky, John A. Wilson from Baltimore, and Frank Smith from

Georgia and Mississippi; as well as white activists, such as the returning native alternative media pioneer Sam Smith. They formed a tight network of community organizers and rivals aligned with—and in competition with—local hot-bloods such as Fauntroy, Hobson, and a radical white lawyer, David A. Clarke. More often than not, their paths crossed on or near U Street.

Tempered by their experiences in confronting white authorities in the South, all were gifted choreographers of confrontations with the police and adept at generating media attention to their causes and to themselves. Barry was particularly adept at calling attention to himself as when, in 1967, he turned a colorful midnight jaywalking arrest near 14th and U streets into a rallying call for opposition to the police occupation of African American neighborhoods.[126] After shouting curses at arresting officers Tommy Tague and Albert Catalano and kicking them in the shins, Barry provoked gathering crowds to chant "Honkey pigs. Let the brother go."[127] After his $1,015 bail was paid by friends, a roughed-up Barry—once viewed by many in the neighborhood as a mere "Bama" (or hick from the South)—emerged from a jail cell at 3:00 a.m. the next morning as a newly minted martyr for the cause of community dignity.[128] Other dramatic incidents would follow, launching a more-than-four-decade political career that would lead Barry to the heights of municipal politics and depths of personal degradation in a crack cocaine sting operation.

Beyond Barry's emergence as the city's dominant politician throughout the final quarter of the twentieth century, his background was not dissimilar to that of many other activists who were arriving in town around the same time. He had been born in Mississippi and had grown up and studied in Tennessee. While he was a student, and was already under Federal Bureau of Investigation (FBI) surveillance, he helped to found the influential radical group SNCC. He came to Washington in June 1965 to launch SNCC's operations in the city, setting up shop on Rhode Island Avenue, NW, close to the neighborhoods then being studied by Elliott Liebow and Ulf Hannerz. He helped to establish PRIDE, Incorporated, a local self-help organization located near the intersection of 16th and U streets, NW.[129] Though he had initially found Washington to be "a strange city," he set out to promote Black Power in a community that remained too conservative to respond to his call. According to later Barry observers Harry S. Jaffe and Tom Sherwood,

> Barry would walk down Fourteenth Street on the edge of the Shaw neighborhood and greet the shopkeepers, who were members in good standing of the local black bourgeoisie.
> "Hey, brother," he would say. "What's happening?"
> "Don't give me that brother bullshit," some would respond. "I'm not your damn brother. Take that shit back down South."[130]

Never prone to backing down, Barry targeted such merchants in his effort "to free D.C. from our enemies, the people who make it impossible for us to do anything about lousy schools, brutal cops, slumlords, welfare investigators who go on midnight raids, employers who discriminate in hiring and a host of other ills that run rampant through our city."[131] Together with a fellow activist, a white Midwesterner, L. D. Pratt, Barry launched the Free D.C. Movement to boycott local businessmen opposed to home rule. Support for home rule was demonstrated by the willingness of a shop owner to sign a petition in favor of home rule, to display a red "Free D.C." emblem in their window, and to contribute money to Barry's organization at the behest of menacing young males who showed up at their door.[132]

Pratt and Barry followed with demonstrations in front of the downtown law offices of members of the powerful Board of Trade, along with a January 1966 boycott of privately owned D.C. Transit buses, opposing an impending fare hike imposed by the disliked New York company owner, O. Roy Chalk.[133] That two-day protest cost the company between 130,000 and 150,000 fares before the transit commission intervened to deny the proposed increase.[134]

Such tactics did little to change minds where it mattered most, in Congress. They offended the sensibilities of many older African Americans, such as Rayford Logan, who would come to reject the term "black" in response.[135] Rather, such actions—and the outrage they generated in response—prompted local media to devote increasing attention to what Barry and his colleagues were doing. As Jaffe and Sherwood would write nearly thirty years later, "the net effect of the Free D.C. Movement on Capitol Hill was negligible, but in the city, the balance of power began to shift."[136]

As Barry and the Free D.C. Movement confronted neighborhood businessmen and white power brokers downtown, the Reverend Douglas Moore and his Black United Front turned to white congregations to demand reparations for slavery and the Jim Crow past. Parish historians of the predominantly white National Baptist Memorial Church in nearby Columbia Heights recorded growing anxiety in response to such initiatives throughout the late 1960s. The National Baptist congregation had responded to requests by Sterling Tucker and the Washington Urban League to assist in organizing the August 1963 March on Washington by encouraging worshippers to participate "as their consciences and talents may prescribe."[137] Unlike many Baptist churches in the city and region, National Baptist had welcomed blacks parishioners into their ranks for some time.[138] Therefore, they felt aggrieved by increasingly assertive demands for financial support—which some saw as "guilt payments"—by Moore and others.

The confrontation between the Black United Front and National Baptist culminated in a dramatic showdown as Moore and National Baptist's pastor, the Reverend George Hart, faced off at a Sunday service in October 1969. Demanding that whites recognize "and know that after over 400 years, the 'boy' is now a full-grown man," Moore demanded compensation. "Too many yesterdays have passed him by," he continued. "We feel it is fair and just that you give $250,000 as your share of what is owed the Black people of this City for past services rendered."[139]

Hart responded that he and the church's parishioners recognize that "our church is by no means perfect in its adjustment to these revolutionary days." However, he maintained, while black nationalism "is a needed corrective for the intransigence of a stubborn racism that is inflexible in granting simple human rights to people, . . . that kind of separation will only result in a polarization of society which will continue animosity that will perpetuate hostility forever."[140]

The confrontation at National Baptist Memorial was also taking place in different forms in other congregations throughout the city. All Souls Unitarian Church a few blocks away at 16th and Harvard streets, NW, just uphill from U Street almost adjacent to Mrs. Henderson's Meridian Park (a.k.a. Malcolm X Park) was experiencing turmoil of its own. Founded in 1821 by John Quincy Adams and John C. Calhoun as First Unitarian Church, All Souls' ministers included many prominent abolitionists among their ranks before the Civil War, such as Edward Everett Hale. Frederick Douglass attended the church, though he never became a member. Wartime minister Reverend William Henry Channing allowed the church to be used as a hospital during the Civil War, and worked to found Miner Normal School and other African American educational institutions in the city. He later would be involved in the establishment of Howard University.

All Souls Church continued its commitment to social activism by supporting the women's suffrage movement late in the nineteenth and early in the twentieth centuries, and it provided some of the few meeting rooms where racially integrated groups could meet during much of the twentieth century. All Souls accepted African Americans into its congregation beginning in 1950. As with neighboring National Baptist Memorial, the parishioners at All Souls could legitimately claim to have been out in front of many fellow white Washingtonians when it came to the issue of race. But the turmoil of the 1960s challenged them to understand that they might not be as forward looking as the times required.

In 1969, All Souls appointed David Eaton as its new pastor.[141] He had grown up in the city and had graduated from Dunbar High School and Howard University as well as the Boston University School of Theology. He had served as pastor of a Methodist church in California before returning to Washington as chaplain at Howard University. He subsequently would become a dean at Federal City College and appeared on local radio and television with growing frequency.

Eaton, a close associate of Julius Hobson Jr., was already an outspoken member of the city's increasingly radicalized younger African American elite. All Souls had recruited Eaton at the suggestion of his predecessor, Duncan Howlett, who had argued that the times called for a powerful and charismatic minister who could serve a "pulpit-centered church" in a time of societal upheaval. Not all parishioners were convinced, using opposition to Eaton's Methodist background as a smokescreen for disquiet over the appointment of an African American as church leader. Eaton would continuously shake the church and the city with his social activism and politically charged pronouncements from the All Souls pulpit until his final sermon on Easter 1992, a few weeks before his death.

Eaton's most controversial sermon took place in May 1970, when he spoke at a Sunday service against a proposed crime bill that would have permitted police officers to break into houses without knocking if they could reasonably believe that evidence would be destroyed or an officer would be endangered by waiting. Taking on this "no knock" clause in the proposed legislation directly, he declared to gasps from the congregation that "I suggest to you and instruct myself . . . [that] any time persons break into your house unannounced, shoot them!"

Throughout this era, such showdowns as those playing themselves out at National Baptist Memorial and All Souls Unitarian churches were transpiring across Washington each Sunday morning. As in the debates over the fate of D.C. public schools—and between black and white business owners and Black Power organizers—both sides were talking past rather than to one another.

Tensions grew in every corner of the neighborhood and of the city, spawning intense reactions in the arts community. The Black Arts Movement, associated with the Black Power Movement, prompted new thinking in African American communities such as U Street.[142] As-yet-nascent Latino and Caribbean communities began to press for expanded rights.[143] And the Fauntroy-led MICCO protests against the ramming of highways for suburbanites through their neighborhood extended to other social concerns.[144]

Demonstration City

Such efforts began to place questions of broader neighborhood physical decay on the agenda, as when Martin Luther King Jr. called Shaw "one of Washington's most neglected areas" during a Fauntroy-organized urban renewal public meeting in March 1967.[145] National, if not city, officials began to notice, with MICCO-sponsored "demonstration city" projects capturing the attention of regional transportation planners.[146] As the Washington historian Howard Gillette Jr. observed, "the emergence of a black power movement in the 1960s necessarily changed the terms of social advocacy. . . . As demographics changed, as organizations crystallized around separate causes, and as the factor of race sharpened the debate over what could and should be done in urban areas, reform efforts splintered."[147] Meanwhile, the city's congressional overseers and their allies on the Board of Trade became increasingly intransigent on the issue of home rule.[148]

The growing racial hostility so palpable in Washington's schools and churches—and on its streets—reflected the escalating deterioration in race relations throughout the country. African Americans pushed for equal rights; resistant whites pushed back in many communities in every state and region. Militancy and public confrontation increased on both sides of the racial divide. Poor inner city residents felt ever more abandoned as economic dynamism began a relocation to the suburbs that would last for decades.[149] Major outbreaks of communal violence erupted in New York and Philadelphia during the summer of 1964, destroyed Watts in Central Los Angeles the following summer, and ravaged Newark and Detroit in 1967.

This self-reinforcing cycle of destruction shocked the nation. President Lyndon Baines Johnson appointed the National Advisory Commission on Civil Disorders in July 1967 to record precisely what had happened the previous summers, and to explore possible policies to divert frustration into less violent means of expression. Illinois governor Otto Kerner chaired the commission, with New York City mayor John V. Lindsay serving as vice chair. The group included nearly a dozen prominent elected officials, union leaders, businessmen, and community and police officials. Their report, released on March 1, 1968, concluded that "our nation is moving toward two societies, one black, one white—separate and unequal."[150] Hardly a major American community would be spared as civil disorders and ghetto uprisings occurred in more than 300 cities throughout the 1960s.[151] The decade became "burn, baby, burn" time across America.

The task of heading off violence in Washington fell to the U.S. secretary of labor, Willard Wirtz, an ardent supporter of Johnson's "Great Society" programs who intended to use federal funds to cure the inner city's core problems. Many of the era's antipoverty programs—such as the Office of Economic Opportunity, the Job Corps, VISTA, Head Start, and Upward Bound—fell within his Cabinet-level portfolio.[152] A number of community-based job creation and housing programs already existed in Washington. In addition to the city's ambitious public housing initiatives, neighborhood groups such as the United Planning Organization (UPO) were running programs reaching out to impoverished Washingtonians. UPO in particular had managed well-run job training initiatives for some time, seeking out ex-convicts and giving them jobs.[153]

Wirtz wanted intermediaries who were closer to "the street." Barry, meanwhile, had joined together with his second wife, Mary Treadwell, and an ex-convict, Rufus "Catfish" Mayfield, to establish their own self-help program, PRIDE, Incorporated.[154] The charismatic Barry seemed to be just the person Wirtz was trying to find. Wirtz gave a grant for a $250,000, month-long pilot project to Barry, Treadwell, and Mayfield following a tense meeting in his office, at which he told Barry to "do it. But do it fast. I want something in a few days."[155] Wirtz's Labor Department soon followed with an additional $1.5 million.[156]

Barry, Treadwell, and Mayfield set up shop near the corner of 16th and U streets in a building that had once been a luxury automobile dealership. Barry's visibility rankled many long-term community leaders, who viewed the young SNCC leader as a parvenu who was given to associating with known street thugs. His success caught the attention of another former SNCC activist, Stokely Carmichael, who showed up with some of his own armed friends one day to claim the building for himself.[157] The resulting standoff ended peacefully, with the building remaining under Barry's control.

Barry, Treadwell, and Mayfield used their newfound resources to their own ends. They built a loyal following among local "street dudes" fresh out of prison. Treadwell eventually would go to prison for stealing thousands of federal dollars from PRIDE, Incorporated.[158] The drama

surrounding PRIDE, Incorporated, heightened the city's growing sense
of apprehension about the future.[159]

While political activism rose and racial animosities deepened, most
U Street residents tried the best they could to simply get on with their
lives. Ulf Hannerz, who was living in the neighborhood at the time,
captured the broader mood in his study *Soulside*. "More often, however,"
he later wrote,

> organized political activities were simply not of a kind which
> most ghetto dwellers would regard as any of their business,
> such as public meetings. When asked if they planned to go to
> some meeting coming up, most people in the Winston Street
> neighborhood were obviously surprised at the idea, and in
> this they seemed to represent well the ghetto as a whole. . . .
> They felt that "black power" may be taken as license for
> unruly teenagers to go around knocking down people, black
> and white, thus starting a white avalanche which would
> come to destroy ghetto lives. . . . Among the younger people,
> on the other hand, many more are willing to listen to the
> black power message and acknowledge that "it makes a lot
> of sense." . . . While the older people are concerned with the
> rebelliousness of the younger men and women, the latter feel
> that the preceding generations have too often been "conned
> by the white man" into complacency which has taken them
> nowhere.[160]

U Street's residents, who were unified by a shared frustration with
whites and a local power structure that denied the city's residents even a
modicum of control over their communities, remained divided as before
by class, education, belief systems, and generations. The pressure cooker
kept boiling, as it had ever since the beginning of racial segregation
nearly a century before. The heroic actions of local residents that led to
a dismantling of Jim Crow laws and practices simultaneously exposed
rawer and rawer nerves running throughout the community.

"The Thin Line Vanishes"

The sidewalks at the corner of 14th and U streets were crowded on the pleasantly warm early spring Thursday evening of April 4, 1968.[161] Commuters scurried to make the multiple bus transfers spread out around the area, shoppers sought products both licit and not, and promenaders paraded around as the evening multitude began to replace those trying to make their ways home after work. Some of the guys hanging out on the corner, chowing down in nearby eateries, or exchanging greetings with a bus driver or shopkeeper undoubtedly were talking about the sermon given by Martin Luther King Jr. the previous Sunday to a congregation of 4,000 at the National Cathedral across town. King proclaimed April 22, at the height of the city's famed Cherry Blossom Festival, as the launch date for his "Poor People's Campaign" of demonstrations at the National Mall and throughout downtown.[162]

For those in the know, the city was on edge, as civil disturbances spread across urban America and ugly confrontations between blacks and whites broke out in Washington with greater frequency. And for those in the know, generational rivalries between civil rights leaders such as King and young radicals such as Barry and Carmichael heightened community instability. But for those not in the know—including many in Congress, at the White House, and in the District Building—the city seemed secure from massive unrest; at least until the summer.[163]

All these worlds crashed violently at 7:16 p.m., when radios throughout the city announced the news that the Reverend Martin Luther King Jr. had been shot in Memphis. For many in the city, their shock was private, screaming and crying in the privacy of their homes and apartments. For others, solitude turned to anguish, and they headed to the streets to find others as worried, angry, and hurt as themselves. The crowd at 14th and U streets began to grow, becoming increasingly restive as the minutes passed. Betty Wolden, a white reporter for NBC News, arrived to find a quiet that was "ominous—like before a hurricane strikes." She left just before the announcement came at 8:19 p.m. that King had died.[164]

Menacing calm turned to shock, which turned to hot anger in a matter of minutes. Thirty or so young black men led by Stokely Carmichael burst into the Peoples Drug Store at the corner to demand that white manager G. Simirtzakis shut down to honor King. Carmichael had told friends a few minutes before that "it's time to end this nonviolence bullshit."[165] "If," he continued, "we must die, we better die fighting back."[166] Simirtzakis closed his store. Carmichael's band continued on to other merchants in the area, gathering angry twentysomething males along the way. Carter's Liquors across the street shut down, as did YanKee Restaurant owner How K. Chen, and Wings 'N' Things night manager Berkeley Chaney.[167]

In contrast, popular WOL disc jockey "Nighthawk" Bob Terry broadcast the message that "This is no time to hate. Hate won't get you anywhere. And let me tell you something too, white man," Nighthawk continued. "Tomorrow, before you get back in that car and go out to that suburban house, you better say something nice to that black man on the job beside you. You'd better stop hating, too." As much as the community loved Nighthawk, Stokely moved the crowd. "Now that Dr. King's dead, we ain't got no way but Stokely's way," one young man declared.[168]

According to white news accounts,

> mostly young men fell in with Carmichael. Many wore light jackets over flashy sports shirts or turtlenecks and slacks. Some had put on raincoats against the on and off again drizzle that had begun. Others were in work clothes or blue collar uniforms. Although it was dark, some did not remove their sunglasses. Many of the men wore their hair in natural Afro style and had goateed beards. Dotted through the growing crowd walking with Stokely were past and present students of nearby Howard University. Tension rose as the crowds were swelled by more and more teenaged youths and adults under thirty.[169]

A block south of U Street along 14th, a short, pudgy man ran up and grabbed Carmichael's arm, screaming in a soft tenor voice, "This is not the way to do it, Stokely. Let's not get anyone hurt. Let's cool it."

Carmichael shouted back to the Reverend Walter Fauntroy that the crowd merely wanted the stores to close. "They killed Dr. King," he exclaimed.[170]

Fauntroy retreated to the Southern Christian Leadership Conference office nearby, telling a plainclothes policeman in an unmarked car that everything would be all right. At 9:25 p.m., as Fauntroy climbed to the conference's second-floor walk-up office, the sound of the Peoples Drug Store window smashing echoed through the night.[171]

As the crowd surged past the Republic Theater, "a stocky fifteen year old boy, wearing dungarees, a tan sweatshirt, and a sailor cap, suddenly punched his fist into one of the movie theater's glass doors. The glass shattered, and a younger boy slipped through the door frame into the theater and came back with a large bag of popcorn. The fifteen-year-old stood by the door, rubbing his fist, which was not cut, and smiled broadly. 'Way to go, kid,' somebody called him."[172]

Carmichael exhorted in return that "this is not the way," as SNCC members tried to calm the crowd. Young men rushed into the Lincoln Theatre demanding that the show stop. After ordering Moy Hon Toon to close his Zanzibar Restaurant, Carmichael knew he had lost control. A middle-aged man kicked out the window of the National Liquor Store, bewailing the white man's evil.[173]

"This is it baby," someone shouted. "The shit is going to hit the fan now. . . . We oughta burn this place down right now. . . . Let's get some white motherfuckers. . . . Let's kill them all."[174]

In desperation, Carmichael cried out, "We're not ready. We'll be back. This ain't the way," and disappeared up the 14th Street hill.[175] But the time for preparing was past; the die was cast.

Civil order collapsed for the next three days, and was only eventually restored after the city was occupied by more than 13,000 federal troops for a dozen days. During the turmoil, twelve people died; hundreds were injured; 7,600 men, women, and children were arrested—90 percent of whom were African American males, 80 percent of whom had lived in the city for at least five years, 80 percent of whom had jobs, and many of which with the federal government; more than 1,000 fires were set; and nearly 700 businesses—large and small, owned by both blacks and

FIGURE 5.2
Seventh and P Streets, NW, in the Aftermath of the April 1968 Violence

Photograph from the Washington Historical Image Collection, Washingtoniana Division,
Martin Luther King Jr. Library, Washington. Used with permission.

whites—were destroyed, with at least 5,000 jobs being lost permanently to the city.[176] Nearly 700 "dwelling units"—apartments and homes— were destroyed, and their residents were left on the street.[177] For weeks— even months—those who remained in the neighborhood had to rely on churches and civic organizations for basic essentials because the stores that sold food and personal items were gone.[178]

According to some estimates, the city's total losses during this twelve-day period exceeded $27 million.[179] Though some small African American enterprises such as Ben's Chili Bowl survived, with "Soul Brother" signs in their windows, far too many other large and small black and white businesses burned to the ground.[180] Once-vibrant commercial corridors along 14th, U, and 7th streets in Northwest, and H Street in Northeast, lay in ruins (figure 5.2).[181] Countless lives were destroyed, even though the number of people who died was remarkably low given the fury of the violence.[182]

Minor outbursts of communal violence followed later in the spring during the breakup of the Poor People's Campaign tent village on the National Mall, known as Resurrection City, which had been encouraged by King.[183] Many local whites and blacks opened their homes to the demonstrators at Resurrection City in the hope of softening some of the tensions that were swirling around the city. Unfortunately, what had started as an effort to express anger and sorrow over the murder of King on April 4 already had become a potent brew of uprising and riot, of nascent revolution and recreational looting, of anger and cynical greed that continued to haunt the tent city. Neither the city, nor U Street, would ever be the same again.

Two Days of Fire

The unrest had followed Carmichael up 14th Street to Mount Pleasant and back down the hill again. The police, who had been caught off guard, were helpless to respond to all the calls for trouble.[184] Belmont TV and Appliance was looted and burned; Sam's Pawnbrokers, Irving's Record Shop, Federated Five and Dime, the Rhodes Five and Ten store; London Custom Shop. . . . Growing crowds of young men and women up and down 14th Street ignored admonitions by Carmichael and SNCC workers for calm. At 10:40 p.m., Carmichael had darted into a Mustang waiting for him and disappeared into the night. By 11 p.m., all the stores around 14th and U had been destroyed.[185]

The mood on the street changed, according to *Washington Post* reporters on the scene, from antiwhite hostility to "the carnival excitement produced by looting."[186] A heavy rain that began around 11:30 helped the police secure the streets. By midnight, the 14th and U area had been sealed off and occupied; areas further north around 14th, Girard, and Kenyon streets were not subdued until several hours later. In a half-dozen hours, 200 stores had suffered damage, 150 stores had been looted, seven fires had been set, 150 adults and 50 juveniles had been arrested, 30 people had been injured, and 1 had died.[187]

According to reporters, "at dawn Friday, with hundreds of policemen still lining the sidewalks, 14th Street was quiet. The rays of the rising sun glinted on those store windows that still contained unbroken glass. White foam, sprayed by street cleaning crews, ran down the steep hill, carrying broken glass and debris along with it. . . . Eye-stinging tear gas still hung in the air. Burglar alarms continued to jangle in an unsettling chorus."[188]

A strange sense of the matter-of-fact had descended on the city. Sam Smith later recalled that he had returned to his Capitol Hill townhouse to find his wife "out back working on our foot-wide strip of garden, listening to reports of looting and arson on a portable radio as the black fog settled in."[189] Others also went about their business, as if Friday, April 5, 1968, was a normal day. Federal offices remained open as if nothing had happened. At 1:30 a.m., with mayhem still ruling 14th Street, city school superintendent William R. Manning, city director of public safety Patrick V. Murphy, and presidentially appointed mayor Walter Washington decided to keep the schools open on Friday to better control the city's 150,000 students.[190]

Howard president James M. Nabrit Jr. immediately understood that his school must honor King. The campus had been tense for weeks, with students occupying the main administration building for four days just two weeks before in a campaign for a greater student voice in university management. Nabrit's hastily organized memorial service let out at 11:45 a.m., just as an impromptu demonstration of several hundred students was beginning on the steps of Frederick Douglass Hall.[191]

During this demonstration, the political rhetoric became ever more heated as the various groups jostled for control of the campus. Stokely Carmichael appeared from the back of the crowd and declared, "Stay off the streets, if you don't have a gun, because there's going to be shooting." He urged those who "were not ready for the thing" to go home, and then he vanished once more.[192]

In retrospect, the decision to keep the city's schools open was a dismaying mistake. Rather than controlling students, the schools concentrated groups of hostile youngsters together. The decision communicated a callous disregard for the profound sorrow felt by most

African Americans over King's assassination. Instead of being cleared, 14th, 7th, and U streets, NW, and H Street, NE, were thronged with overflowing crowds of furious youths with no place to go. Angry students from Howard joined in. By noon, the U Street neighborhood had started to burn once again.[193]

Fire began consuming entire blocks and, with smoke billowing on the horizon, suburban office workers downtown decided to flee at once. Chaos spread despite calls for calm from local leaders like Fauntroy and Barry, and visiting celebrities such as the soul singer James Brown.[194] Roaming youths taunted customers in downtown department stores as well as whites stuck in the worst traffic-jam in the city's history.[195]

Wild rumors of worse destruction spread. When President Johnson was told that Carmichael was leading a band to burn down Georgetown, the colorful president allegedly responded, "Goddamn, I've waited thirty-five years for this day."[196] Within hours, the violence extended to within a dozen blocks of the White House. It was so close, in fact, that Johnson could smell the city burning from his desk in the Oval Office.[197]

Despite such high drama, the overwhelming preponderance of the city remained untouched and calm.[198] As Ulf Hannerz, who was conducting his research at the time, later recorded, "some groups went downtown but looting there was rather limited—as we have noted once before, it was particularly men's fashion stores that were hit—and there was hardly any burning outside the ghetto, where most of it continued to be concentrated on the main shopping streets."[199]

Ironically, Police Chief John B. Layton, Public Safety Commissioner Murphy, Mayor Washington, Undersecretary of the Army David E. McGiffert, Deputy Attorney General (and future secretary of state) Warren Christopher, and other local and federal officials had just placed the finishing touches on a military deployment plan known as "Cabin Guard" in case disturbances broke out in Washington that summer, as they had during previous years in other large American cities.[200] To set their design into operation, Murphy needed to reach the Pentagon to receive the necessary signatures, and then return to the District Building downtown for final authorization from the city. He too became immobilized by the massive traffic jam.

President Johnson and Mayor Washington decided to designate Cyrus Vance—a future secretary of state who had been Johnson's personal representative during the Detroit disturbances the previous summer—to coordinate the police and military response.[201] By about 3:00 p.m.—as the police were outflanked by the crowds around Mount Vernon Square at the edge of downtown—dozens of Jewish merchants along 7th Street watched their livelihoods go up in flames. Forty years later, ninety-seven-year-old Larry Rosen, owner of Smith Pharmacy on upper 14th Street in Columbia Heights, would still ask himself "What did we do to deserve that?" After all, Rosen thought, he did all he could to treat black customers with respect and hired local residents.[202] Eventually, Murphy managed to make it back from Virginia with the requisite signatures, as looters invaded downtown stores and bands of malcontents descended on H Street, NE.[203]

At 4:30 p.m. on Friday, April 5, 1968, 150 troops of the Third Infantry's D Company crossed the Memorial Bridge under the command of Vietnam veteran Captain Leroy Rhode. By 5:00 p.m., D Company had mounted machine guns on the steps of the Capitol, the Third Infantry's troops had surrounded the White House, and the first of 13,000 National Guard and regular Army soldiers from as far away as North Carolina had begun a nearly two-week occupation of the city.[204] Curfews went into effect, checkpoints were established, and the city fell eerily quiet under military control by late Saturday.

Lost in the dramatic scenes on the streets was the fact that the vast majority of the city's African Americans stayed home throughout the unrest, often feeling just as terrorized as white residents.[205] Analysts months later concluded that "roughly 20,000, or about one out of eight residents of the affected area," participated in the riots.[206] Neoconservative commentators such as Fred Siegel are appalled that the figure is as high as one in eight, many of whom appear to have been employees of the federal government.[207] Others, such as Michael Katz, wonder why instances of collective violence are so rare given the social tensions evident in cities such as Washington.[208]

Hannerz caught the mood as calm returned to the city. "On Sunday," he reported, "things were returning to normal. People hurried to do their shopping at those chain stores which were still in existence and which opened for a little while to meet the needs of those customers who have not been able to do shopping in the past days. Some neighborhood people went over to the large shopping streets to see what they looked like; there they could mix with sightseeing white suburbanites, whose movie cameras steadily aimed at the ruins were spinning out of the windows of slow-moving cars."[209]

Washington Post journalists reported at the time that "April 7 was Palm Sunday and Washington's first day of almost complete calm since the assassination of Dr. King. It was a day of new incongruities: families in their finest clothes, walking to church past burned-out buildings, sooty debris, and armed troops; soldiers wearing folded palms in their helmets; sermons touching on the triumphal entry of Christ into Jerusalem, the slaying of a modern black martyr, and the furious destruction of a riot."[210] These seemingly incongruous images would become the norm for the U Street area for a third of a century as hope and despair, destruction and renewal, degradation and dignity came to stand side by side along the neighborhood's half-recovered streets.[211]

The oral historian Dana Lanier Schaffer records that community reactions to what had transpired during those April days of 1968 proved to be as ambiguous as the images from that Palm Sunday. Shaffer records that oral interviews about the events decades later revealed an African American community that

was actually a mix of interrelated communities with some-times competing identities, goals, beliefs, values, and re-actions. While generally united by the common experience of racial injustice, each group's distinct sense of identity led to varying levels of participation in and reactions to this urban unrest. Feeling marginalized during an era of great turmoil, some blacks used destructive violence as both an outlet for their frustration and a political statement demanding change. Others responded to the increasing destruction with determined community activism, while still others stood by in disbelief or disapproval. This variety of experiences before and during the riots continued as African Americans attempted to assess the damage and determine how to move forward in the aftermath.[212]

The diverse African American reactions recorded by Schaffer very much parallel the divergent responses of the U Street community to the larger world around it ever since it took shape at the end of the Civil War. Integrationists, nationalists, rich, poor, recent arrivals, and haughty descendants of the "first freed" divided over strategy and tactics even as they shared their place behind the veil of American racial barriers. Despite these divisions, they nonetheless united around the notion that Washington had become their city for the first time. Their paths crossed, if at all, in the zone of contact that was U Street.

Let Them Eat Watermelon

The question of home rule remained perhaps the most painful wound left festering as the fires of April 1968 burned themselves out. For the majority of Washington's residents, the issue remained as potent as any voting rights dispute in the South throughout the entire decade of the 1960s. Various half-steps toward democratic representation were taken along the way. The city's residents had been allowed to vote in presidential elections since the early 1960s. They gained an elected school board in 1968. In 1971, local residents were extended the right to elect a nonvoting delegate to the U.S. House of Representatives—a position that would be held by the Reverend Walter Fauntroy throughout the 1970s and 1980s, and by Eleanor Holmes Norton ever since.[213]

Such measures mattered little in light of the absence of local electoral control over the District government. Between 1948 and 1966, the U.S. Senate passed numerous "home rule" bills for Washington, only to see their efforts languish before the House Committee on the District of Columbia, where one man—Representative John McMillan of South Carolina—stood in the way. There would be no democratic government for the nation's capital as long as McMillan remained in Congress.[214]

McMillan, an old-line Democratic Party segregationist, gained his congressional seat in northeastern coastal South Carolina in 1939. As the chair of the House District Committee for two dozen years, he held African Americans and Washington residents in contempt. He became evermore intransigent as presidents from both parties—Kennedy, Johnson, and Nixon—tried to find ways to extend home rule to city residents.[215] His contretemps with appointed Mayor Walter Washington were both bitter and legendary. One day, in an especially racist insult, McMillan arranged for a truckload of watermelons to be delivered to the District Building.[216] Because he was seemingly unbeatable in his home district, advocates of home rule had little choice but to wait for McMillan to retire or to die.

However, the new generations of activists who had come to town in the mid-1960s—and had been tempered by the upheavals of 1968—were too impatient to wait for McMillan to leave. The Reverend Walter Fauntroy, Sterling Tucker of the Washington Urban League, and others organized bus trips to McMillan's South Carolina congressional district to mobilize newly enfranchised African American voters to defeat their nemesis.[217] Miraculously, they succeeded, with John Jenrette beating McMillan in the Democratic Primary runoff election of that year by 645 votes. Jenrette eventually lost the seat to Republican Edward L. Young in the general election later that fall.[218]

McMillan's defeat opened the way for African American U.S. representative Charles Diggs—a Democrat from Michigan—to assume the chair of the House Committee on the District of Columbia.[219] The D.C. Home Rule Bill passed in October 1973, following more than five weeks of hearings.[220] The Republican House of Representatives minority leader, Gerald Ford, led a last-ditch effort to kill the bill on the floor of the House. He was pulled away in mid-debate to the White House, where President Richard Nixon proposed nominating him to replace Vice President Spiro Agnew, who had been forced to resign in disgrace following tax evasion charges. Congress passed the home rule bill, with Nixon signing the act into law on December 24, 1973.[221] The city's voters ratified the law via a referendum on May 7, 1974.[222]

The home rule law appeared to create a municipal government much like that found elsewhere across the United States. With an elected mayor and Council, the D.C. charter appeared on the surface to be unexceptional, except for the creation of thirty-six Advisory Neighborhood Commissions, which were intended to give voice to the concerns of micro-level communities across the city consisting of single-member districts representing approximately 2,000 residents (see chapter 7).[223]

Racist Southern Democrats and conservative congressional Republicans nonetheless managed to leave their indelible mark on the final legislation that granted home rule to the District of Columbia.[224] Congress retained the right to have final authority over the city's finances and effective veto authority over its laws. Unlike any other American city of metropolitan scale, Washington would be unable to tax commuters from neighboring states. Finally, the city's court and penal systems would remain in the hands of the federal government. Home rule—as granted to Washington in 1974—proved to be a nearly fatally flawed legislative compromise that has left local officials constantly running up a down escalator ever since.

Congress's control over the city is more than theoretical. As Michael Fauntroy has noted, congressional disapproval of D.C. legislation requires "a simple majority of members voting in either the House or the Senate. Any member of either chamber can introduce a resolution, and all local legislation is open to Congressional challenge."[225]

The ease of intervention opens the door to any number of objections. Fauntroy continues,

> Congressional intervention has many motives. From a lobbyist reporting to a friendly congressional staff member that noise from a neighborhood swimming pool is too loud (resulting in a rider to an appropriations measure mandating a 9 p.m. closing time), to a House member threatening to "savage" an upcoming appropriations bill (because the Mayor was tardy in responding to two letters regarding a potholed bridge), congressional intervention has come from a variety of quarters. . . . The major mechanism for Congress to intervene and erode District home rule has been through the appropriations process.[226]

The final passage of home rule confirmed President Richard Nixon's interest in the city. Within two weeks of his inauguration, Nixon had toured burned out areas along 7th Street, greeting crowds that had gathered at the sight of his long presidential limousine. Stopping before a damaged storefront with an aide standing nearby holding a large rendition of a new shopping center, Nixon told appointed Mayor Walter Washington, "This is our capital city. We want to make it a beautiful city in every way. We will make Washington a model city."[227]

Nixon and his top domestic advisers, John Erlichman and Egil "Bud" Krough Jr., retained their concern for Washington, promoting home rule as best they could until they became enmeshed in the Watergate affair. The city's future seemed bright with a friend in the White House, a powerful enemy removed from Congress, and a new home rule city charter in place.

In the enthusiasm of the moment, many legislative fine points were lost on young community activists such as Dave Clarke, John Wilson, Marion Barry, Ivanhoe Donaldson, and Sterling Tucker (although Julius Hobson Sr. immediately understood that the city once again had been dealt a losing hand). The city's appointed mayor, Walter Washington, retained his office in the city's first municipal elections. Clarke, Barry, Wilson, and Tucker were elected to the newly constituted District of Columbia Council, which they would dominate for two decades. FBI agents assigned to maintain surveillance on the city's leaders recorded dryly that "Negro militants" were becoming elected officials.[228]

Barry eventually emerged as master of the new system. In the first of his four successful mayoral campaigns, he won an intensely fought 1978 race by forcing Mayor Washington from the race and by defeating Tucker, Fauntroy, and several other candidates.[229] On January 2, 1979— following a festive but rain-soaked parade from Malcolm X Park, across U Street, down 16th Street past the White House to the District Building—Supreme Court Justice Thurgood Marshall began a new era in District politics by swearing in Barry as mayor.[230] The street "radicals" who emerged on the streets around U Street during the 1960s were now in charge of the city.

Profile

STOKELY STANDIFORD CHURCHILL
CARMICHAEL KWAME TURE (1941–1998)

Stokely Carmichael (figure 5.3) was born into a working-class family in Port of Spain, Trinidad, on November 15, 1941. His parents moved to New York when he was two, leaving their son in the care of his grandmother and aunts. He joined his parents and four sisters in New York eleven years later, after having attended the prestigious Tranquility School in Trinidad.

The Carmichael family lived in Harlem before moving to the Morris Park neighborhood in the East Bronx. Carmichael lived a dual life as an award-winning student at New York's exceptional Bronx High School of Science while also a member of the largely white Morris Park Dukes youth gang. Upon graduation from high school, he turned down several scholarships from venerable white universities to enroll in Howard University in 1960. A philosophy major, he quickly became a favored student of many faculty members such as the poet Sterling Brown and the sociologist Nathan Hare.

FIGURE 5.3
Stokely Carmichael,
Chairman, Student Nonviolent Coordinating
Committee, May 23, 1966

United Press International Telephoto, New York
World-Telegram and the Sun Photograph Collection,
Library of Congress, Washington. Used with permission.

Carmichael's intellectual interests merged with a growing commitment to radical activism. He joined the Howard-based Nonviolent Action Group (NAG), which was dedicated to confronting racism throughout the city and its suburbs. He played a pivotal role in affiliating NAG with the Student Nonviolent Coordinating Committee, a national civil rights organization. He participated in Freedom Rides throughout the south in 1961, serving the first of several jail terms in Mississippi at that time. As he became a more and more prominent figure in civil rights protests, he earned a reputation as a fiery orator.

Carmichael's bent toward philosophy and activism prompted him to develop an overarching ideology centering on the concept of "Black Power." He became disillusioned by mainstream attempts to gain legal equality for African Americans. Drawing intellectual sustenance from Malcolm X, Kwame Nkrumah, and Frantz Fanon—among many thinkers—he used his speeches and writings to promote socioeconomic independence and black pride. He eventually entered into a tumultuous relationship with the California-based Black Panther Party.

By 1967, Carmichael, a celebrity in his own right, left SNCC and coauthored the seminal book *Black Power* with Charles V. Hamilton. He developed the concept of "institutional racism" and broadly sought to bring intellectual rigor to African American nationalism. Less than a year later, he found himself at the center of the angry crowds that had gathered along Washington's U Street, 14th Street, and 7th Street in April 1968 following the assassination of Martin Luther King Jr.

Carmichael married the South African singer Miriam Makeba in 1968, and they moved to Guinea-Conakry a year later. He sought out the exiled Ghanaian president Kwame Nkrumah as a teacher, and joined the staff of Guinean prime minister Ahmed Sékou Touré. Carmichael changed his name to Kwame Ture in honor of his two distinguished mentors. In 1972, he helped to establish the All-African People's Revolutionary Party and devoted his energy to promoting Pan-Africanism.

Ture lived in Guinea for the rest of his life, despite being imprisoned briefly by the Guinean military regime following Touré's death in 1984. He remained the subject of surveillance by the Central Intelligence Agency throughout most of his time in Africa. He returned to New York for two years to receive treatment for the cancer that would take his life in 1998 following his return to Guinea.

MARION SHEPILOV BARRY JR. (1936–)

Marion Shepilov Barry Jr. (figure 5.4) was born on March 6, 1936, in Itta Bena, Mississippi. He moved to Memphis at the age of eight. His middle name honors the Soviet foreign minister Dimitri Shepilov, who was forced from politics in disgrace after participating in a failed 1957 coup attempt against Communist Party leader Nikita Khrushchev.

Barry graduated from LeMoyne College in Memphis and then served in the U.S. Army and entered a graduate program at Fisk University in Nashville. Following receipt of his master's degree in chemistry from Fisk, he moved to the University of Tennessee's PhD program, for which he successfully completed all the requirements short of the dissertation.

In 1965, Barry traveled to the founding conference of SNCC in Raleigh, where he was elected the organization's first chairman. He then decided against completing his doctoral studies in favor of full-time civil rights activism.

Barry moved to Washington a few months later to establish the D.C. chapter of SNCC. He launched PRIDE, Incorporated, a local self-help organization, together with his second wife Mary Treadwell and Rufus "Catfish" Mayfield. Barry was one of the main catalysts for the "Free D.C. Movement," which protested local businesses opposed to home rule and sponsored a successful January 1966 boycott of D.C. Transit buses.

FIGURE 5.4
Marion S. Barry Jr.

Photograph from the Kiplinger Research Library,
Historical Society of Washington, D.C. Used with permission.

Barry entered electoral politics as Congress established various home rule institutions during the early 1970s. In 1971, the city's voters elected him to its new School Board, upon which he served as president. He subsequently won a seat on the city's first elected D.C. Council in 1974. On March 9, 1977, he was shot critically while stepping off of an elevator in the District Building just as a group of Hanafi Muslims was seizing the building.

Barry ran for the position of mayor in 1978, edging out several other candidates in a hotly contested Democratic Party primary. Well-timed endorsements by the *Washington Post* were widely credited with generating critical support for him among liberal white voters. Barry easily won reelection in 1982, and again in 1986. *City Paper* political columnist "Loose Lips" (who then was actually Ken Cummins) dubbed Barry "mayor for life" at this time.

On January 18, 1990, an FBI "sting operation" caught Barry smoking crack cocaine with Hazel "Rasheeda" Moore in the Vista Hotel. He was charged with three perjury felony counts, ten misdemeanor drug possession counts, and one misdemeanor conspiracy count, and was forced to leave office. He emerged victorious after a highly emotional trial, which split the city along racial lines. The judge declared a mistrial on twelve of the counts. The jury acquitted him on all but one of the remaining charges, convicting him of a single minor misdemeanor charge for possession of cocaine. He subsequently served a six-month term in a Richmond federal penitentiary.

Barry returned to the city following his release from prison and won a seat on the D.C. Council. He ran successfully for a fourth term as mayor in 1995.

Barry retired from politics at the conclusion of his mayoral term in 1999, but he flirted with the notion of running for the D.C. Council again in 2002. In the November 2004 general election, with 96 percent of the votes cast, he won the Ward Eight seat on the D.C. Council, a position he has held ever since, despite having been censured by the D.C. Council in March 2010 for violations of conflict-of-interest laws.

CHAPTER 6

Chocolate City

On Friday nights in Chocolate City, they get busy. They
get busy, and they get fresh, and they get the music rollin'.

—Gil Scott-Heron, 1989[1]

With the advent of home rule for the District of Columbia in 1974, U
Streeters divided over strategy and tactics as city residents gained the
right to elect their own officials for the first time in ninety-nine years.
The fiction writer Edward P. Jones captured these tensions in his short
story "Bad Neighbors," in which he recorded in passing that "Howard
students not D.C. natives were taught from day one never to venture into
Washington neighborhoods except where they could find a better class of
people, meaning white people for the most part."[2] Class divisions still ran
deep in the area.

Washington's African Americans united around the notion that the
city had become theirs, no matter how much local society was segmented
and divided within itself. In many ways, they were right. The 1970 census
revealed that the city was home to an all-time high African American
community of 527,705, representing 70 percent of all residents.[3] As popular
radio announcers proudly proclaimed—and as popular music groups such
as the band Parliament-Funkadelic and the "grandfather of rap" Gil Scott-
Heron affirmed—Washington had become "Chocolate City."[4]

With home rule, many in the community—both blacks and whites,
such as future D.C. Council members Polly Shackleton, Dave Clarke, and
Betty Ann Kane, and such others as the journalist Sam Smith—hoped
that the city would become a model for an alternative American future,
one in which African Americans could shape their own destiny. The first
home rule government filled up with veterans of the civil rights movement
and the racial conflicts of the 1960s. Mayor Walter Washington presided
as the city elder, Sterling Tucker assumed the chair of the new District of

Columbia Council, Julius Hobson staked out his political base through the newly formed D.C. Statehood Party, the Reverend Walter Fauntroy secured his place as the District's congressional delegate, and Marion Barry presided over the School Board before joining the D.C. Council.[5] Their activities were connected to a wave of neighborhood activism, which was fueled in part by federal dollars flowing through community associations participating in the era's "War on Poverty."[6] Not surprisingly, U Street's legacy of activism combined with the pressing need to rebuild following the destruction of April 1968 to spark myriad local initiatives aimed at reinventing the neighborhood.

Nonviolent Land Reform

Walter Fauntroy was well placed to move forward with neighborhood planning. He had been a child of the neighborhood, his New Bethel Baptist Church had long been a major neighborhood institution, and his church coalition—the Model Inner-City Community Organization (MICCO)—had united neighborhood voices with federal funds. MICCO, in fact, secured $92 million from the Nixon administration to support two "Action Years" aimed at redeveloping the 14th, U, and 7th street commercial corridors.[7]

Fauntroy's MICCO was hardly alone in benefiting from the Nixon administration's largess. The United Planning Organization—which had been established in the 1960s as a community action program under the Economic Opportunity Act of 1964—received robust funding from federal agencies as well as from private foundations for a variety of job training, housing, and poverty alleviation programs.[8] Barry's PRIDE, Incorporated, similarly was awarded federal grants, at times after Barry personally browbeat beleaguered administration officials (such as Nixon's director of the Office of Economic Opportunity, Donald Rumsfeld).[9] Rivalries among these groups remained intense.[10]

Under MICCO's plan, local congregations would become responsible for developing the land parcels. MICCO-affiliated churches agreed to acquire land through the power of eminent domain for a "non-violent land reform" during the first Action Year (1970). By the second Action

Year (1971), private developers were to have formed alliances with civic associations and clubs, dividing the not-for-profit community and setting various neighborhood groups against one another.[11] The D.C. Redevelopment Land Agency (RLA), charged with overseeing these developments, began to complain that MICCO represented "primarily the political interests of its founder, D.C. delegate Walter E. Fauntroy, and the financial interests of his supporters rather than the people of Shaw."[12]

Jerome Paige and Margaret Reuss, in their history of Washington urban renewal projects during the period, noted that groups vied for funds and staff to replan and to redevelop 14th Street. The D.C. Model Cities Program competed with MICCO and UPO for neighborhood planning dominance.[13] As Paige and Reuss conclude,

> These three major neighborhood development organizations of the 1960s differed widely in structure and impact. MICCO, which originated from the neighborhoods, was led by a local black elite, pastors and business people. The neighborhood Development Center #1, though staffed by black professionals and activists, built its strength from the block clubs upward. The Model Cities Commission was heavily weighted with establishment representatives at least in the beginning. Both MICCO and the Model Cities program suffered from duplication by the D.C. government of their staffs and authority. All three programs suffered from the tendency of government to terminate programs rather than continuing them with appropriate changes as needed.[14]

MICCO and Fauntroy maintained one significant advantage over their competitors: The member churches had proven ready to make their own, at times significant, contributions to local housing programs.[15] In March 1971, Fauntroy declared that the time had come to "get the dirt flying" and begin construction.[16] RLA officials, similarly impatient, proposed to move to competitive bidding, which threatened to pass control over planning and construction to nonneighborhood groups.[17] *Washington*

Post columnist Eugene Meyer began to criticize Fauntroy, generating support for his resignation.[18] Fauntroy eventually stepped down so that the RLA could extend its support to his now-former coalition.[19]

Despite such theatrics, community planning from the ground up took shape in a neighborhood that had been devastated by communal violence only a few years before. By 1974, the RLA had released a plan for neighborhood business and commercial establishments.[20] Meanwhile, MICCO and other groups hired professional planners to expand the neighborhood's capacity for shaping its own future.[21] This newfound adeptness, in turn, allowed U Street to face down initiatives imposed from the outside by the new home rule District government, by transportation planners developing the regional Metrorail subway and highway systems, and by private developers intent on turning a profit.[22]

Government planners focused on large burned-out blocks along 7th Street, along with destroyed lots near the intersection of 14th and U streets. This corner had particular significance because it demarcated the neighborhood's most symbolically significant public space. Many felt that the public would perceive the neighborhood to be damaged as long as vacant lots remained covered with the rubble of such previously well-known buildings as the Republic Theater.[23]

The city's planners gravitated toward images of the large-scale megaprojects that represented the height of fashion at the time.[24] But the D.C. government did not have the funds required to turn such plans into realities. Federal agencies had retreated from focusing on rebuilding violence-torn neighborhoods in Washington once Nixon and his senior advisers had become embroiled in the Watergate scandal. And Nixon was succeeded in office by a series of presidential administrations with no meaningful interest in the city. Therefore, the key to rebuilding increasingly lay with private developers as Marion Barry came to power after winning the 1978 mayoral race.[25]

One of these would-be developers, Jeffrey Cohen, had returned home to Washington in 1971 to enter law school after graduating from college in Philadelphia. As a local kid who had grown up in Northwest Washington—and had worked in his father's business in Northeast—he knew the city scene well. He set out to launch a career as a developer following his legal studies by picking up smaller properties and renovating them. He took a special interest in the U Street area, in part because the property there had become so devalued following the communal violence of 1968 that even a beginner in real estate like himself could afford to buy it. Like a number of young developers starting up around the city at the time, he wanted to do more than just turn a profit on a few projects. He wanted to give something back to his hometown.

As a child of the city, Cohen understood the neighborhood's special place in African American history and envisioned reviving its stature as the center of Washington commercial and cultural life. He naturally sought to push his plans forward by working with the new city administration, an effort that eventually would lead some critics to claim that he had become far too close to Barry.[26]

Cohen entered a new stage in his fledgling career when he purchased the closed Children's Hospital complex at 13th and V streets with the hope of establishing a rehabilitation hospital combining treatment and hotel facilities for patients and their families modeled along the lines of the Mayo Clinic. His efforts eventually led to the construction of the National Rehabilitation Hospital at Washington Hospital Center farther out in Northwest Washington. The hospital project brought him into closer contact with the U Street community as he began to form alliances with a number of nonprofit community groups. Over time, he gained control of more than 7 acres of land in the neighborhood, including the vacant Lincoln Theatre and the similarly unused Twelfth Street YMCA.

Among Cohen's holdings were several abandoned industrial properties, including the Manhattan Laundry, Thompson's Dairy, and the original Children's Hospital site. To take advantage of these fallow properties, he created a coalition of neighborhood groups and private business interests to develop a proposed apartment-office-retail mixed-use project; nearly half of which (45.7 percent) was to have been owned by twenty-three community-based organizations. And because the project was to be constructed on the sites of already unoccupied buildings, it would have the additional advantage for the neighborhood of not requiring the displacement of local residents. This proposed Samuel C. Jackson Plaza, named after a recently deceased neighborhood activist, would have included 1,200 apartments, 350,000 square feet of office space, and an additional 100,000 square feet of retail property. This megaproject theoretically would have become precisely the sort of public-private retail-residential center envisioned by federal and city planners immediately following the upheavals of 1968.[27]

The scale of Cohen's involvement in the neighborhood generated suspicions about his motives, especially because he was seen by many as being too tightly connected with the increasingly malodorous Barry administration.[28] The effort to build Samuel C. Jackson Plaza collapsed after the city reneged on previous commitments to rent office space in the complex. Cohen nonetheless kept trying to launch various plans to revitalize the neighborhood as a commercially viable symbol of the city's African American community.[29] He is remembered today by many in the neighborhood as one of the very few private investors at the time who tried to work with local groups to revivify the area.

House by House, Block by Block

National approaches to neighborhood revitalization began to change by the time Marion Barry came to power as mayor on January 2, 1979. The Housing and Community Development Act of 1974 ended the Lyndon Johnson–era Model Cities Program, rechanneling federal assistance to cities into block grants to be expended according to local priorities.[30] The more flexible block grants began to have an impact on the ground during Jimmy Carter's administration. Cities across the country quickly switched from large megaprojects to what Alexander von Hoffman has called a "house by house, block by block" approach to neighborhood revitalization.[31]

The amount of government money available for projects in U Street and the greater Shaw area contracted precipitously. The Carter administration and then the Ronald Reagan administration proved to be far less generous toward the area than had their predecessors under presidents Johnson and Nixon. Consequently, less federal attention and fewer federal dollars became available for neighborhood projects. Moreover, the profligate spending habits of Barry's District government left local officials short of funds.

These trends compelled those concerned with rebuilding the city's riot corridors to think more strategically, and to rely more heavily on community organizations for project implementation. Barry took perhaps his single most important decision in the upscaling of the neighborhood by selecting the northwest corner of the intersection of 14th and U streets, NW, as the site for a large municipal office building, which would become known over time as the Frank D. Reeves Municipal Center. When it opened in September 1986, the Reeves Center brought a steady flow of middle-class civil servants and those seeking city services into the area for the first time in many years (figure 6.1).[32] Restaurants, stores, and offices sprang up, initiating what *Washington Post* columnist Courtland Milloy called a "white tornado" sweeping the area "clean of litter and junkies."[33] The opening of the Reeves Center marked a psychological change far beyond its physical presence. The media story line concerning the neighborhood subtly changed from one of decline and decay to one of tentative recovery.

FIGURE 6.1
The Frank D. Reeves Municipal Center at the Time of Its Opening

Photograph from the Kiplinger Research Library, Historical Society of Washington, D.C.
Used with permission.

The District government—now accountable to local voters for the first time in a century—sought innovative ways to invest in the U Street neighborhood. In 1980, when the School Board approved a magnet academic high school serving the entire city, they voted to place it in the U Street area. Overcoming efforts to locate the school in middle-class neighborhoods elsewhere, the board opened Banneker High School near Howard University so that it could draw on nearby university faculty. When Banneker opened in 1984, its nearly all African American student body faced many challenges, ranging from assaults and robberies to abuse on the area's streets.[34] Over time, Banneker has emerged as a rare bright spot in the city's generally declining school system.[35]

Howard University similarly reinvigorated its hospital facilities, opening a medical center on the former site of Griffith Stadium in March 1975. The hospital—which absorbed the functions of the Freedmen's Hospital—became a major medical provider for an otherwise poorly served community. As with the Reeves Building and Banneker High School, the Howard University Medical Center attracted middle-class Washingtonians to the U Street vicinity.[36]

Riding the Green Line

By far the largest public investment in the area proved to be a Metrorail subway line that eventually ran up 7th Street before turning under U Street and continuing uptown under 14th Street. Planning for the subway system's "Mid-City Trunk Line" proved to be especially contentious, with the Reverend Walter Fauntroy, the coalition churches in MICCO, and other community groups playing decisive roles in forcing regional transit authorities to think about how the subway could reshape the U Street neighborhood.

The National Capital Transit Authority initially proposed to serve the "Mid-City" area with a spur off a Connecticut Avenue trunk line, rather than with a main line running under African American neighborhoods directly downtown. But Fauntroy and the Howard University sociologist G. Franklin Edwards convinced the authority's Advisory Board and the National Capital Planning Commission to reconsider their design. Over the course of the 1970s, Fauntroy prompted the planners and the D.C. Council to realign a major Metro trunk line under the Mid-City area at a cost of $3 million above the original cost projection.[37] Yet, given various congressional mandates to provide service to Union Station early in the construction cycle, planning for the Mid-City Line was pushed further and further into the future even as other segments of the Metro system began operation in 1976.[38]

Delays, protests over its construction plans and schedules, troubling engineering reports, and efforts to link its construction to completion of the ill-fated North Central Freeway conspired to delay the construction schedule for what was to become Metrorail's Green Line. Disputes over the location of platforms and entrances added fresh complications along the way. Each delay caused costs to rise, lending support to speculation that this line serving predominantly poor African American communities would never get built. Projected completion dates drifted from 1977 to 1980 to 1984 to 1991.[39]

But Fauntroy and others kept placing as much pressure as they could on the transit authority to honor the commitment to build the Metro line. In August 1985, the Washington Metropolitan Area Transit Authority (WMATA) finally began construction nearly a decade after the system's first line had opened connecting Union Station to the upscale retail and office districts along K Street, NW.[40]

Soil conditions, together with the necessity of reducing costs, prompted WMATA to opt for the highly disruptive cut-and-cover construction technique, rather than tunneling under the streets above the line's route. Thus U Street was converted into a dirty and disruptive construction site for the next half-dozen years.[41] Businesses failed—only Ben's Chili Bowl, Lee's Flower & Card Shop, and the Industrial Bank survived—as Metro construction made it impossible for pedestrians to move along the street. Even those businesses had a tough time, for there was only one convoluted route to Ben's, which reduced its staff to a skeleton crew of a handful of employees. That which was bad for pedestrians proved to be a boon for criminals, who seemingly maneuvered around the building sites with impunity. The historian Zachary Schrag reports that "a block-long stretch of 7th Street turned into a twenty-foot deep garbage pit; residents fretted that children might climb through the shoddy fences and fall in. By the event of completion, a neighborhood resident mourned, 'after five years of construction, the name of the game right now is survival.'"[42]

One good thing about the Metro construction delays was that they enabled planners to work with community leaders to develop more sensitive sitings for the Green Line's tunnels and stations. The result was, in many ways, a triumph of transit-oriented urban design, one fitting for a neighborhood that had been brought to ascendancy by streetcars. The success of Metro planning brought community perspectives to the fore. The problem became how best to harness those successes for neighborhood residents rather than for outsiders with greater economic clout. As Schrag records, the Reverend Jerry Moore, a former WMATA chairman, and Fauntroy were frustrated that the powerful economic forces unleashed by Metro would serve future gentrifiers, most likely whites.[43] Subsequent events would prove their concerns to have been justified. Few casual passers-through the U Street corridor at the time could have guessed what would lay in store.

"Shameful Shaw"

Following Barry's election as mayor in 1978 and Julius Hobson's death the year before, the city's home rule government evolved toward a unified single-party system dominated by the Barry machine.[44] Dubbed "Mayor for Life," Barry began using District payrolls to provide employment to as many African American residents as possible, often with little regard for professional qualifications. Having been convicted of various crimes related to the machine's operations both before and after Barry had become mayor, his former wife Mary Treadwell, his trusted aide Ivanhoe Donaldson, and his girlfriend Karen Johnson all went to jail in 1984, to be followed a few years later by Barry himself.[45] A general air of corrupt incompetence settled over the District government, with the possibility of political competition dissipating with each passing year.[46] By Barry's third term (1987–91), the city provided additional proof of the Argentine novelist Jorge Luis Borges's dictum that single-party systems breed servility and idiocy.[47]

Life on the streets around U Street took its own demoralizing course during this period, as anger and despair grew in the face of what appeared at the time to be continuing economic and physical degradation.[48] The neighborhood attracted all sorts of vice for the same reasons it had attracted all sorts of business a couple of decades before. Illicit entrepreneurs craved the same centrality as those in respectable trades. The area's major streets—7th, 14th, 16th, Georgia Avenue, Florida Avenue, and U Street—gave ready access to every part of the city.

The neighborhood's physical destruction in 1968 combined with the more recent disruptions from subway construction, short hidden alleyways, and an increasingly impoverished population to make U Street and the broader area known as "Shaw" a perfect stalking ground for criminals. These trends converged at a time when a crack cocaine epidemic was driving Washington into the ranks of the most dangerous cities in the United States, with the country's highest murder rate.[49] As one of the characters in George Pelecanos's detective novel *The Sweet Forever* declared about the Third Police District—which encompassed U Street—there was "*always* somthin' goin' on down here."[50]

The arrival of crack cocaine propelled Washington's crime rates to historic levels. Crack came to the city in 1986, after it already had ravaged such cities as Los Angeles, Houston, Detroit, Miami, and New York. Harry S. Jaffe and Tom Sherwood captured these trends when they observed that "adding crack to Washington's dispossessed neighborhoods had the same effect as throwing a match into a bucket of gasoline."[51] Between 1984 and 1989, the proportion of arrested adults testing positive for cocaine increased by 43 percent.[52] Crimes and addiction were spinning out of control.

The dysfunctionality of Barry's D.C. government amplified tendencies toward the flight of the middle class and businesses from central cities, which was generating an economic crisis among most of the nation's large cities. Cases were not being "closed," and criminals increasingly felt that they had a free ride, as the Metropolitan Police Force faced reduced funding, declining numbers, and the hostility of Barry himself.[53] Washington's children were not receiving the training they needed to survive in the formal economy as a highly politicized school system became the focal point for a full-employment program run by Barry's political machine. Public housing projects became sites for open drug markets as the same trends eroding competence in the schools spread to the management of the public housing's stock.[54] And few neighborhoods in the city were more violent than Shaw, which sat in the middle of this growing storm.

A cocaine kingpin, Rayful Edmond III, ran the city's most notorious gang of the era nearby. Edmond passed back and forth through the area from his home base on Orleans and Morton places off Florida Avenue in Northeast Washington.[55] Being located more or less across the street from Gallaudet University, the area's alleys proved to be perfect for scouting the police who, in any event, rarely ventured into the Edmond lair. Customers, meanwhile, had easy access from Florida and New York avenues, both arteries running across major parts of the city and out toward major regional highways. Edmond often was to be found at the Florida Avenue Grill, at 11th and Florida, NW, just north of U Street. He and his colleagues, along with their competitors, fanned out throughout the neighborhood, spreading vice in their wake. They made U Street among the most perilous neighborhoods in the city, region, and nation.

Pelecanos captured the feel of the U Street of the era in his gritty detective novels. Early in *The Sweet Forever*, which was set in the 1980s, he describes a central character, Marcus Clay, watching the "scene unfold" on a U Street neighborhood street. As Clay looked around,

> he saw the familiar, aging residents who came from their two-story 11th Street row houses to see the action. He saw the beat cops who worked his district, one of whom he recognized as a brother who had come out of Cardozo a few years after him. He saw the kid who always stood on the corner at the liquor store, the winos out front. He saw the drug boys leaning against their pretty sports car, just two of the many who were driving middle-class residents out of the city, keeping them away from U, keeping them and their children from patronizing his shop.[56]

Praising the Lord with Good Deeds

Another master novelist, Dinaw Mengestu, described the desperation of the U Street area at the time in a fictional stroll along the streets around nearby Logan Circle: "Few people lived here. Half of the block was entirely burned out or boarded up. There was a unique fear that came with feeling that it was the inanimate objects around you that frightened you most. The crumbling brick facades streaked with black from fires that had raged decades ago didn't need rumors of violence to intimidate. They were frightening enough on their own. Like anything, they had softened with time. All I saw now was how sad and empty they looked—how sad and empty all of these blocks looked."[57]

Despite the depressing streetscape and the visibility of local street crime—with daily accounts of horrific violence on the streets around U Street becoming a common theme for local news broadcasts and newspapers—the U Street of the era was about far more than degradation. As in the Pelecanos account, many longtime residents remained in the neighborhood, even if only as involuntary prisoners of circumstance. The aging owners of two-story row houses, for example, probably couldn't afford to leave even if they had wanted to do so.

Not all U Streeters were looking to move elsewhere. Some—such as John Carlton "Butch" Snipes, the owner of several small businesses in the area, including a deli and convenience store that survived for nearly a decade and a half during the violence and disruptions of the 1970s and 1980s—deepened their commitment to the neighborhood. Snipes became known as "the mayor of U Street" for his food drives for the needy, his sponsorship of the Boys' Clubs and youth athletic teams, and his creation of the Shaw Business and Professional Association. People like Snipes sustained the spirit of the old U against all odds, often in alliance with the neighborhood's churches.[58]

Historically significant congregations joined with temporary storefront chapels in a common struggle to cast a protective social safety net across the area. Congregants often kept their ties to the community through the area's vibrant churches long after they had moved away. Historic Shaw congregations in and around U Street and the vicinity—

such as John Wesley African Methodist Episcopal Zion Church; Shiloh Baptist Church; New Bethel Baptist Church; Fifteenth Street Presbyterian Church; Lincoln Congregational Temple; Saints Paul and Augustine Catholic Church; Augustana Lutheran Church; Luther Place Memorial Church; Elder Lightfoot Solomon Michaux's Temple of Freedom under God, Church of God; and Bishop "Sweet Daddy" McCullough's United House of Prayer for All People—were large, powerful, and increasingly wealthy as their parishioners entered the post–civil rights movement African American middle class.[59] They were joined by the increasingly influential Masjid Muhammad (also known as Muhammad Temple Number 4), founded by the Nation of Islam during the 1930s, and housed after 1960 in a new building near the corner of 4th and P streets, NW, constructed in part with $1.4 million raised by Malcolm X. Other less permanent storefront chapels came and went.[60] Together, these congregations maintained a deep commitment to ameliorating the neighborhood's ills.

These congregations were joined by a number of community-oriented organizations, some of which were creations of Johnson-era "Great Society" programs that had fallen out of fashion by the 1980s. Ibrahim Mumin's Shaw Project Area Committee organized marches against drugs, encouraged local citizens to work more closely with the police, and helped find jobs for local residents. The United Planning Organization similarly thrived with federal and private philanthropic support. Initially a jobs-training initiative, UPO expanded to include early childhood development centers, meal programs for homebound seniors, emergency home weatherization efforts, youth programs, bank-teller training initiatives, antidrug efforts, and a Head Start preschool education program.[61]

UPO's reputation in the community grew when popular radio host Ralph "Petey" Greene joined the UPO staff to devote himself to social work as part of his personal struggle with alcoholism. As his biographer, Lurma Rackley, explained, "Only Petey Greene could inspire people with insults like, 'Stop eating them donuts and get some job training.' He would say he could talk to 'the little people' in their language because he was one of them."[62] And UPO was only one of many community action organizations struggling to sustain U Street and Shaw as a vital and animated community of dignified human beings even as the neighborhood appeared to have been abandoned by official national and local government agencies.

Creatively using a variety of mechanisms to achieve their goals—ranging from minority-banking programs to historic preservation regulations—religious and community groups worked jointly and separately to piece together a variety of initiatives to rebuild, sustain, and nurture the U Street community and those living in it. For example, Howard University faculty members and the LeDroit Park Civic Association, working under the leadership of former mayor Walter Washington and his wife Bennetta Bullock Washington, organized the LeDroit Park Historic District to attract additional capital to their neighborhood.[63] The United House of Prayer for All People renovated Victorian houses around L Street to create the subsidized Madison Homes complex for seniors and other low-income residents, and All Souls Unitarian Church created a housing corporation that built more than 140 low-income housing units on 14th Street, NW.

For its part, UPO developed nearly 2,000 low-income housing units around the neighborhood, and Luther Place Memorial Church constructed the N Street Village, which combined low-cost housing with social services. The nonprofit developer MANNA assisted low- and moderate-income families with owning homes, creating and preserving more than 800 units of affordable housing, including in the historic Whitelaw Hotel. Shaw Junior High School on Rhode Island Avenue and 7th Street was transformed into the Asbury Dwellings, a housing complex for handicapped and elderly neighborhood residents.[64]

Outsiders driving along U Street during the 1970s and 1980s were much more likely to see the disruptive Metro construction, boarded-up storefronts, and narcotics runners that gave rise to the "Shameful Shaw" sobriquet. The area's tawdriness was part—but not all—of the reality of the streets adjacent to U Street and further afield in the Shaw neighborhood generally. Less visible, but no less real, were the community's efforts to fight back—lives were saved, residents succeeded in the face of strong odds that they could not, and the community survived. U Street's religious and social activists of the 1970s and 1980s created a beauty of their own, one that was informed by a wise and humane social intelligence.

The sum of these endeavors proved to be far greater than any individual initiative. They put in place pieces of an urban reality that would make U Street a prime target for revitalization—and gentrification. They guaranteed—at least, they have thus far—that some former residents and other low-income Washingtonians would retain a presence—albeit one that's too small—in the area once the marketplace caught up with the changing realities of the street.

The challenge of understanding these complex processes is rooted in the seemingly undirected nature of what happens in the economic transition from one community equilibrium to another. Writing about another Washington neighborhood affected by the violence of 1968—Adams Morgan—the political scientist Jeffrey Henig observes that "neighborhood gentrification is the result of an accumulation of private market decisions. It is not formally announced, as was public-sector urban renewal; neither its beginning nor its boundaries are unambiguously defined. As a result, neighborhood gentrification is an elusive phenomenon."[65]

It is a difficult process to nurture a revitalized neighborhood so that it maintains the physical and metaphorical space to include those who are less well off but who lived there previously. As Alexander von Hoffman argues,

> No government but a myriad of small private groups has led the drive for community development, a term that encompasses the many and diverse efforts to save the inner city. During the darkest hours, citizens, clergy, and businesspeople have banded together in local nonprofit organizations to halt population flight, abandonment, and capital disinvestment. They have worked not only through churches, government antipoverty agencies, or schools but also through a new kind of association: community development corporations, or CDCs. Operating out of storefronts and sometimes living

rooms, the non-profit organizations ran anticrime programs, developed new homes and retail businesses, instituted job training and day care, and established health care centers. They sometimes failed, but they often succeeded triumphantly.[66]

Incremental change is change nonetheless. If such modification is to benefit those who resided in the area before, those with custodianship for the common good must eschew grand gestures for the hard work of bringing everyone along together. No shopping center or "500-day plan" can replace the difficult process of community building. The fact that so many individuals and institutions became engaged in the fate of U Street provided the area with an opportunity to accumulate renewed vitality. The question that remained unanswered in the 1980s—and remains so today—is whether or not those living in and shaping this restored U Street in the past will have the possibility of benefiting themselves.

The Quiet Storm

In the midst of the social upheavals of these years, music brought together the U Street of "Shameful Shaw" and N Street Village, of Rayful Edmond and Walter Fauntroy, of George Pelecanos and "Butch" Snipes. The music of local stars Roberta Flack, Shirley Horn, Chuck Brown, and Marvin Gaye brought the sounds of U Street to the rest of Washington—and to the world at large. The live music of church choirs, jazz combos, rock bands, and street kids pounding the homegrown go-go rhythms of the city on plastic pails confirmed that U Street had not died. The recorded sounds of rhythm and blues, hip-hop, Stax Records, and Motown on the radio and on vinyl records and tape cassettes created a soundtrack of life on U Street and elsewhere in the city.

The disc jockeys who promoted these sounds may have been the only Washingtonians to reach both the corners of 14th and U and the teenage bedrooms of well-to-do suburban Bethesda, the barbershops of Shaw and the boardrooms of K Street, the headquarters of drug gangs and the offices of top White House aides. Their compass united a city that seemed to share very little other than an allegiance to the local professional football team, the Redskins. In serving such widespread hunger for music, some mom-and-pop radio stations grew to form the core of vast national commercial radio empires. Others passed out of existence or were absorbed by larger broadcasters. In the process, U Street fashioned an African America of the airwaves much as it had nurtured African American vaudeville, theater, basketball, and baseball decades before.

In early 1964, a prison radio announcer, Ralph "Petey" Greene, left a penitentiary near the city with few skills other than a remarkable gift of gab and a voice that sounded great on the radio (figure 6.2).[67] Greene had grown up in Depression-era and wartime Washington's rundown West End and in Georgetown long before either neighborhood became gentrified, raised primarily by his grandmother, Maggie Floyd—better known as A'nt Pig. He attended Stevens Elementary School on 21st Street, NW, Francis Junior High on 23rd Street, NW, and Cardozo High on Clifton Street, NW. Young Petey periodically saw his father (who eventually served prison time in Alcatraz), roamed through the neighborhood, visited friends in black Georgetown, explored Rock Creek Park, hopped on and off of streetcars that took him around the city, and enjoyed various successes playing football and baseball.[68] He dropped out of school at seventeen, a year before he was to graduate, and entered the Army after "two winos" posing as his parents gave false testimony that he was old enough to enlist.[69] He bounced around various Army bases in the States before seeing combat duty in Korea.

FIGURE 6.2
Ralph "Petey" Greene
Holding His Emmy Award

Photograph from the Washington Historical Image Collection, Washingtoniana Division, Martin Luther King Jr. Library, Washington. Used with permission.

Greene returned to the city following his military service with little to recommend him to an employer. He hung out on the streets around U Street, becoming what he himself later called "a wine head bum."[70] He passed in and out of jail on various minor charges for public drunkenness and disturbing the peace before getting arrested on a robbery charge. He eventually ended up in Lorton Penitentiary outside the city after spending two years in the city's jail.[71] Once at Lorton, his life took a fateful turn.

Greene used his gift for conversation to convince the Lorton authorities to allow him to be the emcee of prison talent shows, and to have a show on the prison radio station. The job gave him the perfect cover for an ambitious contraband shell game that he was running to make some extra money from his fellow inmates.[72] His folksy style and humor caught everyone's attention as he used the airways to ingratiate himself with fellow prisoners, guards, and top penitentiary authorities. Dewey Hughes, a superachiever who had climbed his way out of the slums of Southwest Washington, heard Greene while visiting his younger brother Sam, who was serving a long sentence on a rape charge and had little hope of parole. At some point, Sam introduced Petey to Dewey and, in making small talk, Dewey mentioned that he was working at radio station WOL and that Greene should stop by if he was ever released.[73]

Petey, who had already been denied parole once, became desperate to get out. He calculated that he needed to earn the goodwill of prison authorities. One day in the mess hall, he convinced a fellow inmate known as "Baldy" to climb to the top of the prison water tower and threaten to jump. The scam would be that Baldy would ask to speak with Petey, who would talk him down.

The plan worked like a charm.[74] Baldy started the stunt on a day when Donald Clemmer, chief of the Corrections Department, was on the prison grounds. Clemmer, Superintendent Kermit Wheatley, the prison chaplain, and several guards became exasperated at the scene of an inmate threatening to throw himself off a tower. When Baldy said that he would talk to Petey, Greene appeared and played out the scam. Pleased at having avoided the bad publicity of a prison suicide, Clemmer had Greene escorted under guard to the District Building downtown, where he met with staff in the mayor-commissioner's office. When asked how he could be thanked, "Petey nodded humbly, then looked heavenward and silently told A'nt Pig, 'What they don't know is it took me six months to talk that niggah up there.' With an impish grin, he added, 'Think I got a good chance of making parole this time, don't you?'"[75]

Greene was paroled in 1967 and headed straight to Dewey Hughes. Hughes had been part of an effort by WOL management under General Manager John Pace, a white man, to integrate the station. WOL had started broadcasting in 1928 but had been struggling to find a market niche on the increasingly competitive airways of the 1960s. Pace intuitively understood that the African American community represented an untapped market. The station, which was fumbling its way toward one of the first rhythm-and-blues broadcasting formats in the country, was already home to the popular "Nighthawk" Bob Terry, extending its reach deep into black Washington.[76] Dewey convinced Pace to give Greene an audition. Greene cut a tape, which Hughes shared with Pace and the station's African American disc jockeys Sonny Jim Kelsey, Carrol Henson, and "Nighthawk" Bob Terry—a trio known as the "Soul Brothers."[77] Greene won his break, and he immediately connected with the city's African American audience. Terry and Greene cemented their positions as voices of the community in April 1968, when they stayed on the air urging calm throughout the unrest.

Greene faced many internal demons and would fight with alcoholism throughout his career. He helped to start the EFEC—"Efforts for Ex-Convicts"—to assist former prisoners like himself make their way in the community. He worked with the United Planning Organization and, over time, beat his alcoholism with the help of Bishop "Sweet Daddy" McCullough's United House of Prayer for All People.

Having been rebaptized, Greene proselytized the Gospel, eventually moving to religious stations WYCB and WUST.[78] He had become one of the city's most popular media figures by this time, debating white cohost Dick McCormick on an argumentative television show during the late 1960s and launching a wildly successful TV talk show—*Petey Greene's Washington*—in the late 1970s and early 1980s.[79] When he succumbed to cancer in 1984, within days of his fifty-third birthday, more than 20,000 mourners showed up at Union Wesley African Methodist Episcopal Church for his funeral.[80]

WOL's success prompted other local stations to pursue the city's large African American audience. In the years ahead, WPGC-FM, another small station once known by the call letters WBUZ, developed a large listenership. WWRC rebranded itself as WKYS, "the People's Station," riding its way to the top of the charts behind popular announcer Donnie Simpson. The stations added talk radio formats, often with a distinctly political edge. As the white alternative journalist Sam Smith noted, "For blacks, Soul Radio became one major source of communications, particularly WOL, which was relied upon by community organizations to stir up interest and by city officials to calm unrest in between the shouts of DJs like the popular Nighthawk."[81]

The significance of these radio stations extended far beyond U Street—and the city. In 1971, the Washington Post Company donated its radio station WTOP-FM to Howard University (retaining control over WTOP-AM, which would become an all-news station). The dean of Howard's School of Communications, Tony Brown, recruited Catherine Woods from Omaha to run the station, which had been rechristened WHUR-FM. Woods, who married Dewey Hughes, and Brown embraced a popular, sensual jazz music format called "the Quiet Storm" that had been invented by a station intern and future popular disc jockey, Melvin Lindsey, making WHUR the most popular station in the city. Hughes herself became a talk show host, often offending white listeners, as when she vociferously defended Marion Barry following his arrest on cocaine charges.[82]

In 1979, the Hughes couple pooled whatever money they could find to purchase a struggling WOL, which had been damaged by federal investigations into its business dealings. From this base, the couple gained control of eight radio stations in the Washington market. Later, after being divorced from Dewey Hughes, Catherine Hughes further expanded her network, and she eventually owned more than four dozen stations under the Radio One broadcasting company umbrella. Radio One spun off TV One, a partner cable television network oriented toward African American viewers. In February 2008, Hughes' son,

Alfred C. Liggins III, the chief executive of Radio One, announced that the network would relocate to U Street as part of a plan to renovate the historic Howard Theatre.[83]

The Hughes empire did not stand alone. Robert L. Johnson, an African American cable television industry lobbyist, founded the Black Entertainment Television cable network in 1980. Johnson, the ninth of ten children, was born in Hickory, Mississippi, and grew up in Freeport, Illinois. He earned a history degree from the University of Illinois, and a master's degree in international affairs from the Woodrow Wilson School at Princeton University, before arriving in Washington to become a lobbyist.[84] He expanded Black Entertainment Television into a diversified company, extending his business interests into major sports franchises, film companies, and private philanthropy.

Hughes and Johnson placed Washington at the center of the African American media and entertainment industry, much as it had been before World War II. Their reach extended over the entire United States, and into the world at large. And their success rested on a base created by U Street's audiences and personalities, such as Ralph "Petey" Greene and Melvin Lindsey.

The centrality of Soul Radio to the life of the U Street community in the 1960s, 1970s, and 1980s seemed natural. Reflecting on his time conducting the field research that led him to write *Soulside*, the Swedish anthropologist Ulf Hannerz explained, "We see that soul music is not only one of the parts of the soul perspective. By serving also as a running commentary on the other parts, it serves to integrate this thing of shreds and patches into a whole. It gives expression to a great many of the shared understandings of the ghetto, and by giving them an impersonal form—while yet involving intensely personal concerns—soul music also gives them a more official standing as community ideology, above the level of particular personal relationships."[85]

Characters such as Ralph "Petey" Greene and "Nighthawk" Bob Terry were at the center of Hannerz's world as he explored Winston Street and U Street (see chapter 5). Stage performances—which Hannerz notes were often presided over by Greene—became tied to the radio stations, as were conversations about the news and about religion.[86]

"The black radio stations—three in Washington, D.C., WOL, WOOK and WUST," Hannerz concluded,

> have hit music, almost all soul, on their programs more or
> less around the clock, interspersed with newscasts; Sunday
> programming is largely occupied by religious broadcasts
> (mostly services from ghetto churches) and community service
> programs. The radio stations are thus the major channels
> of soul music into the community and thereby contribute
> to strengthening the shared perspective of ghetto dwellers.
> But beyond this, the disc jockeys—who are the leading
> personalities of the community—have their commentaries
> revolving around soulful motifs. The WOL disc jockeys have
> the collective label "the Soul Brothers," and WOOK and
> WUST have followed suit with "the Soul Men," and "the
> Soul Bandits." WOL, the leading station in recent years, has
> had a superman parody serial named "Captain Soul," and one
> of the disc jockeys had a white friend of his elected "honorary
> Negro," with the privilege of burning water melons on white
> persons' front lawns—an inversion of Ku Klux Klan cross
> burning which a ghetto dweller hardly fails to appreciate.
> The disc jockeys express their soulful enjoyment of music in
> cries, shouts, and comments interjected into it, they address
> themselves to the subject of women, and they make references
> to soul food in their running commentaries.[87]

Hannerz had uncovered a community that transcended the ubiquitous physical degradation and destruction so visible to those who drove too quickly down U Street.

Floorboards and Greasepaint

Other performing arts took root in the community as U Street began to recover from the violence of the 1960s and 1970s. Mike Malone and Louis Johnson added a powerful dance component to the D.C. Black

Repertory Company (DCBRC) founded by the nationally renowned actor and Washington native son Robert Hooks. Malone, who grew up in Pittsburgh before entering Georgetown University to earn a degree in French, became a fixture in Washington dance. Malone, who was a tap dancer in his teens, met Josephine Baker while studying at the Sorbonne. He returned to the city to earn a graduate degree in French literature from Howard, and he later entered the graduate program in theater at Catholic University. After a stint on Broadway, he established the Everyman Street Theatre in the late 1960s, and led the DCBRC a few years later. He would teach at Howard until his death in 2006, and he also cofounded the D.C. Public School System's Duke Ellington School of the Arts in 1974, together with Peggy Cooper Cafritz.[88]

Malone teamed up with Louis Johnson to bring modern dance to the city's neighborhoods. Johnson, who had grown up in the U Street area, had gone on to New York to dance with the American Ballet Theater and for Jerome Robbins at the New York City Ballet. His other New York credits included a Tony award for the choreography of *Purlie*, successful choreographic endeavors for the films *Cotton Comes to Harlem* and *The Wiz*, and influential work with the Dance Theatre of Harlem, the Alvin Ailey American Dance Theater, and the Metropolitan Opera. In 1975, he choreographed the Houston Grand Opera's production of Scott Joplin's *Treemonisha*.[89]

Malone and Johnson brought together local dancers and actors for performances promoting the African roots of modern dance at the Smithsonian Institution's Festival of American Folklife, the Carter Barron Amphitheater, the Fort Dupont Outdoor Theatre, the Sylvan Theatre on the National Mall, and Malcolm X Park. Malone's "Black Nativity" became a standard holiday favorite at the Kennedy Center, and his choreography in the 1990s for the Studio Theatre won rave reviews and nominations for the city's theater community's highest honors, and most recognized measure of theatrical success, the Helen Hayes Awards.[90]

According to a Kennedy Center program from June 16, 1973, DCBRC was "developing a Black theater company that is a powerful and vital statement to the Black community; an outlet capable of imparting meaningful ideas."[91] Malone's position at Howard and his long association with the Duke Ellington School of the Arts made him a fixture in the late-twentieth-century Washington arts scene. His participation in the cultural upheavals of the 1970s and 1980s helped to give cultural definition to Washington's claim to be "Chocolate City."

Malone's work in the 1990s with the Studio Theatre also tied him to another development near U Street. By the late 1970s, as the neighborhood struggled against the ravages of high crime and drug dealers, three critically acclaimed theater companies took advantage the area's plummeting rents to open stages that would transform the Washington theater world.[92]

The Source, which opened in 1977, specialized in experimental plays and new works. Before being forced to close by rising rents in 2006, the Source promoted more than 700 plays and was nominated for thirty Helen Hayes Awards from a small theater at 14th and T streets, NW.[93] The company guaranteed that the neighborhood remained a vital center of artistic innovation throughout the disruptions caused by Metro construction, only to fall victim to the gentrification that swept through the area once the Metro line opened. In 2008, the Cultural Development Corporation reopened the facility for the use of several small experimental theater groups in the hope of keeping a presence for theater in the fast-changing neighborhood.[94]

The Source was joined in 1978 by the Studio Theater, founded by Joy Zinoman. The Studio—which began at 1443 Rhode Island Avenue and moved around until it secured the former Peerless and REO automobile showroom at 1333 P Street, just off Logan Circle—has become a major training ground for young actors and is known for its high performance and production values. The company has earned some 200 Helen Hayes Awards, ensuring a central role in Washington theatrical life. Zinoman viewed her company's success as integral to the neighborhood's revitalization, linking the fate of her theater to the well-being of the area and its residents.[95]

In 1980, two New York actors, Howard Shalwitz and Roger Brady, opened the Woolly Mammoth company near the Metro Center subway station. The company moved shortly thereafter to a warehouse on 14th

Street, where it remained for thirteen seasons, until opening a stunning new facility downtown. Having been nominated for more than 130 Helen Hayes Awards, Woolly Mammoth sought out innovative scripts, and it explicitly tried "to forge the future of the art form rather than just preserving its past."[96]

The Source, Studio, and Woolly Mammoth theater companies represented both continuity and change in the neighborhood. Once again, the area surrounding U Street nurtured artistic expression and innovation, transforming the city and the artistic community beyond. They contributed to the neighborhood's tradition of producing beauty in the midst of physical atrophy and hardship.

Simultaneously, they marked a departure from everything U Street had been in the past. These were not African American companies, their founders were not rooted in the community, and their audiences came from elsewhere in the city. They settled along 14th Street because space was available at a price they could afford. Nearly three decades after their arrival, the Studio Theater remains in the general neighborhood (several blocks closer to downtown, near Logan Circle), whereas the Source has been replaced by several smaller experimental companies. Woolly Mammoth moved to its much-admired new facility downtown in 2005. These three groups were early manifestations of a future that combined communities of varied socioeconomic class, race, ethnicity, and sexual orientation at the center of Washington's U Street zone of contact.

Sustaining Hope

The decades following the desegregation decisions of 1954 eviscerated U Street. The members of the area's and the city's African American elites took advantage of access to more up-to-date housing elsewhere in the city. The prestigious African American schools that had attracted those elites to the area fell into the abyss of an increasingly dysfunctional public education system. Impoverished African Americans displaced by urban renewal in Southwest Washington and rural depression in the coastal Carolinas crowded into the area's once-elegant townhouses. Civil disturbances destroyed the neighborhood's physical environment, while a rampaging illicit narcotics trade ravaged its spiritual landscape. U Street's once-vibrant business community lay in ruins. Griffith Stadium was long gone, and the street's great theaters were either closed or on their way out. Most of the famous clubs no longer existed. By the 1980s, U Street—now merely seen as one commercial center of a broader neighborhood known as Shaw—was poorer and more racially homogenous than ever before. Its middle class gone, U street had become the center of Ulf Hannerz's "Soulside."[97]

Yet despite myriad crushing problems, U Street lived. The vigor and creativity of the working-class African American culture that had mesmerized Langston Hughes and Jean Toomer continued to bubble to the surface; the easy conviviality visible at places like Holliday's Pool Hall that once captivated a young Duke Ellington remained. Howard University had no place to go. And the influential churches that had always been the community's backbone stayed in place even as their sprawling congregations commuted from the suburbs.

U Street continued to create beauty along with squalor and anguish. Social inventiveness found a new direction, seeking to redefine social services and housing. Policing and the justice system passed into African American control for the first time with the city's fledgling and imperfect home rule governments. Black Power activists struggled to define what it meant to be "black" in America and in the world, transforming the visual and performing arts.

The emergence of black television programming followed by African American–controlled radio stations redefined U Street's—and Washington's—public space. WOL's Ralph "Petey" Greene, Juwanza Kunjufu, "Yango" Sawyer, and "Nighthawk" Bob Terry—as well as WHUR's Melvin Lindsey and WPFW's Jerry "the Bama" Washington— gave voice to black Washington's working class, speaking a fresh truth. Their audiences shaped the African American community around U Street and around the city. They played critical roles in the city's new community organizations such as the United Planning Organization and Efforts for Ex-Convicts.[98]

U Street continued to bring Washington's blacks and whites crashing together, though in novel ways. Many a white suburban kid learned about the joys of R&B by listening to "Nighthawk," and "the Bama" talked to Washingtonians of all hues and classes throughout the Reagan years. Greene won two Emmy Awards for his television shows, including his impassioned debates with white cohost Dick McCormick on his first TV appearances on WETA-TV in 1969 and 1970.[99] His celebrated talk show *Petey Greene's Washington* pulled large white audiences together with an African American base throughout its run on WDCA-TV between 1976 and 1984. Beginning in the mid-1960s, WDCA and WOOK in Arlington, Virginia, were the first independent television stations in the country to focus primarily on an African American audience. Greene considered a standing ovation following his 1982 commencement address at suburban Montgomery County's predominantly white Walt Whitman High School to be a crowning moment of his life.[100]

Such voices of working-class black Washington reached into the corridors of power. Vice President Hubert Humphrey became a huge "Petey" Greene fan after once hearing his chauffeur surreptitiously listening to Greene's talk show one morning on the way to a day's work at the White House.[101] President Carter invited Greene to a state dinner honoring Yugoslavian president Josip Broz Tito in March 1978. Jerry "the Bama" Washington and his successor "Bama" Nap Turner could count Reagan political Svenghali Lee Atwater, D.C. mayor Marion Barry, *Washington Post* chairman Donald Graham, and future secretary of state Colin Powell among the ranks of their biggest fans.[102] U Street continued to force suspicious and hostile Washingtonians to confront one another; creating new ways of thinking, speaking, and acting in the process.

Despite all its harsh realities, U Street remained Washington's zone of contact throughout the three decades following desegregation. And this era thus was not merely a valley in a once-and-future glorious history that had been lost but somehow was recovered, and miraculously restored, by real estate developers in the 1990s. These years after desegregation were part of a shared history of creativity with what came before—and after.

"Petey" Greene captured the era in describing what he found to be "the most touching thing that ever happened to me." In telling his life story to his biographer, Lurma Rackley, Greene launched into an account of an incident at Ben's Chili Bowl just when U Street seemed to be at its nadir (figure 6.3):

> While I was standing there waiting to get my chili dog half smoke, a nigguh walked up to me with a baby in his hands and he said, "Man, I want you to pray over this baby right now." I said, "Man, I ain't praying over that baby." He said, "Niggah, it ain't my baby. It's that girl's baby back there and as soon as she walked in the door, she said, 'That's Petey Greene, do you know him?' I told her, yeah, I know him, and she said get him to pray over my baby. This woman begged me to bring this baby. Man, I personally could care less about you praying over this baby."
>
> So he called the girl up and three more of them came up and then I could see that they were drug users. The girl was, too. And she had a pretty baby. She said, "Mr. Greene, this is my baby. I listen to you on the radio, along with my mother and everybody. Would you pray over my baby, please, that he won't have no bad luck?"
>
> Now when the conversation gets like this, a complete silence falls. The junkies start to looking. And something in me just seemed like it guided my hand and I put my hand on the baby's head and I began what I thought was going to be a short prayer. I was going to try to pray as low as I possibly could, but when I looked around, I was praying and I was praying loud. I was saying things like, "Father if it's in your power like I know it is, bless this child, bless his mother for having the confidence in me as being one of your workers."
>
> And as I began to pray, everybody got quiet and a funny feeling came over me. It seems as though the prayer was the right prayer and the length of the prayer was long enough for it to be a prayer. Everybody was just at a complete standstill and when I finished, the silence broke when the nigguh turned to the girl and say, "Is you satisfied now?"
>
> She said, "Thank you Mr. Greene." She had tears in her

eyes and two or three of them nigguhs look like they was about to cry. I was sweating.

Now that didn't make me step out of Ben's Chili Bowl and say I am one of God's workers, follow me. But after I got in my car, I just rode and said, "Thank you, Jesus, for preparing me to be able to give that child something to hold onto, and God, many people holding onto your hand 'cause your hand don't never change."[103]

Postsegregation U Street wasn't the same street it had been in the 1920s and 1930s. In many ways, it had been degraded by the social tempest swirling around it. Nonetheless, the era was not a low point between a radiant past and a glorious future. U Street has always managed to give its people something to hold onto, even as it was about to change yet again.

FIGURE 6.3
Ben's Chili Bowl during the 1970s

Photograph from the Kiplinger Research Library, Historical Society of Washington, D.C.
Used with permission.

Profile

Walter Edward Fauntroy (1933–)

Walter E. Fauntroy is a native of the U Street neighborhood (figure 6.4). The son of a housewife and a clerk in the U.S. Patent Office, he grew up in some of the rough-and-tumble nearby streets during the height of the Great Depression and the deprivations of World War II–era rationing. Because he was fearful of crime and the first signs of the drug trade, he sought refuge whenever possible in the New Bethel Baptist Church a couple of blocks south of U Street on 9th Street, NW.

Fauntroy graduated from Dunbar High School in 1952. He attended Virginia Union University in Richmond, drawing on funds raised by New Bethel Baptist Church parishioners at church dinners. He befriended Martin Luther King Jr. while completing his coursework at Virginia Union with distinction before continuing on to earn a degree in divinity from Yale University.

FIGURE 6.4
Walter Fauntroy with Models for Redevelopment of the Shaw Neighborhood

Photograph from the Washington Historical Image Collection, Washingtoniana Division, Martin Luther King Jr. Library, Washington. Used with permission.

Fauntroy returned to the city to become pastor of the New Bethel Baptist Church, the congregation of his youth. The church had been a mainstay of the U Street community since 1915, being particularly known for its work with local youth, its inspirational choir, and its concern with missionary work abroad.

Fauntroy viewed community activism as part of his religious obligations. Following increasing involvement in local Washington protests, King asked Fauntroy to lead the Washington Bureau of the Southern

Christian Leadership Conference. He joined King's inner circle, helping to organize the 1963 March on Washington, the 1965 Selma-to-Montgomery Voting Rights March, and the 1966 Meredith Mississippi Freedom March. President Lyndon Johnson appointed Fauntroy vice chair of the D.C. Council in 1967. He founded the Model Inner City Community Organization, an organization dedicated to protecting the U Street neighborhood from physical destruction through misguided urban renewal and highway projects.

In 1971, Fauntroy was elected the District of Columbia's first nonvoting delegate to the U.S. House of Representatives. He went on to be reelected nine times, serving until 1991. His congressional career was noteworthy for his quest to expand D.C. home rule (including an unsuccessful effort to secure statehood), and for his role as a founding member of the Congressional Black Caucus. In the House, he chaired the Subcommittee on Domestic Monetary Policy and the Subcommittee on International Development, Finance, Trade, and Monetary Policy, as well as serving on the Select Committee to Study Governmental Operations with Respect to Intelligence Activities (chaired by Senator Frank Church). Fauntroy, an accomplished singer, was widely known for bursting into song during political appearances. He retired from Congress in 1991, subsequently running unsuccessfully for D.C. mayor.

Upon leaving elective office, Fauntroy devoted himself to his ministry at New Bethel Baptist Church. His lobbying firm, Walter E. Fauntroy & Associates, represented a number of community-based causes as well as clients intent on advancing racial justice both at home and abroad. Having long been a supporter of the Free South Africa Movement, Fauntroy represented South Africa's African National Congress, and its leader, Nelson Mandela, in the United States. He also continued to be involved in efforts to protect and to improve the U Street neighborhood. He offered his final official sermon to New Bethel congregants on Martin Luther King Jr. Day in 2009, twenty-four hours before Barack Obama was sworn in as president.

CATHERINE L. HUGHES (1947–)

Catherine Elizabeth Woods was born in Omaha to a trombonist and registered nurse, Helen Jones Woods, and an accountant, William Alfred Woods, while her father was studying at Creighton University. The family lived in the Logan Fontenelle Housing Projects.

Catherine enjoyed early academic success as the first African American student at Duchesne Academy of the Sacred Heart, a Roman Catholic girls' school. She began working in the media with a part-time sales job at the African American–owned *Omaha Star* at the age of fourteen. Two years later, her world crumbled when she discovered that she was pregnant. She dropped out of school and married the father of her son Alfred Liggins. The marriage lasted two years, after which she found herself a teenage mother and high school dropout with few prospects. But she was determined to provide for her son's future, and so she pursued her high school education, graduating from the Duchesne Academy in 1964. She subsequently attended the University of Nebraska–Omaha and Creighton University, eventually leaving formal studies for the workplace.

During the early 1970s, Hughes worked for the Reverend Leon H. Sullivan, whose Opportunities Industrialization Center in Omaha received significant foundation funding to promote careers among African American youth. Sullivan became one of the leading advocates of African American "self-help" approaches to overcoming poverty, and as a member of the General Motors Board of Directors, he developed and promoted the "Sullivan Principles," a code of conduct for companies operating in South Africa during the apartheid period. In addition to working for Sullivan, Hughes held a number of jobs in local radio, and promoted African American ownership of local radio stations.

Tony Brown, dean of a newly formed Howard University School of Communications, invited Hughes to join his program on the basis of her success in Omaha. She moved to Washington to lecture and to manage the Howard radio station, WHUR-FM, where she met and married the television producer Dewey Hughes, who had long been active in Washington's African American radio and TV scene. Catherine Hughes promoted the "Quiet Storm" format featuring rhythm-and-blues music with a romantic twist. She simultaneously encouraged African American talk radio formats. WHUR-FM became hugely successful before she left in 1978 to become general manager of WYCB-AM.

In 1979, she and her husband Dewey purchased WOL-AM, a Washington station under investigation by the federal government. They were initially unsuccessful, and her husband left for California, divorcing Catherine in the process. She stayed with WOL, becoming a popular if controversial talk show host. She leveraged her ownership of WOL to launch Radio One, the largest radio broadcasting company oriented toward African Americans. With more than fifty stations in nearly twenty markets across the United States, Radio One became a powerful force in American broadcasting. TV One, a cable and satellite television network, followed in the 1990s.

Radio One joined the exodus from the U Street neighborhood during the 1980s, moving its headquarters to nearby Prince George's County in Maryland. In early 2008, Catherine's son Alfred C. Liggins III, who had become chief executive of Radio One, announced that the company would move back to the U Street area as part of an effort to restore the historic Howard Theatre.

CHAPTER 7

"The New You"

U Street is freestyle. It is about pleasure, excitement.
About music and theatre, jazz and soul, food and fun,
drinks, and more drinks.

—*Skylines*, the Austrian Airlines in-flight magazine, 2008[1]

Saturday, May 11, 1991, was a grand day for U Street. After a long period of construction that had been very disruptive for local residents and businesses (see chapter 6), the Shaw neighborhood's three stations on the Metrorail subway system's Green Line—U Street–Cardozo, Shaw–Howard University, and Mount Vernon Square–UDC (University of the District of Columbia)—were finally opening (figure 7.1 and map 3). But fittingly, everything had not gone as planned. Metro officials, politicians, local clergy, and businesspeople came out for the ribbon cutting to hear D.C. mayor Sharon Pratt Dixon apologize for the day having been so long in coming. (The mayor, who was the former wife of late-1980s D.C. Council chair Arrington Dixon, changed her last name to Kelly after marrying James R. Kelly III in December 1991, at the end of her first year in office). New riders at the Shaw station found a broken escalator and leaks, which presaged the future deterioration of the Metro system as a whole. Most neighborhood residents seemed pleased, however; as thirty-year Shaw resident Hardina Williams explained, "It's going to mean a whole lot because a lot of people here don't drive."[2]

The neighborhood celebrated both the new train service and the freshly paved streets that finally had returned to normal.[3] The Cardozo High School band joined the Shaw and Garnet-Patterson Junior High School bands as well as the McCoullough Sunrisers church band in marching by the pristine stations. The Cardozo-Shaw Neighborhood Association organized a "Taste of U Street" event showing off local restaurants, with

FIGURE 7.1
Metro Construction along U Street

Photograph from the Kiplinger Research Library, Historical Society of Washington, D.C.
Used with permission.

children's and music stages stretched out along U Street. Metro offered free rides to passengers entering the three new stations. The day was festive and full of cheer. U Street was back. But for whom?

For many, the cost had already been too high. Charlie Anderson had closed his Half Dollar Carry-Out just weeks before, after having been in business for a quarter-century. "I feel bad, really bad about it," the seventy-three-year-old Anderson told *Washington Post* writer Linda Wheeler. "Metro would have brought me more customers, but I just couldn't put the landlord off any longer."[4] Faced with revenues collapsing from $250 to $300 a day before Metro construction to under $20 in recent months, Anderson had little choice but to join the more than seventy businesses that had closed during the half-decade of impassable streets and closed sidewalks.

Those that tried to stay open faced the city's increasingly rapacious revenue collectors. Virginia Ali reported that the tax bill for Ben's Chili

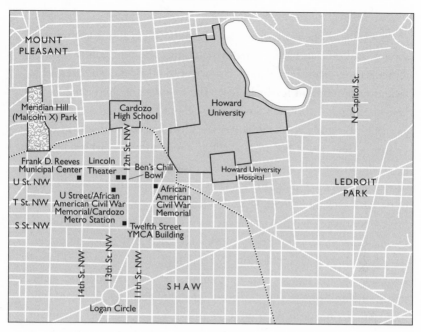

MAP 3
U Street Today
Map by William Nelson.

Bowl had more than doubled, even as steam shovels tore up the sidewalk and street in front of her restaurant, making it impossible for all but the most intrepid customers to find their way to Ben's for its legendary half-smoked hot dog smothered in chili.[5]

Longtime U Street residents wondered if the loudly proclaimed neighborhood renaissance was for them. Why shouldn't they have? As the *Washington Post* Saturday real estate section breathlessly reported at the time, "And now, after being dealt years of hard luck, [the neighborhood is] beginning again to attract young professionals who crave reasonable home prices and are willing to take on the challenges of inner city life. . . . A few businesses have arrived. Price tags on property are climbing. A new community group named for a local street, the French Street Neighborhood Association, is planting trees and fighting crime. Next week, it's conducting its first house tour."

Ironically, all the work that local religious congregations, community groups, and officials had invested in sustaining the community through difficult times made it even more attractive to outsiders, who seemed to lack any appreciation for its history. The founders of the French Street Neighborhood Association so proudly telling reporters that they were planting trees and organizing house tours had few ties to that history.[6]

Just a few years before, in 1983, predominantly white historic preservation activists had touched off a heated row when they sought to extend the Dupont Circle Historic District to incorporate the western edge of the Shaw neighborhood. Shaw residents, led by Ibrahim Mumin and others, beat back what they saw as an intrusion by primarily white, upper-middle-class preservationists to move onto their turf, a neighborhood with little historical connection to Dupont Circle. An angry Mumin declared, "In the area we're talking about, the critical issues are crime, drugs, unemployment, and displacement. All of a sudden, someone who hasn't lifted a finger to do anything purports to be concerned about the community."[7] The proposed extension failed, with Mayor Marion Barry appointing Mumin to the city's historic preservation review board.

Despite the continuing presence of former residents resulting from the creative housing arrangements that had been sponsored by religious and nonprofit organizations, the past's presence seemed to fade as Metro trains began to rumble underneath the neighborhood. The differences between those who were subdued in their reactions to Metro's Green Line and those who were celebrating became increasingly stark. If U Street became "freestyle," could there be any place left for those who had come before?

The Best of Times, the Worst of Times

The good times promised by the opening of Metro's Green Line stood in contrast to the general atmosphere in the city. The trial of Marion Barry on drug charges the previous summer had polarized the city along stark racial lines.[8]

Just the week before, a city often on the edge had been pushed over the precipice of communal violence yet again. As the previous weekend drew to a close, Daniel Enrique Gomez was having some beers with his friend in the Adams Morgan area of the city just uphill from U Street when, at about 7:30 p.m., he was approached by a rookie police officer, Angela Jewell, for violating laws against the public consumption of alcohol.[9] What followed remains unclear—the police claimed Gomez resisted arrest, and eyewitnesses claimed Gomez was already partially handcuffed. In the end, Jewell fired her gun, wounding Gomez. Hundreds of youths tossed rocks and bottles and set police cars on fire in a battle that would last for three nights.[10]

While the confrontation on the streets between Hispanic youths and the police was contained within Adams Morgan and Mount Pleasant, parts of U Street were in a curfew zone sealed off by the police.[11] For the third time in the twentieth century, an area within a mile or two of the intersection of 14th and U had broken out in widespread communal street violence.

Some of the demographic changes that heightened tensions just up the escarpment along 14th and 16th streets were at play around U Street. The African American population was entering a period of decline in older neighborhoods just north of downtown and immediately east of Rock Creek Park.[12] Both Latinos and non-Hispanic whites were moving in, with the latter significantly increasing the area's aggregate income levels. Public drinking became a source of tension between Latino migrants and middle-class residents, two groups that were beginning to reshape formerly African American neighborhoods such as Mount Pleasant.[13] The police were caught in the middle, answering calls from upscale residents to confront Central Americans who looked forward to socializing out-of-doors.

Beyond exposing the anxieties revolving around gentrification, the Mount Pleasant disturbances undercut the authority of newly elected Mayor Sharon Pratt Dixon. For a brief moment, her administration had gained luster by virtue of the simple fact that she was not Marion Barry. However, as time passed, her administration imploded in a cloud of incompetence and unprofessionalism. She never recovered from the tarnish of widespread reports of police ineptitude during the Mount Pleasant events.[14]

"Cash Rules"

As the Mount Pleasant violence abated, midcity neighborhoods once disfigured by the 1968 disturbances—such as Adams Morgan, Mount Pleasant, and U Street—were changing rapidly. This process began well before the arrival of Metro. The small experimental theaters springing up on 14th Street—some of which would evolve into mainstays of the Washington stage scene—were among the first harbingers of new times even as subway construction tore up the neighborhood. Middle-class whites began buying up property. Other changes were taking place as well, suggesting that U Street would be something other than the place to be in African American Washington.

Longtime neighborhood residents became increasingly concerned about what was happening. They noticed improvement, but worried that it was not for them. Maudine R. Cooper, president of the Greater Washington Urban League, noted that "economic revitalization is the only way to get the city going. But there will be casualties."[15] Many in the neighborhood wanted to be sure that they would not be among the dispossessed. As Ernest Drew Jarvis—grandson of former D.C. Council member Charlene Drew Jarvis and great grandson of Dr. Charles Drew— once put it, "The city's hot again. It's vibrant. It's the continuation of the revitalization of the core of the District. I look at that and say, 'These are the neighborhoods I grew up with. This is the city where I will raise my family. I'm not leaving.'"[16]

Just as important, immigrants—including Africans as well as Hispanics—began moving near the area.[17] Tensions grew between these communities and longtime U Streeters. In 2005, when Ethiopian entrepreneurs proposed designating a block of 9th Street between T and U streets as "Little Ethiopia," many African American veterans of the neighborhood rebelled. As seventy-one-year-old Clyde Howard declared, "They haven't paid their dues. Where were they during the [1968] riots? They're Johnny-come-lately. What gives them the right? Just because you opened a store?"[18]

In fact, "just opening a store" might have been part of the problem. Businesses that had once serviced the African American community began to close, as new businesses aimed at immigrants and whites opened up.[19] In a moment of supreme irony, a tanning salon set up shop for a while on U Street between 13th and 14th streets. A neighborhood that was once thought of as a focal point for racial uplift was being replaced by one driven by vulture-like real estate developers. As the Reverend Walter Fauntroy declared to a reporter from the *Washington Post,* "Cash rules in all matters."[20]

This process—widely known as gentrification—was hardly new either to Washington or to African American neighborhoods in other cities around the country. Georgetown—together with Beacon Hill in Boston, the French Quarter in New Orleans, the old quarters of peninsular Charleston, and Old Town Alexandria, Virginia—had been among the first historic neighborhoods in the country to revive as early as the 1940s; to be followed in rapid succession by Capitol Hill, Foggy Bottom, the Kalorama Triangle, Dupont Circle, and other central Washington neighborhoods.[21] Similarly, Harlem in New York and Bronzeville in Chicago had experienced their own transformations at the end of the twentieth century, led in large measure by a rising African American middle class.[22]

Nonetheless, as Jeffrey Henig writes in connection with gentrification in nearby Adams Morgan, experts on cities expected urban change to be synonymous with decline until well into the 1970s.[23] The popular perception of "Shameful Shaw" combined with the disruptions of Metro construction to obscure for most Washingtonians what was taking place on the street. A decade or two later, local residents understood well that urban neighborhoods could be upgraded as well. But for whom?

Henig notes further that gentrification is different from "normal change" in the rapidity of divergence from the past, and in the scope of the transformation that takes place. All aspects of neighborhood life are affected in a compressed time period.[24] As a consequence, the underlying community organization substructure fragments before most residents and outsiders can recognize the impact of gentrification.[25] This is precisely what happened in the U Street neighborhood. Along U Street— as elsewhere in cities undergoing these disruptive changes—many local residents became embittered as their lives were uprooted by forces they could not control.

A *Washington Post* correspondent, Paul Schwartzman, captured this sour mood in a 2006 article examining the neighborhood's "bittersweet renaissance,"[26] writing about longtime area residents W. Norman Wood, Harry "Sonny" Brodgins, and Moses Loften:

> They are among the many homeowners who have lived in Shaw for decades—through the 1968 riots, the crack epidemic, black flight. They are there now for the rebound. Their homes have mushroomed in value, and they are adapting to new neighbors, many of them white and more affluent. And they find themselves confronting a question that arises in any neighborhood where prices skyrocket: Why not sell? But this is not just any neighborhood. These owners are nagged by something deeper and more complicated than how far their wealth would take them or how they would adjust to new surroundings. They fret about the future identity of the neighborhood, a bastion of black culture and history. . . . They know that much of Shaw has been transformed and is gone. But what about the rest? What would become of the black-owned barbershops and shoe shops, the familiar faces who still congregate on the corners? Would the presence of African Americans be erased and eventually forgotten?[27]

A month later, *Washington Post* reporter Teresa Wiltz wrote about a new U Street enthusiast named Shmar. "At 20, almost 21," Wiltz noted,

> Shmar is all about the new U Street. Condos, funky boutiques, hip restaurants. She lives around Eastern Market, but U Street is her home. She has a fiancé at Howard and a job at the Wild Women Wear Red shoe store. Which is where she is standing, right now, hair pouffed up and out in a righteous, 2006 'fro, breaking it down. For Shmar, U Street is. It's poetry readings and veggie burgers at Busboys and Poets. It's boho chic at Wild Women and club girl gear at Pink November. It's a $5,000 sectional in lipstick-red leather

at Urban Essentials. It's the design-award-winning Langston Lofts, with condominiums now reselling for $400,000-plus. It's CakeLove cupcakes and owner Warren Brown's show on the Food Network. It's *Lion King Reloaded*, D.C. youth's take on the original *Lion King*, landing at the Lincoln Theatre in time for Black History Month. It's chilled-out jazz at the Bohemian Caverns and Yerba Buena steaming up the Black Cat with a potent set of Afro-Cuban/funk fusion on a hot summer night. It's the African American Civil War Memorial and affluent whites walking mountain bikes down the block. U Street is renewal and gentrification.[28]

The story of post-Metro U Street—the "New You"—is about the crashing together of the worlds of W. Norman Wood, Harry "Sonny" Brodgins, and Moses Loften on the one hand and of Shmar on the other. It is about how these dramatic changes played out in a District of Columbia that was itself becoming something new and different.

Enter the Control Board

The Dixon administration foundered following the Mount Pleasant disturbances and was damaged further by the constant attention focused on Barry.[29] After being released from jail in 1991, Barry returned to the city to a hero's welcome in the city's poorest neighborhoods across the Anacostia River. Barry dove back into local politics in November 1992, getting himself elected to the Ward Eight D.C. Council seat representing trans-Anacostia. Barry's powerful story of Christian redemption resonated among many of the city's African American poor. He played to African American fears of a white conspiracy to take back the city from them ("the Plan," as it was known on city streets). A haughtily judgmental editorial in the *Washington Post* opposing Barry's election only reconfirmed the suspicion of many that the city's white, corporate interests had plans of their own for its future. By the end of 1994, Barry was about to become mayor of the District of Columbia once again, with a fourth term set to begin in January 1995.[30]

Barry's triumphant return brought him the personal redemption that he so eagerly sought. Yet he could not recover his old political magic. The city had evolved, as had its politics, and much of his traditional political base had moved to nearby Prince George's County in Maryland. Perhaps more important, conservative Republicans had gained control of the House of Representatives at the same time, amplifying congressional hostility toward the city.[31] Barry himself was tired, while the civil rights municipal regime that had taken power at the outset of home rule in the 1970s increasingly was bereft of energy and fresh ideas.

Delegate Eleanor Holmes Norton, the city's nonvoting member of the House of Representatives, filled the local leadership vacuum left by the dissipation of Barry's power. Holmes Norton grew up in the U Street neighborhood and graduated from Dunbar High, experiences she recalls fondly in her memoir *Fire in My Soul*.[32]

Holmes Norton followed in the footsteps of other illustrious U Street achievers, combining professional accomplishment with community activism. She left Washington for college, completing her undergraduate education at Antioch College in Ohio, before receiving an MA and a law degree at Yale during the early 1960s. She became an organizer for the Student Nonviolent Coordinating Committee and participated in the Mississippi Freedom Summer with leading civil rights leaders such as Medgar Evers and Fannie Lou Hamer. Following law school, she served as a law clerk to a Federal District Court judge, A. Leon Higginbotham Jr., and worked as assistant legal director for the American Civil Liberties Union. She became the head of the New York City Human Rights Commission under Mayor John Lindsay, and was appointed as the first female chair of the U.S. Equal Employment Opportunity Commission by President Jimmy Carter. She began teaching law at New York University before joining the faculty of Georgetown University Law Center in Washington. She was elected the city's delegate to the House to replace the departing Walter Fauntroy in 1990 and effectively used her position in Congress to promote city-related causes. Her arrival on Capitol Hill coincided with one of her native city's most delicate political moments.

President Bill Clinton and congressional leaders had wasted no time reining in the newly reelected Barry and the D.C. government, passing Public Law 108-4 in early 1995 establishing the D.C. Financial Responsibility and Management Assistance Authority, known as the "Control Board."[33] The board's five members and their staff under the chairmanship of former Federal Reserve Board member Andrew Brimmer gained control over the city's finances by the end of the summer.

The Control Board generally won praise for bringing order to the city's finances, enabling the authority to pass out of existence ahead of schedule on September 30, 2001.[34] Nearly all the critical figures involved in the board were African American, marking a break with previous congressional interventions in the city's affairs.[35] The macro-level achievements were impressive, reducing the D.C. government's costs by tens of millions of dollars while also dramatically reducing its employment rolls by the thousands.[36] The board's chief financial officer, Anthony Williams, would himself become elected mayor in 1998 following Barry's listless fourth term.[37]

Nonetheless, there were a number of miscues—particularly surrounding the Control Board's ill-fated effort to assume control over the city's public schools under the direction of retired army general Julius W. Becton Jr.[38] The D.C. Council eventually modified, suspended, or terminated several board initiatives—such as an especially inept "master license" program for consultants and freelance contractors.[39] Local evaluations of the board and its actions were highly racialized. As Michael K. Fauntroy observed, "A March 1995 public opinion poll indicated that DC Whites favored the Control Board by a 70 to 26 percent margin; DC Blacks opposed the legislation 31 to 62 percent."[40]

Effective or not, the Control Board's actions combined with increased congressional oversight at a time of conservative Republican ascendancy to give freer rein to economic interests to have their way with the city.[41] The city's economy boomed, real estate prices soared, and the city's capacity to regulate predatory business practices withered just as Metro's new Green Line opened up U Street as the next gentrification frontier. The deck was stacked against efforts to upgrade the neighborhood by improving the lot of those living in it. More and more, the "New You" literally meant a new "You" of new residents and business owners, with old-timers being forced elsewhere.

Who Gets the History?

In 1999, D.C. Council member Charlene Drew Jarvis—the daughter of distinguished Howard University blood plasma specialist Charles Drew—articulated one strategy for integrating the old-timers and newcomers in Shaw in the popular monthly *Washingtonian* magazine.[42] Jarvis, who subsequently would be defeated by newcomer Adrian Fenty in a run for reelection a year later, advocated creating a "civic" consciousness that would be sufficiently broad so as to accommodate and honor a multitude of competing neighborhood realities.

When asked how the down-at-the-heels African American neighborhood around U Street might peacefully absorb an influx of upscale, primarily white residents, Jarvis pointed to the soothing effect of a shared history for "tamp[ing] down the friction, at least between blacks and whites." She continued: "Many black residents know the history. Now white residents who come into the community want to learn. Your neighborhood becomes known not for drug trafficking but for its history."

Jarvis's belief in the unifying possibilities of U Street's history proved to be misplaced in a neighborhood where groups and individuals competed for ownership. The answer to the question of who could assert ownership over history turned out to be as contested as the answer to the question of who could assert ownership over the area's land, buildings, housing, and businesses. Was the area's story one of families, as Rohulamin Quander would declare at a 2004 conference on local history?[43] Was it one of "a focal point of black life in America," as the narrator of a Public Broadcasting System television documentary on the neighborhood proudly proclaimed?[44] Was it local? National? Multiracial? African American? The appropriate answers to all these questions changed depending on who was asking and who was answering.

U Street—as the space where Washington's cultures met, clashed, and came to terms with one another in changing and asymmetrical hierarchies of power and wealth, as Washington's "zone of contact"—represented something different to the diverse groups that claimed an association with the area.[45] Its history had remained a rather straightforward affair when the neighborhood had become a predominantly working-class African American one following the end of Jim Crow in the city; when U Street was downtown Chocolate City. U Street's history would become highly contentious once gentrification placed quite different racial, ethnic, and socioeconomic groups in competition with one another. As one observer of the local scene, Stephanie Barbara Frank, put it, "If we own the story, we own the place."[46] But who were "we" along the U Street of the 1990s? History exacerbated rather than tamped down the frictions that existed in an ever-fragmenting neighborhood.

Few Washingtonians have done more to promote local history than Kathryn Schneider Smith. Her tireless advocacy of the city's history has included an important role in developing the Washington history curriculum in local public schools, leadership of the Historical Society of Washington, D.C., and founding of the local history journal *Washington History*.[47] She has published invaluable source guides on Washington history and has personally encouraged many of the scholars whose publications are cited in the notes to this volume.[48]

In 1996, Smith attended a regional conference devoted to the concept of "cultural tourism." The notion of using culture as a tourist attraction had been enunciated a year earlier at the White House Conference on Travel and Tourism and quickly gained currency in the travel industry. Smith and others—particularly Carmen James Lane, Barbara Wolfson, and Francine Cary of the Humanities Council of Washington D.C., as well as Barbara Franco of the Historical Society—appreciated the potential benefits for the city and its historical and cultural organizations if tourists could be drawn from the well-known attractions around the National Mall into Washington's neighborhoods and downtown.[49] They took the lead in attracting other cultural organizations in the community to establish the D.C. Heritage Tourism Coalition in 1996, which in 2003 was renamed Cultural Tourism D.C. Smith served as the organization's first executive director until early 2005.[50] Within a few years, the group had brought together more than two hundred arts, heritage, cultural, and community organizations to make the history and culture of the city more accessible to tourists and residents by creating walking tours, neighborhood heritage trails, brochures, theme-based citywide cultural events, and other programming that presented the entire city, on and beyond the Mall, as a cultural destination.[51]

Smith long had appreciated the importance of African Americans for Washington history. She began promoting the importance of tourism becoming linked to the special place of African Americans in the city during the 1960s. Her husband, Sam Smith, picked up the idea and pursued it further in a volume promoting statehood for the District of Columbia, observing that tourism remained among the city's least-utilized economic resources. "Today," Smith wrote in 1974, "the Washington tourist is shoddily treated: forced to stand in long lines to visit the major sights; hustled kitsch souvenirs and over-priced food; and carted long distances to suburban motels. Life could be made more pleasant for both the tourist and Washington if the city would provide more services, facilities, recreation, and entertainment for tourists."[52] Smith continued that "the city has totally failed to take advantage of one of its unique assets: its blackness. Properly promoted, Washington could become the Quebec of America, attracting people not just because it is a center of monuments and political power, but because it is culturally unique. This would mean jobs and money for black residents."[53]

The Smiths were ahead of their time. Their focus on tourism as an economic engine for city neighborhoods combined with the city's African American heritage as a primary marketing tool foretold the conceptual framework used by those who established Cultural Tourism D.C. Within this context, the U Street area became an initial focus of Cultural Tourism D.C.'s efforts, in part because of the neighborhood's rich history, and in part because the newly opened Green Line had made U Street more easily accessible to tourists.

When Kathryn Smith was serving as a consultant in the mid-1990s to the Thurgood Marshall Center for Service and Heritage in the newly renovated Twelfth Street YMCA building, she undertook interviewing longtime area residents. She asked them for their suggestions about appropriate exhibitions for the center's new space, and elsewhere in the neighborhood. Her interlocutors spoke passionately about the community's achievements against great odds, urging her to find ways for making this story more widely known.[54] Accordingly, Smith and her colleagues focused on the area's earlier status as a rival to New York's Harlem as the center of national African American culture.

Shortly thereafter, Cultural Tourism D.C. opened the African American Heritage Trail, which stretched across the entire city, as well as the U Street Heritage Trail, titled "City within a City." Both trails mentioned the comparison with the Big Apple. An accompanying local walking tour—"Before Harlem, There Was U Street"—was even more explicit in elevating U Street above Harlem before World War I.[55] The same basic approach to the area's history was taken by the Shaw Ecovillage Project's bicycle tour of the area, as well as in the D.C. Preservation League's applications for historic district recognition.[56]

"Duke's Place"

These efforts led others to follow suit. In 2002, the "Images of America" series of small photograph albums about various towns and neighborhoods around the country added a volume to its series dedicated to U Street. Several articles in the *Washington Post* took an analogous stance, as did a 1999 PBS television special.[57] In 1997, Mobil Oil and several local businesses sponsored the painting of a large portrait of Duke Ellington by the muralist G. Byron Peck on the side of the Mood Indigo memorabilia shop at 1214 U Street, near the U Street Metro station. A dozen years later, the city's residents voted to place an image of Ellington on the back of a new D.C. commemorative quarter to be issued by the U.S. Mint in 2009.[58] U Street was becoming "Duke's Place."

This focus on national personages such as Ellington drew criticism from several directions. For some, such as Frank, Cultural Tourism D.C. selectively presented a neighborhood history that ignored both poorer residents and the accomplishments of the superficially less noteworthy period of the 1970s and 1980s.[59] Historic preservation and cultural heritage activities in the U Street area were "revanchist," in that they facilitated the conversion of Washington's African American historic center into a white middle-class neighborhood.[60] For Frank, Cultural Tourism D.C. filled the void left by the absence of any comprehensive

neighborhood history and "created what remains the dominant narrative
of the neighboring history. . . . That history is simplistic, narrowly focused
on the period between 1920 and 1950, and almost entirely centered on
the black middle-class experience of Greater U Street while betraying its
racial, ethnic, and economic diversity."[61]

However good the intentions of Smith and her colleagues may have
been, Frank continues, as outsiders "their interests, interpretations and
framing with cultural baggage and politics unique to their situation that
do not necessarily coordinate—and may be glaringly at odds—with some
insiders' interests, desires, and especially stories. Participation of insiders
may mitigate such discrepancies, but it does not diminish them."[62]

For others, the abrogation of the U Street story by outsiders is about race
as much as economics, conforming to a larger struggle for neighborhood
dominance in which white "vigilantes" have systematically carried
forward "an attack on black interests." As the longtime African American
neighborhood activist and Advisory Neighborhood Commission
member Lawrence Guyot explained to Frank, "the problem with race
in Washington is that it involves everything. There's nothing done in
Washington that's not done through the prism of race, but there is no
public dialogue which makes it more dangerous, more devastating."[63]
Guyot noted further that battles erupt over history, over liquor license
applications, over housing prices, and over entertainment spots as
newcomers residing in expensive condominiums bring expectations of
suburban calm to a historically raucous neighborhood.

Cultural Tourism D.C. does not ignore the presence of poorer African
Americans and the less glorious periods of the neighborhood's history.
The materials relating to the organization's heritage trail for the larger
Shaw neighborhood are open about the neighborhood's evolving place
in between many of Washington's geographic, social, economic, gender,
and racial divides.[64] A December 2004 conference sponsored by Cultural
Tourism D.C. examining the history of Shaw sought to provide an
opportunity for residents and historians to talk about what was being
left out of representations of the neighborhood's history. The discussion
devoted considerable attention to family and local histories embracing
the entire U Street story, including the years of "Shameful Shaw." The

sessions simultaneously exposed deep divisions within the community over who gets to "tell the story," and whose "story" it should be.[65]

Critics such as Frank and Guyot are correct in seeing efforts to reinvigorate a broad appreciation of the neighborhood's past as part of a larger struggle over who gets to dominate U Street's future by defining who has a legitimate claim to its past. Gentrification has one meaning if well-off middle-class young adults of all races force out working-class African American families, but quite a different one if they are reclaiming for the affluent what always had been a prosperous neighborhood that simply fell on hard times.

The efforts by Smith and others began modestly as they sought to give voice to residents who were proud of their community's history. The stakes involved in this retelling grew enormously as many from both within and outside the neighborhood began to look for ways to leverage the opening of the new Metro stations for economic gain. A distinguished amateur U Street historian, Henry P. Whitehead, and the founder of the U Street Festival, Chauncey Lyles, tried to work with Cultural Tourism D.C. to pull the focus of the effort back to community residents. Cultural Tourism D.C. joined with the U Street Festival Foundation, the Thurgood Marshall Trust, and others to collect oral histories and artifacts, and to hold neighborhood seminars and festivals proclaiming U Street's glorious past.[66] By the late 1990s, Cultural Tourism D.C. had even launched a bus tour of the area.

Smith, Whitehead, the social historian Marya McQuirter, the informal U Street "mayor" John "Butch" Snipes, and a number of African American sculptors and artists joined forces to mount permanent displays telling the neighborhood's stories in the windows of prominent businesses and on a block-long fence left behind from the Metro construction that closed off a vacant lot.[67] That lot—which eventually would become the site of the Ellington Condominium building on the north side of U Street between 13th and 14th streets—was the temporary home of the popular Georgetown Flea Market, which had been forced to relocate when it lost its weekend site across town. Consequently, Washingtonians of many diverse classes, races, and ethnicities discovered the neighborhood's distinguished history as they came in search for bargains on Sundays or merely walked down the street on their daily business every other day of the week. For two and a half years, the display remained on view on the fence, under the sponsorship of the Washington Metropolitan Area Transit Authority, before being moved indoors along the running track in the gym at the Thurgood Marshall Center.

A second, more complicated tension began to emerge as the neighborhood "recovered." Were the neighborhood's many hallowed sites representative of local achievements, accomplishments of the entire city, or national successes? Four prominent history-oriented projects reveal how different interpretations of U Street's significance found expression in the physical restoration of the neighborhood. Two of these projects—the restorations of the Twelfth Street YMCA and of True Reformer Hall—acknowledged the neighborhood; a third—the restoration of the Lincoln Theatre—became contested between the African American community and pressure to serve the city as a whole; and a fourth—a new monument honoring African American Civil War soldiers—sought to honor national achievement.

Restoring Whose History?

As noted in previous chapters, the Twelfth Street YMCA had been a landmark institution for neighborhood children ever since President Theodore Roosevelt set down the cornerstone for the new building in 1908 (figure 7.2). As already noted, the prominent African American architect William Sidney Pittman designed the building, which was constructed with funding provided in part by Julius Rosenwald and John D. Rockefeller at the instigation of President William Howard Taft. The facility housed the first African American YMCA, which had been founded by Anthony Bowen in 1853. The Y, which was named for Bowen in 1972, closed at the Twelfth Street location 1982, moving to a different site near the intersection of 14th and W streets, NW, despite deeply divisive community protests and several lawsuits seeking to block the move.[68] The building stood vacant for many years with its beloved swimming pool and gymnasium slowly collapsing from prolonged exposure to the elements.

Jeffrey Cohen purchased the building in 1985, agreeing to rent the facility to the Shaw Heritage Trust for $1 a year.[69] He turned the building over to the trust, which subsequently faced difficulties in raising the funds required to undertake renovations. Finally, in February 2000, the trust completed the project and reopened the building as the Thurgood Marshall Center for Service and Heritage, providing space to the trust, a small neighborhood museum, and locally oriented social programs.

The Marshall Center has offered invaluable support to the community, promoting both social services and the preservation of the neighborhood's heritage with a focus on community achievements of both national and local significance. In early 2009, the center marked the building's centennial by inviting Thurgood Marshall's widow, Cissy Marshall, and Theodore Roosevelt's great grandson, Kermit Roosevelt, to reenact the original cornerstone-laying ceremony, mounting an exhibit of the items placed there so carefully when the building was built and replacing them with headlines about President Barack Obama's election and inauguration. The center honored a half-dozen black leaders who had shaped the community, including Walter E. Fauntroy, Marion Barry, Thomas B. Hargrave Jr., and Ibrahim C. Mumin. Hargrave, who had been YMCA president at the time the old Y closed, and Mumin, a longtime Shaw community activist, had been on opposite sides of the bitter struggle over the fate of the Y two decades earlier.[70]

FIGURE 7.2
The Twelfth Street YMCA

Photograph by David Hawxhurst /
Woodrow Wilson Center.

Around the corner, the African American architect John A. Lankford's True Reformer Hall—built in 1903 by a Richmond benevolent association to serve as a community center—served as a prominent neighborhood center hosting fiery political meetings, small groups of businessmen, social clubs, lively weekend dances featuring local musicians such as a young Duke Ellington, and the first African American basketball league in the country.[71] The building was home to the Knights of Pythias following World War I and, at the end of the 1930s, to the only branch of the Metropolitan Police Boys Club to admit African American children. When World War II broke out, True Reformer Hall was converted to an armed forces recruiting center and, following the war, became a distribution center for the Metropolitan (Duron) Paint Company.[72]

The Duron Company abandoned the building following the 1968 upheavals. The structure remained vacant until the 1990s, when J. J. Development, Inc., purchased and began to restore it.[73] The Public Welfare Foundation—an organization that gives away nearly $20 million a year to promote a number of self-help initiatives around the world—joined in the restoration effort, moving its headquarters from the Watergate office complex on the Potomac River near Georgetown to U Street in 2001.[74] Since that time, True Reformer Hall has been a positive presence next to the U Street Metro station between 12th and 13th streets across the street from the Lincoln Theatre, fulfilling its original function as a community center (figure 7.3).

The Thurgood Marshall Center and True Reformer Hall have fortified a neighborhood-oriented approach that seeks to build on U Street's past to sustain an economically diverse community rooted in the area's African American heritage. These facilities— and the institutions they make possible—demonstrate that small preservation projects can provide a local counterweight to the powerful forces of gentrification sweeping through the neighborhood.

FIGURE 7.3
The Renovated True Reformer Building with a Mural of Edward Kennedy "Duke" Ellington

Photograph by David Hawxhurst / Woodrow Wilson Center.

The restored Lincoln Theatre across U Street from True Reformer Hall has reemerged from years of degradation to serve as a cultural resource for the broader African American community throughout the city. After it opened in 1922, with more than 1,600 seats, it became one of the most important movie palaces along U Street—which at its height had three major cinemas, the Republic, Lincoln, and Dunbar; a major live performance venue, the Howard; and several smaller establishments that also showed movies, such as the Minnehaha.[75] Like everything else in the area, the Lincoln had fallen on hard times following 1968. For a time, it was part of Jeffrey Cohen's ambitious plans for the neighborhood (see chapter 6), but the city assumed its ownership from the developer in 1991.[76] The city intended to operate it as a 1,350-seat performing arts center under the direction of the Lincoln Theatre Foundation.[77]

The city delivered on its promises. Spurred on by the theater's location across the street from the new U Street Metro station, the Kelly administration dove ahead in moving the process along. Picking up where Cohen had left off, construction crews faced enormous challenges as they discovered a building flooded waist deep from a leaking roof and broken pipes inhabited by hundreds of rats. They nonetheless were able to complete $9 million worth of structural renovations by August 1993. In September, D.C. Council member Frank Smith hosted a "sneak preview" featuring Martha Reeves and the Vandellas to a wildly enthusiastic reception.[78] "Butch" Snipes declared that the renewed theater would be a "shot in the arm to draw people into the area."[79]

More work was necessary to put on the final touches before the Lincoln's grand official reopening in February 1994. That event featured a gala performance of a musical drama honoring Martin Luther King Jr.—*Ain't Got Long to Stay Here*—with a surprise appearance by the legendary Cab Calloway and an official ribbon cutting by Mayor Sharon Pratt Kelly.[80] D.C. Council member Charlene Drew Jarvis spoke for many when she declared, "My heart is fluttering because U Street is where I walked as a child."[81]

The Lincoln Theatre Foundation and the theater's various managers were committed to showcasing African American performances, such as the opening production of *Ain't Got Long to Stay Here*. The Lincoln staged jazz performances, local dance and film festivals, and, following 2005, the Duke Ellington Jazz Festival. The theater sponsored plays such as Carole Mumin's *Where Eagles Fly*, which told the story of an elderly woman who fought to preserve the Shaw neighborhood and promote its history.[82] The theater's custodians viewed their mission as serving the city's African American community, many among whom, like Council member Jarvis, identified the Lincoln with the city of their youth.

However, the theater began to struggle financially within a few years because its programming failed to attract an audience to fill enough seats to make the grand former movie palace economically viable. Initially, the growing revenue gap was closed with grants from the District government. The government, in turn, placed increasing pressure on management to be more ambitious in reaching out to a larger and more diverse Washington metropolitan regional audience. Thus, the struggles between visions of U Street as a restored family-oriented home to African Americans and U Street as an economic resource for the whole city were being played out inside the Lincoln Theatre. In early January 2007—a little more than a week into Mayor Adrian Fenty's new administration in the District Building—Lincoln director Janice Hill told the press that the theater might have to shut down. The District government stepped in with a $200,000 emergency grant, and Council member Jim Graham promoted adding a line item in the annual D.C. government budget to underwrite the theater at $500,000 a year.[83]

Unlike the Thurgood Marshall Center and True Reformer Hall, which have unabashedly neighborhood-oriented missions, the Lincoln Theatre has been caught trying to serve several competing masters. Given the role of the District government in funding the restoration and in keeping the stage lights lit, the Lincoln increasingly has been drawn toward serving a much wider and diverse audience. This process has been an uncomfortable one, highlighting the tensions evident in so many aspects of life in the gentrifying "New You."

Revenue from the theater's September 1993 sneak preview, hosted by D.C. Council member Frank Smith, went to support another project, one that has a clear national mission: the African American Civil War Memorial.[84] Smith, a civil rights activist from Georgia, had been a founding member of the Student Nonviolent Coordinating Committee who came to the city in 1968 to work at the Institute for Policy Studies, a left-leaning think tank near Dupont Circle. He jumped into local politics, getting himself elected to an Advisory Neighborhood Commission position and to the Board of Education before moving to the D.C. Council in 1982 representing Ward One (which includes such midcity neighborhoods as U Street, Shaw, Adams Morgan, and Mount Pleasant). He served four terms, leaving office in 1998 at the height of the city's disaffection with financial strictures imposed by the congressionally appointed Control Board. He immediately threw himself into establishing the memorial.

The memorial, which was built with contributions large and small from African Americans around the country—much as Carter G. Woodson had sustained his Association for the Study of Negro Life and History decades before—rose on land next to the Shaw–Howard University Metro station donated by the transit authority as part of a program to repay the community for the construction-related disruptions of the late 1980s. The effort completed the dream of African American Civil War veteran and Ohio representative George Washington Williams more than a century before. Williams had sought to memorialize the sacrifice of African Americans such as himself who had fought throughout the war in segregated regiments. An eleven-foot statue of six soldiers by the prominent African American sculpture Ed Hamilton stands at the center of a plaza surrounded by polished granite walls engraved with the names of

FIGURE 7.4
The African American Civil War Memorial

Photograph by David Hawxhurst /
Woodrow Wilson Center.

230,000 African Americans and 7,000 white officers who fought with them for the Union cause (figure 7.4).[85]

At the monument's July 1998 dedication ceremony—attended by a multitude that included two thousand descendants of the memorialized soldiers—D.C. Council chairperson Linda Cropp told the crowd that "today we all stand taller. History has not been changed. History has been recognized."[86] The National Park Service eventually assumed responsibility for the site, opening an information center and small museum in nearby True Reformer Hall.[87] With its location adjacent to a Metro station, the monument is sought out by tourists visiting the city, thereby luring them into the neighborhood.

These four projects—the Thurgood Marshall Center, True Reformer Hall, the Lincoln Theatre, and the African American Civil War Memorial—stand along today's U Street giving tangible presence to the varied local realities being reshaped by gentrification. Only the Howard Theatre among the street's major surviving historic buildings remains unrestored.[88] Together, they reflect the emergence of a new community that is wealthier and more connected to the larger world than was the case a generation ago. They simultaneously demonstrate that U Street's "revival" and the rediscovery of its own history have been more complex than the mere assertion of a new economic or racial hegemony. They reveal the centrality of conflict over who gets U Street's history—and over who can claim ownership of the city as a whole—at a time when the era's increasingly unbridled globalizing economy was transforming the city.

A Pragmatic Municipal Regime

Many in the city had found the combination of Marion Barry's fourth term and the imposition of the Control Board by Congress especially dispiriting. Against this demoralized backdrop, Anthony Williams, the Control Board's chief financial officer, was among the few figures whose stock rose quickly. Williams grew up in a poor family in Los Angeles, before entering Yale College and earning both a law degree and a public policy degree from Harvard. He was elected to the City Council in New Haven, Connecticut, and came to Washington to serve as the top accounting official in the U.S. Department of Agriculture. He was, in many ways, the antithesis of Barry.[89]

Williams was one among many pragmatists emerging on the city's political scene as the civil rights activists who came to power at the dawn of home rule (see chapter 5) began to disappear from political life.[90] His financial wizardry for the Control Board caught the attention of Congress and the media, and so his decision to run for mayor in 1998 had an air of inevitability.[91] By the time the dust had settled on the 1998 municipal elections, the bow-tied accountant-mayor Williams presided over the city—along with a gaggle of newcomers on a majority-white District Council, which was a true departure resulting in a new post–civil rights generation of home rule politicians.[92]

These newcomers had appeared thanks to the opportunities offered by the city's new Advisory Neighborhood Commissions (ANCs), which provided a pool of fresh candidates ready to run for higher office as the once seemingly invincible first home rule generation left the scene. The ANCs had been established under the city's home rule charter to give citizens a chance to participate at the neighborhood level in making political decisions. The city was divided into three dozen ANC districts, with each in turn divided into single-member districts for every 2,000 residents.

Most observers had failed to notice what had been taking place with the ANCs because, despite their ambitious participatory intentions, they had always been something of a poor stepchild for the D.C. government, having minimal budgets and no direct powers. Many of the unremunerated ANC seats remained vacant or uncontested. But a few ANCs—especially in wealthier neighborhoods—developed into vehicles for local debate. Community activists grabbed whatever minimal power and authority that might have been vested in their ANC to ward off unwanted interference from "downtown," and to demand improved services for their neighborhoods.[93] Thus, if the first home rule elite had emerged from the early School Board elections of the late 1960s and early 1970s, Washington's post-1998 elected municipal elite—epitomized by the new Council members—had cut their political teeth on the ANCs.

Ward Two Council member Jack Evans initially took this path to city office when he was elected to the Council to replace John A. Wilson, who had just won the race for District Council chair in 1990. In the next several years, Jim Graham, Adrian Fenty, and Sandy Allen were likewise elected to the Council from several of the city's wards—as well as at-large members Phil Mendelson and David Catania—after beginning their political careers by serving on their neighborhood ANC. Having emerged from the most local of local political institutions, this new breed of Council member has proven to be more concerned with the nitty-gritty politics of trash collection, public safety, and zoning than with the larger philosophical issues of social and racial justice that so drove the city's earlier politicians such as Julius Hobson, Dave Clarke, and Walter Fauntroy.[94]

Several leaders of the African American community—especially the powerful ministers and bishops of local churches—remained shocked and silent at these events. Marion Barry quickly calculated that further shifts in local politics might be afoot. Sensing the impending possibility of a majority-white District Council for the first time in modern history, the mayor began to speak out against white candidates for local office. It was Williams, however, who set the tone for the next round of city elections, eventually emerging as the victor.[95] The pivotal race in bringing about regime change took place in centrally located Ward One, the city's most densely populated and ethnically diverse Council district, which included the U Street neighborhood.

Ward One had been represented by only two people since 1974: Dave Clarke, a fiery civil rights lawyer, and Frank Smith Jr., who had first been elected in 1982 when Clarke moved on to take over the Council's chair. As noted above, Smith was a onetime leader of the Student Nonviolent Coordinating Committee in Georgia who arrived in the city in 1968 and went on to become very much a part of the local political scene. By the late 1990s, he had angered many of his longtime labor union supporters by working on the D.C. Council in cooperation with the Control Board to straighten out the city's finances. Moreover, his ward was undergoing profound demographic changes, which undercut the electoral power of African American voters.[96]

Jim Graham, a resident of Ward One, was a nationally recognized AIDS activist and longtime executive director of the city's Whitman-Walker Clinic (a leading HIV/AIDS treatment center) who had worked with Smith in the past.[97] Graham had arrived in Washington following graduation from Michigan State University and the University of Michigan Law School to serve as a clerk for Earl Warren, chief justice of the United States. He had stayed on, earning additional law degrees from Georgetown University and becoming a staff attorney with the U.S. Senate Governmental Affairs Committee under its chair, Senator Abraham Ribicoff. His AIDS work brought him into local affairs.

When Graham decided to run for the Ward One Council seat against Smith, he effectively mobilized the support of the ward's large gay community, piecing together a strong coalition with Latino and other neighborhood-oriented activists. Gays had become a growing presence in this and other midtown neighborhoods. They took on increasingly visible and significant civic roles as the neighborhood continued its demographic and economic transition throughout the 1990s. Graham, much to the consternation of local African American community leaders, collected 48.6 percent of the vote in the September 1998 Ward One Democratic Primary, to Smith's 32 percent.[98]

The November general election completed the turnover of District Council members, as longtime council member Hilda H. M. Mason—who had held down Julius Hobson's former seat for the D.C. Statehood Party—went down to defeat and several outsiders who had won in the earlier Democratic primaries swept into office, together with Williams as mayor.[99] The newcomers made their way from grassroots neighborhood organizations and the ANCs into the District Building. Encountering the city's dysfunctionality in their jobs and daily lives, this new breed of D.C. politician turned to community and neighborhood activism. Their agendas, unlike those of the initial home rule generation, became oriented toward problem solving. They wanted their city to work. Together with Williams, these new Council members brought about a new municipal regime in the District Building. Local politics was increasingly dominated by pragmatic concern for city services and neighborhood quality of life as well as the exigencies of city planning rather than the larger issues of social and racial justice.[100]

The changes sweeping through the city were a consequence of many factors. The congressionally mandated Control Board dramatically restructured the function of city finances and institutions, undercutting the ability of city officials to continue patronage systems that had undergirded the initial home rule government and the Barry administrations.[101] Demographic change had swept through many neighborhoods as the city's white population remained stable, its Asian and Latino populations increased, and its African American population fell. The city reflected larger changes taking place in the country during the 1990s, which emphasized private capital over public expenditures, along with prodevelopment approaches to urban planning.[102] The gentrification of U Street both reflected this broader reorientation of District affairs and reinforced the citywide trends away from a focus on social justice and toward pragmatic problem solving. Graham's defeat of Smith in the ward embracing the U Street neighborhood cemented these changes on the District Council.

Adrian Fenty, the youngest among the new Council members, emerged as one of the most outspoken newcomers. He was particularly vocal during acrimonious debates about the construction of a baseball stadium for the Washington Nationals to be funded by the city. In September 2004, Major League Baseball announced its intention to move a team from Montreal to Washington, contingent upon the city building a "suitable" stadium.[103] A bitter battle ensued, with the new Council members led by Fenty and Catania trying to hold down the cost to the city. Opposition to the expenditure of public funds on the project crossed racial and socioeconomic lines, with more than two-thirds of the city's voters in every part of the city opposing the use of public revenues to fund the proposed ballpark.[104] Barry and Council chair Linda Cropp brokered a last-minute compromise placing a $611 million cap on the city's expenditures for the stadium just before time ran out on its contract with Major League Baseball in late December 2004.[105] The Nationals opened their stadium along the banks of the Anacostia River four years later, with Ryan Zimmerman's dramatic ninth-inning "walk-off" home run lifting them over the Atlanta Braves by a score of 3 to 2.[106]

Within two years, Fenty would use his newfound notoriety to launch a campaign for mayor. Williams decided not to run for a third term, thereby setting up a contest between stadium supporter Cropp and stadium opponent Fenty.[107] Notwithstanding Cropp's long service on the District's School Board and the D.C. Council, Fenty swept both the September 2006 Democratic primary and the November general election, winning every precinct.[108] On January 2, 2007, a month after his thirty-sixth birthday, he was inaugurated mayor of the District of Columbia. He is the son of a well-known biracial couple that owns a popular running shoe store in Adams Morgan, and grew up in Mount Pleasant before heading off to Oberlin College. He returned to the city to study at Howard University Law School and to work as an intern for several national and local officials.

A marathon runner and Blackberry fiend, Fenty represents a fresh generation dedicated to the city yet removed from personal experience with its past battles. On the one hand, he was a child of the city in ways that Mississippi-born Barry and California-born Williams were not. On the other, he paid far less attention to the rituals of race in appointments and in policies than any of his predecessors. He represents a new Washington, one shaped—yet less encumbered—by the past. In this regard, he personifies much of the spirit of the "New You."

"Where Would Jesus Park?"

The new cannot escape so easily from the past.[109] Despite Fenty's initial ability to transcend race and class—and despite his New Age belief in the power of technology and fresh faces—he has been unable to move beyond many of the venomous fights that were playing out in the city's neighborhoods as new prosperity pushed aside those who were there before. Nowhere is this enduring tension between the old and the new more visible than on U Street at the beginning of the twenty-first century.

Although there are people of good faith throughout the U Street community, some especially vocal members of various groups loudly act out their disdain for others who came before and after. The continuing and particularly nasty skirmishes in recent years over parking on Sunday mornings exemplify how tense U Street remains.

As noted above, many area churches have retained their congregations even as their parishioners moved further out in the city and, eventually, into the surrounding suburbs. As they return every Sunday for services, these generations of churchgoers sustain the linkages that have made U Street a special place from its earliest days. Hundreds of families arrive every Sunday morning, often parking wherever they can.[110] No one much cared about having so many cars with Maryland and Virginia license plates double- and tripled-parked when U Street was down on its luck. The crowds reminded people of how alive the area once was.

By the 1990s, newcomers began to move in. Even if the newer residents were religious, they attended church elsewhere. Many, however, viewed Sunday morning as a time to sleep late, run errands, pursue a hobby, or play some sport. As their numbers grew, many newcomers, who were spending a lot of money to rent or to buy their apartments and houses on and around U Street, awoke on Sunday along with other longtime residents to find that they were immobilized for several hours because their cars were blocked by double-parked churchgoers who had driven in from the suburbs.

In this contentious situation, more was at stake than where to put a car. Both groups had diametrically opposed understandings of what was happening—of what U Street was, and could be.[111] For the parishioners, the churches they, their parents, grandparents, and great-grandparents had built represent the very essence of what U Street is about. They were people so attached to the neighborhood that they continued to attend church even though they lived miles away. From their perspective, the new residents didn't belong, and didn't understand where they were. How could they possibly object to having the neighborhood's real community block a traffic lane for a few hours once a week?

For the new residents, the churchgoers were aliens who had given up on the neighborhood long ago and moved out. It was they, the new arrivals, who were genuinely committed to the community because they were living in it; they were the people who had put their money and lives on the line by moving into the area. The suburbanites were the parvenus. The new residents, who were often secular, and thus largely unfamiliar with the centrality of the church to the community in the past, resented these out-of-towners coming in and disrupting their lives.

As always, along U Street, race often underlies these kinds of tensions. The parishioners were African American, whereas the newcomer complainers, for the most part, were not. Other issues entered in as well. The churches at times run subsidized housing and shelter programs for the disadvantaged; many new residents feel as if their neighborhood already has its fair share of such facilities.[112]

The African American churchgoers were deeply offended by the growing presence of a gay culture in the area; the newcomers at times viewed the churches as standard-bearers for a retrograde Protestant fundamentalism. Clashes broke out over liquor licenses, over public behavior, over political candidates. For many, Ward One Council member Jim Graham—who is gay, white, and a tough critic of some of the area's African American–oriented nightclubs—symbolized this divide. How much one supported or opposed Graham often became a litmus test for all sorts of other divisions. Both groups have become resentful of the other; both have a sense of entitlement based on profoundly different worldviews.

After simmering for years, the conflict over Sunday morning parking reached a new stage in the spring of 2006, when the District's Department of Transportation announced that it would begin to ticket illegally parked cars around the city's more than six hundred congregations.[113] Bill Rice, the agency's spokesperson, noted that problems had emerged along 16th Street, NW, and on Capitol Hill in addition to the U Street area. More aggressive ticketing would begin around Logan Circle and U Street, where efforts had been made to identify alternative parking options. The pastor of Metropolitan Baptist Church, the Reverend H. Beecher Hicks, appreciated the city's decision to postpone the enforcement of this new policy until after Easter and Mother's Day. He nonetheless indicated that the overall issue was far from resolved. After all, he noted, "God is not creating new terra firma, you know?"[114]

The battle had been joined. Within a few weeks, Mayor Williams had reversed the policy, appointing a commission to review the question. New neighborhood residents, in turn, were greatly angered. An exasperated Christopher Dyer, a local ANC member, exclaimed that he had "just spent six months of my time in meetings with churches and city government officials and we came up with a solution that seems to work. In Logan Circle, we solved the problem, and without the enforcement going on, people are not going to have any incentive at all to not double park there."[115] The fact that the District Council had exempted itself from its own parking regulations—allowing Council members to park wherever they like throughout the city—only added fuel to the growing fire.[116] The editors of the *Washington Post* weighed in, urging the city to create new parking spots rather than simply issuing more tickets.[117]

Following a moratorium on ticketing, the mayor's task force met throughout a summer of demonstrations and angry denunciations on both sides. Among the various groups taking to the streets and lobbying behind the signs was "Logan Residents for Equitable Enforcement of Parking Regulations," founded by Todd Lovinger. As Lovinger saw it, "Every Sunday—and some week nights—you just knew there was at least a 50/50 chance you'd be blocked in."[118]

By the fall of 2006, the city government had announced a fresh approach, charging each community to "work with the church and the ANC in a collaborative way."[119] Fenty, running for mayor by this time, stated clearly that communities should find new parking spots, on the one hand, and that parking regulations should be enforced, on the other.[120] In fact, additional parking options were created near the largest churches near U Street.

The issue was not totally put to rest, however, because more than automobiles was at stake.[121] The parking wars were part of the larger struggle over who could stake a claim to the neighborhood that was playing out in the conflicts over history, liquor licenses, and any number of other details of urban life. In February 2008, Fenty ordered the police to start ticketing once again, especially around five churches north of Logan Circle and around U Street: Vermont Avenue Baptist, Metropolitan Baptist, Eleventh Street Baptist, Way Back to Pentecost Church, and the Church of Christ.[122] The pastors responded, claiming that heightened enforcement of parking regulations would "turn the city into a one-class, one-race gated community."[123]

Does "Clean" Have to Be White?

Although "playing the race card" might seem a sign of paranoia to some, African Americans with long ties to the U Street area have little trouble finding evidence to support their fears. For example, a postcard advertisement sent to hundreds of potential buyers at the new Ellington Apartments—which towers over U Street between 13th and 14th streets with close to two hundred units—showed cleanliness unusual for the area, and several pedestrians who also were atypical. Despite the fact that the 2000 census had revealed the neighborhood to be 48 percent African American and 36 percent white—and despite the fact that some of the partners building the project were themselves African American—all eight of the pedestrians shown on the postcard were white.[124] Despite demurrals from any number of spokespersons affiliated with the project—and despite the presence of African Americans in other advertising materials for the Ellington—the message seemed clear.[125] Nor was it particularly out of step with other advertisements for condominiums, restaurants, and clubs in the area.

The District government and local developers bet heavily on U Street's "return." Mayor Williams designated U Street to be one of five "corridors" for his D.C. Main Streets program designed to provide additional city funds for sprucing up neighborhoods.[126] Various economic development programs have been more munificent, providing tax breaks and investment incentives to developers running into the tens of millions of dollars. These investments invariably go to companies outside the neighborhood and to new residents moving in from elsewhere. As the real estate section of the *Washington Post* put it one Saturday in 2001, "These are new places and new people—many young, many gay, many white—for the District's U Street corridor. . . . Change has come slowly to the area. . . . This is the next step: Once-empty lots are being filled by expensive new houses and condos, the first in decades to be built on a large scale in the neighborhood."[127] The sales manager at the time for the Lincoln Condominiums explained that "our mission was to have a product offering where the customer would allow certain conditions of the neighborhood not to be a pressing concern for them when they made a buying decision."[128]

What might those conditions be? Given the history of U Street, a longtime African American resident need not be overly anxious about race issues to understand that he or she is part of whatever condition it is that gets in the way of an attractive "product offering."

U Street always has had multiple faces. The neighborhood has been one where different people who really do not think much of one another have been forced to dance together along the city's most jagged edge. Fourteenth Street and Seventh Street long represented quite different realities; Stokely Carmichael and Walter Fauntroy presented different paths into the future; LeDroit whites put up their fences only to have Howard students tear them down the next night. The neighborhood's contested history provides numerous glimpses at what U Street can be at its worst. Contemplating how diverse people have staked a claim to this single patch of real estate offers a reminder of just how remarkable it is that the area has produced great beauty as well as enormous tragedy and incomprehensible folly. Gentrification has not created these divisions so much as exposed nerves that were already too raw.

A Night on the Town

U Street's recent history has not only been about battles between past and present residents and among various sexual, economic, and racial groups. In fact, the neighborhood's history of conflict probably is the farthest thought from the minds of most of its denizens as they seek out the next chic club on a weekend evening. As a 2008 brochure advertising local shops declared, "U Street Is All about You!"[129]

The U Street entertainment scene exploded during the 1990s. New clubs, bars, restaurants, coffee bars, and cupcake shops opened seemingly every month as the decade marched by. Like the theaters that had set up shop during the 1980s, these entrepreneurs were drawn by lower rents. As time passed—and as rents rose—larger, more ambitious venues opened, sometimes driving out earlier clubs. By the decade's end, U Street had become one of the city's premier locales for nightspots.

Thus far, the U Street scene has been distinguished by two characteristics very much in keeping with the area's history. First, the restaurants, bars, and clubs present a remarkable variety of entertainment, from go-go and hip-hop to salsa and R&B, from metal and hard rock to bop and post-bop. As the *New York Times* observed as early as 1996, "This is a Washington not seen on the 6 o'clock news. This is the capital as a hip-hop, acid-jazz, house music, reggae, boogie-down-blues, rocking, bopping four-block weekend party."[130]

More and more people have flooded into the area every night to catch their favorite music, thereby reinforcing U Street's long-standing function as the city's jagged edge, along which people who are quite different from one another come crashing together. A U Street night is not always violence free, as nasty fights spilling out of nightspots have resulted in tragic murders, and as criminals have sometimes targeted inebriated patrons. Given the number of people out on the town on any particular evening—and given the variety of ages, incomes, ethnicities, sexual orientations, and races visible on the streets—the larger story is how well the area has functioned in a city full of invisible barriers keeping people apart.

Second, though many club owners book national groups, several U Street clubs provide critically important opportunities for the city's talent to perform. For more than a decade, Velvet Lounge owner George Saah, for example, has booked both touring bands—such as the Austin-based Modern Skirts—and local groups—such as the Black and Tan Fantasy Band—in an effort "to attract Adams Morgan barflies away from 18th Street, NW, to his pub along a sketchy stretch at Ninth and U streets, NW."[131]

In jazz, the Axis Bar and Grill provides a stage for the always-elegant piano playing of Harry Appleman, while U-Topia often features smooth guitarist Paul Piper. Both Café Nema and Bohemian Caverns give a platform for young players from the University of the District of Columbia and Howard University to cut their teeth in public behind the local jazz group the Young Lions, featuring master piano player Allyn Johnson, standout bassist Kris Funn, and fearsome drummer Quincy Philips.[132] The city's rich history of soul/funk—a local scene that produced Marvin Gaye, Roberta Flack, and the D.C. Playboys, among many performers—is on display at clubs throughout the area.[133] Club U—which was open for several years inside the Reeves Center at 14th and U—featured the distinctive "go-go" groove perfected by local legend Chuck Brown during the 1970s. That club closed following a number of violent incidents and a murder.[134] Though overshadowed in the city by go-go and funk, hip-hop—led by such locals as DJ Kool, 3LG, Fat Rodney, and Head Roc—

often finds its way into U Street venues.[135] The now-defunct Cada Vez and the Cha Cha Lounge offered Latin beats.

Both these characteristics—the diversity of performances and the opportunities provided for local artists—convert U Street from a venue for cultural consumption into a space for cultural production. In other words, U Street is not only where folks have fun—though it is that to be sure. U Street is also the space in which local musicians, comedians, writers, artists, and performers create their new work, as revealed by four venues representing quite different styles: the 9:30 Club at 815 V Street, NW; the Black Cat at 1811 14th Street, NW; Twins Jazz at 1344 U Street, NW; and Busboys and Poets at 2021 14th Street, NW.

The 9:30 Club migrated to U Street in the mid-1990s after opening in 1980 at 930 F Street, NW, downtown. The club became known for discovering new performers, and for mixing them together with well-established acts. Chuck Brown, Cyndi Lauper, Nash the Slash, Fugazi, the Slickee Boys, and other groups sought out opportunities to perform at this post-punk mecca. National Public Radio covered the opening of the new stage in the former WUST Radio Music Hall at 815 V Street, NW, in January 1996, on an evening that featured the Smashing Pumpkins.[136] Bob Dylan, the Red Hot Chili Peppers, and the Beastie Boys have come to U Street to play the 9:30 in recent years. With a capacity of 1,200 people, the 9:30 has provided new talent with an opportunity to create a fan base; and it has given those same musicians the chance to play with some of the biggest names in the music business.

The Black Cat several blocks away has emerged as another favorite venue for the city's independent musicians. Various rooms in the large club provide both small and large stages for local bands, films, and poetry readings. The Mainstage regularly features nationally known and international underground and alternative acts, making the Black Cat the city's primary venue for indie, punk, and garage rock groups. Like the 9:30, the Black Cat has created numerous opportunities for local artists to develop their craft and to win fans. They both nurture creativity while marketing it.[137]

Twins Jazz originally was housed in a small storefront on Colorado Avenue not far east of the Carter Baron Amphitheater along the traditional racial boundary zone of Rock Creek Park. It is owned by Ethiopian twin sisters Kelly and Maze Tesfaye, who opened it in 1987 at the height of the city's racial tensions surrounding the arrest of Marion Barry. The sisters, together with photographer-host Joseph Beasley, welcomed all customers—black, white, Asian, Hispanic, young, old, rich, poor, jazz lovers and jazz novices—to create a preserve of tolerance in a racially polarized community. From the beginning, the sisters booked both national and international acts together with local jazz musicians, giving younger players the chance to explore their music and to learn from old masters. By the late 1990s, the sisters had opened a second club on U Street, which has outlasted their original lounge uptown. As a focal point for the jazz community, Twins preserves U Street's special place in jazz culture and history.[138]

Busboys and Poets combines a restaurant, a space for a "progressive political" bookstore, and a performance area intended by its owner—Iraqi-born immigrant Andy Shallal—to pay homage to Langston Hughes and the broader U Street achievement.[139] It is located in a trendy new apartment building boasting units that sell in the high six figures, the Langston Lofts at 14th and V streets, and has established itself as the heart of a lively poetry scene that explicitly claims links to the neighborhood's past. The Busboys and Poets bookstore is operated by Teaching for Change, a not-for-profit organization dedicated to social justice starting in the classroom.

The open poetry nights in the Busboys and Poets performance space, named the Langston Room, have been wildly popular—especially the Tuesday night poetry series, which has been sold out nearly every Tuesday since September of 2005—with up to 120 listeners straining to hear what the next poet will have to say upon reaching the open mike.[140] "And there's nothing new here," *Washington Post* writer Ellen McCarthy reported in 2007,

> nothing that wasn't happening 10 years ago. And seventy years before that. And ever since the dawn of humanity. It's just some folks talking. Telling stories. Wrapping thoughts into words. There's no computer animation or big-screen explosions or digital remixing or precious YouTube kitsch. There's nothing

new here. Nothing except this particular talking, these stories, these thoughts, and these words. . . . They talk sometimes about the ones who came before them. About how, before their grandparents could even imagine their parents, Langston Hughes walked these streets and Zora Neale Hurston lived here. But just as often they talk about heartbreak, redemption, survival. . . . And their followers, standing when there's no more room to sit, holler in support.[141]

Shallal eventually opened up two additional locations, one in the Shirlington area of Arlington, Virginia, and the other just off New York Avenue and 5th streets, NW.[142]

The 9:30 Club, Black Cat, and Twins, together with Busboys and Poets, reach out to very different audiences and "demographics." Yet they have much in common. They provide invaluable places for creativity in a city far too reliant on imposing rules rather than breaking them. They blend together local talent and nationally known names, to the benefit of both. They bring people who otherwise would have scant contact with one another crashing together. They represent many more bars and clubs and restaurants and small halls on and around U Street that similarly make discovery possible.

U Street continues to enrich Washington by nurturing those who create beauty. The neighborhood has done this for the past two decades in part because rents have been low enough to enable innovative theater directors, music promoters, club owners—and the actors, performers, and artists they present—to pursue their dreams. Rumors abound that one club or another will be driven out by rising rents, or that a national producer will come in with national groups on tour to force out local entrepreneurs and performers. There is little question that gentrification threatens to undermine the very characteristics that have made the area so creative—its diversity and its openness to local performers.

The task for the future will be how best to ensure that creative energy will continue to course through the neighborhood even as it becomes home to expensive condominiums and pricey restaurants. Some older stores try to adapt and contend with the newcomers. Faced with stiff competition from upscale Whole Foods a block or two away, the Best D.C. Supermarket on 14th Street has added expensive zinfandels and designer chocolate bars to its traditional stock of white bread and Cheez Whiz. One customer charges veggie sticks on her Gold Card; the next pays for his beef jerky with food stamps.[143]

Other neighborhood mainstays have never been able to adjust to the area's new realities. The hip-hop club State of the Union, the African American women's bookstore and poetry venue Sisterspace, and the R&B club Republic Gardens are gone.[144] As the closures of these clubs demonstrate, failure to meet this challenge will dissipate the very vitality that has made U Street so attractive to so many Washingtonians and out-of-towners. The District government has undertaken some limited efforts to provide "historic businesses" with property tax relief, but these measures seem to be insufficient to save many of the older, more quirky establishments that have given the "New You" character.[145]

Busboys and Poets owner Andy Shallal put it well when lamenting the homogenization threatening the area in 2008. "In the rush to create this instant renaissance," he cautioned readers of a neighborhood newspaper, "we're really tripping over ourselves at the cost of losing our local flavor."[146] If space must be found to enable former residents to remain in the area so that it can continue its role as the city's meeting ground, so too must space be found for local performers and artists to create beauty of diverse kinds.

Beauty in the Face of Folly

By the end of the first decade of the twenty-first century, on any given Saturday night, dozens of venues present some sort of live performance along U Street and nearby streets. Some of the city's trendiest restaurants and bars line the streets, catching the attention of travel writers from the *New York Times* to Austrian Airlines.[147] "Black Broadway" is back— only without some of the "black"—as U Street has become a playground for an emerging Washington that is younger and more diverse racially, ethnically, and culturally than the city has ever been before. In other words, here is a neighborhood—and a city—better personified by Mayor Fenty than by Mayor Barry.

This is the good news. The bad news has been that working-class African Americans who, in many ways, invented and have sustained the street as a creative center have had an increasingly difficult time maintaining their presence in the neighborhood—and in the city. Perhaps even worse news would be if the spunky and gritty clubs that characterize the area become just as rare in the years ahead as the working-class culture that first created them. The good news is that U Street did not become what Southwest Washington became; the bad news is that no one has quite figured out how to improve a neighborhood while keeping the original residents in place.

Another piece of good news is that the neighborhood's identification with its African American past provides core meaning to what the street can become. Those promoting the neighborhood embrace, rather than cover over, African American cultural achievement. In this sense, U Street has preserved that aspect of Washington that makes the city so much more than its image as merely the seat of American power.

Critics have decried the commodification of U Street history by Kathryn Schneider Smith and others. From this perspective, as Stephanie Barbara Frank concludes, "the role of historic preservation and cultural heritage activities in the Greater U Street neighborhood is a revanchist one. The efforts guised as those meant to preserve the neighborhood have instead put into motion the refashioning of the former 'heart of black Washington' into a white middle-class neighborhood."[148]

This charge rings hollow in the case of Smith, who has done more than nearly any other Washingtonian of her generation to focus attention on the rich complexity of the city's history, always with local communities in the forefront of her mind.[149] She—as well as Cultural Tourism D.C. and the Humanities Council of Washington, D.C.—explicitly sought to use the neighborhood's history to draw tourists from the National Mall deeper into the city, as was described earlier in the chapter. They did so in order to try to save an important history before it was lost. Smith, for example, points to the sad state of the Carter G. Woodson house at the time, which was boarded up and covered with graffiti. Their intent was to bring new visitors, jobs, and dollars to local businesses and cultural and historic sites while working closely with local people to frame how that history would be presented.[150]

In the end, Cultural Tourism D.C.—and its various partners—did not have it within their power to stave off pressures to gentrify an area that was full of exceptionally attractive Victorian row houses set along tree-lined streets located within a few minutes' walk of a new Metro line. Once those assets were "commodified," neither Cultural Tourism D.C. nor others concerned with local history could control who got to "own" the story.

The marketing of U Street and its past has produced far more serious "commodifiers." Once the neighborhood's story was being told again, real estate agents, developers, and entrepreneurs of all stripes sensed an opportunity to capitalize on what the street had been. It is they—not Smith, the Humanities Council, and Cultural Tourism D.C.—who denuded U Street's story of texture and meaning; it is they who have deified Duke Ellington and Langston Hughes in order to turn a profit.

Ellington and Hughes are, of course, more than worthy of praise. Their increasingly ubiquitous presence in the new imagery of the neighborhood nonetheless raises two issues. First, both left town for New York as quickly as they could. Ellington recalled his childhood in the city with some fondness in later years; Hughes detested the place.[151]

Second, Ellington and Hughes represent but a small, safe corner of a vast and troubled story. Neighborhood anger over racial and economic injustice does not play quite as well in brochures peddling million-dollar condominium apartments. Otherwise, in addition to the Ellington, new residents might be able to move into buildings named "the Stokely" or "the Julius" after Stokely Carmichael and Julius Hobson. More than Smith and her colleagues, local media and travel writers have reduced the street's story line to a singular tale of recovered greatness. In doing so, they have left out far too many contradictions and heroic figures who have come and gone during the past century and a half.

U Street is about more than the genius of an Ellington or a Hughes. The neighborhood has been from the very beginning a "zone of contact," in which the city's diverse communities have come clashing together. To borrow from Mary Louise Pratt, who first developed that notion nearly two decades ago, U Street throughout its history has been replete with the improvised relationships and "co-presence" of people separated by the intractable conflicts of race, ethnicity, faith, gender, sexual orientation, and class.[152] As they have pursued their causes or pleasures, have clashed or sought to cooperate, they have found ways to do so with a particular sense of purpose. In ways large and small, these many residents have proclaimed their deep human right to be in this place at this time—the contrabands of the Civil War in their encampments, the economically diverse homeowners of the 1870s in their brick homes, the brilliant Frances Grimké from his pulpit at the Fifteenth Street Presbyterian Church, the acerbic William Calvin Chase in the pages of the *Washington Bee*, the flashy Sportin' Daniels "stylin'" down U Street at the height of the Depression, the curmudgeonly Carter G. Woodson from his *Journal of Negro History*, the magisterial Mary Church Terrell and Mary McLeod Bethune on their picket lines, the fearsomely angry Gardner "Bish" Bishop in his barber shop, the burned-out Jewish merchants in government offices trying to reclaim their loses after 1968, and the straightlaced Walter Fauntroy at neighborhood meetings.[153]

Throughout its history, U Street has been where the aggrieved and the displaced have staked out their possession of the city. They have done so ever since the street and its community first took shape fifteen decades ago. Their lives are not the material for real estate advertisements and restaurant menus. Nevertheless, their legacies have made such self-promotion possible. In the end, the beauty of individual and collective accomplishment born of a creative social intelligence has made U Street an indispensable corner of Washington—and American—urban soil.

The sum of these endeavors has proven to be far greater than any individual initiative, which is the most important lesson to be derived from the experience of U Street and other zones of contact. The challenge of understanding these complex processes is rooted in the seemingly undirected nature of what happens in the economic transition from one community equilibrium to another. If such modification is to benefit those who resided in the area before—as should be the goal of any transition from a protected traditional economy to an open globalized one, whether on a neighborhood, city, national, or regional scale—those with custodianship for the common good must eschew grand gestures for the hard work of bringing everyone along together.

The distinguished urbanists Phil Wood and Charles Landry eloquently argue in their book *The Intercultural City* that successful cities more often than not have historically been diverse cities.[154] Diversity in and of itself, they continue, is not a sufficient condition for urban success; this is so even at a time when global forces are creating unprecedented human multiplicity in cities throughout the world. "For cities to unlock the benefits of cultural diversity—to realize the diversity advantage or dividend—they need to become more intercultural," Wood and Landry argue. "They need to become stages upon which the free interplay of different skills, insights and cultural resources may take its course."[155]

Neighborhoods such as U Street—and thousands of similar jagged urban edges—are the necessary proving grounds where the diverse become transformed into an intercultural resource. They are where accomplished cities become successful. Like wetlands in the natural environment, such mixing bowls of urban diversity often appear to outsiders to be little more than wastelands. They are the first places to be rebuilt, redesigned, reconceived, and reconstituted when "reformers" think about "improving" a city. Yet this is a terrible mistake. Like wetlands, contact zones are among the most productive corners of the urban environment. Like wetlands, such communities must be revitalized from time to time for them to continue to enrich the city at large.

Among urban specialists, such analogies with ecosystems are leading to a borrowing of terminology from biological science, with the notion of "community resilience" gaining a certain fashion in contemporary discussions of the city. As with many concepts drawn from the natural sciences by the social sciences ("sustainability," to cite just one more example), the term "resilience" has a high degree of indeterminacy. This lack of definition is not necessarily limiting, for it permits people from different ideological and political positions to attach a different meaning to the same term.

As notions of "community resilience" gain wider currency in discussions about the challenges of urban life, those using the term are less and less precise about its meaning.[156] Even so, the growing number of commentators and social observers utilizing the concept seek to highlight an important dimension to urban life that is exemplified by neighborhoods and communities such as U Street.[157] More precisely, what is it that allows communities to adapt in the aftermath of natural disasters and violent conflict so they can thrive once more?

"Resilience" has gained adherents among urban specialists because the concept implies organic, incremental, bottom-up approaches to addressing pressing social ills. Successful communities become those that are inclusive rather than exclusive; those that accumulate small-scale additions in social and economic capital rather than gamble with overarching, top-down abstractions to pursue community enhancement. Communities such as Washington's U Street seem in many ways to affirm the importance of resilience in urban life. This is a neighborhood that has reinvented itself many times over, serving as an epitome of bottom-up social change.

U Street—and neighborhoods like it—offer counterexamples to the resilience model as it has emerged in recent years as conflict as well as accommodation stands at the center of their histories. They reveal how the wellspring of resilience is the need to survive within what Lewis Mumford perceptively labeled the "purposive social complexity" of urban life.[158] Resilience lies in pragmatism—what Edward C. Banfield has called a "culturally ingrained willingness to tolerate behavior that is in some degree offensive."[159]

How different, then, is the "New You" from the old? Superficially, it is dramatically so. The buildings are taller, and their residents are whiter, than a century ago. There were no tanning salons along U Street when "Washington was in vogue."

Beneath the surface, however, the distance from the old U to the new may not be quite so far after all. U Street represents an example of the surprising semiotic stability that the perceptive Russian urban thinker Vyacheslav Glazychev argues is essential to understanding how cities function.[160] For Glazychev, an essential mystery of urban life remains how neighborhoods retain their essential character despite changes in population, building size, physical structures, and economic reorganization. His observation prompts the question: Are today's "urban adventurers" and yuppie-buppie U Streeters really all that much different from the "upper-class colored people" a young Langston Hughes found to be "as unbearable and snobbish a group of people as I have ever come in to contact with anywhere" more than eight decades ago?[161]

This book argues that U Street has been important precisely because it has always served as a zone of contact among the divergent racial, cultural, and economic communities that define Washington as a city. Class along with race have long been defining cleavages running through the heart of U Street. The neighborhood has been a jagged edge along which people so profoundly different that they often could not stand being with one another have come knocking together. Gentrification has meant that the corner of 14th and U streets, NW, has reemerged as the city's central crossroads.

After a few decades of heading to Georgetown to congregate when times call for communal celebration, Washingtonians of all ages, races, and classes now turn once again to the very spot where the violence broke out in 1968. This was where supporters ran when Adrian Fenty won his pivotal primary in September 2006. Similarly, 14th and U was the place to which Washingtonians turned when Barack Obama was elected president on November 4, 2008.

Election Day 2008 had been tense in Washington, as many local voters waited in line for hours to cast their ballots. Obama's supporters—and there were many in a city where 93 percent of all votes cast went to him—couldn't quite believe that something would not go wrong to snatch victory away at the last moment.[162] Disappointing initial results from neighboring Virginia—where many of the city's residents had worked long and hard for the Democratic nominee—heightened a sense of unease. By 11:00 p.m., the wait was over. Within minutes of the polls closing in California, news agencies began to call the Illinois senator the victor. A dozen minutes later, Senator John McCain was well into his concession speech in Arizona.

U Street had been busy all night, as the bars were full of election watchers. Dozens congregated on the corner of 14th Street as the final confirmation of victory came. Fifteen minutes later, these dozens had turned into hundreds, as they had in April 1968. The hundreds were thousands within half an hour. Traffic came to a halt as a surging crowd of every human size, age, shape, and color began dancing in the street.

Life stopped, as it had just forty years before—only now in joy rather than in rage.

A second, more partisan group—also in the hundreds—quickly gathered in front of the White House to heckle outgoing President George W. Bush. Singing the chorus to Steam's 1969 hit "Na Na Hey Hey Kiss Him Goodbye,"[163] "strangers hugged. People danced in clusters. The air became saturated with the sound of honking cars horns from all points of the compass. Police stayed back, remaining barely perceptible on the periphery."[164]

At Ben's Chili Bowl, elated customers sang along to the Temptations' 1964 hit "My Girl," which was playing over and over again on Ben's famous jukebox. Ecstatic patrons changed the chorus as they belted out the old pop favorite. "What can make me feel this way? O-bama, talkin' 'bout Obama!" they sang over and over and over again.[165] The Ali family, which has owned the place since it opened, changed the sign

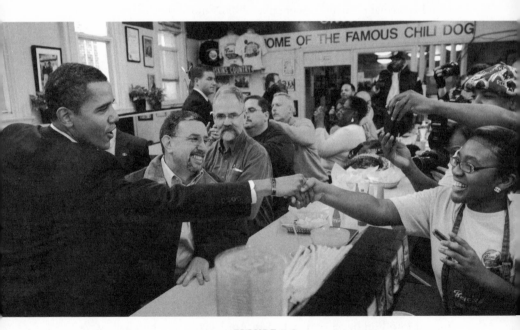

FIGURE 7.5
President-Elect Barack Obama at Ben's Chili Bowl

Photograph by Linda Davidson / Getty Images. Used with permission.

over the cash register that reads "The only person who gets free food here is Bill Cosby," with the additional words, "and the Obama family." In fact, Obama would join Mayor Fenty at Ben's for a half-smoke and cheese fries two months later on his first Saturday living in Washington, and pay the bill himself (figure 7.5).[166] As the excitement at Ben's demonstrates, the music that brought Nighthawk and Petey such fame when U Street was indisputably "Soulside" continued to provide the backdrop for people's lives.

Bands of Obama-ites roved up and down 14th and 16th streets, passing from revenge to rapture. Brooklyn native Victoria Cabrera told one blogger that "she was driving from Maryland back into the city tonight when she saw masses of people pouring onto the streets from one of the residence halls of historically black Howard University."[167] Another blogger on the popular Web site *DCist* recorded that she was "still processing what happened last night. One minute, I was gathered in a living room with friends, watching election returns come in. The next minute, Barack Obama had been declared the winner, his moving acceptance speech was over, and I was in the middle of the intersection at 14th and U streets, NW, with thousands of other city residents, yelling, singing, high-fiving, and hugging total strangers."[168] The violence of 1968 was being played out in reverse. Washington was healing itself with each passing minute.

Nothing worth celebrating would have occurred on the night of November 4, 2008, had it not been for a century and a half of creative social and political activism among the institutions and residents of Washington's U Street. Surely, everyone at 14th and U that evening stood on the shoulders of millions of other Americans—past and present—from throughout the country and beyond who had struggled for an American transformation. This particular spontaneous gathering held special meaning, taking place as it did at the very place where so much bitterness had remained on display for so long.

Returning to the lambent wisdom of Olga Grushin expressed in this book's epigraph, U Street has produced genuine beauty in response to human folly—the beauty of Duke Ellington's music; of Charles Drew's medical innovations; of Langston Hughes, Edward Christopher

Williams, and Jean Toomer's poetry and prose; of Charlie Houston, Ralph Bunche, and Thurgood Marshall's analytic brilliance; of Mary Church Terrell and Mary McLeod Bethune's activism; of Walter Fauntroy's commitment to community; of "Petey" Greene's and David Chappelle's wicked humor; and of the poetry scene of the first decade of the twenty-first century.[169]

Is the "New You" just a superficial commercialized sham replacing the authentic old U Street? Perhaps this is the case. As Nadine Gordimer has observed, "The past has no wholeness, it has been etiolated by revised explanations of it, trampled over by hindsight."[170] The "New You" is, in many ways, an etiolated vision of the old U. U Street's elder, jazz historian, and radio personality Jamal Muhammad might have been closer to the truth when he observed that, while people of different races and ethnicities coexist along today's U Street without commingling, such coexistence might be a first step toward something new. "One day," he suggests, "there will be real diversity, and people will frequent the area and color won't matter. We will all just hang out because we have the same interest socially."[171]

Rather than lamenting contemporary reality with the assurance of a rant on a blog, this book urges every reader to step back and ask Olga Grushin's question instead: In the face of all of this new silliness and stupidity, is U Street still a place where people come and go as they make the world richer and purer by adding more beauty to it? There is, indeed, no higher mission for an urban community to fulfill. Throughout its history until this very day, U Street has been one of the very few urban communities that rightfully can claim to have done so. The value of its future incarnations will be found in whether or not the people who make U Street "new" will continue to add beauty to the world.

KATHRYN SCHNEIDER SMITH (1939–)

Kathryn Schneider Smith, a native of Milwaukee, moved to Washington in 1965 to serve as assistant press secretary to Senator Gaylord Nelson. She previously worked in public relations and publications at the State Historical Society of Wisconsin after graduating from the University of Wisconsin with a degree in journalism. She was immediately struck upon arrival in Washington by the absence of a sense of place and of local history.

Once in Washington, she met and married the alternative media journalist Sam Smith. Sam, who had grown up in the city and in Philadelphia, returned to his home town upon graduating from Harvard and serving in the Coast Guard. He declined job offers from mainstream newspapers in order to devote his energies to launching a community paper, the *Capitol East Gazette*. He was drawn to local politics, participating in the activities of the Student Nonviolent Coordinating Committee, the Free D.C. Movement, and the growing antiwar movement. He was a close collaborator with Julius Hobson, helping to found the D.C. Statehood Party. His activism became national in scope when he helped to found the Green Party. In 1984, he transformed the *Gazette* into the *Progressive Review*.

Kathryn, a community-based historian, earned her master's in American studies at George Washington University. She became increasingly active in promoting scholarship on the history of Washington, and in finding ways to disseminate the findings of that scholarship to the general public through the schools, historical society, teaching, tours, and writing. She was a leader in the development of history curricula for the D.C. Public Schools, an initiative which resulted in the 1983 publication of the standard text used for Washington history—*City of Magnificent Intentions: A History of the District of Columbia*. Her volume *You in History* explored the role of family and neighborhood in creating the past, while *Washington at Home* introduced the city as a collection of neighborhoods rather than as merely the official seat of national power.

Kathryn became involved in the activities of the Columbia Historical Society shortly after arriving in the city. The society had been founded in 1894 by local white notables to collect materials about the city's history as understood by their racial community. In 1952, Ulysses S. Grant III became president of the society's board and helped bring about the purchase of the Heurich Mansion—a Victorian-style faux castle just off of Dupont Circle. The building served as the society's headquarters and major repository of its various collections until 2003, when it relocated to the former D.C. Public Library on Mount Vernon Square.

By working closely with society director Jane North as the chair of its Board of Trustees between 1989 and 1993, Smith helped to revivify the organization and to expand its scope to incorporate all communities in the city, regardless of race, confession, or ethnicity. They simultaneously oversaw the renaming of the group as the Historical Society of Washington, D.C. In particular, Smith and North expanded the society's mission to add prominence to the city's African American community. Kathryn was the founding editor of the society's magazine dedicated to the city's past, *Washington History.*

During the 1990s, Kathryn helped to found Cultural Tourism D.C., a coalition of neighborhood arts organizations dedicated to promoting the cultural riches of the city "beyond the monuments" as well as on the National Mall. Cultural Tourism D.C. has long been deeply involved in promoting the history of U Street.

Adrian M. Fenty (1970–)

Adrian M. Fenty was born in Washington to a biracial couple living in the Mount Pleasant neighborhood up the escarpment from U Street. His parents—who own and operate Fleet Feet, a popular running shoe store in Adams Morgan—had been active in D.C. politics.

Fenty graduated from Oberlin College and Howard University Law School before entering politics as an intern for Senator Howard Metzenbaum (D-Ohio), the city's Democratic delegate to Congress Eleanor Holmes Norton, and Representative Joseph P. Kennedy II (D-Mass.). He subsequently joined the staff of D.C. Council member Kevin Chavous, before running for a seat on the local ANC (4C) in the uptown Northwest neighborhood of Crestwood.

In 2000, Fenty ran successfully against veteran Ward Four Council member Charlene Drew Jarvis, just as a number of community activists and ANC members were challenging the older generation of city politicians who were formed by the civil rights movement. Jarvis, the daughter of Dr. Charles Drew, personified the legacy of the established Washington African American elite that had dominated city affairs for decades. Like Fenty, other newcomers to the District Council were making their mark by focusing on the practical irritations of living in the city. Fenty surprised longtime observers of the city's political scene by handily defeating the distinguished Jarvis through a determined door-to-door campaign.

Fenty emerged as an aggressive presence on the District Council, gaining visibility together with other former neighborhood activists such as David Catania as vociferous critics of proposals to build a Major League Baseball stadium. The stadium deal—orchestrated by Mayor Anthony Williams—garnered little support among the city's residents. Fenty, viewed by supporters and opponents alike as an assertive "thirtysomething" policy wonk who carried three BlackBerry communication devices, was easily reelected to his Ward Four Council seat in 2004.

Fenty announced his candidacy for mayor in June 2005. The race tightened after Mayor Williams announced that he would not seek a third term. District Council chair Linda Cropp, another mainstay of the local political scene, emerged as the frontrunner. Her vacillation on the stadium issue appeared to be waffling in the face of Fenty's strong opposition. Her final endorsement carried the wildly unpopular project forward at the last moment.

Fenty's campaign quickly gained momentum and, on September 12, 2006, he emerged as the victor in the critical Democratic Party Primary by winning all 142 precincts as well as large majorities in both the white and African American communities. On January 2, 2007, the thirty-six-year-old Fenty became the youngest mayor in the city's history and the second-youngest mayor in the country.

Fenty's term in office has been marked by major shake-ups in key city government agencies. His appointments of Police Chief Cathy L. Lanier, a white officer who had served as the commander in Fenty's neighborhood, and School Chancellor Michelle Rhee, a Korean-American education reformer, surprised many old hands on the city scene. Fenty was able to gain direct control of the city's public schools in 2007 and, with Rhee, initiated major reforms of public education.

Fenty and his supporters frequently have used the "New You" as a symbol of the city's regeneration. Several celebrations of Fenty's victory in 2006 took place along U Street, while the popular restaurant Busboys and Poets at 14th and V streets, NW, has become a frequent venue for the mayor's breakfast and lunch meetings.

NOTES

---◈---

INTRODUCTION

1. Rohulamin Quander as quoted by Cultural Tourism D.C., *What's the Story? A Deeper Look at the History of Greater Shaw in Washington, D.C. in the Context of the National African American Experience—Conference Proceedings, December 7–8, 2004* (Washington, D.C.: Cultural Tourism D.C., 2005).

2. For an eloquent exposition of the lives of slaves in Washington, see Fergus M. Bordewich, *Washington: The Making of the American Capital* (New York: Amistad, 2008).

3. For more on the story of the planning of Washington, see Scott W. Berg, *Grand Avenues: The Story of the French Visionary Who Designed Washington, D.C.* (New York: Pantheon Books, 2007).

4. A concise overview of congressional policies toward the District of Columbia is given by Steven J. Diner, *Democracy, Federalism, and the Governance of the Nation's Capital, 1790–1974*, Studies in D.C. History and Public Policy 10 (Washington, D.C.: Center for Applied Research and Urban Policy, University of the District of Columbia, 1987).

5. Amartya Sen, *Identity and Violence: The Illusion of Destiny* (New York: W. W. Norton, 2006), 105–6.

6. Ibid., 106.

7. The divisional designation of "NW" for the Northwest quadrant of the District of Columbia will be omitted from this point forward. There are also U Streets in the Northeast and Southeast quadrants, but not in Southwest Washington. Readers should know that this definition both extends the story beyond a more traditional understanding of "U Street" as embracing an area running from 3rd to 14th streets, NW, and is used elastically to capture an entire neighborhood rather than specific urban blocks. By doing so, this study reaches out to include Howard University and LeDroit Park to the east as well as the Strivers' Section between 15th and 18th streets, NW, to the west. This generous definition opens up greater possibility for exploring the various pernicious racial and class boundaries that have defined the city since its birth.

8. Edward Kennedy "Duke" Ellington, *Music Is My Mistress* (Garden City, N.Y.: Doubleday, 1973), 14–17.

9. This is obvious from the materials and sources identified by Kathryn Schneider Smith and Marya McQuirter, *A Guide to the Historical Resources of Shaw* (Washington, D.C.: Thurgood Marshall Center for Service and Heritage, 1996).

10. For further discussion of Arbat's mythical role in Moscow's cultural landscape, see Stephen V. Bittner, *The Many Lives of Khrushchev's Thaw: Experience and Memory in Moscow's Arbat* (Ithaca, N.Y.: Cornell University Press, 2008).

11. In justifying the term "Secret City" as the title of her monumental history of African American Washington (the first of its kind), Constance McLaughlin Green noted that the label was "first assigned to the Negro city in an anonymous article in *Crisis* in 1932." Green observed further that "virtually from the beginning, white citizens of the District of Columbia manifestly were acquainted with only the most obvious facts about how free Negros lived and knew almost nothing about what they thought. . . . Colored Washington was psychologically a secret city all but unknown to the white world round about." Constance McLaughlin Green, *The Secret City: A History of Race Relations in the Nation's Capital* (Princeton, N.J.: Princeton University Press, 1967), vii–viii.

12. Juan Williams, "14th and U When Being There Meant Being Somebody," *Washington Post Magazine*, February 21, 1988.

13. Teresa Wiltz, "U Turn: The Fabled D.C. Street That Played Host to Duke Ellington and Pearl Bailey Reinvents Itself Once More," *Washington Post Magazine*, March 5, 2006.

14. Kathleen M. Lesko, Valerie Babb, and Carroll R. Gibbs, *Black Georgetown Remembered: A History of Its Black Community from the Founding of "The Town of George" in 1751 to the Present Day* (Washington, D.C.: Georgetown University Press, 1991), 10–11, 138–54.

15. Laura Bergheim, *The Washington Historical Atlas: Who Did What When and Where in the Nation's Capital* (Rockville, Md.: Woodbine House, 1992); Sandra Fitzpatrick and Maria R. Goodwin, *The Guide to Black Washington: Places and Events of Historical and Cultural Significance in the Nation's Capital*, rev. illus. ed. (New York: Hippocrene Books, 2001), 120–24, 134–35, 143–44.

16. David Taylor, "It All Began One Night Near U Street," *Washington Post*, January 7, 2007; Fitzpatrick and Goodwin, *Guide to Black Washington*, 124–25.

17. Brad Snyder, *Beyond the Shadow of the Senators: The Untold Story of the Homestead Grays and the Integration of Baseball* (New York: Contemporary Books, 2003).

18. Ibid.

19. Fitzpatrick and Goodwin, *Guide to Black Washington*, 144–46.

20. Bob Kuska, *Hot Potato: How Washington and New York Gave Birth to Black Basketball and Changed America's Game Forever* (Charlottesville: University of Virginia Press, 2004), 1–5.

21. The U Street neighborhood's role as a launching ground for civil rights activism throughout the twentieth century (and before) is discussed in Jessica Weiss, "Portrait of a Community: Life in Shaw," *Janus Undergraduate History On-Line Journal of the University of Maryland* (2005).

22. Fitzpatrick and Goodwin, *Guide to Black Washington*, 88–90, 177; Lonnell Aikman, *The Southern Shaw–Striver Cultural Resources Survey, Phase II: Final Report* (Washington, D.C.: Traceries, 1993); Kimberly Prothro Williams, *Strivers' Section Historic District* (Washington, D.C.: D.C. Preservation League, 1999).

23. Fitzpatrick and Goodwin, *Guide to Black Washington*, 147. U Street residents and institutions are visible throughout this history of the *Brown* and other major civil rights cases of the mid–twentieth century. See, e.g., Richard Kluger, *Simple Justice: The History of* Brown v. Board of Education *and Black America's Struggle for Equality* (New York: Alfred A. Knopf, 2004).

24. Willard B. Gatewood, *Aristocrats of Color: The Black Elite, 1880–1920* (Bloomington: Indiana University Press, 1990), 260–61.

25. Jonathan Scott Holloway, *Confronting the Veil: Abram Harris Jr., E. Franklin Frazier, and Ralph Bunche, 1919–1941* (Chapel Hill: University of North Carolina Press, 2002), 40–41; Fitzpatrick and Goodwin, *Guide to Black Washington*, 95–96.

26. On the seminal role of Washington in the "Harlem Renaissance," see James A. Miller, "Black Washington and the New Negro Renaissance," in *Composing Urban History and the Constitution of Civic Identities*, ed. John J. Czaplicka, Blair A. Ruble, and Lauren Crabtree (Washington, D.C., and Baltimore: Woodrow Wilson Center Press and Johns Hopkins University Press, 2003), 219–41; and Fitzpatrick and Goodwin, *Guide to Black Washington*, 157–58.

27. E.g., see the original Nick Stefanos mysteries series: George P. Pelecanos, *A Firing Offense* (New York: St. Martin's Press, 1992); George P. Pelecanos, *Nick's Trip* (New York: St. Martin's Press, 1993); and George P. Pelecanos, *Down by the River Where the Dead Men Go* (New York: St. Martin's Press, 1995).

28. See Edward P. Jones, *Lost in the City* (New York: William Morrow, 1992).

29. For more information about the Davis home in the Strivers' Section, see Benjamin O. Davis Jr., *Benjamin O. Davis, Jr.: American—An Autobiography* (Washington, D.C.: Smithsonian Institution Press, 1991); and Fitzpatrick and Goodwin, *Guide to Black Washington*, 179–80. Norton's memoirs, *Fire in My Soul*, offer a charming account of the enriching life for children around mid-twentieth-century U Street. See Joan Steinau Lester, Eleanor Holmes Norton, and Coretta Scott King, *Fire in My Soul* (New York: Simon & Schuster, 2004), 29–58.

30. Fitzpatrick and Goodwin, *Guide to Black Washington*, 86–87, 105–6; Marya Annette McQuirter, *African American Heritage Trail, Washington, D.C.* (Washington, D.C.: Cultural Tourism D.C., 2003), 43–45; Henrietta R. Hatter, "History of Miner Teachers College," MA thesis, Howard University, Washington, 1939; James

N. Saunders, "The Origin and Development of the Colored Public Evening Schools in the District of Columbia," MA thesis, Howard University, Washington, 1941.

31. Paul K. Williams, *Greater U Street*, Images of America Series (Charleston: Arcadia, 2005), 13–17; Fitzpatrick and Goodwin, *Guide to Black Washington*, 108–9.

32. Marquita Jones and Alexander M. Padro, *Shaw Historic Bicycle Tour* (Washington, D.C.: Ecovillage Project and Shaw Main Streets, 2004); Kimberly Prothro Williams, *Greater U Street Historic District* (Washington, D.C.: D.C. Preservation League, 2003).

33. Yasunari Kawabata, *The Scarlet Gang of Asakusa*, trans. Alisa Freedman (Berkeley: University of California Press, 2005), 30.

34. Robert Alter, *Imagined Cities: Urban Experience and the Language of the Novel* (New Haven, Conn.: Yale University Press, 2005), 17.

35. Jason Wilson, *Buenos Aires: A Cultural History* (Northampton, Mass.: Interlink Books, Inc., 2007), 215.

36. Mary Louise Pratt, "Arts in the Contact Zone," *Profession 91*: 33-40, republished by David Bartholomae and Anthony Petrosky, eds., *Reading the Lives of Others* (Boston: Bedford Books, 1995), 180–95.

37. Mary Louise Pratt, *Travel Writing and Transculturation* (New York: Routledge, 1992), 6–7.

38. Kevin J. Mumford, *Interzones: Black/White Sex Districts in Chicago and New York in the Early Twentieth Century* (New York: Columbia University Press, 1997), xi.

39. Stephanie Barbara Frank, "'If We Own the Story, We Own the Place': Cultural Heritage, Historic Preservation, and Gentrification on U Street," MA thesis, University of Maryland, College Park, 2005, 38–39.

40. Kathryn S. Smith, "Remembering U Street," *Washington History* 9, no. 2 (1997–98): 28–53.

41. See, e.g., Chris Shott, "2004: The Year D.C. History Died," *Washington City Paper*, December 24, 2004; and David Plotz, "L'Enfant Terrible: The Real Reason the City Museum Failed," *Washington City Paper*, December 24, 2004.

42. Green, *Secret City*.

43. D.C. Redevelopment and Land Agency, *Shaw Neighborhood Shopping Center* (Washington, D.C.: D.C. Redevelopment Land Agency, 1974).

44. Walker Percy, "Why I Live Where I Live," in *Signposts in a Strange Land*, by Walker Percy and ed. Patrick Samway (New York: Picador, 1991), 3–9; the quotation here is on 3.

45. Pep Subirós, "Barcelona: Cultural Strategies and Urban Renewal, 1979–1997," in *Composing Urban History*, ed. Czaplicka, Ruble, and Crabtree, 291–320.

46. A provocative exploration of this point is made by John Vlach, "Looking behind the Marble Mask: Varied African American Responses to Difficult History in Washington, D.C.," in *Composing Urban History*, ed. Czaplicka, Ruble, and Crabtree, 31–57.

47. Natan M. Meir, "Jews, Ukrainians, and Russians in Kiev: Intergroup Relations in Late Imperial Associational Life," *Slavic Review* 65, no. 3 (2006): 475–501; the quotation here is on 498.

48. U.S. National Capital Planning Commission, *Shaw School Urban Renewal Area Landmarks* (Washington, D.C.: U.S. National Capital Planning Commission, 1968).

CHAPTER 1

1. Joseph West Moore, *Picturesque Washington: Pen and Pencil Sketches* (Providence: J.A. & R.A. Reid, 1884), 247–48.

2. Constance McLaughlin Green, *Washington: A History of the Capital, 1800–1950, Volume One: Village and Capital, 1800–1878* (Princeton, N.J.: Princeton University Press, 1962), 3–22. For an overview of L'Enfant's plan for the city and the complexities of its realization, see Scott W. Berg, *Grand Avenues: The Story of the French Visionary Who Designed Washington, D.C.* (New York: Pantheon Books, 2007). For more about the remarkable Banneker, see Charles A. Cerami, *Benjamin Banneker: Surveyor, Astronomer, Publisher, Patriot* (New York: John Wiley & Sons, 2002).

3. Marcia McAdoo Greenlee, "A Methodology for the Identification, Study and Evaluation of Afro-American Historic Places," PhD dissertation, George Washington University, Washington, 1982, 30–63.

4. On Washington at the outbreak of Civil War, see Green, *Washington*, 230–43.

5. This discussion is based on John Karl Byrand, "Changing Race, Changing Place: Racial, Occupational, and Residential Patterns in Washington, D.C., 1880–1920," PhD dissertation, University of Maryland, College Park, 1999, 45–53; and Thomas R. Johnson, "The City on the Hill: Race Relations in Washington, D.C., 1865–1885," PhD dissertation, University of Maryland, College Park, 1975, 7–9. Also see Lois Horton, *Washington, D.C.: From Civil War Town to Modern City* (Washington, D.C.: Associates for Renewal in Education, 1979).

6. Johnson, "City on the Hill," 24–25.

7. Federal Writers' Project, Works Progress Administration, *Washington: City and Capital*, American Guide Series (Washington, D.C.: U.S. Government Printing Office, 1937), 69.

8. Constance McLaughlin Green, *The Secret City: A History of Race Relations in the Nation's Capital* (Princeton, N.J.: Princeton University Press, 1967), 13–54; Richard C. Wade, "Foreword," in *Free Negroes in the District of Columbia, 1790–1846*, by Letitia Woods Brown (New York: Oxford University Press, 1972), v–vii; the citation here is on vi.

9. Brown, *Free Negroes*, 7–10.

10. Ibid., 14.

11. Green, *Secret City*, 33.

12. Allan Johnston, *Surviving Freedom: The Black Community of Washington, D.C., 1860–1880* (New York: Garland, 1993), 76–77.

13. Ibid., 92–93; Brown, *Free Negroes*, 12–14; Willard B. Gatewood, *Aristocrats of Color: The Black Elite, 1880–1920* (Bloomington: Indiana University Press, 1990), 72–80.

14. Brown, *Free Negroes*, 129–42; Green, *Secret City*, 13–54.

15. Charlotte J. Shifrin, "Minstrelsy in Washington, D.C.: The First Decade," MA thesis, American University, Washington, 1987; Marye L. Taylor, "Washington Drinking Places, 1855–1917," MA thesis, George Washington University, Washington, 1980; Chancellor Williams, "The Economic and Social Status of the Free Negro in the District of Columbia, 1830–1862," MA thesis, Howard University, Washington, 1935.

16. Sandra Fitzpatrick and Maria R. Goodwin, *The Guide to Black Washington: Places and Events of Historical and Cultural Significance in the Nation's Capital*, rev. illus. ed. (New York: Hippocrene Books, 2001), 147, 153–57, 176; Kathleen M. Lesko, Valerie Babb, and Carroll R. Gibbs, *Black Georgetown Remembered: A History of Its Black Community from the Founding of "The Town of George" in 1751 to the Present Day* (Washington, D.C.: Georgetown University Press, 1991), 10–11, 138–54; Brown, *Free Negroes*; Stanley Harrold, *Subversives: Antislavery Community in Washington, D.C., 1828–1865* (Baton Rouge: Louisiana State University Press, 2003); Linda M. Arnold, "Congressional Government of the District of Columbia, 1800–1846," PhD dissertation, Georgetown University, Washington, 1974; Paul Phillips Cooke, "From Emancipation to Citizenship: Blacks in Washington, 1862–1887," in *First Freed: Washington, D.C. in the Emancipation Era*, ed. Elizabeth Clark-Lewis (Washington, D.C.: AP Foundation Press, 1998), 69–82; Lillian G. Dabney, "History of Schools for Negroes in the District of Columbia, 1807–1947," PhD dissertation, Catholic University, Washington, 1949; Michael Andrew Fitzpatrick, "Shaw, Washington's Premier Black Neighborhood: An Examination of the Origins and Development of a Black Business Movement, 1880–1920," MA thesis, University of Virginia, Charlottesville, 1989, 67; Michael Andrew Fitzpatrick, "'A Great Agitation for Business': Black Economic Development in Shaw," *Washington History* 2, no. 2 (1990–91): 49–73; Johnston, *Surviving Freedom*, 81–83; Herbert Kingley Lodder, "The Response of White Protestantism to Negroes in Washington, D.C., 1865–1965," MA thesis, Columbia University, New York, 1965; Marya Annette McQuirter, *African American Heritage Trail, Washington, D.C.* (Washington, D.C.: Cultural Tourism D.C., 2003), 10–11; Thelma Randall, "Foreword: Past Is Prologue," in *First Freed*, ed. Clark-Lewis, ix–x; La Vonne M. Siegel, "Myrtilla Miner: Educator and Founder of the Colored Girls Schools in Washington, D.C.," MA thesis, George Washington University, Washington, 1970; Benjamin Lee Swinson, "Historical Development of Public School Education Programs in Washington, D.C., 1858–1982," PhD dissertation, George Washington University,

Washington, 1985; Olive Taylor, "The Protestant Episcopal Church and the Negro in Washington, D.C.: A History of the Protestant Episcopal Church and Its Nexus to the Black Population from the Seventeenth through the Nineteenth Centuries," PhD dissertation, Howard University, Washington, 1973; Thomas B. Hargrave Jr., *Private Differences—General Good: A History of the YMCA of Metropolitan Washington* (Washington: YMCA of Metropolitan Washington, 1985), 17–21.

17. Regina T. Akers, "Freedom without Equality: Emancipation in the United States, 1861–1863," in *First Freed*, ed. Clark-Lewis, 20–39; Nina Honemond Clarke, *History of the Nineteenth-Century Black Churches in Maryland and Washington, D.C.* (New York: Vantage Press, 1983).

18. This account of the founding of the Washington YMCAs, and the role of Anthony Bowen in that process, is based upon Hargrave, *Private Differences—General Good*, 3–21, 28–32, 43–44.

19. James Huntington Whyte, *The Uncivil War: Washington during the Reconstruction, 1865–1878* (New York: Twane, 1958), 17.

20. Byrand, "Changing Race, Changing Place," 45–53; Johnson, "City on the Hill," 7–9; James Borchert, *Alley Life in Washington: Family, Community, Religion, and Folklife in the City, 1850–1970* (Urbana: University of Illinois Press, 1980), 5–7.

21. Alan Lessoff, *The Nation and Its City: Politics, "Corruption," and Progress in Washington, D.C., 1861–1902* (Baltimore: Johns Hopkins University Press, 1994), 40; Elizabeth Clark-Lewis, "Introduction," in *First Freed*, ed. Clark-Lewis, xiv–xxiv; David Taft Terry, "A Brief Moment in the Sun: The Aftermath of Emancipation in Washington, 1862–1869," in *First Freed*, ed. Clark-Lewis, 30–66; Akers, "Freedom without Equality."

22. Clark-Lewis, "Introduction"; Terry, "Brief Moment in the Sun"; Johnston, *Surviving Freedom*, 62–69.

23. Shane White and Graham White, *Stylin': African American Expressive Culture from Its Beginnings to the Zoot Suit* (Ithaca, N.Y.: Cornell University Press, 1998), 155.

24. This discussion is based on Johnston, *Surviving Freedom*, 112–14; Green, *Washington*, 272–90; and Green, *Secret City*, 55–74. The federal government paid District slaveholders up to $300 per slave, in an experiment that proved too expensive to be repeated after the war in other slave-owning states and jurisdictions. For a discussion of Emancipation in the District, see Johnson, "City on the Hill," 14–16. For a discussion of conditions among arriving fugitive slaves, see ibid., 32–37.

25. Thomas C. Battle, "Published Resources for the Study of Blacks in the District of Columbia: An Annotated Guide," PhD dissertation, George Washington University, Washington, 1982; Johnston, *Surviving Freedom*, 114–77; Federal Writers' Project, *Washington*, 75; William B. Edelin, "The District of Columbia in the Civil War," MA thesis, Howard University, Washington, 1925.

26. Major General Oliver Otis Howard describes the confusion over the status of fugitive slaves at the outbreak of the Civil War in his autobiography; Oliver Otis Howard, *Autobiography of Oliver Otis Howard, Volume II* (New York: Baker & Taylor, 1907), 163–73.

27. Ibid., 169.

28. Ibid., 171.

29. For further discussion of the emergence and use of the term "contraband" as applied to African Americans, see Kate Masur, "A Rare Phenomenon of 'Philological Vegetation': The Word 'Contraband' and the Meanings of Emancipation in the United States," *Journal of American History* 94, no. 4 (2007): 1050–84.

30. Whyte, *Uncivil War*, 15.

31. Ibid.; Fitzpatrick and Goodwin, *Guide to Black Washington*, 148; Thomas Holt, Cassandra Smith-Parker, and Rosalyn Terborg-Penn, *A Special Mission: The Story of the Freedmen's Hospital, 1862–1962* (Washington, D.C.: Howard University Press, 1975), 2–5; Johnston, *Surviving Freedom*, 155–61; Katherine (Kate) Mazur, "Reconstructing the Nation's Capital: The Politics of Race and Citizenship in the District of Columbia, 1862–1878," PhD dissertation, American Culture, University of Michigan, Ann Arbor, 2001, 105.

32. "Barry Farms," an experimental agricultural community for freed slaves sponsored by the ubiquitous Major General Oliver O. Howard in Southeast Washington across the Anacostia River from what would become Downtown D.C., was among these suburban areas; Howard, *Autobiography*, 414–22. For more on the outplacement of "contrabands" to outlying locations, see Johnston, *Surviving Freedom*, 121–22; Holt, Smith-Parker, and Terborg-Penn, *Special Mission*, 5–7; Johnson, "City on the Hill," 36–37, 169–70; and Mazur, "Reconstructing the Nation's Capital," 81.

33. Various interpretations of the Freedmen's Bureau's record may be found in such general historiographies of the period as Eric Foner, *Reconstruction: America's Unfinished Revolution, 1863–1877* (New York: Harper & Row, 1988); John Hope Franklin, *Reconstruction: After the Civil War* (Chicago: University of Chicago Press, 1961); Leon F. Litwack, *Been in the Storm So Long: The Aftermath of Slavery* (New York: Alfred A. Knopf, 1979); and C. Vann Woodward, *The Strange Career of Jim Crow* (New York: Oxford University Press, 1974). A thoughtful analysis of the bureau's record in Washington is given by Mazur, "Reconstructing the Nation's Capital," 49–79. The Freedmen's Hospital, together with Howard University, established following the war by the Bureau's commissioner, Major General Oliver O. Howard, firmly secured this new corner of the nation's capital for African American elites.

34. John A. Carpenter, *Sword & Olive Branch: Oliver Otis Howard* (Pittsburgh: University of Pittsburgh Press, 1964).

35. Howard, *Autobiography*, 208.

36. Holt, Smith-Parker, and Terborg-Penn, *Special Mission*; Fitzpatrick and Goodwin, *Guide to Black Washington*, 108–9, 114–15.

37. Green, *Secret City*, 81.

38. Ibid., 308–9. For an overview of the history of Howard University, see Rayford W. Logan, *Howard University: The First Hundred Years, 1867–1967* (Washington, D.C.: Howard University Press, 1968).

39. Fitzpatrick and Goodwin, *Guide to Black Washington*, 101–9; Harry G. Roninson III, *The Long Walk: The Place-Making Legacy of Howard University* (Washington, D.C.: Moorland-Spingarn Research Center, Howard University, 1996).

40. Howard, *Autobiography*, 394–99.

41. Logan, *Howard University*; Letitia W. Brown and Elsie M. Lewis, *Washington in the New Era, 1870–1970* (Washington, D.C.: National Portrait Gallery, 1972), 25–28; Whyte, *Uncivil War*, 237–61. The bureau's support eventually would become a liability as congressional Southern Democrats gained renewed strength over time. Many Southerners viewed the university as having been financed by the reallocation of the property and wealth illegally seized following the war by the federal government. Therefore, in their minds, Howard University was an illegitimate institution. Such congressional attitudes greatly complicated the task of managing the institution once Reconstruction had come to an end.

42. Paul A. Groves and Edward K. Muller, "The Evolution of Black Residential Areas in Late-Nineteenth-Century Cities," *Journal of Historical Geography* 1, no. 2 (1975): 169–91.

43. Paul A. Groves, "The 'Hidden' Population: Washington Alley Dwellers in the Late Nineteenth Century," *The Professional Geographer* 26, no. 3 (1974): 270–76; Byrand, "Changing Race, Changing Place"; Borchert, *Alley Life;* Johnston, *Surviving Freedom*, 8–9; John P. Radford, "Patterns of White-Nonwhite Residential Segregation in Washington, D.C. in the Late Nineteenth Century," MA thesis, University of Maryland, College Park, 1982.

44. Charles Frederick Weller, *Neglected Neighbors: Stories of Life in the Alleys, Tenements and Shanties of the National Capital* (Philadelphia: John C. Winston, 1909), 9. Other American cities of the era had alleys and alley dwellers. Weller's description correctly captures the peculiarity of the Washington alley. Unlike other American cities, in which alleys were small thoroughfares providing service entrances to buildings on larger streets, the Washington alley and its inhabitants were often hidden within the heart of particularly large blocks. This enclosed environment converted the Washington alley into a secret community hidden to all who did not know it was there. To better understand this contrast, readers may wish to consult Mary Ellen Hayward's history of alley houses in nearby Baltimore: Mary Ellen Hayward, *Baltimore's Alley Houses: Homes for Working People since the 1780s*

(Baltimore: Johns Hopkins University Press, 2008). In most instances, the Baltimore alley dwelling was a diminutive version of the more traditional Baltimore row house. For further discussion of that architectural and social structure, see Charles Belfoure and Mary Ellen Hayward, *The Baltimore Rowhouse* (New York: Princeton Architectural Press, 1999).

45. D.C. Cheek and A. Friedlander, "Pottery and Pig's Feet: Space, Ethnicity, and Neighborhood in Washington, D.C., 1880–1940," *Historical Archeology* 24, no. 1 (1990): 34–60.

46. Borchert, *Alley Life*.

47. Elizabeth Clark-Lewis, *Living In, Living Out: African American Domestics in Washington, D.C., 1910–1940* (Washington, D.C.: Smithsonian Institution Press, 1994); Fitzpatrick, "Shaw."

48. Brown and Lewis, *Washington*, 18–24.

49. This discussion is based on Johnson, "City on the Hill," 42–90.

50. Steven J. Diner, *Democracy, Federalism, and the Governance of the Nation's Capital, 1790–1974*, Studies in D.C. History and Public Policy 10 (Washington, D.C.: Center for Applied Research and Urban Policy, University of the District of Columbia, 1987), 4–14; Whyte, *Uncivil War*, 17–20; Michael K. Fauntroy, *Home Rule or House Rule? Congress and the Erosion of Local Governance in the District of Columbia* (Lanham, Md.: University Press of America, 2003), 29–33; Charles Wesley Harris, *Congress and the Governance of the Nation's Capital: The Conflict of Federal and Local Interests* (Washington, D.C.: Georgetown University Press, 1995), 3–5; Mazur, "Reconstructing the Nation's Capital," 13.

51. Diner, *Democracy*, 7–8, 13–14.

52. Ibid., 4–15.

53. Lesko, Babb, and Gibbs, *Black Georgetown Remembered*, 20–23.

54. Whyte, *Uncivil War*, 17–20.

55. Ibid., 49; Mazur, "Reconstructing the Nation's Capital," 179.

56. Diner, *Democracy*, 13.

57. Ibid., 14–15; Johnston, *Surviving Freedom*, 194–98.

58. Whyte, *Uncivil War*, 35–53; Robert Harrison, "Race, Radicalism, and Reconstruction: Grassroots Republican Politics in Washington, D.C., 1867–74," *American Nineteenth Century History* 3, no. 3 (2002): 73–96; the citation here is on 74–79.

59. Dorothy E. Greene, "Negro Suffrage in the District of Columbia," MA thesis, Howard University, Washington, 1936.

60. Whyte, *Uncivil War*, 61; Sara B. Collins, "Sayles J. Bowen and District of Columbia Problems of Reconstruction," MA thesis, American University, Washington, 1954.

61. Johnson, "City on the Hill," 59–65.

62. Mazur, "Reconstructing the Nation's Capital," 312–16.

63. Whyte, *Uncivil War*, 19–20.

64. Ibid., 34–35.

65. Johnson, "City on the Hill," 74–77.

66. Harrison, "Race, Radicalism, and Reconstruction," 80; Johnston, *Surviving Freedom*, 25, 59–64, 84–85.

67. Harrison, "Race, Radicalism, and Reconstruction," 82.

68. Ibid., 83–84; Lodder, "Response of White Protestantism to Negroes"; Melvin Roscoe Williams, "Blacks in Washington, D.C., 1860–1870," PhD dissertation, Johns Hopkins University, Baltimore, 1976, 46–74.

69. Mazur, "Reconstructing the Nation's Capital," 18–19.

70. Ibid, 20.

71. Johnson, "City on the Hill," 77–90.

72. Whyte, *Uncivil War*, 82.

73. Ibid., 84–89.

74. Johnson, "City on the Hill," 81–84.

75. Harrison, "Race, Radicalism, and Reconstruction," 77–79; 86–88.

76. Howard, *Autobiography*, 423–44.

77. Johnson, "City on the Hill," 128–49; Lesko, Babb, and Gibbs, *Black Georgetown Remembered*, 39–42.

78. Byrand, "Changing Race, Changing Place," 46.

79. Diner, *Democracy*, 16–20; Whyte, *Uncivil War*, 90–145; Lois E. Horton, "The Development of Federal Social Policy for Blacks in Washington, D.C. after Emancipation," PhD dissertation, Brandeis University, Waltham, Mass., 1977.

80. For further discussion of Shepherd's relationship with the Board of Public Works, see William A. Maury, *Alexander "Boss" Shepherd and the Board of Public Works* (Washington, D.C.: George Washington University Press, 1975).

81. For more about the career of Montgomery Meigs, see the collection of articles published by the United States Capitol Historical Society: William C. Dickinson, Dean A. Herrin, and Donald R. Kennon, eds., *Montgomery C. Meigs and the Building of the Nation's Capital* (Athens: Ohio University Press, 2001).

82. Christhard Schrenk and Peter Wanner, "Adolf Cluss in Heilbronn: His Formative Years," in *Adolf Cluss: Architect from Germany to America*, ed. Alan Lessoff and Christof Mauch (Washington, D.C.: Historical Society of Washington, D.C., and Stadarchiv Heilbronn in association with Berghahn Books, 2005), 10–30; Sabine Freitag, "Years of Apprenticeship and Travel: Adolf Cluss and the Revolution of 1848 in Mainz," ibid., 31–42; Sabina W. Dugan, "Adolf Cluss: From German Revolutionary to Architect for America's Capital," ibid., 43–54.

83. Cynthia R. Field, "Cluss's Masterwork: The National Museum Building," in *Adolf Cluss*, ed. Lessoff and Mauch, 131–42; Tanya Edwards Beauchamp, "Schools

for All: Adolf Cluss and Education," ibid., 143–56; Helen Tangires, "Adolf Cluss and Public Market Reform," ibid., 157–67.

84. Rochard Longstreth, "Adolf Cluss, the World, and Washington," in *Adolf Cluss*, ed. Lessoff and Mauch, 103–18.

85. Alan Lessoff, "Adolf Cluss and Washington's Public Works," in *Adolf Cluss*, ed. Lessoff and Mauch, 119–29.

86. Green, *Washington*, 338–62.

87. Ibid., 46.

88. Lessoff, *Nation and Its City*, 44–71.

89. The prototypical "pragmatic pluralist" of the era, Chicago mayor Carter Henry Harrison Sr., successfully built boosterish business-immigrant coalitions even as he lived a private life embedded in his city's snooty "upper crust." For a discussion of the concept of "pragmatic pluralism," see Blair A. Ruble, *Second Metropolis: Pragmatic Pluralism in Gilded Age Chicago, Silver Age Moscow, and Meiji Osaka* (Washington, D.C.: Woodrow Wilson Center Press; Cambridge: Cambridge University Press, 2001; Baltimore: Johns Hopkins University Press, 2004); for a discussion of Harrison as a prototypical "pragmatic pluralist," see 320–33.

90. Lessoff, *Nation and Its City*, 76–77.

91. Ibid., 75–100.

92. Ibid., 74.

93. Whyte, *Uncivil War*, 176–236.

94. Fauntroy, *Home Rule or House Rule?* 29–33; Harris, *Congress*, 3–5; Mazur, "Reconstructing the Nation's Capital," 338–87.

95. Mazur, "Reconstructing the Nation's Capital," 390.

96. Whyte, *Uncivil War*, 267–78; Diner, *Democracy*, 21–22.

97. Diner, *Democracy*, 20–23; H-DC/DC History, "A Timeline of Washington DC History," H-DC Discussion Web site, http://www.h-net.org/~dclist/timeline.1.html.

98. Gatewood, *Aristocrats of Color*, 39–68.

99. Mark Perry, *Lift Up Thy Voice: The Grimké Family's Journey from Slaveholders to Civil Rights Leaders* (New York: Viking, 2001), 261.

100. Lessoff, *Nation and Its City*, 100–129.

101. Mazur, "Reconstructing the Nation's Capital," 196. Mazur explicates the intricate relationship and contradictions between the movements for women's and for black male suffrage; ibid., 190–225.

102. Lessoff, *Nation and Its City*, 118.

103. These points are made by Beverley B. Goodpasture, among many authors, in "Alexander Robey Shepherd: A Reputation Rehabilitated," MA thesis, Georgetown University, Washington, 1964.

104. This general modernization of the city is discussed in *City of Magnificent Intentions: A History of the District of Columbia*, by D.C. History Project (Washington, D.C.: Intac, 1983), 118–94.

105. Shepherd, himself, moved on to silver mining in Mexico. For an account of his time there, see his son's memoirs: Grant Shepherd, *Silver Magnet: Fifty Years in a Mexican Silver Mine* (New York: E. P. Dutton, 1938).

106. "For Outgoing Mayor, an Icon to Remember the District," *Washington Post*, December 14, 2006.

107. This argument is made by the historian James Huntington Whyte, among many observers; see Whyte, *Uncivil War*, 278–79.

108. In 1966, the National Capital Planning Commission would designate the area as "Shaw" after a local junior high school that was itself named after the Civil War hero Robert Gould Shaw, commander of the Massachusetts Fifty-Fourth Regiment, the first African American combat unit in the Civil War. Subsequent historiography has tended to reflect the commission's appellation of the district as a unified neighborhood. The U Street corridor, as defined in this study, runs through the northern reaches of the Shaw neighborhood as defined by the commission. The area of this study extends further west to 16th Street, and east to embrace LeDroit Park and other areas adjacent to Howard University. For definitions of the Shaw neighborhood, see Byrand, "Changing Race, Changing Place," 23; and Jane Freundel Levey, Paul K. Williams, Richard T. Busch, J. Brendan Meyer, Anne W. Rollins, and Joan M. Mathys, *Midcity at the Crossroads: Shaw Heritage Trail* (Washington, D.C.: Cultural Tourism D.C., 2006).

109. Byrand, "Changing Race, Changing Place," 47.

110. Fitzpatrick and Goodwin, *Guide to Black Washington*, 84–86.

111. David L. Lewis, *District of Columbia: A Bicentennial History* (New York and Nashville: W. W. Norton, 1976), 151–52; Kathryn Allamong Jacob, *Capital Elites: High Society in Washington, D.C., after the Civil War* (Washington, D.C.: Smithsonian Institution Press, 1995), 162–64.

112. Laura Bergheim, *The Washington Historical Atlas: Who Did What When and Where in the Nation's Capital* (Rockville, Md.: Woodbine House, 1992), 238.

113. Jacob, *Capital Elites*, 192–93; Paul K. Williams, *Greater U Street*, Images of America Series (Charleston: Arcadia, 2005), 30–31; Jeffrey R. Henig, *Gentrification in Adams Morgan: Political and Commercial Consequences of Neighborhood Change*, Center for Washington Area Studies 9 (Washington, D.C.: George Washington University, 1982), 13.

114. Bergheim, *Washington Historical Atlas*, 242–43; Paul K. Williams and Kathryn S. Smith, *City within a City: Greater U Street Heritage Trail* (Washington, D.C.: Historical Society and D.C. Heritage Tourism Collection, 2001), 26–31.

115. Bergheim, *Washington Historical Atlas*, 242–43.

116. Ibid.

117. Lewis, *District of Columbia*, 141–43.

118. Byrand, "Changing Race, Changing Place," 45–47.

119. Johnston, *Surviving Freedom*, 54–59.

120. Borchert, *Alley Life*, 4.

121. Ibid.

122. Johnston, *Black Community of Washington*, 6.

123. Ibid., 7.

124. Ibid., 54.

125. Jacqueline Moore, *Leading the Race: The Transformation of the Black Elite in the Nation's Capital, 1880–1920* (Charlottesville: University of Virginia Press, 1999); Audrey Elisa Kerr, "Two Black Washingtons: The Role of Complexion in the Oral History of District of Columbia Residents, 1863–1963," PhD dissertation, University of Maryland, College Park, 1998; Perry, *Lift Up Thy Voice*, 251–53.

126. Lodder, "Response of White Protestantism to Negroes."

127. Greenlee, "Methodology," 64–137.

128. Howard, *Autobiography*, 452–543.

CHAPTER 2

1. Langston Hughes, *The Big Sea*, republished in *The Collected Works of Langston Hughes, Volume 13: The Big Sea*, ed. Joseph McLaren (Columbia: University of Missouri Press, 2002), 164.

2. This is a point he acknowledges himself; ibid., 165.

3. Michael Andrew Fitzpatrick, "Shaw, Washington's Premier Black Neighborhood: An Examination of the Origins and Development of a Black Business Movement, 1880–1920," master's thesis, Department of History, University of Virginia, Charlottesville, 1989, 17. Also see Michael Andrew Fitzpatrick, "'A Great Agitation for Business': Black Economic Development in Shaw," *Washington History* 2, no. 2 (1990–91): 49–73.

4. One incident among several that convinced Ralph Bunche to forgo a senior appointment in the Truman administration's State Department following World War II revolved around the refusal of a local pet cemetery to permit the burial of his family dog in a section reserved for the pets of white people. Brian Urquhart, *Ralph Bunche: An American Life* (New York: W. W. Norton, 1993), 109.

5. Willard B. Gatewood, *Aristocrats of Color: The Black Elite, 1880–1920* (Bloomington: Indiana University Press, 1990), 9–13.

6. Hughes, *Big Sea*, 165.

7. Sandra Fitzpatrick and Maria R. Goodwin, *The Guide to Black Washington: Places and Events of Historical and Cultural Significance in the Nation's Capital*, rev. illus. ed. (New York: Hippocrene Books, 2001), 107–8.

8. John Karl Byrand, "Changing Race, Changing Place: Racial, Occupational, and Residential Patterns in Shaw, Washington, D.C., 1880–1920," PhD dissertation, University of Maryland, College Park, 1999, abstract.

9. Thomas R. Johnson, "The City on the Hill: Race Relations in Washington, D.C., 1865–1885," PhD dissertation, University of Maryland, College Park, 1975, 396.

10. Ibid., 396–97.

11. Ibid., 398.

12. These nondiscrimination laws were quietly dropped from the District of Columbia Code in 1901. Civil rights activists such as Mary Church Terrell and Annie Stein (cochairs of the Coordinating Committee for the Enforcement of the D.C. Anti-Discrimination Laws) rediscovered the laws during the 1940s. They drew on them to pursue legal strategies which resulted in a 1953 Supreme Court decision in *District of Columbia v. Thompson Co.* concerning Thompson's Restaurant, which ended legal discrimination in the city's public accommodations. These earlier laws also played important roles in other pivotal Supreme Court decisions, such as *Hurd v. Hodge* in 1948 and *Brown v. Board of Education of Topeka* in 1954. For an additional discussion of the role played by the abandoned anti-discrimination laws of the 1870s, see Marvin Caplan, "Eat Anywhere," *Washington History* 1, no. 1 (Spring 1989): 24–39. Additional supportive material for exploring both trends are identified by Thomas C. Battle, "Published Resources for the Study of Blacks in the District of Columbia: An Annotated Guide," PhD dissertation, George Washington University, Washington, 1982.

13. See Constance McLaughlin Green, *The Secret City: A History of Race Relations in the Nation's Capital* (Princeton, N.J.: Princeton University Press, 1967), 119–54; and Carl Abbott, "Dimensions of Regional Change in Washington, D.C.," *American Historical Review* 95, no. 5 (December 1990): 1367–93.

14. Although the scholarship on Jim Crow is extensive, readers unfamiliar with the term would be well served to begin learning about this sad period of American history from C. Vann Woodward's classic lectures presented at the University of Virginia in 1954 as the James W. Richard Lectures in History. These lectures were published under the title *The Strange Career of Jim Crow* in 1955. One of many editions of this classic volume is C. Vann Woodward, *The Strange Career of Jim Crow* (New York: Oxford University Press, 1974). Readers new to the topic should also consult the encyclopedic study of the era by Rayford W. Logan, *The Negro in American Life and Thought: The Nadir, 1877–1901* (New York: Dial Press, 1954).

15. Fitzpatrick, "Shaw," 18.

16. For a discussion of this legal history, see Richard Kluger, *Simple Justice: The History of* Brown v. Board of Education *and Black America's Struggle for Equality* (New York: Alfred A. Knopf, 1976).

17. This is a point made using similar words by Fitzpatrick, "Shaw," 19.

18. James O. Horton, "Jim Crow and the Response: Protest and Community Building," in *What's the Story? A Deeper Look at the History of Greater Shaw in Washington, D.C. in the Context of the National African American Experience. Conference Proceedings, December 7–8, 2004,* ed. Cultural Tourism D.C. (Washington, D.C.: Cultural Tourism D.C., 2005), 20–22.

19. C. Van Woodward, "Yes, There Was a Compromise of 1877," *Journal of American History* 60, no. 2 (1973): 215–23.

20. Johnson, "City on the Hill," 254–86.

21. These general processes are discussed by D.C. History Project, *City of Magnificent Intentions: A History of the District of Columbia* (Washington, D.C.: Intac, 1983), 304–434.

22. Green, *Secret City*, 33, 200.

23. Ibid.; Byrand, "Changing Race, Changing Place," 202–4.

24. Lewis Newton Walker Jr., "The Struggle and Attempts to Establish Branch Autonomy and Hegemony: A History of the District of Columbia Branch National Association for the Advancement of Colored People, 1912–1942," PhD dissertation, University of Delaware, Newark, 1979, 5–7.

25. Paul A. Groves and Edward K. Muller, "The Evolution of Black Residential Areas in Late-Nineteenth-Century Cities," *Journal of Historical Geography* 1, no. 2 (1975): 169–91.

26. Constance McLaughlin Green, *Washington: A History of the Capital, 1800–1950* (Princeton, N.J.: Princeton University Press, 1962), viii.

27. Marcia McAdoo Greenlee, "A Methodology for the Identification, Study and Evaluation of Afro-American Places," PhD dissertation, George Washington University, Washington, 1982, 64–67.

28. Ibid., 63–137.

29. Ibid., 179–80.

30. Ibid., 73–79.

31. Ibid., 71–73.

32. Fitzpatrick and Goodwin, *Guide to Black Washington*, 84–99, 177–80.

33. Paul Laurence Dunbar, "Negro Life in Washington," *Harper's Weekly*, January 13, 1900, 32.

34. Greenlee, "Methodology," 120–21, 181.

35. Ibid., 135–37.

36. Allan Johnston, *Surviving Freedom: The Black Community of Washington, D.C.: 1860–1880* (New York: Garland, 1993), 6–7.

37. Fitzpatrick, "Shaw," 6–8.

38. Ibid., 17–20.

39. Dunbar, "Negro Life," 32.

40. Charles Frederick Weller, *Neglected Neighbors: Stories of Life in the Alleys, Tenements, and Shanties of the National Capital* (Philadelphia: John C. Winston, 1909), 1–9.

41. Paul A. Groves, "The 'Hidden' Population: Washington Alley Dwellers in the Late Nineteenth Century," *Professional Geographer* 26, no. 3 (1974): 270–76; the citation here is on 270.

42. I discuss this phenomenon in greater detail elsewhere: Blair A. Ruble, *St. Petersburg's Courtyards and Washington's Alleys: Officialdom's Neglected Neighbors*, Kennan Institute Occasional Paper 285 (Washington, D.C.: Woodrow Wilson International Center for Scholars, 2003). Previous editions of this article may be found in Catalan in *Ciutat real, ciutat ideal: Significat i funió s l'espai urbá modern*, ed. Pep Subirós (Barcelona: Centre de Cultura Contemporània de Barcelona, 1998); as well as in a Russian translation by Vyachislav Glazychev and Grigorii Kaganov, appearing in *Real'nost' i Sub"ekt* (Saint Petersburg) 6, no. 2 (2000): 56–64; and *Vestnik Instituta Kennan v Rossii* (Moscow) 2 (2002): 53–66.

43. Byrand, "Changing Race, Changing Place," 15–16; Weller, *Neglected Neighbors*, 37–46.

44. Groves, "'Hidden' Population," 275.

45. The story of the alleys segregating by race before the rest of the city is told by John P. Radford, "Patterns of White-Nonwhite Residential Segregation in Washington, D.C., in the Late Nineteenth Century," MA thesis, University of Maryland, College Park, 1982.

46. James Borchert, *Alley Life in Washington: Family, Community, Religion, and Folklife in the City, 1850–1970* (Urbana: University of Illinois Press, 1980), 42–45, 219.

47. Ibid., 219–20; Byrand, "Changing Race, Changing Place," 145–46.

48. Borchert, *Alley Life in Washington*, 11–12.

49. Walker, "Struggle and Attempts to Establish Branch Autonomy," 14–15.

50. Howard Gillette Jr., *Between Justice and Beauty: Race, Planning, and the Failure of Urban Policy in Washington, D.C.* (Baltimore: Johns Hopkins University Press, 1995), 109–13.

51. Ibid., 113–16.

52. Ibid., 109–13.

53. Ibid., 116–22.

54. Weller, *Neglected Neighbors*.

55. Ibid., 316–17.

56. Ibid., 317.

57. There were, in fact, fitful efforts to raise the issue of District Home Rule in the years leading up to and following World War I. Steven J. Diner, *Democracy, Federalism, and the Governance of the Nation's Capital, 1790–1974*, Studies in D.C. History and Public Policy 10 (Washington, D.C.: Center for Applied Research and Urban Policy, University of the District of Columbia, 1987), 32–36.

58. Jerome S. Paige and Margaret M. Reuss, *Safe, Decent and Affordable: Citizen Struggles to Improve Housing in the District of Columbia, 1890–1982*, Studies in D.C. History and Public Policy 6 (Washington, D.C.: Center for Applied Research and Urban Policy, University of the District of Columbia, 1983), 2–11 .

59. Borchert, *Alley Life in Washington*, 45–46.

60. Ibid.

61. Ibid., 52.

62. Ibid.

63. Lyndsey Layton, "Alley Homes Fight for Respect—and Trash Pickup," *Washington Post*, May 29, 2006.

64. Julia A. Whiters, "The Attitude of the *Washington Post* toward the Negro, 1941–1942," MA thesis, Howard University, Washington, 1945.

65. Romaine F. Scott, "The Negro in American History, 1877–1900, as portrayed in the Washington *Evening Star*," MA thesis, Howard University, Washington, 1948; Virginia C. Scott, "The American Negro as Portrayed in the *Evening Star*, 1904–1912," MA thesis, Howard University, Washington, 1952.

66. Ruble, "St. Petersburg's Courtyards and Washington's Alleys"; and Borchert, *Alley Life in Washington*, 220–23.

67. Borchert, *Alley Life in Washington*, 117.

68. Ibid., 223.

69. Greenlee, "Methodology," 204.

70. Gatewood, *Aristocrats of Color*, 343–47.

71. Green, *Secret City*, 179.

72. Ibid., 178–79; Marye L. Taylor, "Washington Drinking Places, 1855–1917," MA thesis, George Washington University, Washington, 1980; Byrand, "Changing Race, Changing Place," 142; Stephanie Barbara Frank, "'If We Own the Story, We Own the Place': Cultural Heritage, Historic Preservation, and Gentrification on U Street," MA thesis, University of Maryland, College Park, 2005, 59–65.

73. Jacqueline Moore, *Leading the Race: The Transformation of the Black Elite in the Nation's Capital, 1880–1920* (Charlottesville: University of Virginia Press, 1999), 117–19; Evelyn Brooks Higgenbotham, *The Righteous Discontent: The Women's Movement in the Black Baptist Church, 1880–1920* (Cambridge, Mass.: Harvard University Press, 1993).

74. The transformation of domestic service and the significance of those changes for the city's African American women are explored in the work of Elizabeth Clark-

Lewis. See, e.g., Elizabeth Clark-Lewis, "From 'Servant' to 'Dayworker': A Study of Selected Household Service Workers in Washington, D.C., 1900–1926," PhD dissertation, University of Maryland, College Park, 1983; Elizabeth Clark-Lewis, *Living In, Living Out: African American Domestics in Washington, D.C., 1910–1940* (Washington, D.C.: Smithsonian Institution Press, 1994); and Elizabeth Clark-Lewis, "'For a Real Better Life': Voices of African American Women Migrants, 1900–1930," in *Urban Odyssey: A Multicultural History of Washington, D.C.*, ed. Francine Curro Cary (Washington, D.C.: Smithsonian Institution Press, 1996), 91–112.

75. Spencer R. Crew, "Melding the Old and the New: The Modern African American Community, 1930–1960," in *Urban Odyssey*, ed. Cary, 208–27.

76. Fitzpatrick, "Shaw," 23.

77. Ibid., 23–26.

78. Byrand, "Changing Race, Changing Place," 25.

79. Fitzpatrick, "Shaw," 47–55; Fitzpatrick and Goodwin, *Guide to Black Washington*, 165–70.

80. Nina Honemond Clarke, *History of the Nineteenth-Century Black Churches in Maryland and Washington, D.C.* (New York: Vantage Press, 1983), 16–17.

81. "Roosevelt Is Square," *Washington Bee*, December 5, 1908; Byrand, "Changing Race, Changing Place," 200–201; Paul K. Williams and Kathryn S. Smith, *City within a City: Greater U Street Heritage Trail* (Washington, D.C.: Historical Society of Washington, D.C., and D.C. Heritage Tourism Coalition, 2001), 16; Frank, "'If We Own the Story,'" 59–65; Fitzpatrick and Goodwin, *Guide to Black Washington*, 144–46.

82. William H. Jones, *Recreation and Amusement among Negroes in Washington, D.C.: A Sociological Analysis of the Negro in an Urban Environment* (Westport, Conn.: Negro Universities Press, 1927), 55–62; Fitzpatrick and Goodwin, *Guide to Black Washington*, 131–32.

83. "It's the New Emancipation Proclamation," *Washington Bee*, May 28, 1910; Fitzpatrick, "Shaw," 59–60; Fitzpatrick and Goodwin, *Guide to Black Washington*, 165–70; Marya Annette McQuirter, *African American Heritage Trail, Washington, D.C.* (Washington, D.C.: D.C. Cultural Tourism, 2003), 8–11; Paul K. Williams, *Greater U Street*, Images of America Series (Charleston: Arcadia, 2005), 127–30; Williams and Smith, *City within a City*, 8–14.

84. Fitzpatrick, "Shaw," 76–77.

85. Diner, *Democracy*, 27. Marya McQuirter has pointed out that there were some exceptions to this general rule, especially among the earliest African American neighborhood organizations, such as those representing Deanwood and Hillsdale, which also called themselves "citizen" associations. The distinction between white "citizen" and black "civic" groups became more entrenched following the formation of the Federation of Civic Associations as an umbrella group for African American

community groups in 1921. For further discussion, see Marya Annette McQuirter, "Claiming the City: African Americans, Urbanization, and Leisure in Washington, D.C., 1902–1957," PhD dissertation, University of Michigan, Ann Arbor, 2000, 140.

86. These relationships are explored by Alan Lessoff, *The Nation and Its City: Politics, "Corruption," and Progress in Washington, D.C., 1861–1902* (Baltimore: Johns Hopkins University Press, 1994).

87. Mark Twain (Samuel L. Clemens) and Charles Dudley Warner, *The Gilded Age: A Tale for To-day* (New York: Harpers & Brothers, 1873).

88. Diner, *Democracy*, 24–30.

89. Lessoff, *Nation and Its City,* 199–201; Diner, *Democracy*, 31–32.

90. Lessoff, *Nation and Its City,* 201–32.

91. Ibid., 233–67; Diner, *Democracy*, 26–27; Howard Gillette Jr., "Washington, D.C., in White and Black: The Social Construction of Race and Nationhood," in *Composing Urban History and the Constitution of Civic Identities*, ed. John J. Czaplicka and Blair A. Ruble (Washington, D.C., and Baltimore: Woodrow Wilson Center Press and Johns Hopkins University Press, 2003), 192–210 (the citation here is on 196–98).

92. "Oyster to Judson: The Little Napoleon Strikes a Strong Defense of His Position," *Washington Bee*, April 12, 1911; and Fitzpatrick, "Shaw," 20–21.

93. Gatewood, *Aristocrats of Color*, 37–39.

94. Byrand, "Changing Race, Changing Place," 138.

95. McQuirter, *African American Heritage Trail*, 12–14; Kathryn S. Smith, "Remembering U Street," *Washington History* 9, no. 2 (1997–98): 28–53.

96. Fitzpatrick and Goodwin, *Guide to Black Washington*, 84–99, 177–80.

97. Adam McKible is an English professor at New York City's John Jay College who has dedicated his career to promoting the study of African American literature. Edward Christopher Williams, *When Washington Was in Vogue: A Love Story*, with commentary by Adam McKible and Emily Bernard (New York: Amistad/HarperCollins, 2003).

98. "Edward Christopher Williams, 1871–December 24, 1929," on the "Black Renaissance in Washington, D.C. Website," District of Columbia Martin Luther King Jr. Public Library, http://www.dclibrary.org/blkren/bios/williamsec.html.

99. Byrand, "Changing Race, Changing Place," 8, 197–99, 251–55; Jacqueline Mae Moore, "A Drop of African Blood: The Washington Black Elite from 1880 to 1920," PhD dissertation, University of Maryland, College Park, 1994.

100. Green, *Washington*, 101–7; Moore, *Leading the Race*, 1–8.

101. Audrey Elisa Kerr, "Two Black Washingtons: The Role of Complexion in the Oral History of District of Columbia Residents, 1863–1963," PhD dissertation, University of Maryland, College Park, 1998.

102. Moore, *Leading the Race*, 2; Johnston, *Surviving Freedom*, 66–67; Green, *Secret City*, 119–54.

103. Moore, *Leading the Race*, 3.

104. "Public Men and Thought by the Sage of the Potomac," *Washington Bee*, October 15, 1910.

105. Johnson, "City on the Hill," 330–47; Gatewood, *Aristocrats of Color*, 301–6.

106. Moore, *Leading the Race*, 61–62.

107. Ibid., 68–69. Mu-So-Lit stood for Music, Social, and Literary. See Fitzpatrick and Goodwin, *Guide to Black Washington*, 146–47; and Federal Writers' Project, Works Progress Administration, *Washington: City and Capital*, American Guide Series (Washington, D.C.: U.S. Government Printing Office, 1937), 79.

108. Moore, *Leading the Race*, 62; Gatewood, *Aristocrats of Color*, 47–48.

109. Moore, *Leading the Race*, 161–86; Gatewood, *Aristocrats of Color*, 210–46; Elizabeth Clark-Lewis, *Living In, Living Out*, 147–72; Zachery R. Williams, "In Search of the Talented Tenth: Howard University Intellectuals and the Dilemmas of Race in Academia, 1926–1970," PhD dissertation, Bowling Green State University, Bowling Green, Ohio, 2003, 115–21.

110. Clarke, *History of the Nineteenth-Century Black Churches*; Johnston, *Surviving Freedom*, 58–59; Gatewood, *Aristocrats of Color*, 167–71.

111. Moore, *Leading the Race*, 16–21, 70–85.

112. Fitzpatrick and Goodwin, *Guide to Black Washington*, 153–57; Gatewood, *Aristocrats of Color*, 260–61, 286–87; Walker, "Struggle and Attempts to Establish Branch Autonomy," 11–16; Reginald Blaxton, "The American Negro Academy: Black Excellence 100 Years Ago," *American Visions*, February–March 1997; Mark Perry, *Lift Up Thy Voice: The Grimké Family's Journey from Slaveholders to Civil Rights Leaders* (New York: Viking, 2001); Darryl M. Trimiew, *Voices of the Silenced: The Responsible Self in a Marginalized Community* (Cleveland: Pilgrim Press, 1993); Letitia W. Brown and Elsie M. Lewis, *Washington in the New Era, 1870–1970* (Washington, D.C.: National Portrait Gallery, 1972), 22–25.

113. Blaxton, "American Negro Academy"; Williams, "In Search of the Talented Tenth," 17–19; Jonathan Scott Holloway, *Confronting the Veil: Abram Harris Jr., E. Franklin Frazier, and Ralph Bunche, 1919–1941* (Chapel Hill: University of North Carolina Press, 2002), 19–23.

114. Blaxton, "American Negro Academy"; Fitzpatrick and Goodwin, *Guide to Black Washington*, 156–57.

115. Moore, *Leading the Race*, 17–18.

116. Ibid., 83–84.

117. Amir N. Muhammad, *The History of Masjid Muhammad and the Early Muslims in the Washington, DC Area* (Washington, D.C.: FreeMan Publications, 2009), 17.

118. Moore, *Leading the Race*, 21–24; Johnson, "City on the Hill," 314–39; Jean M. Pablo, "Washington, D.C. and Its School System, 1900–1906," PhD dissertation, Georgetown University, Washington, 1974; Lillian G. Dabney, "History

of Schools for Negroes in the District of Columbia, 1807–1947," PhD dissertation, Catholic University, Washington, 1949; Hedrick Smith, *Duke Ellington's Washington*, television program, Public Broadcasting System, February 7, 2000.

119. Moore, *Leading the Race*, 22–23; Mary Gibson Hundley, *The Dunbar Story (1870–1955)* (New York: Vantage Press, 1965); Jane Freundel Levey, Paul K. Williams, Richard T. Busch, J. Brendan Meyer, Anne W. Rollins, and Joan M. Mathys, *Midcity at the Crossroads: Shaw Heritage Trail* (Washington, D.C.: Cultural Tourism D.C., 2006), 3–4, and Rayford W. Logan, *Howard University: The First Hundred Years, 1867–1967* (Washington, D.C.: Howard University Press, 1968).

120. David L. Lewis, *District of Columbia: A Bicentennial History* (New York and Nashville: W. W. Norton and American Association for State and Local History, 1976), 105–10.

121. Logan, *Howard University*.

122. Moore, *Leading the Race*, 86–111.

123. Mary Church Terrell, *A Colored Woman in a White World* (Washington, D.C.: Ransdell, 1940), 174–85.

124. Moore, *Leading the Race*, 87–88; Logan, *Howard University*.

125. Moore, *Leading the Race*, 88.

126. Miner was founded in 1851, and it was absorbed into the University of the District of Columbia seven decades later. See McQuirter, *African American Heritage Trail*, 45; and Fitzpatrick and Goodwin, *Guide to Black Washington*, 105–6.

127. Edward Kennedy "Duke" Ellington, *Music Is My Mistress* (Garden City, N.Y.: Doubleday, 1973), 11.

128. Moore, *Leading the Race*, 26–31.

129. Laurence J. W. Hayes, "The Negro Federal Government Worker: A Study of His Classification Status in the District of Columbia, 1883–1938," MA thesis, Howard University, Washington, 1941.

130. In fact, Washington was more assertive in his pursuit of African American interests than many characterized him at the time. For an overview of the national debate, see Kluger, *Simple Justice*, 68–80. For a discussion of how these debates were reflected within the Washington black community, see Moore, *Leading the Race*, 26–31.

131. Moore, *Leading the Race*, 132–60.

132. Ibid., 136–39; Fitzpatrick, "Shaw," 20–23.

133. Narris Mosley Ethridge, "The Black Architects of Washington, D.C., 1900–Present," PhD dissertation, Catholic University, Washington, 1979; Angela W. Winand, "Weighed upon a Scale: African-American Women, Class and Consumer Culture in New Orleans and Washington, D.C., 1880–1950," PhD dissertation, University of Michigan, Ann Arbor, 2003.

134. Byrand, "Changing Race, Changing Place," 138.

135. Ibid., 42–46.

136. Kathryn Schneider Smith and Marya McQuirter, *A Guide to Historical Resources of Shaw* (Washington, D.C.: Thurgood Marshall Center for Service and Heritage, 1996).

137. Richard W. Woodward, "Study of a Washington, D.C. Negro Newspaper: *The Washington Bee*, 1900–1922," MA thesis, Catholic University of America, Washington, 1950; Fitzpatrick, "Shaw," 33–43; Gatewood, *Aristocrats of Color*, 167–71.

138. Fitzpatrick, "Shaw," 36–38.

139. Ibid., 68–74.

140. Green, *Washington*, 200–260; Perry, *Lift Up Thy Voice*, 263–303; Gatewood, *Aristocrats of Color*, 315–20.

141. Moore, *Leading the Race*, 137.

142. "The Whitelaw Apartment," *Washington Bee*, July 19, 1919; Patricia M. Cook, "'Like the Phoenix': The Rebirth of the Whitelaw Hotel," *Washington History* 7, no. 1 (1995): 5–23; Laura Bergheim, *The Washington Historical Atlas: Who Did What When and Where in the Nation's Capital* (Rockville, Md.: Woodbine House, 1992), 253; McQuirter, *African American Heritage Trail*, 11; Williams, *Greater U Street*, 126; Cultural Tourism D.C., *Historic Neighborhoods: U Street / Shaw* (Washington, D.C.: Cultural Tourism D.C., 2005); Frank, "'If We Own the Story,'" 51–58.

143. Moore, *Leading the Race*, 51–69; Brown and Lewis, *Washington in the New Era*, 25–26; James A. Miller, "Literary Washington and the New Negro Renaissance," in *What's the Story?* ed. Cultural Tourism D.C.

144. Bergheim, *Washington Historical Atlas*, 248; McQuirter, *African American Heritage Trail*, 10; Fitzpatrick and Goodwin, *Guide to Black Washington*, 122–24, 170.

145. Williams, *Greater U Street*, 54–55; Bergheim, *Washington Historical Atlas*, 249–50; Moore, *Leading the Race*, 58–59; McQuirter, *African American Heritage Trail*, 9; Frank, "'If We Own the Story,'" 65–69; Fitzpatrick and Goodwin, *Guide to Black Washington*, 171.

146. Bob Kuska, *Hot Potato: How Washington and New York Gave Birth to Black Basketball and Changed America's Game Forever* (Charlottesville: University of Virginia Press, 2004), 25–29.

147. Bergheim, *Washington Historical Atlas*, 259; McQuirter, *African American Heritage Trail*, 45; Fitzpatrick and Goodwin, *Guide to Black Washington*, 114–15.

148. Williams and Smith, *City within a City*; Cultural Tourism D.C., *Greater U Street Historic District* (Washington, D.C.: Cultural Tourism D.C., 2005); Smith, *Duke Ellington's Washington.*

149. Moore, *Leading the Race*, 32–50.

150. Dunbar, "Negro Life," 32.

151. This point is forcefully argued by Moore, *Leading the Race*, 32–50.

152. Gatewood, *Aristocrats of Color*, 51–52.

153. Elizabeth Clark-Lewis, *First Freed: Washington, D.C. in the Emancipation Era* (Washington, D.C.: AP Foundation Press, 1998), 75.

154. Byrand, "Changing Race, Changing Place," 292.

155. Fitzpatrick and Goodwin, *Guide to Black Washington*, 119–20.

156. Jean Toomer, *Cane* (New York: Liveright, 1993; orig. pub. by Boni & Liveright, 1923), 39.

157. The denizens of Seventh Street intuitively understood an observation made in 2003 by the geographer Don Mitchell, who wrote, "The right to the city is never guaranteed and certainly never freely given." Don Mitchell, *The Right to the City: Social Justice and the Fight for Public Space* (New York: Guildford Press, 2003), 42.

158. Jean Toomer was born in Washington on December 26, 1894, and died in Pennsylvania on March 30, 1967. For more information about her life, see Scott W. Williams, "A Jean Toomer Biography Website," http://www.math.buffalo.edu/~sww/toomer/toomerbio.html.

159. Bergheim, *Washington Historical Atlas*, 238–39.

160. Lewis, *District of Columbia*, 161–62.

161. Ibid.; Ellington, *Music Is My Mistress*, 14–17.

162. Hughes, *Big Sea*, 167.

163. Ibid., 166–67. The reference to having an overcoat or not refers in part to Hughes's bitterness at having his mother uninvited to a formal dinner honoring the poet by one of U Street's literary society because she did not have the proper attire.

164. Toomer, *Cane*, 50.

165. Perry, *Lift Up Thy Voice*, 291–96.

166. Ibid., 293.

167. Ibid., 285–91; Beverly Washington Jones, "Quest for Equality: The Life of Mary Eliza Church Terrell, 1863–1954," PhD dissertation, University of North Carolina, Chapel Hill, 1980.

168. Terrell, *Colored Woman*, 232.

169. Perry, *Lift Up Thy Voice*, 297–98.

170. Ibid.

171. Robert L. Zangrando, "About Lynching," in *The Reader's Companion to American History*, ed. Eric Foner and John A. Garraty (New York: Houghton Mifflin, 1991), 684–86. Also see Timothy V. Kaufman-Osborn, "Capital Punishment as Legal Lynching?" in *From Lynch Mobs to the Killing State: Race and the Death Penalty in America*, ed. Charles J. Ogletree Jr. and Austin Sarat (New York: New York University Press, 2006), 21–54 (the citation here is on 27–36).

172. David S. Cecelski and Timothy B. Tyson, editors, *Democracy Betrayed: The Wilmington Race Riot of 1898 and Its Legacy* (Chapel Hill: University of North Carolina Press, 1998).

173. Perry, *Lift Up Thy Voice*, 300–301; Fitzpatrick and Goodwin, *Guide to Black Washington*, 156–57; Thabiti M. Anayabwile, *The Faithful Preacher: Recapturing the Vision of Three Pioneering African-American Pastors* (Wheaton, Ill.: Crossway Books, 2006).

174. Perry, *Lift Up Thy Voice*, 300–301.

175. Ibid., 302–4.

176. Ibid., 305.

177. Ibid., 303.

178. W. E. Burghardt Du Bois, *The Souls of Black Folk: Essays and Sketches* (Chicago: A. C. McLurg, 1903).

179. Perry, *Lift Up Thy Voice*, 306–14.

180. Ibid., 316–39.

181. Ibid., 318.

182. Ibid., 319.

183. Ibid., 320–24; Walker, "Struggle and Attempts to Establish Branch Autonomy," 16–18; Kluger, *Simple Justice*, 110–14.

184. President Theodore Roosevelt ordered the dishonorable discharge of 167 black soldiers, removing all claims to salaries, pensions, and commendations. Roosevelt's proclamation revoked the Congressional Medals of Honor that previously had been awarded to 6 of the 167 soldiers. In 1972, President Richard M. Nixon reversed Roosevelt's actions, pardoning the Brownsville soldiers on the basis of new evidence revealing that the original charges had been manufactured by whites resentful of the presence of African American military personnel in their community. John D. Weaver, *The Brownsville Raid* (New York: W. W. Norton, 1970).

185. Perry, *Lift Up Thy Voice*, 324–33.

186. Carolyn Amonitte Stubbs, "Angelina Weld Grimké: Washington Poet and Playwright," PhD dissertation, George Washington University, Washington, 1978.

187. Perry, *Lift Up Thy Voice*, 324–33.

188. Ibid., 329–37; Paula J. Giddings, *Ida: A Sword among Lions—Ida B. Wells and the Campaign against Lynching* (New York: Amistad, 2008), 472–80; Kluger, *Simple Justice*, 91–100.

189. Hazen D. Turner, "A History of the District of Columbia Branch of the National Association for the Advancement of Colored People, 1913–1950," PhD dissertation, University of Maryland, College Park, 1954; Gatewood, *Aristocrats of Color*, 315–20.

190. Walker, "Struggle and Attempts to Establish Branch Autonomy," 196–213.

191. The definitive account of this conflict is ibid., 10–99.

192. Ibid., 99–161; Perry, *Lift Up Thy Voice*, 330–37.

193. Walker, "Struggle and Attempts to Establish Branch Autonomy."

194. Terrell, *Colored Woman*, 234.

195. Perry, *Lift Up Thy Voice*, 340.

196. Green, *Secret City*, 172–75.

197. Greenlee, "Methodology," 140; "Democratic Party Duplicity," *Washington Bee*, October 3, 1908.

198. McQuirter, *African American Heritage Trail*, 4.

199. I would like to acknowledge the research of interns Ariana Curtis, Kimberly Painter, and Rickita T. Perry in the preparation of this discussion of the Washington Race Riots of 1919, and express my gratitude for their assistance.

200. Fitzpatrick and Goodwin, *Guide to Black Washington*, 121.

201. Byrand, "Changing Race, Changing Place," 204–5.

202. Bergheim, *Washington Historical Atlas*, 252–53.

203. Washington's white Protestants were particularly concerned about emboldened African American behavior. See Herbert Kingley Lodder, "The Response of White Protestantism to Negroes in Washington, D.C., 1865–1985," MA thesis, Columbia University, New York, 1967; and McQuirter, "Claiming the City," 153–58.

204. Roberta Cardwell, "The Washington Riot of 1919," MA thesis, Howard University, Washington, 1971.

205. For an authoritative account of the two-week-long Chicago riots that began on July 27, 1919, see William M. Tuttle Jr., *Race Riot: Chicago in the Red Summer of 1919* (New York: Athenaeum, 1970). For a brief overview of these events, see Blair A. Ruble, *Second Metropolis: Pragmatic Pluralism in Gilded Age Chicago, Silver Age Moscow, and Meiji Osaka* (Washington, D.C., and Baltimore: Woodrow Wilson Center Press and Johns Hopkins University Press, 2001), 258–64.

206. Walker, "Struggle and Attempts to Establish Branch Autonomy," 102–5.

207. Ibid., 106–11.

208. Lewis, *District of Columbia*, 74. For a concise narrative of the day to day events between July 19 and 23, 1919, see Cardwell, "Washington Riot."

209. James Weldon Johnson, "The Riots: An N.A.A.C.P. Investigation," *The Crisis*, September 1919, 241–43 (the citation here is on 243); "Service Men Negroes in Race Riot at Capital," *New York Times*, July 21, 1919.

210. Lewis, *District of Columbia*, 74; Cardwell, "Washington Riot."

211. "This Nation's Gratitude: The Colored Americans' Reward for Fighting for 'World Democracy,'" *Washington Bee*, July 26, 1919.

212. "Denouncing Wave of Crime Here, Officials, Ministers and Others Declare Police Are Too Few," *Washington Post*, July 21, 1919; "Riots Taken Up by Congress," *Washington Post*, July 22, 1919.

213. "Race Riots Renewed," *Washington Post*, July 21, 1919.

214. "Detective Sergeant Wilson Victim; Other Officers Hurt; Negro Runs Amuck, Wounding Many in Fight," *Washington Post*, July 22, 1919.

215. "Street Rioting in Check, Is Belief of Authorities, after 4 Are Killed and 11 Are Dangerously Wounded," *Evening Star*, July 22, 1919; "Martial Law Asked in Resolution Offered in Congress Today," *Washington Times*, July 22, 1919.

216. See, e.g., "Desperadoes Shoot as Car Speeds Past U.S. Hospital," *Washington Times*, July 21, 1919; "Flash News Briefs in Detail: Stirring Scenes," *Washington Times*, July 23, 1919; and "'Sniping Negress' Held for Slaying," *Washington Times*, July 23, 1919.

217. "Flash News Briefs in Detail: Stirring Scenes."

218. "Gen. Haan in Command after Wilson Confers with Baker on Riots," *Washington Post*, July 23, 1919; "Asks a Riot Inquiry," *Washington Post*, July 23, 1919; "Negroes Call on Wilson to Act on Mob Violence; Fear Outbreaks Elsewhere," *Washington Post*, July 23, 1919; "Public Order and Safety," *Washington Post*, July 23, 1919.

219. Green, *Washington*, 266; "Rioters in Courts," *Washington Post*, July 23, 1919; "Hears 11 Riot Cases," *Washington Post*, July 24, 1919; "Complete List of Those Arrested in Race Rioting," *Washington Times*, July 24, 1919; "Capital of the Nation in Disgrace: Partial List of Arrests," *Washington Bee*, July 26, 1919.

220. Green, *Washington*, 266; Walker, "Struggle and Attempts to Establish Branch Autonomy," 111–15; Bergheim, *Washington Historical Atlas*, 252–53; "Race Clashes Ended," *Washington Post*, July 25, 1919; "End to Street Rioting Reached, It Is Thought; One Killed Last Night," *Evening Star*, July 23, 1919; "Troops Ready to Act If Rioting Is Resumed in Capital, Says Haan," *Evening Star*, July 24, 1919; "2,000 Troops Remain Here to Keep Riot Spirit Down," *Washington Times*, July 24, 1919.

221. "Toll of Dead and Wounded in Last Night's Rioting," *Washington Times*, July 23, 1919; Bergheim, *Washington Historical Atlas*, 252–53. By comparison, thirty-eight people—including thirty-three blacks—were killed in the Chicago riots a week later that required 6,200 state militia troops to subdue. Tuttle, *Race Riot*, 12–31.

222. Green, *Washington*, 266; Walker, "Struggle and Attempts to Establish Branch Autonomy," 111–12; Lewis, *District of Columbia*, 74; Greenlee, "Methodology," 153–54.

223. Fitzpatrick, "Shaw," 76–77.

224. "They Started It," *Washington Bee*, July 26, 1919.

225. Fitzpatrick, "Shaw," 77.

226. Greenlee, "Methodology," 154.

227. Johnson, "Riots," 242.

228. "Negroes Call on Wilson to Act on Mob Violence; Fear Outbreaks Elsewhere," *Washington Post*, July 23, 1919; "Riots Elsewhere, Forecast by Negro," *Washington Post*, July 25, 1919; "Calls for Rights Probe," *Washington Post*, July 26,

1919; "Call Riots Here Big Conspiracy," *Washington Post*, July 28, 1919; "Colored
Mass Meeting to Draw Up Resolutions of Protest Against Riot," *Evening Star*, July
21, 1919; "Protection Is Asked by Colored Citizens," *Evening Star*, July 22, 1919.

229. "The Rights of the Black Man," *Washington Bee*, August 2, 1919.

230. Miller, "Literary Washington."

231. Hughes, *Big Sea*, 165.

232. Terrell, *Colored Woman*, 425.

CHAPTER 3

1. Helen Nicolay, *Our Capital on the Potomac* (New York: Century Company,
1924), 463.

2. Genna R. McNeil, "Charles Hamilton Houston (1895–1950) and the Struggle
for Civil Rights," PhD dissertation, University of Chicago, Chicago, 1975.

3. Richard Kluger, *Simple Justice: The History of* Brown v. Board of Education
and Black America's Struggle for Equality (New York: Alfred A. Knopf, 1976), 105–7.

4. Ibid., 107–8; Mary Gibson Hundley, *The Dunbar Story (1870–1955)* (New
York: Vantage Press, 1965).

5. Kluger, *Simple Justice*, 108–9.

6. Ibid., 109–11.

7. Ibid., 114–16.

8. Ibid., 115–16.

9. Ibid.

10. Houston, Hastie, and many of the remarkable men and women discussed
in this chapter were photographed by Addison N. Scurlock and his sons, Robert
and George. Addison opened a family photography studio at 9th and U streets,
NW, in 1911. Following World War II, Robert and George ran the Capital School
of Photography from 1948 to 1952. Among their students was *Washington Post*
photographer Jacqueline Bouvier, who met her future husband, Representative John
F. Kennedy, on a school photo assignment. Robert established Custom Craft Studies
following the closure of the school in 1952. Having a "Portrait by Scurlock" was a
sure sign that a member of the U Street community had arrived. Addison died in
1964. Robert moved the studio to 18th Street, where it remained until his death in
1994. Throughout this era, the Scurlocks' photos provide a chronicle of U Street and
Washington history. The Scurlock studio archives are available at the Archives Center
of the National Museum of American History of the Smithsonian Institution, and at
the Moorland-Spingarn Research Center at Howard University. Jane Freundel Levy,
"The Scurlock Studio," *Washington History* 1, no. 1 (1989): 41–57; Laura Bergheim,
*The Washington Historical Atlas: Who Did What When and Where in the Nation's
Capital* (Rockville, Md.: Woodbine House, 1992), 161.

11. Kluger, *Simple Justice*, 125–29.

12. Ibid., 124–25.

13. The broad impact on African American education of Howard University's emergence as a graduate training center is explored in Michael R. Winston, "Through the Back Door: Academic Racism and the Negro Scholar in Historical Perspective," *Daedalus* 100, no. 3 (1971): 678–719.

14. Kluger, *Simple Justice*, 124; Jonathan Scott Holloway, *Confronting the Veil: Abram Harris, Jr., E. Franklin Frazier, and Ralph Bunche, 1919–1941* (Chapel Hill: University of North Carolina Press, 2002), 48–49.

15. Kluger, *Simple Justice*, 124–25.

16. Holloway, *Confronting the Veil*, 45–47.

17. See ibid., 46–47; and Zachery R. Williams, *In Search of the Talented Tenth: Howard University Public Intellectuals and the Dilemmas of Race, 1926–1970* (Columbia: University of Missouri Press, 2009), 20–34.

18. For a discussion of Howard's built environment and role in encouraging the emergence of an African American architectural profession, see Narris Mosley Ethridge, "The Black Architects of Washington, D.C., 1900–Present," PhD dissertation, Catholic University of America, Washington, 1979; and Federal Writers' Project, Works Progress Administration, *Washington: City and Capital*, American Guide Series (Washington, D.C.: U.S. Government Printing Office, 1937), 513–16.

19. Kluger, *Simple Justice*, 124; Williams, *In Search of the Talented Tenth*, 47–51.

20. Holloway, *Confronting the Veil*, 49–50; also see 40–47.

21. Zachery R. Williams, "In Search of the Talented Tenth: Howard University Intellectuals and the Dilemmas of Race in Academia, 1926–1970," PhD dissertation, Bowling Green State University, Bowling Green, Ohio, 2003, 96–101.

22. Harry G. Robinson III, *The Long Walk: The Place-Making Legacy of Howard University* (Washington, D.C.: Moorland-Spingarn Research Center, Howard University, 1996).

23. Holloway, *Confronting the Veil*; Letitia W. Brown and Elise M. Lewis, *Washington in the New Era, 1870–1970* (Washington, D.C.: National Portrait Gallery, 1972), 25–28.

24. Holloway, *Confronting the Veil*, 31.

25. Ibid., 31–32.

26. Kluger, *Simple Justice*, 125.

27. Ibid., 126.

28. Holloway, *Confronting the Veil*, 176.

29. Kluger, *Simple Justice*, 173–80.

30. Ibid., 127.

31. Ibid., 127–35.

32. Ibid., 130; Lillian G. Dabney, "History of Schools for Negroes in the District of Columbia, 1807–1947," PhD dissertation, Catholic University of America, Washington, 1949, 110–12.

33. Kluger, *Simple Justice*, 123.

34. This legal history is engagingly retold by Kluger, *Simple Justice*.

35. Mara Cherkasky, "'For Sale to Colored': Racial Change on S Street NW," *Washington History* 8, no. 2 (1996–97): 41–57.

36. Concerning the Twelfth Street YMCA, see Thomas B. Hargrave Jr., *Private Differences—General Good: A History of the YMCA of Metropolitan Washington* (Washington, D.C.: YMCA, 1985), 89–96. Concerning the other venues, see Bergheim, *Washington Historical Atlas*, 253; and Thomas Cornell Battle, "Published Resources for the Study of Blacks in the District of Columbia: An Annotated Guide," PhD dissertation, George Washington University, Washington, 1982.

37. Edward Kennedy "Duke" Ellington, *Music Is My Mistress* (Garden City, N.Y.: Doubleday, 1973), 14–17.

38. Jacqueline Goggin, *Carter G. Woodson: A Life in Black History* (Baton Rouge: Louisiana State University Press, 1991).

39. Sandra Fitzpatrick and Maria R. Goodwin, *The Guide to Black Washington: Places and Events of Historical and Cultural Significance in the Nation's Capital*, rev. illus. ed. (New York: Hippocrene Books, 2001), 81, 119.

40. Hazen D. Turner, "A History of the District of Columbia Branch of the National Association for the Advancement of Colored People, 1913–1950," PhD dissertation, University of Maryland, College Park, 1954; Lewis N. Walker, "The Struggles and Attempts to Establish Branch Autonomy and Hegemony: A History of the District of Columbia Branch of the National Association for the Advancement of Colored People, 1912–1942," PhD dissertation, University of Delaware, 1979; Larry W. Mixon, "The Fight to Make Democracy Real: The Los Angeles, Washington, and Detroit NAACP Branches during the 1940s," MA thesis, University of Maryland, College Park, 1975.

41. Julia A. Whithers, "The Attitude of the 'Washington Post' toward the Negro, 1941–1942," MA thesis, Howard University, Washington, 1945; Richard W. Woodward, "The Study of a Washington, D.C. Negro Newspaper, *The Washington Bee*, 1900–1922," MA thesis, Catholic University of America, Washington, 1950; Hayward Farrer, *The Baltimore Afro-American, 1892–1950* (Westport, Conn.: Greenwood Press, 1998).

42. James W. Quander and Rohulamin Quander, *The Quander Quality: The True Story of a Black Trailblazing Diabetic* (Blandon, Ore.: Robert D. Reed, 2006), 221.

43. For a discussion of the relationship between class and race in African American urban communities, see Derek S. Hyra, "Racial Uplift? Intra-Racial Class Conflict and the Economic Revitalization of Harlem and Bronzeville," *City & Community* 5, no. 1 (2006): 71–92.

44. Williams, "In Search of the Talented Tenth," 14.

45. Kluger, *Simple Justice*, 513–14.

46. Ibid., 514–16.

47. Ibid., 517–18.

48. Ibid., 518–19; Marya Annette McQuirter, *African American Heritage Trail, Washington, D.C.* (Washington, D.C.: Cultural Tourism D.C., 2003).

49. Kluger, *Simple Justice*, 521–23.

50. Ibid.

51. D.C. History Project, *City of Magnificent Intentions: A History of the District of Columbia* (Washington, D.C.: Intac, 1983), 468–70.

52. Ibid., 523–34.

53. This was because *Brown* was decided on a constitutional argument that applied only to states, and hence, not to D.C.; ibid., 703–49.

54. The story of the trio's time at Howard is told by Holloway, *Confronting the Veil.*

55. Ibid., 1–34, 67–87.

56. Winston, "Through the Back Door."

57. Holloway, *Confronting the Veil*, 3–4.

58. Ibid., 127–37, 157–63; Joseph D. McNair, *Ralph Bunche* (Chanhassen, Minn.: Child's World, 2002), 22.

59. Holloway, *Confronting the Veil*, 126–36.

60. Ibid., 180–84; Anthony Sampson, *Mandela: The Authorised Biography* (London: HarperCollins, 1999), 23.

61. This discussion of Logan's biography is based on *Rayford W. Logan and the Dilemma of the African-American Intellectual*, by Kenneth Robert Janken (Amherst: University of Massachusetts Press, 1993).

62. According to Kenneth Robert Janken, "the 'bad Negroes with Ph.D.s' were a cohort of young radical intellectuals in the 1930s who sought alternatives to what they considered to be the tired, inadequate program and tactics of the NAACP." Ibid., 111.

63. Rayford W. Logan, *Howard University: The First Hundred Years, 1867–1967* (Washington, D.C.: Howard University Press, 1968). The process of Logan's authorship—and his eventual dismissal from the project just prior to its completion—is discussed in greater detail by Williams, "In Search of the Talented Tenth," 118–21.

64. Rayford W. Logan, *The Betrayal of the Negro, from Rutherford B. Hayes to Woodrow Wilson*, New Paperback Edition (New York: Da Capo Press, 2001); Rayford W. Logan, ed., *What the Negro Wants* (Chapel Hill: University of North Carolina Press, 1944).

65. Janken, *Rayford W. Logan*, 228–38.

66. Concerning the intellectual lineage between Frazier's scholarship on the family and Moynihan's controversial claim that black urban poverty was related to

family disorganization and pathological culture resulting from slavery and racism, see Holloway, *Confronting the Veil*, 202–5. The highly visible Bunche, who closed out his distinguished career as a United Nations undersecretary-general, was frequently subject to pointed barbs about being "insufficiently black." Arthur P. Davis, a fellow faculty member at Howard, once declared that "there [are] bandana-handkerchief-headed Negroes, and silk-handkerchief-headed Negroes, but Ralph is a cellophane-handkerchief-headed Negro—you have to get off at a certain angle to see him." Ibid., 157–58.

67. Brian Urquhart, *Ralph Bunche: An American Life* (New York: W. W. Norton, 1993), 452.

68. Ibid., 430–33.

69. Holloway, *Confronting the Veil*, 200–202.

70. Ibid., 195–218.

71. Christopher Buck, *Alain Locke: Faith and Philosophy* (Los Angeles: Kalimat Press, 2005); McQuirter, *African American Heritage Trail*, 17.

72. Nor were their reactions unique to African Americans. Similar divisions were being played out in Quebec in the struggles between the pro-Federalist stance of Pierre Elliott Trudeau and his lifelong intellectual and political battles with sovereigntist rival René Lévesque—see Graham Fraser, *René Lévesque and the Parti Québécois in Power* (Montreal: McGill–Queen's University Press, 1984); and Andrew Cohen and J. L. Granatstein, *The Life and Legacy of Pierre Elliott Trudeau* (Toronto: Vintage Canada, 1999)—as well as in South Africa, between the more nationalist inclination of Pan Africanist Congress leader Robert Sobukwe and the increasingly antinationalist position of African National Congress leader Nelson Mandela—Leonard Thompson, *A History of South Africa* (New Haven, Conn.: Yale University Press, 2000); and Sampson, *Mandela*.

73. For further information concerning Woodson's early years, see Goggin, *Carter G. Woodson*, 1–65.

74. Ibid., 21–22.

75. Winston, "Through the Back Door," 686.

76. Goggin, *Carter G. Woodson*, 26.

77. Ibid., 34–48.

78. Ibid., 26–31.

79. Ibid., 50–51.

80. Ibid., 50–57.

81. Ibid., 34–45.

82. Jane Freundel Levey, Paul K. Williams, Richard T. Busch, J. Brendan Meyer, Anne W. Rollins, and Joan M. Mathys, *Midcity at the Crossroads: Shaw Heritage Trail* (Washington, D.C.: Cultural Tourism D.C., 2006), 16–20; Federal Writers' Project, *Washington*, 85.

83. Goggin, *Carter G. Woodson*, 66–81.
84. Ibid., 72–75.
85. Ibid., 84–95.
86. Ibid., 108–13.
87. Ibid., 111–39.
88. Janken, *Rayford W. Logan*, 214–20.
89. "Boycott Conducted by Negro Alliance," *Washington Post*, September 3, 1933.
90. Goggin, *Carter G. Woodson*, 155–56.
91. Jacqueline Moore, *Leading the Race: The Transformation of the Black Elite in the Nation's Capital, 1880–1920* (Charlottesville: University of Virginia Press, 1999), 132–60.
92. Ibid., 136–39; Michael Andrew Fitzpatrick, "Shaw, Washington's Premier Black Neighborhood: An Examination of the Origins and Development of a Black Business Movement, 1880–1920," MA thesis, Department of History, University of Virginia, Charlottesville, 1989, 20–43; Michael Andrew Fitzpatrick, 'A Great Agitation for Business': Black Economic Development in Shaw," *Washington History* 2, no. 2 (1990–91): 49–73; Willard B. Gatewood, *Aristocrats of Color: The Black Elite, 1880–1920* (Bloomington: Indiana University Press, 1990), 167–71.
93. Moore, *Leading the Race*, 137.
94. Goggin, *Carter G. Woodson*, 163–64.
95. Walker, "Struggles and Attempts to Establish Branch Autonomy," 170.
96. Ibid., 170–71.
97. Goggin, *Carter G. Woodson*, 163–64.
98. Constance McLaughlin Green, *The Secret City: A History of Race Relations in the Nation's Capital* (Princeton, N.J.: Princeton University Press, 1967), 229–30.
99. Holloway, *Confronting the Veil*, 50–51.
100. "Boycott Forces Hamburger Grill to Rehire Three," *Washington Tribune*, August 31, 1933.
101. Fitzpatrick and Goodwin, *Guide to Black Washington*, 172–73.
102. Ibid.; "A&P Hires Two Clerks," *Washington Tribune*, September 28, 1933; "Luncheonette Manager Denies Charge by Negro Alliance," *Washington Tribune*, September 13, 1933; "New Jobs Being Secured by New Negro Alliance," *Washington Tribune*, September 21, 1933.
103. Holloway, *Confronting the Veil*, 52–53; Farrer, *Baltimore Afro-American*, 90–92; "Common Sense and Justice," *Washington Post*, August 9, 1938.
104. Fitzpatrick and Goodwin, *Guide to Black Washington*, 142.
105. Holloway, *Confronting the Veil*, 52.
106. Fitzpatrick and Goodwin, *Guide to Black Washington*, 172–73.
107. Ibid.

108. Walker, "Struggles and Attempts to Establish Branch Autonomy," 172–73; Bergheim, *Washington Historical Atlas*, 246–47; "Labor Board Wins Review of Greyhound Suit," *Washington Post*, November 23, 1937.

109. Michele F. Pacifico, "A History of the New Negro Alliance of Washington, D.C., 1933–1941," MA thesis, George Washington University, Washington, 1983; Walker, "Struggles and Attempts to Establish Branch Autonomy," 173–74; Holloway, *Confronting the Veil*, 55–56.

110. Holloway, *Confronting the Veil*, 59–63. One of the most infamous trials of the Jim Crow era, the Scottsboro Case, revolved around accusations against nine black teenagers for raping two white women in Scottsboro, Alabama. International protests arose after the nine defendants were sentenced to the death penalty. The U.S. Supreme Court eventually overturned the death sentences. One of the women later denied the charges. All nine eventually were acquitted, pardoned, paroled, or escaped after serving years in prison. The protests served to outrage and to radicalize the African American community. For more information about the case, see Dan T. Carter, *Scottsboro: A Tragedy of the American South* (Baton Rouge: Louisiana State University Press, 1969).

111. Walker, "Struggles and Attempts to Establish Branch Autonomy," 177–78.

112. Ibid., 164–65.

113. Ibid., 174–87.

114. Marya Annette McQuirter, "Claiming the City: African Americans, Urbanization, and Leisure in Washington, D.C., 1902–1957," PhD dissertation, University of Michigan, Ann Arbor, 2000, 232–77.

115. Ibid., 278–82.

116. Beverly Washington Jones, "Quest for Equality: The Life of Mary Eliza Church Terrell, 1863–1954," PhD dissertation, University of North Carolina, Chapel Hill, 1980; Angela W. Winand, "Weighed upon a Scale: African American Women, Class and Consumer Culture in New Orleans and Washington, D.C., 1880–1950," PhD dissertation, University of Michigan, Ann Arbor, 2003.

117. McQuirter, *African American Heritage Trail*, 14.

118. Mary Church Terrell, *A Colored Woman in a White World* (Washington, D.C.: Ransdell, 1940).

119. D.C. History Project, *City of Magnificent Intentions*, 468–69.

120. Debra Newman Ham, "Foreword," ibid., 7–21.

121. Jessica Weiss, "Portrait of a Community: Life in Shaw," unpublished paper, University of Maryland Undergraduate History Conference, College Park, March 17, 2005.

122. McQuirter, *African American Heritage Trail*, 4–6.

123. Information about research materials relating to these organizations may be found in *A Guide to the Historical Resources of Shaw*, by Kathryn Schneider and Marya McQuirter (Washington, D.C.: Thurgood Marshall Center for Service and Heritage, 1996).

124. Marcia McAdoo Greenlee, "A Methodology for the Identification, Study and Evaluation of Afro-American Places," PhD dissertation, George Washington University, Washington, 1982.

125. Laurence J. W. Haynes, "The Negro Federal Government Worker: A Study of His Classification Status in the District of Columbia, 1883–1938," MA thesis, Howard University, Washington, 1941.

126. Green, *Secret City*, 200.

127. D.C. History Project, *City of Magnificent Intentions*, 439–43.

128. Carole Adams Kolker, "Migrants and Memories: Family, Work and Community among Blacks, Eastern European Jews, and Native Born Whites in an Early Twentieth Century Washington, D.C. Neighborhood," PhD dissertation, George Washington University, Washington, 1996; Amy Louise Trout, "Settlement Work in Washington, D.C. during the Progressive Era," MA thesis, George Washington University, Washington, 1986.

129. Spencer R. Crew, "Melding the Old and the New: The Modern African American Community, 1930–1960," in *The Urban Odyssey: A Multicultural History of Washington, D.C.*, ed. Francine Curro Cary (Washington, D.C.: Smithsonian Institution Press, 1996), 208–27; the citation here is on 208–11.

130. Ibid., 216–17; Stanley J. Smith, "A History of Race Relations in the District of Columbia since Pearl Harbor," MA thesis, Catholic University of America, Washington, 1949.

131. Crew, "Melding the Old and the New," 218–27.

132. Ibid., 215–17.

133. Ibid., 255–63; Urquhart, *Ralph Bunche*, 94–109; Holloway, *Confronting the Veil*, 78–82.

134. Green, *Secret City*, 262–63, 285–87.

135. Urquhart, *Ralph Bunche*, 109–10.

136. Ibid., 49; Benjamin O. Davis, *Benjamin O. Davis, Jr.: American—An Autobiography* (Washington, D.C.: Smithsonian Institution Press, 1992).

137. Janken, *Rayford W. Logan*, 128–34. Concerning the role of the Twelfth Street YMCA in these events, see Hargrave, *Private Differences—General Good*, 98–100.

138. Roy L. Brooks et al., *Civil Rights Litigation: Cases and Perspectives* (Durham, N.C.: Carolina Academic Press, 2006).

139. Elizabeth Clark-Lewis, "'For a Real Better Life': Voices of African American Women Migrants, 1900–1930," in *Urban Odyssey*, ed. Cary, 97–112; the citation here is on 102–3.

140. Ibid.

141. Elizabeth Clark-Lewis, *Living In, Living Out: African American Domestics in Washington, D.C., 1910–1940* (Washington, D.C.: Smithsonian Institution Press, 1994), 166–69.

142. Kathryn S. Smith, "Remembering U Street," *Washington History* 9, no. 2 (1997–98): 28–53; the citation here is on 38.

143. Herbert Kingley Lodder, "The Response of White Protestantism to Negroes in Washington, D.C., 1865–1965," MA thesis, Columbia University, New York, 1965.

144. Bergheim, *Washington Historical Atlas*, 253.

145. Fitzpatrick and Goodwin, *Guide to Black Washington*, 112–14.

146. Steven J. Diner, *Democracy, Federalism, and the Governance of the Nation's Capital, 1790–1974*, Studies in D.C. History and Public Policy 10 (Washington, D.C.: Center for Applied Research and Urban Policy, University of the District of Columbia, 1987), 37–46.

147. Ibid., 39–42.

148. Ibid., 42–44.

149. Ibid., 44–46.

150. Jerome S. Paige and Margaret M. Reuss, *Safe, Decent and Affordable: Citizen Struggles to Improve Housing in the District of Columbia, 1890–1982*, Studies in D.C. History and Public Policy 6 (Washington, D.C.: Center for Applied Research and Urban Policy, University of the District of Columbia, 1983), 4–17.

151. Barbara G. H. Fant, "Slum Reclamation and Housing Reform in the Nation's Capital, 1890–1940," PhD dissertation, George Washington University, Washington, 1982.

152. William R. Barnes, "The Origins of Urban Renewal: The Public Housing Controversy and the Emergence of a Redevelopment Program in the District of Columbia, 1942–1949," PhD dissertation, Syracuse University, Syracuse, 1977.

153. Howard Gillette Jr., *Between Justice and Beauty: Race, Planning, and the Failure of Urban Policy in Washington, D.C.* (Baltimore: Johns Hopkins University Press, 1995), 135–50.

154. Paige and Reuss, *Safe, Decent and Affordable*, 8–9.

155. D.C. History Project, *City of Magnificent Intentions*, 452–60.

156. Gillette, *Between Justice and Beauty*, 151–69; Frederick Gutheim and Wilcomb E. Washburn, *The Federal City: Plans and Realities* (Washington, D.C.: Smithsonian Institution Press, National Capital Planning Commission, and U.S. Commission of Fine Arts, 1976), 44–67; Kluger, *Simple Justice*, 511.

157. Michael K. Fauntroy, *Home Rule or House Rule? Congress and the Erosion of Local Governance in the District of Columbia* (Lanham, Md.: University Press of America, 2003), 103–4.

158. Gillette, *Between Justice and Beauty*, 157–58.

159. Ibid., 154.

160. Rackman Holt, *Mary McLeod Bethune: A Biography* (Garden City, N.Y.: Doubleday, 1964).

161. Caroline LaDelle Bennett, ed., *Annotated Bibliography of Mary McLeod Bethune's "Chicago Defender" Columns, 1948–1955* (Lewiston, N.Y.: Edwin Mellen Press, 2001).

162. Bergheim, *Washington Historical Atlas*, 255.

163. McQuirter, *African American Heritage Trail*, 45.

164. Henrietta R. Hatter, "History of Miner Teachers College," MA thesis, Howard University, Washington, 1939; Federal Writers' Project, *Washington*, 73.

165. McQuirter, *African American Heritage Trail*, 13; Bergheim, *Washington Historical Atlas*, 257.

166. Crew, "Melding the Old and the New," 224.

167. James N. Saunders, "The Origin and Development of the Colored Public Evening Schools in the District of Columbia," MA thesis, Howard University, Washington, 1941; Benjamin L. Swinson, "The Historical Development of Public School Adult Education Programs in Washington, D.C., 1858–1981," PhD dissertation, George Washington University, Washington, 1985.

168. Allan Keiler, *Marian Anderson: A Singer's Journey* (New York: Scribner, 2000), 181–217.

169. Urquhart, *Ralph Bunche*, 99–100.

170. "Pastures' Benefit for Colored Denied," *Washington Post*, February 11, 1933.

171. "Letter to the Editor: True Friend of the Colored Race, Washington," *Washington Post*, March 29, 1936.

172. Holloway, *Confronting the Veil*, 64–65.

173. Bergheim, *Washington Historical Atlas*, 250–51.

174. Crew, "Melding the Old and the New," 208–9.

CHAPTER 4

1. Mark Caldwell, *New York Night: The Mystique and Its History* (New York: Scribner, 2005), 352.

2. Juan Williams, "14th and U When Being There Meant Being Somebody," *Washington Post Magazine*, February 21, 1988.

3. These stories are recounted in photographs in *Greater U Street*, by Paul K. Williams, Images of America Series (Charleston: Arcadia, 2002).

4. Marya Annette McQuirter, "Claiming the City: African Americans, Urbanization, and Leisure in Washington, D.C., 1902–1957," PhD dissertation, University of Michigan, Ann Arbor, 2000, 4.

5. Ibid.

6. Ibid., 7–8.

7. Ibid., 9–11.

8. James Freeman, "Great, Good, and Divided: The Politics of Public Space in

Rio de Janeiro," *Journal of Urban Affairs* 30, no. 5 (2008): 529–56; the quotation here is on 551.

9. McQuirter, "Claiming the City," 1. For Ellington's recollections as recounted in the introduction to this volume, see Edward Kennedy "Duke" Ellington, *Music Is My Mistress* (Garden City, N.Y.: Doubleday, 1973), 6–18.

10. McQuirter, "Claiming the City," 180–82.

11. Ibid., 12–55.

12. Ibid., 19.

13. Ibid., 25.

14. Ibid., 27.

15. Ibid., 29–42.

16. Ibid., 2–3.

17. William H. Jones, *Recreation and Amusement among Negroes in Washington, D.C.: A Sociological Analysis of the Negro in an Urban Environment* (Westport, Conn.: Negro Universities Press, 1927), 112–18. Further information about these theaters may be found on the National Park Service's Greater U Street Historic District Web site, http://www.cr.nps.gov/nr/travel/wash/dc63.htm. Further information about historic walking tours through the neighborhood are given by Paul K. Williams and Kathryn S. Smith, *City within a City: Greater U Street Heritage Trail* (Washington, D.C.: Historical Society of Washington, D.C., and D.C. Heritage Tourism Coalition, 2001).

18. McQuirter, "Claiming the City," 113–14.

19. Jones, *Recreation and Amusement*, 199–20; Tamara Lizette Brown, "Lingering Lights from America's Black Broadway: Negro Renaissance to the Black Arts Movement, African-American Theatrical Dance in Washington, D.C.," PhD dissertation, Howard University, Washington, 2004, 9.

20. Jones, *Recreation and Amusement*, 125–31. Further information about these dance halls is given by Marya Annette McQuirter, *African American Heritage Trail, Washington, D.C.* (Washington, D.C.: Cultural Tourism D.C., 2003), 9.

21. Laura Bergheim, *The Washington Historical Atlas: Who Did What When and Where in the Nation's Capital* (Rockville, Md.: Woodbine House, 1992), 252.

22. David A. Taylor, "It All Began One Night Near U Street," *Washington Post*, January 7, 2007.

23. The theater historian Henry P. Whitehead compiled a collection of memorabilia from the U Street cabarets, clubs, and theaters. Some of the posters, fliers, tickets, and newspaper articles in his collection were published by Henry P. Whitehead, *Remembering U Street: There Was a Time* (Washington, D.C.: Remembering U Street, Inc., 1994).

24. Jones, *Recreation and Amusement*, 131–34.

25. Ibid., 134.

26. Ibid., 136.

27. Ibid., 135–40.

28. Ibid., 88.

29. Ibid., 161–62.

30. Ibid., 162–63.

31. McQuirter, "Claiming the City," 186–88.

32. Ibid., 204–5.

33. Ibid., 209–10.

34. Bettye Gardner and Bettye Thomas, "The Cultural Impact of the Howard Theatre on the Black Community," *Journal of Negro History* 55, no. 4 (1970): 253–65.

35. As reported by ibid., 254.

36. Ibid., 254–55.

37. Sandra Fitzpatrick and Maria R. Goodwin, *The Guide to Black Washington: Places and Events of Historical and Cultural Significance in the Nation's Capital*, rev. illus. ed. (New York: Hippocrene Books, 2001), 122–23.

38. Gardner and Thomas, "Cultural Impact of the Howard Theatre," 255–56.

39. Ibid., 257–59.

40. Ibid., 258–59.

41. Bergheim, *Washington Historical Atlas*, 249–50.

42. Mark Opasasnick, *Washington Rock and Roll: A Social History* (Tinicum, Pa.: Xlibris, 2003), 24–50.

43. Gardner and Thomas, "Cultural Impact of the Howard Theatre," 260–62.

44. Ibid.

45. McQuirter, "Claiming the City," 94–102; Stephanie Barbara Frank, "'If We Own the Story, We Own the Place': Cultural Heritage, Historic Preservation, and Gentrification on U Street," MA thesis, University of Maryland, College Park, 2005, 65–69.

46. McQuirter, "Claiming the City," 108–11.

47. Ibid., 112–15.

48. Loften Mitchell, *Black Drama: The Story of the American Negro in the Theater* (New York: Hawthorn, 1967).

49. Brown, "Lingering Lights from America's Black Broadway," 10, 76–80.

50. Ibid., 80.

51. Carol Blair Vaughan, "Clayton 'Peg Leg' Bates: Monoped Master of the Art of Tap Dance," MA thesis, American University, Washington, 1991.

52. Brown, "Lingering Lights from America's Black Broadway," 46–48.

53. For further discussion of the place of Washington in the "Harlem" Renaissance and the New Negro Movement, see James A. Miller, "Black Washington and the New Negro Renaissance," in *Composing Urban History and the Constitution*

of Civic Identities, ed. John J. Czaplicka and Blair A. Ruble (Washington, D.C., and Baltimore: Woodrow Wilson Center Press and Johns Hopkins University Press, 2003), 219–41.

54. Brown, "Lingering Lights from America's Black Broadway," 52–53.

55. Carolyn Amonitte Stubbs, "Angelina Weld Grimké: Washington Poet and Playwright," PhD dissertation, George Washington University, Washington, 1978.

56. Brown, "Lingering Lights from America's Black Broadway," 327.

57. Ibid., 127–34.

58. Erin Trouth, "Russian Influence on American Dance," in *Culture/Kultura: Russian Influences on American Performing Arts and Sports*, ed. Kennan Institute (Washington, D.C.: Kennan Institute, Woodrow Wilson International Center for Scholars, 2004), 13–15.

59. Ibid., 4–5.

60. This account of Williams' career is adapted from that given by Brown, "Lingering Lights from America's Black Broadway," 137–44.

61. Ibid., 147–49.

62. Tamara Brown, "Highlights from America's Black Broadway," *Negro History Bulletin* 59 (1996).

63. Brown, "Lingering Lights from America's Black Broadway," 148–79.

64. Ibid., 168–69.

65. Ibid., 169–71.

66. Ibid., 192–95.

67. Ibid., 198–215.

68. Ibid., 327–28.

69. Bob Kuska, *Hot Potato: How Washington and New York Gave Birth to Black Basketball and Changed America's Game Forever* (Charlottesville: University of Virginia Press, 2004), 1–14.

70. Ibid., 10–11.

71. Ibid., 11–12.

72. Ibid., 12–15.

73. Ibid., 15.

74. David K. Wiggins, "Edward Henderson," in *Encyclopedia of Ethnicity and Sports in the United States*, ed. George B. Kirsch, Othello Harris, and Claire E. Nolte (Westport, Conn.: Greenwood Press, 2000), 211–12.

75. Kuska, *Hot Potato*, 14–15.

76. E.g., *The Negro in Sports* (1939, 1949) and *The Black Athlete: Emergence and Arrival* (1968). See Wiggins, "Edward Henderson," 212.

77. Kuska, *Hot Potato*, 1–3.

78. Ibid.

79. Ibid.

80. Ibid., 4–5.

81. Ibid., 5–6.

82. Ibid., 5–7.

83. Ibid., 28–29.

84. Ibid., 38–40.

85. Ibid., 46–47.

86. Ibid., 136–61.

87. Ibid., 163–79.

88. Ibid., 164–66.

89. Bergheim, *Washington Historical Atlas*, 259–60.

90. Fitzpatrick and Goodwin, *Guide to Black Washington*, 114–55.

91. Brad Snyder, *Beyond the Shadow of the Senators: The Untold Story of the Homestead Grays and the Integration of Baseball* (New York: Contemporary Books, 2003), 3–4.

92. Ibid., 4–5.

93. Fitzpatrick and Goodwin, *Guide to Black Washington*, 114–55.

94. Jones, *Recreation and Amusement*, 29.

95. Snyder, *Beyond the Shadow of the Senators*, 10–12.

96. Jones, *Recreation and Amusement*, 79–86.

97. Ibid., 80.

98. Ibid.

99. Ibid., 80–81.

100. Ibid., 81–82.

101. Ibid., 83.

102. Ibid., 83–84.

103. Fitzpatrick and Goodwin, *Guide to Black Washington*, 112–33.

104. Ibid., 113.

105. Federal Writers' Project, Works Progress Administration, *Washington: City and Capital*, American Guide Series (Washington, D.C.: U.S. Government Printing Office, 1937), 86, 710.

106. Fitzpatrick and Goodwin, *Guide to Black Washington*, 112–33.

107. Ibid., 114; Snyder, *Beyond the Shadow of the Senators*, 11–12.

108. Bergheim, *Washington Historical Atlas*, 259–60.

109. Ibid.

110. Snyder, *Beyond the Shadow of the Senators*, 198.

111. The pass was already well on its way to becoming an integral part of the college game before Baugh proved its success in the National Football League. The forward pass—often misassociated with the Knute Rockne Notre Dame teams of the 1920s—was first developed by the legendary Carlisle Indian School teams of the first decades of the twentieth century. For further discussion of this history, see Sally

Jenkins, *The Real All Americans: The Team That Changed a Game, a People, a Nation* (New York: Doubleday, 2007).

112. Thom Leverro, *Hail Victory: An Oral History of the Washington Redskins* (Hoboken, N.J.: John Wiley & Sons, 2006), 16–41.

113. Whit Canning and Dan Jenkins, *Sam Baugh: Best There Ever Was* (Fort Worth: Fort Worth Star-Telegram, 1997).

114. The Redskins rode Baugh's strong arm to a fourth-quarter victory, winning by a score of 20–14. The always imperious Marshall resented having the public address system used to page senior military personnel as the realization of war swept through the capital city. See Burt Solomon, *The Washington Century: Three Families and the Shaping of the Nation's Capital* (New York: HarperCollins, 2004), 49; and Snyder, *Beyond the Shadow of the Senators*, 100–101.

115. Henry W. Thomas, *Walter Johnson: Baseball's Big Train* (Washington, D.C.: Phenom Press, 1995).

116. Snyder, *Beyond the Shadow of the Senators*, 12–13.

117. See Williams, *Greater U Street*.

118. Snyder, *Beyond the Shadow of the Senators*, xi–xii, 13–14.

119. Ibid., xi–xii.

120. Ibid., 91–96.

121. Ibid., 67–74.

122. Kuska, *Hot Potato*, 180–85.

123. Lacy's career is recounted throughout the history of Washington baseball by Snyder, *Beyond the Shadow of the Senators*.

124. Ibid., 59–64.

125. Ibid., 94.

126. Ibid., 113–20.

127. Ibid., 88–90.

128. Jules Tygiel, *Baseball's Great Experiment* (New York: Oxford University Press, 1983).

129. Snyder, *Beyond the Shadow of the Senators*, 107.

130. Ibid., 112.

131. Ibid., 180.

132. Ibid., 285.

133. Ibid.

134. Ibid., 283.

135. Ibid., 288.

136. Ibid., 289.

137. Ibid., 33–86.

138. Ibid., 87.

139. Ibid., 88–89.

140. Ibid., 104–6.

141. Ibid., 113.

142. Ibid.

143. Ibid., 132–47.

144. Ibid., 177–84.

145. Ibid., 270–79.

146. Ibid., 271–72.

147. Florence Murray, ed., *The Negro Handbook 1949* (New York: Macmillan, 1949), 354–56.

148. Federal Writers' Project, *Washington*, 89.

149. Rita Lierti, "'We Were Ladies, We Just Played Basketball Like Boys': African American Womanhood and Competitive Basketball at Bennett College, 1928–1942," *Journal of Sports History* 26 (1999): 567–48.

150. Brown, "Highlights from America's Black Broadway."

CHAPTER 5

1. This observation was made concerning his life in Paris on the eve of World War II. Langston Hughes, *I Wonder As I Wander*, republished in *The Collected Works of Langston Hughes, Volume 14: I Wonder As I Wander*, ed. Joseph McLaren (Columbia: University of Missouri Press, 2003), 387.

2. Eric W. Weiss, "Tax Relief Proposed for Historic Businesses," *Washington Post*, January 26, 2006.

3. Fred Siegel, *The Future Once Happened Here: New York, D.C., L.A. and the Fate of America's Big Cities* (San Francisco: Encounter Books, 1997), 109–11.

4. This is from a 1957 editorial, as quoted by Howard Gillette Jr., *Between Justice and Beauty: Race, Planning, and the Failure of Urban Policy in Washington, D.C.* (Baltimore: Johns Hopkins University Press, 1995), 163.

5. Frederick Gutheim and Wilcomb E. Washburn, *The Federal City: Plans and Realities* (Washington, D.C.: Smithsonian Institution, National Capital Planning Commission, and U.S. Commission of Fine Arts, 1976), 44–67.

6. Ronald M. Johnson, "LeDroit Park: Premier Black Community," in *Washington at Home: An Illustrated History of Neighborhoods in the Nation's Capital*, ed. Kathryn Schneider Smith (Washington, D.C.: Columbia Historical Society and Windsor Publications, Inc., 1988), 139–47.

7. Ben W. Gilbert and the Staff of the *Washington Post*, *Ten Blocks from the White House: Anatomy of the Washington Riots of 1968* (New York: Frederick A. Praeger, 1968), 3.

8. Marcia M. Greenlee, "Shaw: Heart of Black Washington," in *Washington at Home*, ed. Smith, 119–29.

9. Gillette, *Between Justice and Beauty*, 161–68.

10. Paul K. Williams, *Greater U Street*, Images of America Series (Charleston: Arcadia, 2002), 105–20.

11. D.C. History Curriculum Project, *City of Magnificent Intentions: A History of the District of Columbia* (Washington, D.C.: Intac, 1983), 438.

12. Carl Abbott, "Dimensions of Regional Change in Washington, D.C.," *American Historical Review* 95, no. 5 (1990): 1367–93 (the citation here is on 1385); Dennis E. Gale, *Washington, D.C.: Inner-City Revitalization and Minority Suburbanization* (Philadelphia: Temple University Press, 1987), 12.

13. Robert Manning, "Multicultural Washington, D.C.: The Changing Social and Economic Landscape of a Post-Industrial Metropolis," *Ethnic and Racial Studies* 21, no. 2 (1998): 328–54 (the citation here is on 338).

14. D.C. History Curriculum Project, *City of Magnificent Intentions*, 438–41.

15. Gale, *Washington*, 54–57.

16. Ibid., 56–58; Jeffrey R. Henig, *Gentrification in Adams Morgan: Political and Commercial Consequences of Neighborhood Change*, Center for Washington Area Studies, Washington Studies Series 9 (Washington, D.C.: George Washington University, 1982); Frank H. Wilson, "Gentrification in the Central Area Neighborhoods: Population and Housing Change in Washington, D.C., 1970–1980," PhD dissertation, University of Michigan, Ann Arbor, 1985. In retrospect, these were only the first of a series of neighborhoods that would experience private restoration and investment during the last half of the twentieth century. U Street's turn would come in the 1990s.

17. Abbott, "Dimensions of Regional Change," 1376–77. For further discussion of these trends, see Blair A. Ruble, *Creating Diversity Capital: Transnational Migrants in Montreal, Washington, and Kyiv* (Washington, D.C., and Baltimore: Woodrow Wilson Center Press and Johns Hopkins University Press, 2005), 68–76.

18. Gale, *Washington*, 18–20; Duane R. Taylor, *Home Rule in the District of Columbia: The First 500 Days* (Washington, D.C.: University Press of America, 1977).

19. Constance McLaughlin Green, *The Secret City: A History of Race Relations in the Nation's Capital* (Princeton, N.J.: Princeton University Press, 1967), 200; Krishna Roy, "Socio-Demographic Profile," in Council on Latino Agencies / Consejo de Agencias Latinas, *The State of Latinos in the District of Columbia* (Washington, D.C.: Council on Latino Agencies / Consejo de Agencias Latinas, 2002), 1–30 (the citation here is on 5).

20. Mara Cherkasky, "'For Sale to Colored': Racial Change on S Street NW," *Washington History* 8, no. 2 (1996–97): 41–57.

21. Green, *Secret City*, 321–36.

22. Stan R. Nikkel, "A Study in the Development and Structure of an Interracial Neighborhood in Washington, D.C.," PhD dissertation, University of Maryland, College Park, 1973.

23. D.C. History Curriculum Project, *City of Magnificent Intentions*, 443–48.

24. Ibid.; Sandra Fitzpatrick and Maria R. Goodwin, *The Guide to Black Washington: Places and Events of Historical and Cultural Significance in the Nation's Capital*, rev. illus. ed. (New York: Hippocrene Books, 2001), 85–86.

25. Fitzpatrick and Goodwin, *Guide to Black Washington*, 85–86.

26. Herbert Kingley Lodder, "The Response of White Protestantism to Negroes in Washington, D.C., 1865–1965," MA thesis, Columbia University, New York, 1967.

27. D.C. History Curriculum Project, *City of Magnificent Intentions*, 449–50.

28. Ibid., 450–51.

29. Ibid., 27–30.

30. Fitzpatrick and Goodwin, *Guide to Black Washington*, 81.

31. Ibid., 183; Laura Bergheim, *The Washington Historical Atlas: Who Did What When and Where in the Nation's Capital* (Rockville, Md.: Woodbine House, 1992), 244.

32. Elliot Liebow, *Tally's Corner: A Study of Negro Streetcorner Men* (Boston: Little, Brown, 1967), 17–18.

33. Sam Smith, *Captive Capital: Colonial Life in Modern Washington* (Bloomington: Indiana University Press, 1974), 16–17.

34. Ibid., 116–19; Audrey Elisa Kerr, "Two Black Washingtons: The Role of Complexion in the Oral History of District of Columbia Residents, 1863–1963," PhD dissertation, University of Maryland, College Park, 1998; Siegel, *Future Once Happened Here*, 79.

35. Green, *Secret City*, 1.

36. Spencer R. Crew, "Melding the Old and the New: The Modern African American Community, 1930–1960," in *Urban Odyssey: A Multicultural History of Washington, D.C.*, ed. Francine Curro Cary (Washington, D.C.: Smithsonian Institution Press, 1996), 208–27 (the citation here is on 216).

37. George W. Carey, Leonore MacOmber, and Michael Greenberg, "Educational and Demographic Factors in the Urban Geography of Washington, D.C.," *Geographical Review* 58, no. 4 (1968): 515–37.

38. Kinzo Yamamoto, "Assimilation of Migrant Negroes in the District of Columbia: A Study of the Effect of Length of Residence on Urban Life Adjustment," PhD dissertation, Pennsylvania State University, State College, 1971.

39. Green, *Secret City*, 3–4.

40. Alan Ehrenhalt, *The Lost City: Discovering the Forgotten Virtues of the Community in the Chicago of the 1950s* (New York: Basic Books, 1995); Siegel, *Future Once Happened Here*, 5–6.

41. Joseph Berger, *The World in a City: Traveling the Globe through the Neighborhoods of the New New York* (New York: Ballantine Books, 2007).

42. Siegel, *Future Once Happened Here*, 10.

43. Ulf Hannerz, *Soulside: Inquiries into Ghetto Culture and Community* (New York: Columbia University Press, 1969).

44. Ibid., 11.

45. Ibid., 7.

46. Green, *Secret City*, 1.

47. Gillette, *Between Justice and Beauty*, 163.

48. D.C. History Curriculum Project, *City of Magnificent Intentions*, 452–60.

49. These laws were the District of Columbia Redevelopment Act of 1945, the National Housing Act of 1949, and the National Capital Planning Act of 1952. Ibid., 452.

50. Ibid.

51. Zachery M. Schrag, "The Freeway Fight in Washington, D.C.: The Three Sisters Bridge in Three Administrations," *Journal of Urban History* 30, no. 5 (2004): 648–73.

52. D.C. History Curriculum Project, *City of Magnificent Intentions*, 157–59.

53. Jerome S. Paige and Margaret M. Reuss, *Safe, Decent and Affordable: Citizen Struggles to Improve Housing in the District of Columbia, 1890–1982*, Studies in D.C. History and Public Policy 6 (Washington, D.C.: Center for Applied Research and Urban Policy, University of the District of Columbia, 1983), 20.

54. Harry S. Jaffe and Tom Sherwood, *Dream City: Race, Power and the Decline of Washington, D.C.* (New York: Simon & Schuster, 1994), 29.

55. Ibid.

56. D.C. History Curriculum Project, *City of Magnificent Intentions*, 460–61.

57. Siegel, *Future Once Happened Here*, 10.

58. "Urbicide" is the destruction (or homicide) of an urban neighborhood or city supporting a socioeconomic, ethnic, racial, or religious group. For further discussion of this concept, see Martin Shaw, "New Ways of the City: 'Urbicide' and 'Genocide,'" in *Cities, War, and Terrorism: Towards an Urban Geopolitics*, ed. Stephen Graham (London: Blackwell, 2004), 141–53.

59. Gillette, *Between Justice and Beauty*, 163–64.

60. Sofie M. M. A. Geschier, "'So There I Sit in a Catch-22 Situation': Remembering and Imagining the Trauma in the District Six Museum," in *Imagining the City: Memories and Cultures in Cape Town*, ed. Sean Field, Renate Meyer, and Felicity Swanson (Cape Town: HSRC Press, 2007), 37–56 (the citation here is on 40).

61. Gillette, *Between Justice and Beauty*, 163–64.

62. Ibid., 163; D.C. History Curriculum Project, *City of Magnificent Intentions*, 463.

63. D.C. History Curriculum Project, *City of Magnificent Intentions*, 460.

64. Green, *Secret City*, 324; Greenlee, "Shaw."

65. Green, *Secret City*, 324.

66. Bergheim, *Washington Historical Atlas*, 246.

67. Greenlee, "Shaw."

68. Paige and Reuss, *Safe, Decent and Affordable*, 20.

69. Greenlee, "Shaw."

70. As explained in the 1961 report *A Plan for the Year 2000* released by the National Capital Park and Planning Commission and the National Capital Regional Planning Council, the goal ostensibly was to shorten commuting distances for suburban white collar workers, and to increase pedestrian traffic by moving the city's office district closer to in-town middle-class areas. This plan is discussed by Gale, *Washington*, 35.

71. Paige and Reuss, *Safe, Decent and Affordable*, 20.

72. This account is based on ibid., 20–26; and Gillette, *Between Justice and Beauty*, 173–89.

73. Fauntroy, who had been named vice chair of the council, abstained from voting on the MICCO proposals.

74. Liebow describes his field research at the outset of his book. Liebow, *Tally's Corner*, 4–28.

75. Ibid., 11.

76. Ibid., 18.

77. Ibid., 24.

78. Ibid., 21–22.

79. Ibid., 22. Liebow draws on the concept of "effortless sociability" from Josephine Klien, *Samples from English Cultures* (London: Routledge, 1967), vol. 1, 142.

80. Liebow, *Tally's Corner*, 23.

81. Ibid., 214.

82. This point is emphasized in the discussion of these issues by D.C. History Curriculum Project, *City of Magnificent Intentions*, 486.

83. Paul Hanly Furfey, *The Subculture of the Washington Ghetto* (Washington, D.C.: Bureau of Social Research, Department of Sociology, Catholic University of America, 1972), 21.

84. Ibid., 26.

85. Ibid., 7–8.

86. Ibid., 10–12.

87. Brett Williams, *Upscaling Downtown: Stalled Gentrification in Washington, D.C.* (Ithaca, N.Y.: Cornell University Press, 1988).

88. Ibid., 3.

89. Ibid.

90. Ibid., 41–42.

91. Ibid., 47.

92. Ulf Hannerz, *Soulside*, 19–33.

93. Ibid., 12–16.

94. Ibid., 19–28.

95. Ibid., 28.

96. Ibid., 35–57.

97. Ibid., 34.

98. For a general biography for Julius Hobson, see the recounting of Hobson's story by Burt Solomon, *The Washington Century: Three Families and the Shaping of the Nation's Capital* (New York: HarperCollins, 2004).

99. Ibid., 173.

100. Martina Pinkney Matthews, "The Politics of Julius W. Hobson, Sr., and the District of Columbia Public School System," PhD dissertation, Ohio State University, Columbus, 1981.

101. Solomon, *Washington Century*, 229–30.

102. Smith, *Captive Capital*, 261.

103. Jaffe and Sherwood, *Dream City*, 49–50.

104. D.C. History Curriculum Project, *City of Magnificent Intentions*, 482–83.

105. Donald Earl Collins, "'A Substance of Things to Come': Multiculturalism, Desegregation and Identity in African American Washington, D.C., 1930–1960," PhD dissertation, University of Michigan, Ann Arbor, 1997, 397–433.

106. Megan Greenwell, "Md., Va. School Systems Ranked in Nation's Top 5: Report Places the District Behind All States," *Washington Post*, January 10, 2008.

107. Beverly E. Reid, "Desegregation of the Public Schools of the District of Columbia, 1954–1959," MA thesis, Howard University, Washington, D.C., 1971; and Edwin Knoll, "The Truth about Desegregation in Washington, D.C., Public Schools," *Journal of Negro Education* 22, no. 2 (1959): 92–113.

108. Reid, "Desegregation," 20–45.

109. Anna Kinsman, *The Politics of Knowledge: Public Schools in the Nation's Capital* (New York: Peter Land, 2003), 39.

110. Ibid., 39–41.

111. Ibid., 42–43.

112. Thornell K. Page, "A Study of the District of Columbia Public Schools Desegregation Policies, 1954–1967," PhD dissertation, Virginia Polytechnic Institute, Blacksburg, 1978.

113. Matthews, "Politics of Julius W. Hobson, Sr.," 88–90.

114. Smith, *Captive Capital*, 184–85; D.C. History Curriculum Project, *City of Magnificent Intentions*, 491–92.

115. Solomon, *Washington Century*, 171–78.

116. Kinsman, *Politics of Knowledge*, 46–50.

117. Matthews, "Politics of Julius W. Hobson, Sr.," 88–90.

118. Ibid.

119. Ibid; Solomon, *Washington Century*, 178–82.

120. D.C. History Curriculum Project, *City of Magnificent Intentions*, 511–12.

121. Smith, *Captive Capital*, 186–87.

122. Benjamin Lee Swinson, "Historical Development of Public School Adult Education Programs in Washington, D.C., 1858–1982," EdD dissertation, George Washington University, Washington, 1985.

123. Kinsman, *Politics of Knowledge*, 46–50.

124. This account is based on "Explosion of Hate," *Time Magazine,* December 7, 1962. Also see Kinsman, *Politics of Knowledge*, 44–45.

125. D.C. History Curriculum Project, *City of Magnificent Intentions*, 491–97. Further discussion of the March on Washington is given by Juan Williams, *Eye on the Prize: America's Civil Rights Years, 1954–1965* (New York: Penguin Books, 1987), 197–206.

126. Jaffe and Sherwood, *Dream City*, 31–35.

127. Ibid., 33.

128. Ibid., 34.

129. For further discussion of Barry's background, see Ruble, *Creating Diversity Capital*, 116–77.

130. Jaffe and Sherwood, *Dream City*, 40–41.

131. Steven J. Diner, *Democracy, Federalism, and the Governance of the Nation's Capital, 1790–1974*, Studies in D.C. History and Public Policy 10 (Washington, D.C.: Center for Applied Research and Urban Policy, University of the District of Columbia, 1987), 52.

132. Ibid.; Jaffe and Sherwood, *Dream City*, 43–47.

133. Jaffe and Sherwood, *Dream City*, 47–48.

134. Smith, *Captive Capital*, 239–41.

135. Kenneth Robert Janken, *Rayford W. Logan and the Dilemma of the African-American Intellectual* (Amherst: University of Massachusetts Press, 1993), 226–27.

136. Jaffe and Sherwood, *Dream City*, 47.

137. John W. Wann, *A Compilation and History of National Baptist Memorial Church (Formerly Immanuel Baptist Church), Washington, D.C., 1906 to about 1976* (Washington, D.C.: National Baptist Memorial Church, 1976), 121–27.

138. Ibid., 243–49.

139. Ibid., 267–69.

140. Ibid., 269–72.

141. For more on the history of All Souls Church, consult its Web site at www .all-souls.org. A biography of David Eaton with information about the "Take the Blindfold Off the Lady" sermon may be found on the Web site of the Unitarian Universalist Association at http://www25.uua.org/uuhs/duub/articles/davidheaton

.html. Thomas Hargrave has written about the impact of the sermon as well in an unpublished manuscript; see Thomas B. Hargrave Jr., "Take the Blindfold Off the Lady: Rev. David Eaton's Fire from the All Souls' Pulpit," unpublished manuscript, August 2009.

142. Tamara Lizette Brown, "Lingering Lights from America's Black Broadway: Negro Renaissance to the Black Arts Movement, African-American Concert-Theatrical Dance in Washington, D.C.," PhD dissertation, Howard University, Washington, 2004, 276–320.

143. Olivia Cadaval, *Creating a Latino Identity in the Nation's Capital: The Latino Festival* (Washington, D.C., self-published, 1998); Olivia Cadaval, "The Latino Community: Creating an Identity in the Nation's Capital," in *Urban Odyssey*, ed. Cary, 231–49; Berket H. Selassie, "Washington's New African Immigrants," in *Urban Odyssey*, ed. Cary, 264–75; Keith Q. Warner, "From 'Down the Way Where the Nights Are Gay': Caribbean Immigration and the Bridging of Cultures," in *Urban Odyssey*, ed. Cary, 250–63.

144. Howard Gillette Jr., "Washington, D.C., in White and Black: The Social Construction of Race and Nationhood," in *Composing Urban History and the Construction of Civic Identities*, ed. John J. Czaplicka and Blair A. Ruble (Washington, D.C., and Baltimore: Woodrow Wilson Center Press and Johns Hopkins University Press, 2003), 192–210.

145. Jessica Weiss, "Portrait of a Community: Life in Shaw," paper presented at the Janus Undergraduate History Conference, University of Maryland, College Park, March 17, 2005, 26–27.

146. Zachary M. Schrag, *The Great Society Subway: A History of the Washington Metro* (Baltimore: Johns Hopkins University Press, 2006), 209–12.

147. Gillette, "Washington, D.C.," 193.

148. Diner, *Democracy*, 54–56.

149. Gilbert et al., *Ten Blocks from the White House*, 5–6.

150. National Advisory Commission on Civil Disorders, *Report* (Washington, D.C.: U.S. Government Printing Office, 1968), 1.

151. Janet L. Abu-Lughod, *Race, Space and Riots in Chicago, New York, and Los Angeles* (New York: Oxford University Press, 2007), 3–4.

152. Jaffe and Sherwood, *Dream City*, 52–62.

153. UPO had been established in December 1962 to provide community services. Information on its founding and development over the past half-century may be found on the organization's Web site, www.upo.org.

154. Siegel, *Future Once Happened Here*, 79–81.

155. Jaffe and Sherwood, *Dream City*, 58; Jonetta Rose Barras, *The Last of the Black Emperors: The Hollow Comeback of Marion Barry in the New Age of Black Leaders* (Baltimore: Bancroft Press, 1998), 125–32.

156. Siegel, *Future Once Happened Here*, 80.

157. Ibid.

158. Vernon Loeb, "Barry Brings Halt to Turbulent D.C. Saga," *Washington Post*, May 22, 1998; Barras, *Last of the Black Emperors*, 34.

159. D.C. History Curriculum Project, *City of Magnificent Intentions*, 483–85.

160. Hannerz, *Soulside*, 167.

161. The phrase "The Thin Line Vanishes," used as this section's title, is the title of chapter 3 in *Ten Blocks from the White House*, by Gilbert et al., 45.

162. Jaffe and Sherwood, *Dream City*, 67–68.

163. Gilbert et al., *Ten Blocks from the White House*, 1–13; Faye P. Haskins, "*The Evening Star*'s Coverage of the 1968 Riots," *Washington History* 19 & 20 (2007–8): 51–67.

164. Gilbert et al., *Ten Blocks from the White House*, 14.

165. Jaffe and Sherwood, *Dream City*, 68.

166. Gilbert et al., *Ten Blocks from the White House*, 14.

167. Ibid., 15–17.

168. Ibid., 18.

169. Ibid., 18.

170. Jaffe and Sherwood, *Dream City*, 71.

171. Gilbert et al., *Ten Blocks from the White House*, 18–19.

172. Ibid.

173. Ibid.

174. Ibid.

175. Ibid., 20–21.

176. Ibid., 120, 150–91; Jaffe and Sherwood, *Dream City*, 81. The death toll was so low in large measure due to Mayor Walter Washington's order that the police not shoot looters, a decision made over the staunch opposition of Federal Bureau of Investigation director J. Edgar Hoover. In later life, Washington was especially proud of his refusal to bend to Hoover's will. His subsequent accounts of his confrontation with Hoover over the issue are retold by Sam Smith in his online memoir, "Multitudes" (http://prorev.com/mmfire.htm).

177. D.C. History Curriculum Project, *City of Magnificent Intentions*, 498.

178. Ibid. White churches joined with African American congregations to provide basic services and to promote the slow process of community healing. See, e.g., Wann, *Compilation and History of National Baptist Memorial Church*, 251–65.

179. Gilbert et al., *Ten Blocks from the White House*, 120.

180. Hannerz, *Soulside*, 174. The story of Ben's survival in particular has become legendary. See, e.g., Weiss, "Portrait of a Community," 31. In fact, the protection provided by such impromptu self-defense mechanisms as posting a "Soul Brother" sign in the window appears to have been inconsistent at best as large numbers of African American–owned businesses were destroyed along with everything else that stood in the path of the spreading fires.

181. Gilbert et al., *Ten Blocks from the White House*, 32–33.

182. Wann, *Compilation and History of National Baptist Memorial Church*, 251–65.

183. Ibid., xiii–xiv, 192–218; D.C. History Curriculum Project, *City of Magnificent Intentions*, 499.

184. Hannerz, *Soulside*, 172–75.

185. Gilbert et al., *Ten Blocks from the White House*, 23–25.

186. Ibid., 24.

187. Ibid., 28–30.

188. Ibid., 30.

189. Smith, *Captive Capital*, 126.

190. Gilbert et al., *Ten Blocks from the White House*, 46–47.

191. Ibid., 61–68.

192. Ibid., 64–65; Jaffe and Sherwood, *Dream City*, 73–74.

193. Gilbert et al., *Ten Blocks from the White House*, 48–53.

194. Jaffe and Sherwood, *Dream City*, 76–77.

195. Gilbert et al., *Ten Blocks from the White House*, 57–58, 71–73.

196. Solomon, *Washington Century*, 184.

197. Jaffe and Sherwood, *Dream City*, 77; Gilbert et al., *Ten Blocks from the White House*, 79.

198. This point is underscored by Barrye La Troye Price in a perceptive doctoral dissertation examining the federal intervention in the city. Barrye La Troye Price, "King to King: A Study of Civil Unrest and Federal Intervention from 1968 to 1992," PhD dissertation, Texas A&M University, College Station, 1997.

199. Hannerz, *Soulside*, 173.

200. Gilbert et al., *Ten Blocks from the White House*, 11–12.

201. Ibid., 74–77.

202. "Memories of Mayhem and Mercy," *Washington Post*, April 7, 2008.

203. Gilbert et al., *Ten Blocks from the White House*, 87–90. For further discussion of the especially damaging impact of the unrest on the Jewish community, see, e.g., Hasia R. Diner and Steven J. Diner, "Washington's Jewish Community: Separate But Not Apart," in *Urban Odyssey*, ed. Cary, 138–53; and Carole Adams Kolker, "Migrants and Memories: Family, Work and Community among Blacks, Eastern European Jews, and Native Born Whites in an Early Twentieth Century Washington, D.C. Neighborhood," PhD dissertation, George Washington University, Washington, 1996.

204. Gilbert et al., *Ten Blocks from the White House*, 87–113; Jaffe and Sherwood, *Dream City*, 80–81; Price, "King to King," 84–101.

205. Richard Guy Sedlack, "Riots as Disasters: An Exploratory Case Study of Selected Aspects of the Civil Disturbance in Washington, D.C., April 1968," PhD dissertation, University of Maryland, College Park, 1973.

206. Gilbert et al., *Ten Blocks from the White House*, 224–25.

207. Siegel, *Future Once Happened Here*, 77–78.

208. Michael B. Katz, "Why Don't American Cities Burn Very Often?" *Journal of Urban History* 34, no. 2 (January 2008): 185–208.

209. Hannerz, *Soulside*, 175.

210. Gilbert et al., *Ten Blocks from the White House*, 113.

211. These images can be confirmed in recent promotion of the area as a cultural and historic destination. See, e.g., Williams, *Greater U Street*, 105–27; Bergheim, *Washington Historical Atlas*, 252–53; Fitzpatrick and Goodwin, *Guide to Black Washington*, 101–60; and Jane Freundel Levey, as well as Paul K. Williams, Richard T. Busch, J. Brendan Meyer, Anne W. Rollins, and Joan M. Mathys, *Midcity at the Crossroads: Shaw Heritage Trail* (Washington, D.C.: Cultural Tourism D.C., 2006), 24. Similar messages are to be found in Hedrick Smith's documentary about the U Street neighborhood that was broadcast by the Public Broadcasting System; see Hedrick Smith, *Duke Ellington's Washington*, documentary film, Public Broadcasting System, February 7, 2000.

212. Dana Lanier Schaffer, "The 1968 Washington Riots in History and Memory," *Washington History* 15, no. 2 (2003–4): 5–33 (the citation here is on 6).

213. D.C. History Curriculum Project, *City of Magnificent Intentions*, 501–8; Diner, *Democracy*, 56–58.

214. D.C. History Curriculum Project, *City of Magnificent Intentions*, 508–12.

215. Gillette, *Between Justice and Beauty*, 190.

216. Jaffe and Sherwood, *Dream City*, 44–66.

217. Michael K. Fauntroy, *Home Rule or House Rule? Congress and the Erosion of Local Governance in the District of Columbia* (Lanham, Md.: University Press of America, Inc., 2003), 7n8.

218. State of South Carolina Election Commission, *Report of the South Carolina State Election Commission* (Columbia: State Election Commission, 1973), 575, 583.

219. Jaffe and Sherwood, *Dream City*, 99–102; Diner, *Democracy*, 60–61; Taylor, *Home Rule*; Charles Wesley Harris, *Congress and the Governance of the Nation's Capital: The Conflict of Federal and Local Interests* (Washington, D.C.: Georgetown University Press, 1995), 6–10.

220. Jaffe and Sherwood, *Dream City*, 102–5.

221. Ibid., 103.

222. Ibid., 104.

223. D.C. History Curriculum Project, *City of Magnificent Intentions*, 517.

224. Fauntroy, *Home Rule or House Rule?* 76–81; Harris, *Congress*, 11–65; Smith, *Captive Capital*, 167.

225. Fauntroy, *Home Rule or House Rule?* 81.

226. Ibid., 89.

227. Jaffe and Sherwood, *Dream City*, 89–90.
228. As quoted in ibid., 93.
229. Barras, *Last of the Black Emperors*, 131–32.
230. Jaffe and Sherwood, *Dream City*, 125–27.

CHAPTER 6

1. This is from the introduction to the song "Washington, D.C.," performed in concert in 1989. This song, which was published by White Metal Music, Ltd., in 1994, is available on Gil Scott-Heron's album *Minister of Information*, released in compact disc format by Peak Top Records in 1994.

2. Edward P. Jones, "Bad Neighbors," in *All Aunt Hagar's Children*, by Edward P. Jones (New York: Amistad/HarperCollins, 2006), 347–73; the quotation here is on 355.

3. Krishna Roy, "Socio-Demographic Profile," in *The State of Latinos in the District of Columbia*, ed. Council on Latino Agencies / Consejo de Agencias Latinas (Washington, D.C.: Council on Latino Agencies / Consejo de Agencias Latinas, 2002), 1–30; the citation here is on 5.

4. For a discussion of the "Chocolate City" moniker, see Matthew Taylor's review of a documentary film of the same name made by Ellie Walton and Sam Wild in 2007; Matthew Taylor, "Chocolate City," *Washington Street Sense*, February 20–March 4, 2008, 11.

5. Barry's tenure as School Board president coincided with the tenure of the highly controversial African American educator Barbara Sizemore as school superintendent. Tensions between Sizemore and Barry—as well as between Sizemore and the white community—accelerated the school system's decline. Burt Solomon, *The Washington Century: Three Families and the Shaping of the Nation's Capital* (New York: HarperCollins, 2004), 262–73. Also see Sam Smith, *Captive Capital: Colonial Life in Modern Washington* (Bloomington: Indiana University Press, 1974), 20–23.

6. Smith, *Captive Capital*, 66–68.

7. Jerome S. Paige and Margaret M. Reuss, *Safe, Decent and Affordable: Citizen Struggles to Improve Housing in the District of Columbia, 1890–1982*, Studies in D.C. History and Public Policy 6 (Washington, D.C.: Center for Applied Research and Urban Policy, University of the District of Columbia, 1983), 21.

8. Ibid.

9. Fred Siegel reports about how African American television producer Rich Adams described Barry's "mau-mauing" of government officials such as Rumsfeld. According to Siegel, "if someone questioned Barry's good intentions, his response, said Adams, imitating Barry, was as follows: 'Don't ask honky motherfucker, because if you do, we're going out on the street, and we're going to start a riot and say that

the white man is trying to destroy black economic progress,' Adams concluded." Fred Siegel, *The Future Once Happened Here: New York, D.C., L.A. and the Fate of America's Big Cities* (San Francisco: Encounter Books, 1997), 83.

10. Howard Gillette Jr., *Between Justice and Beauty: Race, Planning, and the Failure of Urban Policy in Washington, D.C.* (Baltimore: Johns Hopkins University Press, 1995), 173–81.

11. Paige and Reuss, *Safe, Decent and Affordable*, 21–22.

12. Ibid.

13. Ibid., 23–25.

14. Ibid., 25.

15. Ibid.

16. Gillette, *Between Justice and Beauty*, 185.

17. Ibid., 185–86.

18. Ibid., 186.

19. Ibid., 187–88.

20. D.C. Redevelopment Land Agency, *Shaw Neighborhood Shopping Center* (Washington, D.C.: D.C. Redevelopment Land Agency, 1974).

21. Zachary M. Schrag, *The Great Society Subway: A History of the Washington Metro* (Baltimore: Johns Hopkins University Press, 2006), 206–14.

22. Lois Horton, *Washington, D.C.: From Civil War Town to Modern City* (Washington, D.C.: Associates for Renewal in Education, 1979); Frederick Gutheim and Wilcomb E. Washburn, *The Federal City: Plans & Realities* (Washington, D.C.: Smithsonian Institution, National Capital Planning Commission, and Commission on Fine Arts, 1976), 44–67; National Capital Planning Commission, *Shaw School Urban Renewal Area Landmarks* (Washington, D.C.: National Capital Planning Commission, 1968).

23. Harry S. Jaffe and Tom Sherwood, *Dream City: Race, Power and the Decline of Washington, D.C.* (New York: Simon & Schuster, 1994), 158–59.

24. Ibid., 174–75; D.C. Redevelopment Land Agency, *Shaw Neighborhood Shopping Center*; Gillette, *Between Justice and Beauty*, 185–86.

25. Jaffe and Sherwood, *Dream City*, 158–60.

26. Ibid.

27. Ibid.

28. Ibid.

29. John Mintz, "Shaw Redevelopment Project Launched: Developer, City, Community Join in Long-Awaited Program," *Washington Post*, November 26, 1986; Bill Dedman, Joel Glenn Brenner, "Cohen, City Near Agreement on No-Bid Building Contract," *Washington Post*, June 13, 1990; Miles Maguire, "Cohen Filing Irks U Street Residents," *Washington Times*, September 7, 1990; Miles Maguire, "City Wants to Cancel Shaw Deal," *Washington Times*, November 2,

1990; Miles Maguire, "City Lets Cohen Off, Seeks New Developer," *Washington Times*, November 20, 1990.

30. Alexander von Hoffman, *House by House, Block by Block: The Rebirth of America's Urban Neighborhoods* (New York: Oxford University Press, 2003), 12–13.

31. This shift in national policy is elegantly explored in ibid.

32. Tom Sherwood, "Reeves Municipal Center Dedicated," *Washington Post*, September 28, 1986; Paul K. Williams and Kathryn S. Smith, *City within a City: Greater U Street Heritage Trail* (Washington, D.C.: Historical Society of Washington, D.C., and D.C. Heritage Tourism Coalition, 2001), 32; Sandra Fitzpatrick and Maria R. Goodwin, *The Guide to Black Washington: Places and Events of Historical and Cultural Significance in the Nation's Capital*, rev. illus. ed. (New York: Hippocrene Books, 2001), 175; Marcia M. Greenlee, "Shaw: Heart of Black Washington," in *Washington at Home: An Illustrated History of Neighborhoods in the Nation's Capital*, ed. Kathryn Schneider Smith (Washington, D.C.: Columbia Historical Society and Windsor Publications, 1988), 119–29 (the citation here is on 128).

33. As quoted by Schrag, *Great Society Subway*, 218.

34. Dennis E. Gale, *Washington, D.C.: Inner-City Revitalization and Minority Suburbanization* (Philadelphia: Temple University Press, 1987), 102–4.

35. E.g., Banneker was the only public high school in the District of Columbia to have been selected as a "Blue Ribbon School" by the U.S. Department of Education in 2007. For more information on this designation, see the Public School Review Web site, http://www.publicschoolreview.com/blueribbon_schools/stateid/DC.

36. Thomas Holt, Cassandra Smith-Parker, and Rosalyn Terborg-Penn, *A Special Mission: The Story of Freedmen's Hospital, 1862–1962* (Washington, D.C.: Academic Affairs Division, Howard University, 1975).

37. Schrag, *Great Society Subway*, 106–8.

38. Ibid., 214.

39. Ibid., 215.

40. Ibid., 216–17.

41. Linda Wheeler, "Nightmare on U Street: Metro Work Puts Up Barriers to Business," *Washington Post*, April 15, 1987; Nell Henderson, "Shaw Area Residents Outraged by Metro Excavation Hazards: Green Line Delays, Disputes Fuel Anger," *Washington Post*, April 24, 1990; Pam McClintock, "Shaw Residents, Businesses Upset by Metro Hole, Delay," *Washington Times*, April 25, 1990; Stephen C. Fehr, "Green Line Contractor Promises to Rebuild 2 Streets by May," *Washington Post*, August 7, 1990; Nell Henderson, "Federal Report Cites Metro in Green Line Delay," *Washington Post*, August 7, 1990; Linda Wheeler, "Light at the End of Metro Tunnel: Shaw Community Gets a Glimpse of Long-Awaited Green Line," *Washington Post*, December 11, 1990.

42. Schrag, *Great Society Subway*, 217.

43. Ibid., 218–19.

44. Siegel, *Future Once Happened Here*, 75–114.

45. Ibid., 104.

46. Jonetta Rose Barras, *The Last of the Black Emperors: The Hollow Comeback of Marion Barry in the New Age of Black Leaders* (Baltimore: Bancroft Press, 1998), 130–33.

47. Jorge Luis Borges, "*Sur 142*, August 1946," as reported by Edwin Williamson, *Borges: A Life* (New York: Viking, 2004), 295.

48. Siegel, *Future Once Happened Here*, 26.

49. Jaffe and Sherwood, *Dream City*, 200–229.

50. George P. Pelecanos, *The Sweet Forever: A Novel* (New York: Little, Brown, 1998), 9.

51. Jaffe and Sherwood, *Dream City*, 209.

52. Ibid.

53. Barry reduced the size of the force to its smallest number in years—3,612 officers in 1981. These trends are discussed in detail by Jaffe and Sherwood, *Dream City*, 210–12.

54. Ibid., 212.

55. Ibid., 204–5.

56. Pelecanos, *Sweet Forever*, 31.

57. Dinaw Mengestu, *The Beautiful Things That Heaven Bears* (New York: Riverhead Books, 2007), 162–63.

58. Patricia Sullivan, "Obituaries: 'Mayor of U Street' John 'Butch' Snipes, 71," *Washington Post*, June 29, 2006.

59. Nina Honemond Clarke, *History of the Nineteenth-Century Black Churches in Maryland and Washington, D.C.* (New York: Vantage Press, 1983).

60. Concerning the work of the Nation of Islam in the neighborhood, and more generally in the city, see Amir N. Muhammad, *The History of Masjid Muhammad and the Early Muslims in the Washington, DC Area* (Washington, D.C.: FreeMan Publications, 2009).

61. Concerning the work of the Shaw Project Area Committee, see Vincent Taylor, "Shaw Activist Stays Busy," *Washington Afro-American*, June 4, 1983. Information concerning the evolution of UPO's programs may be found on the United Planning Organization's Web site, www.upo.org.

62. Lurma Rackley, *Laugh If You Like, Ain't a Damn Thing Funny: The Life Story of Ralph "Petey" Greene as told to Lurma Rackley* (Tinicum, Penn.: Xlibris, 2007), 271; for more about Greene's social work with UPO and other organizations, see 240–81.

63. Ronald M. Johnson, "LeDroit Park: Premier Black Community," in *Washington at Home*, ed. Smith, 139–47; the citation here is on 146.

64. Information on these various projects can be found in a variety of sources, including the Web sites for the organizations mentioned here—e.g., MANNA, www.mannadc.org; N Street Village, www.nstreetvillage.org; and the United House of Prayer for All Peoples, www.tuhopfap.org. Concerning the reopening of the Whitelaw, see Patricia Cook, "'Like the Phoenix': The Rebirth of the Whitelaw Hotel," *Washington History* 7, no. 1 (1995): 5–23; Peter F. Sisler, "Former Fans Register Joy at New Plan for Old Hotel," *Washington Times*, February 26, 1992; and Nancy L. Ross, "The Whitelaw Is Back: A Historic Hotel Is Readied for a New Generation of Residents," *Washington Post*, November 12, 1992. Some projects are described by Laura Bergheim, *The Washington Historical Atlas: Who Did What When and Where in the Nation's Capital* (Rockville, Md.: Woodbine House, 1992), 247–54.

65. Jeffrey R. Henig, *Gentrification in Adams Morgan: Political and Commercial Consequences of Neighborhood Change*, Center for Washington Area Studies Series 9 (Washington, D.C.: George Washington University, 1982), 28.

66. Von Hoffman, *House by House*, 2.

67. The Ralph "Petey" Greene story is told in the 2007 film *Talk to Me* (Kasi Lemmons, director; Sidney Kimmel Entertainment, 2007), as well as in Ralph "Petey" Greene's incomplete autobiography; see Rackley, *Laugh If You Like, Ain't a Damn Thing Funny*.

68. Rackley, *Laugh If You Like, Ain't a Damn Thing Funny*, 40–104.

69. Ibid., 108.

70. Ibid., 186.

71. Ibid.

72. Ibid., 213–14.

73. Ibid., 222–23.

74. Ibid., 28–36.

75. Ibid., 34.

76. For more information on WOL, see its Web site, www.wolam.com.

77. Rackley, *Laugh If You Like, Ain't a Damn Thing Funny*, 223–24.

78. Ibid., 258–64.

79. Ibid., 225–29.

80. Ibid., 285–328.

81. Smith, *Captive Capital*, 27.

82. Hughes later repudiated her former position, calling Barry a "master pol," who creates "the smoke and mirrors to make it seem like he is" trying to help people. Barras, *Last of the Black Emperors*, 5.

83. Anita Huslin, "Jazzed Up about Reviving D.C. Landmark: Development Projects Near Howard Theater Aim to Resurrect Cultural Hub," *Washington Post*, February 25, 2008.

84. "Robert Johnson and Oprah Winfrey Make *Forbes'* List of 400 Richest People in America," *Jet*, October 22, 2001.

85. Ulf Hannerz, *Soulside: Inquiries into Ghetto Culture and Community* (New York: Columbia University Press, 1969), 150.

86. Ibid., 151–52.

87. Ibid.

88. Yvonne Shinhoster Lamb, "Director and Teacher Mike Malone: Nurtured D.C. Black Theater Scene," *Washington Post*, December 6, 2006.

89. For more about the career of Louis Johnson, see Jennifer Dunning, "Louis Johnson: 'I Love Dance—Any Kind of Dance,'" *New York Times*, September 28, 1975; and Saul Goodman, "Brief Biographies: Louis Johnson," *Dance Magazine*, August 1956.

90. Jacqueline Trescott, "A Man for All Stages: Mike Malone, Director with an Eye for Excellence," *Washington Post*, December 6, 2006; Tamara Lizette Brown, "Lingering Lights from America's Black Broadway: Negro Renaissance to the Black Arts Movement, African-American Concert-Theatrical Dance in Washington," PhD dissertation, Howard University, Washington, 2004, 296–325.

91. This is as cited by William L. Tribby, "*The Blacks*, by Jean Genet, D.C. Black Repertory Company, Eisenhower Theater, John F. Kennedy Center for the Performing Arts, Washington, D.C., June 16, 1973," *Educational Theatre Journal* 25, no. 4 (1973): 513–14.

92. Gale, *Washington*, 64.

93. Trescott and Horowitz, "Debt-Ridden Source Theatre Closes."

94. Jessica Gould, "Nonprofit Offers Tours of Renovated Source," *Dupont Current*, March 19, 2008.

95. More information about the Studio Theatre may be found on its Web site, www.studiotheatre.org.

96. Don Shewey, "Wild and Woolly (Woolly Mammoth Theatre, Washington, D.C.)," *Advocate*, September 1999. Also see the Woolly Mammoth Theatre's Web site, www.woollymammoth.net.

97. Hannerz, *Soulside*.

98. Rackley, *Laugh If You Like, Ain't a Damn Thing Funny*, 222–82.

99. Ibid., 225–29.

100. Ibid., 275–78.

101. Ibid., 14–15.

102. Marc Fisher, "Nap Turner, Mixing Sunshine with the Blues," *Washington Post*, June 18, 2004.

103. Rackley, *Laugh If You Like, Ain't a Damn Thing Funny*, 237–38.

CHAPTER 7

1. Ernst Schmiederer, "Washington, D.C., USA: Die Wiedergeburt der U; U Street Rises Again," *Skylines*, January 2008, 36–45; the quotation here is on 36.

2. Stephen C. Fehr, "Long-Awaited Green Line Gets the Go," *Washington Post*, May 12, 1991.

3. Linda Wheeler, "Welcoming Green Line," *Washington Post District Weekly*, May 16, 1991; Jim Keary, "Openings Herald New Era: Ventures Gain with Subway Nearby," *Washington Times*, May 10, 1991.

4. Linda Wheeler, "Metro Brings Despair, Hope; Shaw Paid Heavy Price Waiting for Green Line," *Washington Post*, May 6, 1991).

5. Ibid.

6. Rene Sanchez, "Ellington's Old Neighborhood Seems Ready for Renaissance," *Washington Post*, May 4, 1991.

7. Mumin was quoted by Anne Chase, "Shaw Leaders Oppose Plans for Historic District," *Washington Post*, April 27, 1983.

8. Vincent McCraw, "He's Baaack—A Confident Barry Returns to the Fray," *Washington Times*, May 14, 1990; Jon Cohen, "Guess Who's Coming to Lunch," *Washington City Paper*, January 26, 1990; Jonetta Rose Barras, *The Last of the Black Emperors: The Hollow Comeback of Marion Barry in the New Age of Black Leaders* (Baltimore: Bancroft Press, 1998), 133–40; Fred Siegel, *The Future Once Happened Here: New York, D.C., L.A., and the Fate of America's Big Cities* (San Francisco: Encounter Books, 1997), 115–31; Harry S. Jaffe and Tom Sherwood, *Dream City: Race, Power and the Decline of Washington* (New York: Simon & Schuster, 1994), 269–95.

9. Gabriel Escobar and Nancy Lewis, "For Every Witness, Yet Another Account of the 'Real' Story," *Washington Post*, May 13, 1991.

10. Nancy Lewis and James Rupert, "D.C. Neighborhood Erupts after Officer Shoots Suspect: Crowd of Hundreds Confronts Police, Sets Cruisers Ablaze in Mt. Pleasant," *Washington Post*, May 6, 1991; Carlos Sanchez and Rene Sanchez, "Dixon Imposes Curfew on Mt. Pleasant Area after Clash for a Second Night: Skirmishes, Looting Spread under Cloud of Tear Gas," *Washington Post*, May 7, 1991; "Curfew Leaves Mount Pleasant Area Quieter: Sporadic Incidents Reported on 3rd Night," *Washington Post*, May 8, 1991; Gary Fields, "Dixon Declares Curfew: Rioters Rampage Again in NW," *Washington Times*, May 8, 1991); Rene Sanchez, "3rd Night of Curfew Quiet but Uneasy in Mt. Pleasant Area," *Washington Post*, May 9, 1991; Keith Harriston, "Life Gets Back on Track in Mt. Pleasant: Dixon Lifts Curfew but Police Maintain Strong Presence in Area," *Washington Post*, May 10, 1991.

11. Harrison, "Life Gets Back on Track."

12. Jaffe and Sherwood, *Dream City*, 304–5; Jennifer Gilligan Twombly, "An Exploration of Neighborhood Racial Change in the Washington, D.C. Metropolitan

Area and an Analysis of Factors Influencing Racial Stability," PhD dissertation, George Washington University, Washington, 2001.

13. Debbi Wilgoren, "A Core of City, Old-Timers, Recent Arrivals Seek a New Balance: Population Shifts Leave Some Poorer Residents Worried," *Washington Post*, July 10, 2003.

14. Harrison, "Life Gets Back on Track."

15. Paul Schwartzman and Robert E. Pierre, "From Ruins to Rebirth: Condos and Cafés Have Replaced Gutted Shops, but Who's Profiting?" *Washington Post*, April 6, 2008.

16. "Memories of Mayhem and Mercy," *Washington Post*, April 7, 2008.

17. Keith Q. Warner, "From 'Down the Way Where the Nights are Gay': Caribbean Immigration and the Bridging of Cultures," in *Urban Odyssey: A Multicultural History of Washington, D.C.*, ed. Francine Curro Cary (Washington, D.C.: Smithsonian Institution Press, 1996), 250–63; Berket H. Selassie, "Washington's New African Immigrants," in *Urban Odyssey*, ed. Cary, 264–75; Frank H. Wilson, "Gentrification in the Central Area Neighborhoods: Population and Housing Change in Washington, D.C., 1970–1980," PhD dissertation, University of Michigan, Ann Arbor, 1985; Robert Manning, "Multicultural Washington, D.C.: The Changing Social and Economic Landscape of a Post-Industrial Metropolis," *Ethnic and Racial Studies* 21, no. 2 (1998): 328–54; Elizabeth Chacko, "Washington, D.C.: From Biracial City to Multiethnic Gateway," in *Migrants to the Metropolis: The Rise of Immigrant Gateway Cities*, ed. Marie Price and Lisa Benton-Short (Syracuse: Syracuse University Press, 2008), 203–25.

18. Paul Schwartzman, "Shaw Shuns 'Little Ethiopia': Black Leaders Note Immigrants' Pride But Resist Designation," *Washington Post*, July 25, 2005.

19. Paul Schwartzman, "A Bittersweet Renaissance: Longtime Shaw Residents Ponder: Cash Out or Stay," *Washington Post*, February 23, 2006; Linda Wheeler, "A Whole New U: Businesses Spring Up along Historic Street in NW," *Washington Post*, December 26, 1995.

20. Schwartzman, "Bittersweet Renaissance."

21. Dennis E. Gale, *Washington, D.C.: Inner-City Revitalization and Minority Suburbanization* (Philadelphia: Temple University Press, 1987), 54- 57.

22. Derek S. Hyra, "Racial Uplift? Intra-Racial Class Conflict and the Economic Revitalization of Harlem and Bronzeville," *City & Community* 5, no. 1 (2006): 71–92. For further discussion of these issues, also see Derek S. Hyra, *The New Urban Renewal: The Economic Transformation of Harlem and Bronzeville* (Chicago: University of Chicago Press, 2008).

23. Jeffrey R. Henig, *Gentrification in Adams Morgan: Political and Commercial Consequences of Neighborhood Change*, Center for Washington Areas Studies,

Washington Studies Series 9 (Washington, D.C.: George Washington University, 1982), 2–3.

24. Ibid., 4–6, 64–65.

25. Ibid., 64–65.

26. Schwartzman, "Bittersweet Renaissance."

27. Ibid.

28. Teresa Wiltz, "U Turn: The Fabled D.C. Street That Played Host to Duke Ellington and Pearl Bailey Reinvents Itself Once More," *Washington Post Magazine*, March 8, 2006.

29. Michael K. Fauntroy, *Home Rule or House Rule? Congress and the Erosion of Local Governance in the District of Columbia* (Lanham, Md.: University Press of America, Inc., 2003), 155–66.

30. These events are reviewed in the lively account of Barry's "comeback" by Barras, *Last of the Black Emperors*, 185–208. Also see Howard Gillette Jr., "Washington, D.C., in White and Black: The Social Construction of Race and Nationhood," in *Composing Urban History and the Construction of Civic Identities*, ed. John J. Czaplicka and Blair A. Ruble (Washington, D.C., and Baltimore: Woodrow Wilson Center Press and Johns Hopkins University Press, 2003), 192–210. The author's analysis of these events is discussed in greater detail by Blair A. Ruble, *Creating Diversity Capital: Transnational Migrants in Montreal, Washington, and Kyiv* (Washington, D.C., and Baltimore: Woodrow Wilson Center Press and Johns Hopkins University Press, 2005), 121–29. For contemporary views on the events, see District Staff, "The Year in Review, 1993: Times of Dissension, Fear and Despair; Moments of Unity, Courage, and Hope," *Washington Post District Weekly*, December 30, 1993; and District Staff, "'94: The Year That Barry Came Back; City Also Seeks Redemption," *Washington Post District Weekly*, December 29, 1994.

31. Krishna Roy, "Socio-Demographic Profile," in *The State of Latinos in the District of Columbia*, ed. Council of Latino Agencies / Consejo de Agencias Latinas (Washington, D.C.: Council of Latino Agencies / Consejo de Agencias Latinas, 2002), 1–20, esp. figure 1.1 on p. 5. Also see Charles Wesley Harris, *Congress and the Governance of the Nation's Capital: The Conflict of Federal and Local Interests* (Washington, D.C.: Georgetown University Press, 1995), 65–169; and Gillette, "Washington, D.C."

32. Joan Steinau Lester, Eleanor Holmes Norton, and Coretta Scott King, *Fire in My Soul* (New York: Simon & Schuster, 2004).

33. Fauntroy, *Home Rule or House Rule?* 167–94; Barras, *Last of the Black Emperors*, 180–82.

34. Carol O'Cleireacain, *The Orphaned Capital: Adopting the Right Revenues for the District of Columbia* (Washington, D.C.: Brookings Institution Press, 1997); U.S. General Accounting Office, *Report of the Ranking Minority Member,*

Subcommittee on the District of Columbia, Committee on Government Reform, House of Representatives: District of Columbia: Reporting Requirements Enacting by Congress (GAO-01-1134), September 2001 (Washington, D.C.: U.S. General Accounting Office, 2001).

35. Barras, *Last of the Black Emperors*, 180–82; Gillette, "Washington, D.C."

36. Barras, *Last of the Black Emperors*, 180–82.

37. Ibid., 203–8.

38. Bill Miller, "In Her Court, an Open-and-Shut Case: Christian Shows D.C. Schools Litigants That She's Serious about Safety," *Washington Post*, August 24, 1997; Loose Lips, "Gen. Becton's Waterloo," *Washington City Paper*, August 29–September 4, 1997; Maria Tukaeva, "The Damage That Can't Be Repaired: When My D.C. School Was Closed, Windows of Opportunity Shut, Too," *Washington Post*, November 9, 1997; Debbi Wilgoren, Valerie Strauss, and David A. Vise, "One Year Later, Becton Still Struggles," *Washington Post*, November 18, 1997; "Q&A with Julius Becton, Jr.," *Washington Post*, April 14, 1998; Anna Kindsman, *The Politics of Knowledge: Public Schools in the Nation's Capital* (New York: Peter Land, 2003), 98–166.

39. Consumer and Regulatory Affairs, District of Columbia Government, "News Release: City Council Votes on Master Business License Repeal Act; Master Business License Deadline Extended," June 11, 2003.

40. Fauntroy, *Home Rule or House Rule?* 182.

41. Ibid., 183–94.

42. This is as quoted by Harry Jaffe, "Mocha Town," *Washingtonian*, November 1999, 164.

43. This is as quoted by Cultural Tourism D.C., ed., *What's The Story? A Deeper Look at the History of Greater Shaw in Washington, D.C. in the Context of the National African American Experience—Conference Proceedings, December 7–8, 2004* (Washington, D.C.: Cultural Tourism D.C., 2005).

44. Hedrick Smith, *Duke Ellington's Washington*, television program, Public Broadcasting System, February 7, 2000.

45. Mary Louise Pratt, "Arts in the Contact Zone," *Profession 91*, 33–40, as republished in *Reading the Lives of Others*, ed. David Bartholomae and Anthony Petrosky (Boston: Bedford Books, 1995), 180–95.

46. Stephanie Barbara Frank, "'If We Own the Story, We Own the Place': Cultural Heritage, Historic Preservation, and Gentrification on U Street," MA thesis, University of Maryland, College Park, 2005.

47. The excellent textbook produced by Smith and her colleagues in 1983—D.C. History Curriculum Project, *City of Magnificent Intentions: A History of the District of Columbia* (Washington, D.C.: Intac, 1983)—still offers as concise and multidimensional a presentation of Washington history as is available anywhere.

48. See, e.g., Kathryn Schneider Smith and Marya McQuirter, *A Guide to the Historical Resources of Shaw* (Washington, D.C.: Thurgood Marshall Center for Service and Heritage, 1996).

49. This account is based on Stephanie Barbara Frank's interviews with Kathryn Schneider Smith, as reported by Frank, "'If We Own the Story,'" 26–27.

50. Personal correspondence with Kathryn Schneider Smith, October 13, 2009.

51. For further information on Cultural Tourism D.C., see the organization's Web site, www.culturaltourismdc.org.

52. Sam Smith, *Captive Capital: Colonial Life in Modern Washington* (Bloomington: Indiana University Press, 1974), 279.

53. Ibid.

54. This account is based on personal communication with Kathryn Schneider Smith, June 2009.

55. See Marya Annette McQuirter, *African American Heritage Trail, Washington, D.C.* (Washington, D.C.: Cultural Tourism D.C., 2003); Paul K. Williams and Kathryn S. Smith, *City within a City: Greater U Street Heritage Trail* (Washington, D.C.: Historical Society of Washington, D.C., and D.C. Heritage Tourism Coalition, 2001); Cultural Tourism D.C., "Historic Neighborhoods: U Street," http://www.culturaltourismdc.org/information2550/information.htm?area=2529; and National Park Service, "Greater U Street Historic District," http://www.cr.nps.gov/nr/travel/wash/dc63.htm.

56. See, e.g., Marquita Jones and Alexander M. Padro, *Shaw Historic Bicycle Tour* (Washington, D.C.: Shaw Ecovillage Project and Shaw Main Streets, 2004); Lonnell Aikman, *The Northern Shaw–Striver Cultural Resources Survey Project, Phase II: Final Report* (Washington, D.C.: Traceries, 1993); Kimberly Prothro Williams, *Greater U Street Historic District* (Washington, D.C.: D.C. Preservation League, 2003); and Kimberly Prothro Williams, *Strivers' Section Historic District* (Washington, D.C.: D.C. Preservation League, 1999).

57. Many of these developments are discussed by Jessica Weiss, "Portrait of a Community: Life in Shaw," paper presented at Janus Conference, University of Maryland Undergraduate History Conference, College Park, 2005. Also see Paul K. Williams, *Greater U Street*, Images of America Series (Charleston: Arcadia, 2002); Juan Williams, "14th and U: When Being There Meant Being Somebody," *Washington Post Magazine*, February 21, 1988; Wiltz, "U Turn"; and Smith, *Duke Ellington's Washington*.

58. Dana Lanier Schaffer, "The 1968 Washington Riots in History and Memory," *Washington History* 15, no. 2 (2003–4): 5–33 (the citation here is on 27); Mary Beth Sheridan, "Jazzy D.C. Quarter to Feature Ellington," *Washington Post*, December 12, 2008.

59. Frank, "'If We Own the Story.'"

60. Ibid., 72.

61. Ibid.

62. Ibid., 82.

63. Lawrence Guyot has been outspoken on these issues in a number of forums. This particular statement is from Frank's study; ibid., 44.

64. Jane Freundel Levey, Paul K. Williams, Richard T. Busch, J. Brendan Meyer, Anne W. Rollins, and Joan M. Mathys, *Midcity at the Crossroads: Shaw Heritage Trail* (Washington, D.C.: Cultural Tourism D.C., 2006).

65. This account is based on personal communication with Kathryn Schneider Smith, June 2009. Also see Cultural Tourism D.C., *What's the Story?*

66. Frank, "'If We Own the Story,'" 34–35; Jonetta Rose Barras, "Old Shaw's Glorious Echoes; U Street Area Is Latest Stop for Author Researching Race Relations," *Washington Times*, December 9, 1993; Henry P. Whitehead, *Remembering U Street: There Was a Time* (Washington, D.C.: Remembering U Street, Inc., 1994).

67. This account is based on personal communication with Kathryn Schneider Smith, June 2009. Also see Frank, "'If We Own the Story," 34–35; and Natalie Hopkinson, "New to U," *Washington Post*, October 29, 1999.

68. Frank, "'If We Own the Story,'" 59–65; Thomas B. Hargrave Jr., *Private Differences—General Good: A History of the YMCA of Metropolitan Washington* (Washington, D.C.: YMCA of Metropolitan Washington, 1985), 137–38.

69. Hargrave, *Private Differences—General Good*, 165–69.

70. Concerning the 2009 ceremonies, see Ian Shapira, "Marshall Center Holds On to History: Old and New Time Capsules Help Trace Nation's Racial Past, Changes," *Washington Post*, February 8, 2009. Concerning the broader programs of the Marshall Center, see Frank, "'If We Own the Story,'" 59–65. This small neighborhood museum has proven to be more resilient than a simultaneous effort to launch a City Museum in the former D.C. Public Library at Mount Vernon Square. That effort failed, with the City Museum closing shortly after opening in 2004 as a consequence in part of congressional failure to appropriate a promised contribution from the federal government. David Plotz, "L'Enfant Terrible: The Real Reason the City Museum Failed," *Washington City Paper*, December 24, 2004). More information about the Marshall Center can be found on its Web site, www. thurgoodmarshallcenter.org.

71. Sandra Fitzpatrick and Maria R. Goodwin, *The Guide to Black Washington: Places and Events of Historical and Cultural Significance in the Nation's Capital*, rev. illus. ed. (New York: Hippocrene Books, 2001), 170.

72. Ibid.

73. Linda Wheeler, "A Building of the People; On U St., Blacks Created a Powerful Symbol," *Washington Post*, January 18, 1999; Williams, *Greater U Street*, 121.

74. Further information may be found about the Public Welfare Foundation on the organization's Web site, www.publicwelfare.org.

75. Laura Bergheim, *The Washington Historical Atlas: Who Did What When and Where in the Nation's Capital* (Rockville, Md.: Woodbine House, 1992), 250–51.

76. "D.C. Takes Ownership of Lincoln Theatre," *Washington Times*, November 17, 1991.

77. Linda Wheeler, "D.C. to Finish Lincoln Theatre Restoration," *Washington Post*, August 15, 1991.

78. Laura Outerbridge and Matt Neufeld, "Jazzing Up the Lincoln," *Washington Times*, September 15, 1993; Matt Neufeld, "Raising the Curtain on a New Shaw," *Washington Times*, September 15, 1993.

79. Outerbridge and Neufeld, "Jazzing Up the Lincoln."

80. Roxanne Roberts, "The New Jewel of U Street; Lincoln Theatre's Gala Return," *Washington Post*, February 5, 1994; Toni Marshall, "Born-Again Lincoln Theatre Applauded—Renovated Hall Draws 1,200 for Gala Reopening," *Washington Times*, February 5, 1994; Toni Marshall, "Raising Curtain at Restored Theater," *Washington Times*, February 7, 1994.

81. Roberts, "New Jewel."

82. Linda Wheeler, "A Neighborhood Takes Center Stage; Shaw Playwright Brings Troubled NW Area's Rich History to Life at the Lincoln," *Washington Post*, March 10, 1995.

83. Paul Schwartzman, "Storied Stage Could Go Dark; U Street Venue on Brink of Going Broke, Director Says," *Washington Post*, January 9, 2007; Keith L. Alexander, "City's Grant of $200,000 a 'Good Band-Aid,' Official Says," *Washington Post*, January 17, 2007.

84. Outerbridge and Neufeld, "Jazzing Up the Lincoln."

85. Ronald J. Hansen, "Another Lesson in History of Civil War: Shaw Monument Hails Union's Black Soldiers," *Washington Times*, July 19, 1988; Linda Wheeler, "In Touch with the Past: Memorial to Black Civil War Troops Unveiled—Black Civil War Contributions Remembered as Statue Unveiled," *Washington Post*, July 19, 1998; Linda Wheeler, "Celebrating the Civil War's Forgotten Ones: Statue of Black Troops to Be Unveiled Today," *Washington Post*, July 18, 1998.

86. Hansen, "Another Lesson."

87. Linda Wheeler, "New Problem Forces More Delay for Black Civil War Memorial," *Washington Post*, May 20, 1999.

88. However, new plans were announced by the District and Radio One in early 2008. Anita Huslin, "Jazzed Up about Reviving D.C. Landmark: Development Projects near Howard Theatre Aim to Resurrect Cultural Hub," *Washington Post*, February 25, 2008.

89. For further discussion of the rise of Anthony Williams in D.C. politics, see Barras, *Last of the Black Emperors*, 185–208.

90. The author's analysis of these events is discussed in greater detail in Ruble, *Creating Diversity Capital*, 113–23.

91. Barras, *Last of the Black Emperors*, 203–8.

92. The author's analysis of these events is discussed in greater detail in Ruble, *Creating Diversity Capital*, 128–34.

93. Ibid.

94. Ibid.

95. Ibid.; "The 1998 Election," *Washington Post*, November 5, 1998.

96. The author's analysis of these events is discussed in greater detail in Ruble, *Creating Diversity Capital*, 128–36.

97. For Graham's official biography, see his Web site, www.grahamone.com.

98. District of Columbia Board of Elections and Ethics, "Final and Complete Election Results for September 15, 1998 Primary," available at http://www.dcboee .org. Concerning the considerable ill will between some African American activists and Graham, see James Jones, "The Graham Crusade," *Washington City Paper*, December 2–8, 2005.

99. Vanessa Williams, "Election Lacks Spark, Voter Enthusiasm; Only 39% of D.C. Electorate Turns Out," *Washington Post*, November 5, 1998; David Montgomery, "D.C.'s New-Look Council Pledges an Activist Agenda," *Washington Post*, November 5, 1998.

100. Clay Risen, "Off the Mall: Throwing Off the Reins of Federal Control, the City of Washington, D.C. Makes Grand Plans for Its Neglected Neighborhoods," *Metropolis* 23, no. 11 (July 2004): 62, 65.

101. These changes are discussed in detail by Fauntroy, *Home Rule or House Rule?* 167–94; and O'Cleireacain, *Orphaned Capital*.

102. Fauntroy, *Home Rule or House Rule?* 129–67.

103. The author's analysis of these events is discussed in greater detail in Ruble, *Creating Diversity Capital*, 136–43.

104. Lori Montgomery, "Still Tallying Hits and Errors," *Washington Post*, January 6, 2005.

105. David Nakamura and Thomas Heath, "Amended Deal on Stadium Approved: Council Seals Return of Baseball to D.C.," *Washington Post*, December 22, 2004; Associated Press, "D.C. Mayor Signs Legislation for Baseball," December 29, 2004.

106. Dave Sheinin and Daniel LeDuc, "A 'Storybook Ending': Homer Gives Nationals a Memorable Close to $611 Million Stadium Opener," *Washington Post*, March 31, 2008; Barry Svrluga, "The Face of the Franchise Becomes a Hero of the Night," *Washington Post*, March 31, 2008.

107. David Nakamura, "Cropp and Fenty Have Pursued Their Legislative Agendas by Opposite Means," *Washington Post*, August 21, 2006; Marc Fisher, "Fenty Emerges as an Action Hero," *Washington Post*, August 24, 2006.

108. Lori Montgomery, "In Sweep, Fenty Draws on Uniting to Conquer," *Washington Post*, September 14, 2006; District of Columbia Board of Elections and Ethics, "Final and Complete Election Results for November 7, 2006, General Election," available at http://www.dcboee.org.

109. The section title "Where Would Jesus Park?" is taken from an article appearing in the *Washington City Paper*; see Franklin Schneider, "Where Would Jesus Park? City Goes Easy on Car-Driving Logan Circle Congregations," *Washington City Paper*, March 7–13, 2008.

110. Ibid.

111. See, e.g., Bill Broadway, "A Place to Worship, No Place to Park; Near New Convention Center, Congregants Driving from Suburbs Compete for Fewer Spaces," *Washington Post*, October 11, 2003.

112. Christine Spolar, "Some Logan Circle Residents Circle the Wagons," *Washington Post*, May 16, 1992.

113. Amy Doolittle, "Sunday Double-Parking Falls from Grace," *Washington Post*, January 10, 2006.

114. Paul Schwartzman, "Ticketing near Churches to Begin; Residents' Protests Prompt Parking Crackdown in Logan Circle," *Washington Post*, March 17, 2006.

115. Amy Doolittle, "Parking Reversal Angers Residents; Enforcement Seen as Key," *Washington Times*, April 25, 2006.

116. Ibid.

117. "Peaceful Solutions to the Parking Wars," *Washington Post*, April 23, 2006.

118. Schneider, "Where Would Jesus Park?"

119. Amy Doolittle, "Double-Parking Solutions Offered; Panel Urges Sunday Enforcement," *Washington Times*, October 5, 2006.

120. Ibid.

121. Eric M. Weiss, "Parking Solutions Examined in District; Among the Options: Higher Meter Fees," *Washington Post*, July 15, 2005.

122. Schneider, "Where Would Jesus Park?"

123. Ibid.

124. Dave Jamieson, "Great Migration: Apartment Flier Takes the Color out of U Street," *Washington City Paper*, May 28–June 4, 2004.

125. Ibid.

126. Chris Baker, "U-Turn for the Better," *Washington Times*, May 6, 2002; Nikita Steward, "Radio One in Talks with D.C. Officials over Return to City: Deal Turns on $22 Million in Funding," *Washington Post*, September 25, 2007.

127. Daniela Deane, "Going Upscale on U Street; Wave of High-Priced

Housing Developments Brings Praise, Concern for Once-Blighted Neighborhood," *Washington Post*, March 24, 2001.

128. Ibid.

129. The brochure captured the self-centered attitude of many newcomers perfectly, urging youthful shoppers to "forget mindless mall shopping or traveling to New York. Quality and style are now available just down the street. U Street, it's so you!" U Street merchant brochure, July 2008.

130. Karen De Witt, "Why U Street Is Ultimate Place for Night Life—Clubs, Restaurants Draw Diverse Mix of Party Crowds," *New York Times*, October 24, 1996.

131. Dawn Kopecki, "After Tough Lessons, Quick Sales, Club Owner Finds Keeper in Velvet," *Washington Times*, July 21, 1997.

132. For more on the Young Lions, see the *DCist* Web site, http://dcist.com.

133. Mark Opasasnick, *Washington Rock and Roll: A Social History* (Tinicum, Pa.: Xlibris, 2003).

134. On the history of D.C. go-go music, see Alona Wartofsky, "What Go-Goes Around," *Washington Post*, June 3, 2001; as well as Kop Lornell and Charles C. Stephenson Jr., *The Beat: Go-Go's Fusion of Funk and Hip-Hop* (New York: Billboard, 2001). On the demise of Club U, see Yolanda Woodlee, "Club U to Stay Shut until April Hearings: D.C. Seeks Permanent Liquor License Loss," *Washington Post*, March 5, 2005.

135. Tia L. Smith-Cooper, "Contradictions in a Hip-Hop World: An Ethnographic Study of Black Women Hip-Hop Fans in Washington, D.C.," PhD dissertation, Ohio University, Athens, 2006.

136. Benjamin Forgey, "A Big Hand for the New 9:30; An Old Fan Orchestrates Rock Venue's Makeover," *Washington Post*, January 5, 1996; Richard Harrington, "25 Years Later, It's Still 9:30," *Washington Post*, May 27, 2005.

137. More on the Black Cat can be found on its Web site, www.blackcatdc.com.

138. More extensive accounts of the Twins story are given by Blair Ruble, "From 'Chocolate City, Vanilla Suburbs' to 'Rocky Road,'" *Washington Afro-American*, October 16–22, 2004; and Courtland Milloy, "Jazz Provides Sisters with Key to Success," *Washington Post*, May 27, 1998.

139. Sandra Boyd, "What's in a Store's Name?" *Washington Post*, April 22, 2007.

140. Ann Geracimos, "Politics on Menu at Restaurant; Busboys Makes Room for Poetry and Drama at Its Two Locations," *Washington Times*, January 7, 2008.

141. Ellen McCarthy, "The Word Is Out," *Washington Post*, August 24, 2007.

142. Geracimos, "Politics on Menu."

143. Karen Paul-Stern, "Standing in the Express Lane for Change," *Washington Post*, May 19, 2008.

144. All three venues featured prominently in a *Washington Post* review of where to go in the neighborhood in October 1999; see Hopkinson, "New to U."

145. Eric M. Weiss, "Tax Relief Proposed for Historic Businesses," *Washington Post*, January 26, 2006.

146. Jessica Gould, "On U Street, Restaurant Celebrates Cultural Legacy," *Northwest Current*, April 2, 2008.

147. See, e.g., Ian Urbina, "Escape: A Winter Day Out in Washington, D.C." *New York Times*, January 18, 2008; and Schmiederer, "Washington, D.C., USA."

148. Frank, "'If We Own the Story,'" 26–30, 72.

149. Smith made clear her interest in promoting "the whole history" of the area in a December 2004 conference sponsored by Cultural Tourism D.C. at the Thurgood Marshall Center for Service and Heritage at the renovated Twelfth Street / Anthony Bowen YMCA Building. "There is no doubt," she declared, "that Greater Shaw is historically significant. Yet for many who love this area, who want to see it celebrated, shared, preserved, there remains a set of important questions: What is the whole story? What parts of it are nationally and internationally significant? How is its history shared with African American communities elsewhere in the nation, and how is it unique? How and where can this history be shared?" Kathryn S. Smith, "What's the Story? Introduction," in *What's the Story?* ed. Cultural Tourism D.C., 5. Also see Kathryn Schneider Smith and Marya McQuirter, *A Guide to the Historical Resources of Shaw* (Washington, D.C.: Thurgood Marshall Center for Service and Heritage, 1996).

150. This account of motivation is based on a personal communication with Kathryn Schneider Smith, June 2009.

151. As is readily apparent in their memoirs. See, e.g., Edward Kennedy "Duke" Ellington, *Music Is My Mistress* (Garden City, N.Y.: Doubleday, 1973); and Langston Hughes, *The Big Sea*, republished in *The Collected Works of Langston Hughes, Volume 13: The Big Sea*, ed. Joseph McLaren (Columbia: University of Missouri Press, 2002).

152. Mary Louise Pratt, *Travel Writing and Transculturation* (New York: Routledge, 1992), 6–7.

153. They have, in the concept of Don Mitchell, staked out their "right to the city." For a discussion of this concept, see Don Mitchell, *The Right to the City: Social Justice and the Fight for Public Space* (New York: Guilford Press, 2003), 34–42.

154. Phil Wood and Charles Landry, *The Intercultural City: Planning for Diversity Advantage* (London: Earthscan, 2008), 319.

155. Ibid., 244.

156. These observations are based on the discussions at an international conference on "community resilience" in the contemporary city held at the Woodrow Wilson Center in Washington, December 7–9, 2008.

157. For the debate on "community resilience" in recent years, see, e.g., M. Alberti, J. M. Marzluff, E. Shulenberger, G. Bradley, C. Ryan, and C. Zumbrunner, "Integrating Humans into Ecology: Opportunities and Challenges for Studying Urban Ecosystems," *Bioscience* 53, no. 12 (2003): 1169–79; A. A. Batabyal, "The Concept of Resilience: Retrospect and Prospect," *Environment and Development Economics* 3, no. 2 (2001): 221–62; and D. R. Godschalk, "Urban Hazard Mitigations: Creating Resilient Cities," *Natural Hazards Review* 4 (2003): 136.

158. Lewis Mumford, "What Is a City?" in *The Lewis Mumford Reader*, ed. Donald L. Miller (New York: Pantheon Books, 1986), 104–7; the quotation here is on 107.

159. Edward C. Banfield, "Introduction," in *Civility and Citizenship in Liberal Democratic Societies*, ed. Edward C. Banfield (New York: Paragon House, 1992), xii.

160. Vacheslav Glazychev, *Urbanistika* (Moscow: Europa, 2008), 192.

161. Hughes, *Big Sea*, 165.

162. The D.C. vote tally is drawn from several reports, including www.cnn.com/politics, on November 6, 2008.

163. The chorus "Na Na Na, Hey Hey Hey, Goodbye" has become a perennial favorite among victorious sports fans since the song's release on the Fontana label in late 1969.

164. Joel Achenbach, "All-Night Party at the White House," Achenblog, http://voices.washingtonpost.com/achenblog/2008/11.

165. Marc Fisher, "Rapture in the Streets as Multitudes Cheer Obama and Celebrate America," *Washington Post*, November 6, 2008.

166. N. C. Aizenman and Martin Weil, "Eat at Ben's, See the President Elect," *Washington Post*, January 11, 2009; Amy Argetsinger, "Washington Life: Obama Gets a Half-Smoke at Ben's Chili Bowl," *Washington Post*, January 11, 2009; Jeff Zeleny and David M. Herszenhorn, "Obama Again Raises Estimate of Jobs His Stimulus Plan Will Create or Save," *New York Times*, January 10, 2009.

167. Kevin Anderson, "Washington Celebrates Obama Victory," *The Guardian* (London), November 5, 2008, http://www.guardian.co.uk/world/deadlineusa/2008/nov/05/uselections2008-barackobama1.

168. This is as reported by *DCist*, http://dclist.com/2008/11/05/washington_dc_celebrates_obama_vict./php.

169. Olga Grushin, *The Dream Life of Sukhanov* (New York: G. P. Putnam's Sons, 2005), 345.

170. Nadine Gordimer, *The Pickup* (New York: Farrar, Straus & Giroux, 2001), 33.

171. Sandra Butler-Truesdale, "Citizen Journalism: Paying Homage to U Street," *Washington Times*, October 14, 2009.

ACKNOWLEDGMENTS

As is true of any author who labors on a project of this scale, I have been highly dependent in my work on the goodwill and sound advice of too many others to mention in a brief note such as this. I owe an incalculable debt to my many friends and colleagues who have patiently answered my questions, read what I have written, and encouraged me on this intellectual journey.

In particular, I would like to take this opportunity to express my gratitude to a handful who have been particularly active in extending a helping hand with this project: Virginia Ali, Ben's Chili Bowl; Alfred Austin, great grandson of *Washington Bee* publisher W. C. Chase; Judith Bauer, tour guide extraordinaire; Lydia Charles, Cultural Tourism D.C.; Jeffrey N. Cohen, JNC Enterprises, Inc.; William Frucht, Yale University; Howard Gillette Jr., Rutgers University, Camden, N.J.; Thomas B. Hargrave Jr., the YMCA of Metropolitan Washington (retired); Evelyn Higginbotham, Harvard University; Lois Horton, George Mason University; Jerry Hough, Duke University; Laura Kamoie, American University and *Washington History;* Amy Kunz, Latin American Youth Center, Washington; Jane Freundel Levey, Cultural Tourism D.C.; Elizabeth Clark Lewis, Howard University; Marya McQuirter, the D.C. Humanities Council; James A. Miller, George Washington University; Ibrahim Mumin, Mumin Associates; Walter Reich, George Washington University; Zachary Schrag, George Mason University; the Reverend Sandra Butler-Truesdale, historian, writer, and curator of the Emma Mae Gallery; Diana Varat, University of California, Los Angeles; Donna Wells, Moorland-Spingarn Research Center, Howard University; Brett Williams, American University; Thomasina W. Yearwood, Thurgood Marshall Center Trust, Inc.; and my Woodrow Wilson Center colleagues, Lauren Herzer, Margaret Paxson, Philippa Strum, George Liston Seay, and Megan Yasenchak. The always professional and friendly staff of the Woodrow Wilson Center Press—Joseph Brinley, Yamile Kahn, and

Melody Wilson—have been wonderful and generous colleagues throughout the process of researching and writing this work, while the copy
editor, Alfred Imhoff, has improved nearly every sentence of the final
manuscript and the designer, Michelle Furman, has added verve.

Kathryn Schneider Smith, the indefatigable historian of Washington
and its multifarious neighborhoods, has been an especially encouraging
and thoughtful reviewer and critic throughout the life of this project.
Like all who toil on Washington history, I am forever in her debt.

Working full time as the administrator of a large academic program,
my research depends more than most on the energy, skill, and enthusiasm
of hard-working interns. I can hardly express sufficient gratitude to my
research assistants who have worked on this project, including Bridgett
Balliett, Ariana Curtis, Elizabeth Hipple, Renée Lariviere, Raughley D.
Nuzzi, Kimberly Painter, Rickita T. Perry, and Jonathan Zuk. Raughley
D. Nuzzi is largely responsible for the wonderful photographic images
presented in the previous pages.

My interns and I would like to thank the helpful and thoughtful staffs
of the Washingtoniana Collection at the Martin Luther King Jr. Library
of the District of Columbia, the Moorland-Spingarn Library at Howard
University, the Kiplinger Research Library at the Historical Society of
Washington, D.C., and the Library of Congress.

My greatest debt remains to the tens of thousands of souls who have
lived in, worked in, played in, and shaped the remarkable community
about which I am writing. As these souls have demonstrated, and as I
have explained, U Street in the Northwest quadrant of Washington has
been one of the most protean patches of earth on the North American
continent for a century and a half. I close these acknowledgments by
expressing the utmost respect for all who have lived in the neighborhood
and for their contributions to the city that I have been so fortunate to
inhabit. Drawing on the luminous language of Olga Grushin, they indeed have made the planet richer and purer by adding beauty to a world
replete with injustices, horrors, and stupidity.

INDEX

Notes are indicated by n following the page number.
Bold page numbers indicate profiles, and italic page numbers indicate photographs.

establishment of, 20; in Great
Depression, 123; in healing process
after race riots, 363n178; loyalty of
those moving from neighborhood,
164, 239, 289–92; and middle
class, 59; in period between World
Wars, 65–67; political impact of,
29; social services provided by,
174; and Sunday parking, 289–92;
sustaining Shaw area and U Street
community, 239–43
citizen associations, 61, 331–32n85
City College of New York, 165
City Museum, 377n70
*City of Magnificent Intentions: A History
of the District of Columbia* (D.C.
History Curriculum Project),
375–76n47
civic associations, 61, 331–32n85
Civic Federation, 55
Civil Rights Act of 1875, 49
Civil Rights Act of 1964, 201
civil rights movement, 8, 80, 101–5,
200–206
civil unrest. *See* violence
Civil War, 19, 21–22; monument
honoring African American soldiers
in, 278, 282–84, *283*
Clark, Kenneth B., 164
Clarke, David A., 202, 222, 227, 286
Clemmer, Donald, 245
Cleveland, Grover, 153
Clifford, Carrie, 63
clubs: "block clubs," 187;
entertainment, 295–98; literary
and academic, 65; social, 139
Club U, 295
Cluss, Adolf, 33
Cohen, Jeffrey, 230–32, 279, 281
Cold War, 181
Colored Actors' Union, 143

Colored Exhibitors' Association,
142, 143
A Colored Woman in a White World
(Terrell), 77, 94, 119
Colored Women's League, 94
Columbia Heights, 38
Columbia Historical Society, 310
Columbia Teachers College, 199
Columbia University, 148, 165, 195
commissioner system, 35
Committee of Fair Employment
Practice, 122
Committee of Safety, 80
Committee on Housing of the
Washington Council of Social
Agencies, 125
commodification of U Street, 300–301
Communist Party, 119
Community Chest, 121
community development corporations
(CDCs), 242–43
community organizing, 120–23,
188, 285
community resilience, 15, 303–4,
382n156, 383n157
Compromise of 1850, 20
Compromise of 1877, 35, 50
concerts, outdoor, 153
Congregational Church, 31
Congressional Black Caucus, 258
congressional oversight of District of
Columbia, 27–28, 35, 124
consultants' master license program,
271
contact zone. *See* zone of contact
contraband communities of fugitive
slaves, 22–23, 26, 320n32
Control Board, 271, 284, 285, 287–88
Cooper, Anna Julia, 9, 127, **129–30**
Cooper, Maudine R., 266
CORE, 201

football, 71, 151, 153, 156–57,
353n111
Forbes Field, 162
Ford, Gerald, 220
Fort Totten, 178
Fortune, T. Thomas, 80
Fox theater, 143
Francis Junior High, 243
Franco, Barbara, 273
Frank, Stephanie Barbara, 273, 275,
277, 300
Frank D. Reeves Municipal Center,
233, 233–34
Frankfurter, Felix, 97, 102
Franklin, Aretha, 142
Franklin, John Hope, 97, 104, 164
Frazier, E. Franklin: on Howard
University faculty, 97, 107; research
on family, 343–44n66; social
science radicalism of, 101, 108, 110
free blacks: Barry Farms (experimental
agricultural community for freed
slaves), 320n32; in prebellum
Washington, 19, 20–21
Free D.C. Movement, 203–4
Freedmen's Bureau, 23–24, 44, 320n33
Freedmen's Hospital, 9, 24, 25, 59,
164, 173, 234
freelance contractors' master license
program, 271
Freeman, James, 134
French Street Neighborhood
Association, 263–64
Frelinghuysen University, 9, 127, 130
fugitive slaves, 6, 22–26, 320n26
Furfey, Paul Hanly, 191

gangs, 238
Gardiner, Lisa, 147
gay community, 140, 287
Gaye, Marvin, 142, 243

gentrification: community
organizations disrupted by, 267;
in Georgetown, 177; historic
preservation vs., 15, 277, 280;
Metro influence on, 251; as private
market process, 242; and racial
tensions, 294
Georgetown, 27, 28, 177, 182, 267
Georgetown Flea Market, 277
Georgetown University, 240
George Washington University, 9
Gibson, Ernest, 187
Gibson, Josh, 7, 9, 162, 170
The Gilded Age (Twain & Warner), 61
Gillette, Howard, Jr., 207
Glazychev, Vyacheslav, 304
Gomez, Daniel Enrique, 265
Gompers, Samuel, 7, 9
Gone with the Wind (movie), 128, 133
Gordimer, Nadine, 308
Gordon, John, 80
Graham, Donald, 254
Graham, Jim, 286–87, 288
Graham, Philip, 183
Grant, Ulysses S., 32–33, 45–46
Grant, Ulysses S., III, 125–26, 310
Grays (baseball team). See Homestead
Grays
Great Depression: and baseball, 158,
161; and economic nationalism,
117; employment impact of, 123,
139–40; government response to,
124; social sciences impact of, 108
Great Society programs, 240
Green, Constance McLaughlin, 12, 59,
314n11
Greene, Ralph "Petey," 240, 244, 244–
46, 248, 253, 254–56, 370n67
Greenlee, Marcia McAdoo, 19, 41, 52,
53, 58
Green Line (Metro), 174, 234–36, 261

high schools. *See* schools; *and specific
    school by name*
highway system, 175–79, 182–83
Hill, Oliver W., 165
Hilyer, Andrew, 69, 116
Hines, Earl, 142
Hispanics, 265, 266, 287
Historical Society of Washington,
    D.C., 310
historic preservation, 16, 278, 280–84,
    300
history, sharing of, 272–84, 300
Hobson, Julius, Sr., 195–99, *196,* 202,
    222, 228, 236
Hobson, Julius "Hobie," Jr., 197, 205
Holliday, Frank, 4
Holliday poolroom, 74, 76, 104
Holloway, Jonathan Scott, 100–101
Holmes Norton, Eleanor, 8, 219,
    270
home rule: and Advisory
    Neighborhood Commissions
    (ANCs), 285; demand for, 124,
    219–20, 258, 330n57; effect of
    lack of, 183, 187; effect of passage
    of, 227–28, 253; passage of D.C.
    Home Rule Bill (1973), 220–21;
    suspension of, 32, 46
Homestead Grays (baseball team),
    160–63, 169–70
Hon Toon, Moy, 212
Hooks, Robert, 250
Hoover, J. Edgar, 363n176
hope for community renewal, 252–56
Horace, Gregory, 8
Horn, Shirley, 243
Horne, Lena, 142
House Committee on the District of
    Columbia, 219–20
Housing Act of 1937, 125
Housing Act of 1954, 187

Housing and Community
    Development Act of 1974, 232
housing problems, 124–25, 238, 241
Houston, Charles Hamilton, 95–97,
    96, 101–3, 106, 118, 164
Howard, Clyde, 266
Howard, Oliver Otis, 23, 24, 37, *43,*
    43–44, 320n26
Howard Big Five, 150
Howardettes, 136
Howard Players, 141, 144, 146, 168
Howard School of Religion, 165
Howard Theatre, *75;* cultural impact
    of, 76, 136–37, 140–44; Michaux
    saves from bankruptcy, 12, 123,
    156; opening of, 70; restoration
    needs and plans for, 248, 284
Howard Theatre Foundation, 144
Howard University: African American
    presidents of, 97, 99; and
    architecture, 341n18; basketball,
    149, 150; Board of Regents, 79; as
    "Capstone of Negro Education,"
    99–101; Dance Group/Dance
    Ensemble, 168; Department of
    Theatre Arts, 147; desegregation of
    higher education's effect on, 173;
    football, 153; Founder's Library,
    136; Hospital, 12, 173; Law
    School, 101–5, 107, 131, 165; and
    LeDroit Park Historic District,
    241; Library, 63, 136; Medical
    Center, 234; in mid–twentieth
    century, 164; and New Negro
    Movement, 144; origins of, 9, 24–
    25, 44, 59, 205; public celebrations
    sponsored by, 72; racial pride, role
    in, 68; racism, struggle with, 105;
    during Reconstruction, 321n41;
    School of Communications, 247;
    Service Project, 187; Small Business

New Deal Carry-Out Shop, 190–91
New Gospel movement, 156
New Negro Alliance, 116, 118–19,
    122
New Negro Movement, 144
New Negro Renaissance, 168
New Rochelle apartment house, 140
New York City Ballet, 250
New York Times on U Street
    entertainment scene, 294–95, 299
New York Yankees, 158
Niagara Movement, 80–81, 90
Nichols, D. B., 23
9:30 Club, 296, 298
Nixon, Richard, 220, 222, 228, 230,
    337n184
Nonviolent Action Group, 223
nonviolent protests, 8, 117–19
Norris-LaGuardia Anti-Injunction Act
    of 1932, 118
North, Jane, 310
North Central Freeway, 235
Northwest quadrant, 177, 182, 313n9
Norton, Eleanor Holmes. *See* Holmes
    Norton, Eleanor
N Street Village, 241

Obama, Barack, 305–7, *306*
Office of Economic Opportunity, 208,
    228
old-timers vs. newcomers, 272–75,
    290
Organic Act of 1878, 34, 50, 61
Oriental Gardens, 138
Ovington, Mary White, 81

Pace, John, 246
Paige, Jerome, 183, 229
Paige, Leroy "Satchel," 160, 162
Paradise Café, 138
parking on Sunday mornings, 289–92

Parks, Gordon, 164
"passing," 128, 158
Passow, A. Harry, 199
Paula, Carlos, 160
Payne, Dabuek, 66
Pearl Harbor, 155, 157
Peck, G. Byron, 275
Pei, I. M., 183
Pelecanos, George, 8, 237, 238, 239
penny savers' clubs, 123
People's Party, 196
Percy, Walker, 13
performing arts, 142, 163, 249–52.
    See also dance; music; theaters
Perry, Mark, 78–79
pet cemeteries, 326n4
Petey Greene's Washington (TV talk
    show), 246, 254
philosophical split between Du Bois
    and Booker T. Washington, 69–70,
    76–77, 114, 334n130
Phoenix Inn, 138
Phyllis Wheatley YWCA, 113
picketing: of white businesses, 117–19;
    of white-only theaters, 128, 133
Pilgrim Hall, 150
Pinchback, Pickney Benton Stewart,
    73
Pittman, William Sidney, 37, 278
A Plan for the Year 2000 (National
    Capital Park and Planning
    Commission), 359n70
Plessy v. Ferguson (1896), 50
police force, 369n53
poolrooms, 4–5, *5*
"Poor People's Campaign" (1968), 210,
    214
population growth of Washington
    African Americans, 20, 51, 120–21,
    176, 177, 227
Porgy and Bess (Gershwin), 128, 140

ABOUT THE AUTHOR

Blair A. Ruble is the director of the Kennan Institute of the Woodrow Wilson Center, where he also serves as program director for Comparative Urban Studies. He worked previously at the Social Science Research Council and the National Council for Soviet and East European Research. A native of New York, he received his MA and PhD in political science from the University of Toronto, as well as an AB with highest honors in political science from the University of North Carolina at Chapel Hill.

He has edited more than a dozen volumes and is the author of five monographs. His book-length works include a trilogy examining the fate of Russian provincial cities during the twentieth century: *Leningrad: Shaping a Soviet City* (University of California Press, 1990); *Money Sings: The Changing Politics of Urban Space in Post-Soviet Yaroslavl* (Woodrow Wilson Center Press and Cambridge University Press, 1995); and *Second Metropolis: Pragmatic Pluralism in Gilded Age Chicago, Silver Age Moscow, and Meiji Osaka* (Woodrow Wilson Center Press and Johns Hopkins University Press, 2001). His latest monograph—*Creating Diversity Capital: Transnational Migrants in Montreal, Washington, and Kyiv* (Woodrow Wilson Center Press and Johns Hopkins University Press, 2005)—examines the changes in cities brought about by the recent arrival of large transnational communities.

BOOKS BY BLAIR A. RUBLE

Creating Diversity Capital: Transnational Migrants in Montreal, Washington, and Kyiv

Second Metropolis: The Politics of Pragmatic Pluralism in Gilded Age Chicago, Silver Age Moscow, and Meiji Osaka

Money Sings: The Politics of Urban Space in Post-Soviet Yaroslavl

Leningrad: Shaping a Soviet City

Soviet Trade Unions: Their Development in the 1970s

BOOKS COEDITED BY BLAIR A. RUBLE

Urban Diversity: Space, Culture, and Inclusive Pluralism in Cities Worldwide

Cities after the Fall of Communism: Reshaping Cultural Landscapes and European Identity

Global Urban Poverty: Setting the Agenda

Two Centuries of Russian-American Relations: Scholarship and Education. A Collection of Articles (in Russian)

Rebounding Identities: The Politics of Identity in Russia and Ukraine

Russia's Engagement with the West: Transformation and Integration in the Twenty-first Century

Moscow at the Turn of the Twentieth Century: View of the Past from Far Away (in Russian)

Composing Urban History and the Constitution of Civic Identities

Fragmented Space in the Russian Federation

Preparing for the Urban Future: Global Pressures and Local Forces

Russian Housing in the Modern Age: Design and Social History

A Scholars' Guide to Humanities and Social Sciences in the Soviet Successor States: The Academies of Sciences of Russia, Armenia, Azerbaidzhan, Belarus, Estonia, Georgia, Kazakhstan, Kirghizstan, Latvia, Lithuania, Moldova, Tadzhikistan, Turkmenistan, Ukraine, and Uzbekistan

Trade Unions in Communist States

A Scholars' Guide to Humanities and Social Sciences in the Soviet Union: The Academy of Sciences of the USSR and the Academies of Sciences of the Union Republic

Industrial Labor in the U.S.S.R.